Read This First:
CENTRAL & SOUTH AMERICA

CONNER GORRY

LONELY PLANET PUBLICATIONS
melbourne ◆ oakland ◆ london ◆ paris

MEXICO, CENTRAL & SOUTH AMERICA

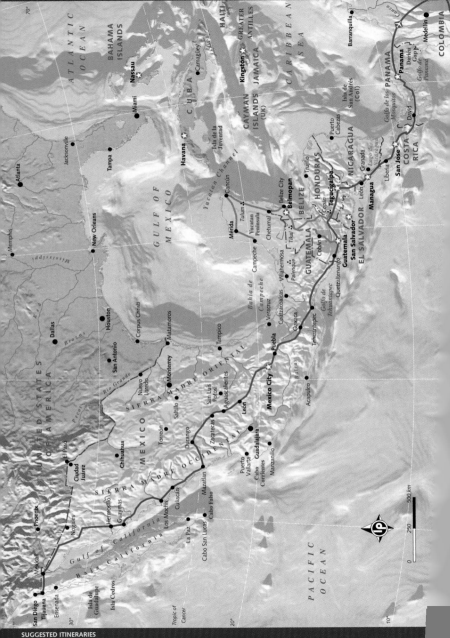

SUGGESTED ITINERARIES

The Gringo Trail   La Ruta Maya: Guatemala, Belize, & the Yucatán

The Andes: Bolivia, Ecuador, Peru & Chile ———— Brazil

Read This First: Central & South America
1st edition – April 2000

Published by
Lonely Planet Publications Pty Ltd ACN 005 607 983
192 Burwood Rd, Hawthorn, Victoria 3122, Australia

Lonely Planet Offices
Australia PO Box 617, Hawthorn, Victoria 3122
USA 150 Linden Street, Oakland, CA 94607
UK 10a Spring Place, London NW5 3BH
France 1 rue du Dahomey, 75011, Paris

Printed by
The Bookmaker Pty Ltd
Printed in China

Photographs
The images in this guide are available for licensing from Lonely Planet Images.
email: lpi@lonelyplanet.com.au

Front cover photograph
Stone pavilion at Tikal, Guatemala (Martin Wheater, LPI)

ISBN 1-86450-067-0

LEGEND ▶▶

BOUNDARIES
International
Regional
Disputed

HYDROGRAPHY
Ocean, Coastline
River, Creek
Intermittent River, Creek
Lake
Salt Lake
Spring, Rapids
Waterfalls
Swamp

MAP SYMBOLS
○ **CAPITAL**	National Capital	
⊙ **Capital**	Regional Capital	
● **City**	City	
● **Town**	Town	
● **Village**	Village	

✕ Airport ∩ Cave
⁂ Archaeological Site ☩ Lighthouse
✕ Battle Site ▲ Mountain or Hill
⊼ Beach ☂ National Park
⋈ Border Crossing)(Pass
🐘 Zoo

TRANSPORT & ROUTES
Ferry Route
Flight Path
One Week Itinerary
Two Weeks Itinerary
Three Weeks Itinerary
One Month Itinerary
Two Months Itinerary

AREA FEATURES
Park, Reserve
Other Countries
Reef

CONTENTS

▶▶

contents

THE AUTHOR

Conner Gorry

It all started in Vieques, Puerto Rico more than 20 years ago. On that seminal trip, Conner first realised there was a world outside of suburban strip malls and pre-pubescent pap. The Dominican Republic and Culebra followed (islands kick ass!) and it wasn't long before the imp was hooked. A BA in Latin American Studies and an MA in International Policy took up a substantial chunk of time, highlighted by an unforgettable adventure to Cuba. She currently lives and writes in San Francisco, though Manhattan and Havana are always beckoning. She has worked on the Lonely Planet titles *Guatemala*, *Guatemala, Belize & Yucatan*, and *Out To Eat San Francisco*.

From the Author

Everyone always coos and ahs when you tell them you work at home, but it's a lifestyle that requires a super harmonious and supportive environment – luckily our little nest above the Taqueriá is just that. The most important ingredients of this harmony are provided by my great friend and co-conspirator Koch, without whom I'd probably still be in the thick of the New York rat race and miserable. Lest you forget baby, you are the best.

My family is also the best. They've been through it all with me and they'll never let me forget it! My mom was the first one to introduce me to Latin America and for this and a million other things, I am indebted to her. My sister Carolyn is always a wealth of insight and was through the course of writing this (benevolent) beast as well. Thanks to my brother Brian for being my biggest cheerleader (the one woman show is in the works – quit nagging!) and Bruce and Jeremiah who are paragons of courage. I'm dedicating this book to you guys.

Last but in no sense least, I'd like to thank the whole LP crew. This includes Brigitte Barta in the Oakland office who showed incredible confidence and derring-do by suggesting me for this assignment. Where she left off, Peter Cruttenden and Anne Mulvaney took over and I learned a lot while working on this book with these and other folks at LP Australia. The cartographers, designers, editors, marketers and everyone else involved with this and every LP title work their butts off (you can barely imagine) and to them I'd like to offer kudos all around. You guys rock!

This book would not have been possible without the unflagging support of Orange Sunshine, our beloved iMac.

THIS BOOK

▶▶

From the Publisher

Martine Lleonart oversaw the content and design development of the series based on the original structure and content devised by Peter Cruttenden. Margaret Jung was responsible for developing the design of the series based on an original design produced by Penelope Richardson. Margaret laid out this book and Penelope designed the cover. Guillaume Roux designed the photographic spread. Anne Mulvaney edited this title with assistance from Graham Fricke, Russ Kerr and Peter Cruttenden. Cartographer Jim Miller produced the maps with the assistance of Jackie Rae, Paul Piaia, Lisa Borg, Natasha Velleley and Piotr Czajkowski. Paul Clifton advised on cartography issues. Csanad Csutoros supplied the climate charts and Tim Uden helped out with Quark. Tamsin Wilson and David Kemp gave advice on design matters and Vicki Beale checked the artwork.

Isabelle Young and Leonie Mugavin wrote the health content, and the following LP authors provided anecdotes from their travels: Scott Doggett, Carolyn Hubbard, Nancy Keller, James Lyon, Jeff Rothman and Chris Rowthorn.

Much of the information in this guide (particularly the country profiles) has been drawn and adapted from existing Lonely Planet titles. Thanks to the following authors for their fine work: Chris Rowthorn and Peter Cruttenden (*Read This First: Asia & India*), Izaskun Arretxe (*Spanish Phrasebook*), Mark Balla (*Brazilian Phrasebook*), Wayne Bernhardson (*Chile & Easter Island, Mexico, South America on a shoestring* and *Argentina, Uruguay & Paraguay*), Tom Brosnahan (*Central America on a shoestring, Guatemala, Belize & Yucatán* and *Mexico*), Anna Cody (*Latin American Spanish Phrasebook*), Scott Doggett (*Mexico* and *Panama*), Andrew Draffen (*Brazil* and *South America on a shoestring*), Krzysztof Dydynski (*Colombia, South America on a shoestring* and *Latin American Spanish Phrasebook*), Susan Forsyth (*Mexico*), Beatrice Glattauer (*Latin American Spanish Phrasebook*), Mark Honan (*Mexico*), Carolyn Hubbard (*Central America on a shoestring*), Allison Jones (*Spanish Phrasebook*), Robyn Jones (*Brazil*), Nancy Keller (*Central America on a shoestring, Guatemala, Belize & Yucatán* and *Mexico*), James Lyon (*Mexico* and *South America on a shoestring*), Chris McAsey (*Brazil*), María Massolo (*South America on a shoestring*), Angela Melendro (*Latin American Spanish Phrasebook*), John Noble (*Mexico*), Leonardo Pinheiro (*Brazil*), Rob Rachowiecki (*Central America on a shoestring* and *South America on a shoestring*), Barbara Reioux (*Central America on a shoestring*), Maria Roca (*Latin American Spanish Phrasebook*), Nick Selby (*Brazil*) and Dianne Swaney (*Bolivia* and *South America on a shoestring*).

FOREWORD

This book is designed to help you to research and prepare for a trip to Central and South America. It contains much of the advice that we'd like to include in our regular travel guides, but cannot due to space limitations. It's a compilation of lessons learned by Lonely Planet travel writers and readers on innumerable trips across the continent, and includes detailed advice on planning your route, buying your ticket, choosing and packing your gear, and surviving your first night on the road. Even more importantly, it contains plenty of advice on day-to-day living while you're on the road – things that hold true across the continent – from finding a decent room, keeping your valuables safe and getting around on some very different forms of transport. In short, this book is the one we wish we'd had before we set out on our first trip.

Writing a travel book that tries to bring all the countries of Central and South America under one roof is a risky undertaking. The continent is so large, and its countries and cultures so diverse, that it is almost impossible to come up with generalisations which apply throughout. The best thing is to consider this book as a first step – like coming upon a new house and taking a peek in the window. As the planning for your trip gets underway, and as you determine the regions you will be visiting, other sources of information – particularly country-specific guidebooks – will help you further along.

This book includes country profiles that provide the basic details and highlights of countries in Central and South America. These can be used to plan your route, calculate your budget and figure out what visas you must get before setting out. These sections won't replace the greater detail you'll need from guidebooks once you're there, but they should serve as a solid start to planning your trip and learning about the cultures you are heading to.

We've also included itineraries for each of the countries. The routes we've selected take in the major sights and attractions, plus a few places further off the beaten track, but if you do some further research and come up with your own specific route, you'll find the aspects of the region that appeal most to your particular tastes and you'll generally have a more rewarding time.

Also included are loads of web site references and addresses in recognition of the increasing role these resources play in travel planning and information. Inevitably, by the time you read this book, some of these links will have changed or disappeared. A keyword search should give you the site's new address.

If you combine the information in this book with some imagination and a healthy sense of adventure, you can't help but fall in love with the place. Remember, the sooner you get started the sooner you'll be stepping off a plane.

The Lonely Planet Story

The story begins with a classic travel adventure – Tony and Maureen Wheeler's 1972 journey across Europe and Asia to Australia. Useful information about the overland trail did not exist at that time, so Tony and Maureen published a guidebook to meet a growing need among the backpacker community.

Written at a kitchen table and hand collated, trimmed and stapled, *Asia on the Cheap* became an instant local bestseller, inspiring thoughts of another book. A further 18 months in South-East Asia resulted in their second guide, *South-East Asia on a shoestring*, which they put together in a backstreet Chinese hotel in Singapore in 1975. The 'yellow bible' as it quickly became known to backpackers around the world, soon became *the* guide to the region. As we go to print, it has sold almost 750,000 copies.

Today Lonely Planet publishes more than 450 titles, including city guides, diving guides, city maps, phrasebooks, trekking guides, wildlife guides, travel atlases and travel literature. The company is the largest independent travel publisher in the world; with offices in Melbourne, Oakland, London and Paris.

However, some things haven't changed. Our main aim is still to help make it possible for adventurous travellers to get out there – to explore and better understand the world. At Lonely Planet we believe that travellers can make a positive contribution to the countries they visit – if they respect their host communities and spend their money wisely. Since 1986 a percentage of the income from each book has been donated to aid projects and human rights campaigns across the world.

Warning & Request

Things change – prices go up, schedules change, good places go bad and bad places go bankrupt – nothing stays the same. So, if you find things better or worse, recently opened or long since closed, please tell us and help make the next edition even more accurate and useful. We genuinely value your feed-back. Julie Young coordinates a well travelled team that reads and acknowledges every letter, postcard and email and ensures that every morsel of information finds its way to the appropriate authors, editors and cartographers for verification.

Everyone who writes to us will find their name in the next edition of the appropriate guide book. They will also receive the latest issue of *Planet Talk*, our quarterly printed newsletter, or *Comet*, our monthly email newsletter. Subscriptions to both newsletters are free. The very best contributions will be rewarded with a free guidebook.

Excerpts from your correspondence may appear in new editions of Lonely Planet guidebooks, the Lonely Planet web site, *Planet Talk* or *Comet*, so please let us know if you don't want your letter published or your name acknowledged.

Send all correspondence to the Lonely Planet office closest to you:

Australia: PO Box 617, Hawthorn, Victoria 3122
USA: 150 Linden St, Oakland, CA 94607
UK: 10A Spring Place, London NW5 3BH
France: 1 rue du Dahomey, 75011 Paris

Or email us at: talk2us@lonelyplanet.com.au

For news, views and updates see our web site: www.lonelyplanet.com

INTRODUCTION

As any old travel hand will tell you, Latin America has it all. Whether you're interested in mountain climbing, skiing, archaeology (actual and armchair), surfing (real and digital), or just some good old relaxing in a hammock overlooking the ocean or mountains, there will be somewhere in Mexico, Central or South America to meet the challenge. In Latin America you'll find some of the most biodiverse rainforest on earth, where thousands of species dwell together in a stunning primordial landscape, plus indigenous cultures that thrive throughout the region despite encroaching modernity. Add Andean peaks, Mayan ruins and tropical beaches to the mix and you have the makings of an awesome adventure.

From precolonial temples and salsa lessons to jungle hikes and Indian markets, there are myriad enticing reasons to explore this part of the world. Suffice to say that this region is a thrilling travel destination, and travellers will find it accessible for two reasons. Firstly, Spanish is an easy foreign language to learn. Portuguese is spoken only in Brazil, and even the severely language-challenged will find a Portuguese or Spanish phrasebook sufficient for getting around and striking up a conversation. Indigenous tongues (spoken exclusively in parts of Latin America) are another story, but if you've got so far off the beaten track that no one speaks Spanish or Portuguese, you're probably doing something right.

The other beauty of Latin American travelling is that buses are ubiquitous. Most locals travel by bus, meaning many destinations are served often and affordably. Plus, bus rides are a great opportunity to meet new folk.

Flights, both domestic and between Mexico, Central and South America are largely a bargain. If you're visiting big countries like Peru or Argentina, or covering a region, flying to and from interest points is a good time-saving strategy. Trains are an option in some countries, and can be dramatic and death-defying (the Devil's Nose route in Ecuador comes to mind). Boat travel is exciting, and in some regions the only option.

Generally speaking, Latin America is affordable. At the end of the dirt track where few travellers have ventured before, it can be downright cheap. With some exceptions, in most Latin American countries US$10 to US$15 a day will keep you clean, well fed and with a place to rest your head. Camping, cooking your own food, riding on buses and other such budgeting tactics are realistic options that can bring down costs considerably.

Latin America is brimful with highlights – the Mayan ruins of Tikal in Guatemala, Belize's coral reef, the Costa Rican rainforest, the fjords of Patagonia, Machu Picchu in Peru, the Galápagos Islands, to name just a few. These places are unique, so you could well be sharing your special experience with throngs of other tourists. Don't despair! Go anyway and make your dreams come true. Often there is a backdoor or little used side entrance to a great attraction, and you can always find pockets of like-minded people wherever you are.

In travel you have to take the good with the bad, come what may. In Latin America, this could mean 10 sweating hours in the back of a bus to reach a pristine river with limestone pools of every blue hue cascading down through the rainforest. It will be worth the discomfort because that river experience will be among the most serene and memorable of your life.

PLANNING ▶▶

What Kind of Trip?

At the outset, you'll need to decide whether you want to go on an organised tour, travel independently, or combine both options.

ORGANISED TOURS

The main advantage of an organised tour is that it enables you to reach out-of-the-way destinations with a minimum of hassles (eg trips to the Galápagos Islands or into the Amazon). Trips that present a logistical or bureaucratic nightmare if attempted independently can be made smooth if arranged by professionals. These could be trips to far-flung destinations, to places regulated by the government, or those requiring specialised equipment, eg white-water rafting. Organised tours are usually all-inclusive, meaning the agency or operator with whom you book your tour minds all the details and you just have to get yourself safely to the point of departure. An organised tour also provides instant travel companions, and some tour guides also double as translators.

The bad news is that organised tours are more expensive than travelling independently and certainly more restricting. If the accommodation, transport, food or guide provided are unsatisfactory to you or other participants, expect a lot of friction. Being on a tour makes it very difficult leave if you're not having a good time, and prevents you from lingering in a place you particularly enjoy. Some travellers find tours hard to tolerate because of these restrictions and the nature of forced group interaction.

Before you book an organised tour, shop around. Ask a lot of questions, especially about the itinerary and guide. This is very important because even if the other travellers are awful and the food poor, a good guide can make or break a trip – after all, you can always steal moments away from the group but you may not be able to understand the meaning of pre-Columbian hieroglyphs without an interpreter. Tours that specialise in activities that interest you, such as birdwatching or mountain climbing, are more likely to attract like-minded people and to create a rewarding travel experience than a generalised tour will.

Australia
  Intrepid Travel
    (☎ 1300-360 667, www.intrepidtravel.com.au) 11 Spring St, Fitzroy, Vic 3065

UK
  Encounter Overland
    (☎ 020-7370 6951, www.encounter.co.uk) 267 Old Brompton Rd, London SW5 9LA
  Exodus
    (☎ 020-8675 5550, www.exodustravels.co.uk) 9 Weir Rd, London SW12 OLT

USA
   Global Exchange
    (☎ 415-255-7296, www.globalexchange.org) 2017 Mission St 303, San Francisco, CA 94110
   Journeys International
    (☎ 1-800-255-8735, www.journeys-intl.com) 107 April Drive, Suite 3, Ann Arbor, MI 48103

International
   Ecotour (www.ecotour.org/ecotour.htm)
   Serious Sports (www.serioussports.com/core.html)
   Specialty Travel (http://specialtytravel.com)

GOING IT ALONE

Travelling alone can seem frightening, lonely and daring when you're snug at home thinking about a trip. Probably it will be all of these things at one time or another. But solo travel is also a rewarding and dynamic challenge that taps energy and skills you won't know you possess until you hit the road.

Finding food and shelter and negotiating transport day after day in a strange land is hard work, and having no one to share that burden can be a drag. Still, there are great benefits to travelling alone. You can go where you want, when you want. Every little decision isn't up to a committee, it's up to you. There is no need to assuage egos, attend to hidden agendas or take someone else's budget into consideration. It's all you, both the mistakes and the triumphs.

In fact you probably won't stay alone for long anyway. Though lonely stretches are inevitable, it's easy to hook up with other travellers in Latin America. Puerto Viejo (Costa Rica), Cuzco (Peru) and Antigua (Guatemala) are all good places to start out alone because they're full of other independent travellers. Solo adventurers will find it surprisingly easy to meet people on the road. When you're by yourself, you have to make an effort to find companionship, and the search will lead you down unexpected paths to new experiences and friends.

If you like the idea of travelling solo but are not sure how you'd handle the reality, try a test trip near home. Camping is a good litmus because it's rough around the edges (like most of Latin America). If you find yourself going psycho after a few days alone, then it's time to start looking for a travel companion.

TRAVELLING WITH FRIENDS

If hitting the road alone doesn't appeal to you, consider travelling with a friend or two. You already share a common history and trust each other. Travelling with a friend has practical advantages too: rooms and food will be cheaper and communal packing can lighten your loads. Travelling as a team is more efficient too: as one person guards the backpacks the other can inspect a hotel room, buy train tickets or hail a taxi. Best of all, travelling with a friend means you have a shoulder to cry on if the going gets tough and an ally if circumstances get dicey.

Best friends won't necessarily make the best travelling companions. Consider the tastes, proclivities, finances and attitudes of your prospective travelling partner before you make firm plans together. Give some thought to levels of comfort – does one person like a daily long, hot bath, while the other splashes their armpits once in a while? Do you have the same ideas about budget? Money can be a very touchy subject, especially if one persons wants to stay in more comfortable (and expensive) accommodation than the other. Do you have similar destinations and activities in mind? If one of you wants to hit the beach and the other dreams of trekking through the jungle, problems could arise if neither is willing to pursue their interests independently. You can't know for sure who will make the best travelling partner, but you can narrow the uncertainty. Go on a short trip to see how you get along together.

If you're travelling in a group, two or three is probably a manageable maximum; otherwise, you're contending with too many personalities, needs and wants for everyone to be satisfied.

Travelling with a lover or spouse is the greatest challenge of all, and will expose characteristics, both ugly and admirable, you never knew existed in both you and your significant other. The trials and joys of travel can make or break a relationship, and there's only one way to find out. You'll either come back single or with new and rich memories woven into your relationship.

Testing the Relationship

Lots of young couples set off together to foreign climes, but many come back separately – travel can be a tough testing ground for personal relationships. People who have lived together for years suddenly discover glaring incompatibilities as they set out on their trip of a lifetime.

When you're travelling together, you probably spend more time in each other's company than any couple ever would at home. Some of this time will be spent in difficult circumstances – on long, uncomfortable bus trips, or in cramped and sweaty hotel rooms – sometimes tired, hungry or exasperated. And how will you cope with all the shared decisions? Is it worth US$12 to stay in the concrete boxes called Paradise Bungalows? Do we trust a guy selling Rolex watches on the street? Will we get cholera eating this stuff? The couples who have it together agree on most things, whether it's trying marinated fish from a street stall or embarking on a seven day jungle trek. The feuding couples bicker over a cheap trinket, and spend the evening sniping at each other as the sun sets superbly over the Pacific Ocean.

As at home, a partner offers security and financial advantages. The security of a relationship really means something when you're in a crowded, chaotic bus station, and one person can sit on the luggage while the other buys the tickets. As for the economics, two people can't travel as cheaply as one, but they can often travel as cheaply as 1½.

The greatest advantage of travelling with your partner comes when you see something intriguing or really amazing. It's pretty much an instinct to turn to the person next to you and say, 'Isn't that whatever?!', and it's sure nice if that person gives a damn.

And if your relationship survives the road test, you might just look back on that marathon bus trip with the crazy driver, the inquisitive kids and the sleazy passengers as a high point of your life together. And that none-too-clean little guesthouse, with the flickering light and the swaying mosquito net, may yet be one of the most romantic places on earth.

James Lyon
LP Author, Australia

STAYING FRIENDS ON THE ROAD

If you can respect each other's privacy, space and travel goals with some measure of consistency, you'll be well on your way to a positive travel experience. For example, if you like to get up at the crack of dawn and roam the empty streets, while your travel mate prefers to sleep in, don't assume you can set the alarm. Teamwork is essential while travelling and you'll need to practise it daily.

Some days are better than others and no trip is free of arguments. Fights usually happen when you're stranded on the side the road in a downpour, having missed the last bus of the day, and tempers flare.

If one of you is still angry after some time and it seems like a break is in order, take one! Head off alone for the day or hook up with some other travellers for a spell to clear the air. Chances are you'll both be feeling the need for space and you can agree on a time and place to meet after a few days apart. This might be a good time to try solo travel if you've ever had an interest. When you hook up again, you'll have had totally different experiences and new ideas to talk about.

FINDING SUITABLE TRAVEL PARTNERS

If none of your friends or family is ready to blaze a trail through Latin America, don't fret. There are lots of other people out there packed and ready to go – you just have to find them. Good places to start looking for travel partners are in the classified ads sections of travel magazines (especially the *South American Explorer*, published by the South American Explorers Club; see the Magazines section later in this chapter for details) where people are looking to connect with partners. Travel web sites and electronic bulletin boards serve the same purpose, as do old-fashioned bulletin boards at colleges, universities or food co-ops. Arrange a meeting with the person before you set off together, perhaps taking a minitrip together to see if you're compatible.

Taking an organised tour, joining a volunteer program or studying Spanish are other options for improving your chances of meeting like-minded people on the road (see the Thematic Trips and Work & Travel sections later in this chapter for some pointers). Throughout Latin America the Gringo Trail – a well beaten track running from Mexico to Tierra del Fuego at the southern tip of Argentina – includes places frequented by foreigners, eg Isla Mujeres on the Yucatán Peninsula, Panajachel in Guatemala, the Cayes in Belize, Lake Titicaca in Peru and Bolivia, and most of Costa Rica. You'll find plenty of company in any of these places.

Your Route

Where you go in Latin America and how you get there will depend largely on time and money. With unlimited quantities of both, you could travel the entire length of the western hemisphere and still be captivated by the time you reach Tierra del Fuego. Needless to say, few are so fortunate, so it's important to decide on what you want to see most before setting off.

Some people prefer to explore one country in depth, usually flying in and out of the capital city and travelling by bus to sites of interest. Others take on a grander scheme and fly into one country and out of another further down the road. The massive Alaska to Argentina odyssey has been in vogue lately and you'll probably meet some of this hard-core contingent on your travels. These types of trips are best served by around-the-world or open-jaw plane tickets, which allow you to fly into one country and depart from another (see the Tickets & Restrictions entry in the Tickets & Insurance chapter for details).

If your preference is to fly into a city and branch out from there, you should decide whether Mexico, Central or South America is your ideal destination. While it is possible (and encouraged!) to take in all three, crossing the land bridge from Panama to Colombia is tricky and time-consuming, as most of the route is through thick, unmarked jungle. If Central America is your choice, consider starting in Antigua (Guatemala) or San José (Costa Rica). Both these cities are abuzz with international backpackers, and buses to anywhere on the isthmus are available. In South America, travel hubs include Lima (Peru), Rio de Janeiro (Brazil) and Caracas (Venezuela). This last is often the cheapest air destination because it's the gateway to the continent.

Travelling overland by motorcycle or car is possible, but not always practical. The paperwork and myriad border crossings will tax your patience; as well, travelling through the Darién Gap between Panama and Colombia is a major hassle because there is no road connecting the two countries and you will need to ship your vehicle around the Gap. The route has been done, however; see the Car & Motorcycle section in the While You're There chapter for more information about driving in Latin America. A good resource is *Driving the Pan-American Highway to Mexico and Central America* by Raymond F & Aubrey Pritchard. Some very hale and hearty folks travel by bicycle, and you may want to consider this option. See Bicycle Touring in the While You're There chapter for more.

Public transportation is another option and eliminates the worry of parking, paperwork and vehicular theft. A combination of buses and planes can give you a good taste of a region, and flying between far-flung points of interest will save time. Planes can spare your nerves too, as the buses in Latin America are not always punctual, efficient or even running! Plane tickets can usually be purchased in the country for less than you'd pay if you booked the flights while still at home (see Getting Around in the While You're There chapter for more transport details).

The following sections describe possible routes for getting to and travelling through Mexico, Central and South America. As everyone has different tastes, make sure you design a route that takes in the sites and activities that appeal to you. Remember that volcanoes can erupt, tectonic plates shift, El Niño can wreak havoc and political and financial crises are always possible, so it's a good idea to check out the current situation before you take off (see the Useful Web Sites section of this chapter for some research pointers). For highlights and suggested itineraries of specific countries, see the country profiles later in this book.

OVERLAND ROUTES

No doubt about it, plane travel is efficient. It's a fantastic and liberating feeling to hop on a plane and a few hours later be someplace totally foreign. Still, watching the transition of a landscape from mountains to sea and experiencing the different lifestyles in those separate environments is a marvel of travel and fairly easily accomplished in Latin America.

It's important not to get caught at a border without a visa, immunisations or enough cash to satisfy the authorities, so research the paperwork needed for crossing between countries (see the Passports & Visas chapter and the country profiles for information on visas and border crossings).

The Gringo Trail: Mexico to Peru & Beyond

The popular Gringo Trail, linking many points of interest to foreign backpackers – hence the name – runs from Mexico to Peru and then south through Bolivia, Chile and Argentina. The route can be lengthened or shortened according to your time, budget, mode of travel and desires. If you want to go for the whole enchilada, you should plan at least a three month trip, although even then you'll miss out on some of the grandeur and regret your trip wasn't longer still. To really have a look around and absorb the Latin American experience, six months is a better target.

Border crossings do not present a problem, but keep in mind that crossing the Darién Gap between Panama and Colombia is very difficult (see the country profiles for more details). Also keep in mind that in Colombia, violence against tourists is an unfortunate reality. Violent attacks, including kidnapping and murder, have occurred in recent years and most informed sources consider it unsafe to travel there, although independent travellers who have been there do report positive experiences. Check with your embassy, the Colombian consulate, news sources and other travellers before deciding on an adventure in Colombia (see also the Colombia profile).

After travelling the start of the Gringo Trail through Mexico, there are several crossings along the lengthy frontier shared by Mexico and Guatemala (see the relevant country profiles later in this book for details), or you can cross from the Yucatán Peninsula to Belize at either Subteniente López, near Chetumal or La Unión. From Belize you can cross to Guatemala at Benque Viejo del Carmen or Punta Gorda (a sea route with ferries to Lívingston or Puerto Barríos).

Guatemala is a fascinating place and you'll want to explore a bit. The main travellers hang-outs are Tikal, Quetzaltenango, Panajachel and Antigua. A good, quick side trip from eastern Guatemala is to the ruins of Copán in Honduras. From Guatemala, you can head to Honduras or swing through El Salvador to points south. Both these routes have border crossings along the Interamericana that are well trodden and straightforward. If that is hackneyed for you, there are plenty of 'unofficial' crossings through the jungle and seafaring crossings.

Many travellers pass quickly through Nicaragua and El Salvador to Costa Rica and then after chilling out in Costa Rica for a while, head to Panama to get to Ecuador and Peru. You can do that, but El Salvador, Nicaragua and Panama are interesting destinations in their own right. A good, popular and cheap option enabling you to avoid the Darién Gap is to fly to Colombia from

Panama or Isla San Andrés (off the coast of Nicaragua, but owned by Colombia). Still, that puts you in Colombia and for safety reasons you may want to fly into Venezuela, Peru or Ecuador instead. If you do opt to fly into Colombia, you can cross into Ecuador at Tulcán.

In Ecuador, the Gringo Trail runs through Otavalo, Quito, Cuenca and points south until crossing into Peru at either Huaquillas or Macará. In Peru, the two key travel destinations are Cuzco, near Machu Picchu and Puno, near Lake Titicaca. You'll want a good amount of time in Peru to do it justice. This is the basic route, but you can keep going through Bolivia and Chile all the way to Tierra del Fuego at the tip of the continent. From Peru you can cross Lake Titicaca into Bolivia or head south into Chile at Arica. The Bolivian route provides more options because you can cross over into Paraguay, Brazil, Chile or Argentina before wending your way south. The best approach to Patagonia and Tierra del Fuego is by air, land or sea from Argentina.

La Ruta Maya: Guatemala, Belize & the Yucatán

This is a mini-Gringo Trail really, with an emphasis on visiting the major Mayan ruins. Starting in Guatemala (having flown into Guatemala City or travelled by bus from Mexico, Costa Rica or Panama), there are many sites, but the big draw is Tikal in the northern region of Petén. The archaeological site is in a 575 sq km park, much of it virgin rainforest.

From Tikal, you can easily visit the ruins of Copán in Honduras on a two day jaunt. Although the setting is not as spectacular as Tikal, Copán is a major archaeological excavation. Back in Guatemala, head into Belize; though the archaeological attractions are slight, there are fantastic beaches, snorkelling and diving in the Cayes. Lastly, you can cross over to Mexico's Yucatán Peninsula, where there are many major sites, including Palenque and Tulum. See the Belize, Guatemala and Mexico profiles for details of border crossings between these three countries.

You would need to allow at least three weeks to a month to see most of these major sites, but Tikal, Copán and a short hop into Belize can be squeezed into two well organised weeks.

The Andes: Bolivia, Ecuador, Peru & Chile

If you're drawn to mountains, you'll swoon before the majesty of the Andes. Bolivia can be described as the Tibet of the Americas, Ecuador is like a less expensive version of Peru (and also boasts the Galápagos Islands), Machu Picchu and Lake Titicaca in Peru are phenomenal, and the massive Andean crest in Chile is almost always within sight – surfing and skiing on the same day is not impossible here. All manner of alpine sports are available this part of the world and if you want to extend your Andean trip, head into Argentina and Patagonia (spanning Argentina and Chile).

Starting in Quito, Ecuador's capital, you can travel down to Cuenca and Vilcabamba before crossing into Peru at Macará or Huaquillas. Lima is about

24 hours or so down the road by bus, from where you can go to Cuzco and Machu Picchu and then on to Lake Titicaca. Here you can cross into Bolivia at either Yunguyo or Desaguadero, or continue south in Peru to cross into Chile at Tacna-Arica.

This route deserves a good six to eight weeks, though tack on an extra week or so if you plan to head to the Galápagos (plus an extra US$1000 if you want to visit this expensive destination).

Brazil

Almost as big as the USA, you could travel around Brazil for months without stopping in the same town twice. Brazil is not only big, it's bustling – two out of thee Brazilians are urbanites – and has a lot to offer. This is the only Portuguese-speaking country on the continent, so high school Spanish will help only a little here. It seems the world flocks to Brazil and specifically Rio de Janeiro in spring for Carnaval. Even so, this raucous, racy party is only one of the many good reasons to visit this country. Some others are its art, music and dancing, its beaches and its Amazonian rainforest. If you're in this part of the world, include the awesome Iguazú Falls in your itinerary, located at the conjunction of the Brazilian and Argentine borders. Domestic air passes allow you five flights in 21 days, so you can see a good portion of this phenomenal country in three weeks. If you have another week or two and some extra money and gumption, consider adding a side trip to Suriname, Guyana or French Guiana. The interiors of all three offer some of the world's best opportunities to experience virgin rainforest and its wild flora and fauna. For more details, see the Brazil, Suriname, Guyana and French Guiana profiles later in this book.

Routes in Mexico, Central & South America

Two Weeks to One Month
- Any single country in Central or South America
- Mexico
- Argentina & Chile
- La Ruta Maya

Two to Three Months
- Mexico, Guatemala, Honduras & Costa Rica
- Ecuador, Peru, Bolivia & Chile
- Venezuela, Guyana, French Guiana, Suriname & northern Brazil

Three to Six Months
- Belize, Guatemala, Honduras, El Salvador, Nicaragua, Costa Rica & Panama
- Mexico, Guatemala, Honduras, Costa Rica, Ecuador & Peru (via the Gringo Trail)
- Ecuador, Peru & Brazil (Amazonian rainforest)

Six Months to One Year
- Yucatán to Tierra del Fuego (via the Gringo Trail)
- The entire South American continent

Thematic Trips

If you're an enthusiast of one type or another, chances are that your interest can be pursued in Latin America. Planning a trip around a hobby or activity is a sure-fire way to meet people with similar pursuits and broaden your travelling experience, and can be pursued independently or as part of an organised tour.

Studying Spanish while living with a local family is popular, as are bird-watching, mountain climbing and surfing. Anyone interested in archaeology and things cosmic will find plenty to interest then throughout the region, as the Mayans, Incans and their descendants relied heavily on celestial movements and signs to structure their life cycles; there are many fascinating archaeological sites throughout Mexico, Central and South America. Likewise, orchid enthusiasts will not be bored: Latin America grows some of the rarest orchids in the world. Consult the activities section of a good guidebook, and see the country profiles later in this book, to assess the options. Specialised books are available on all sorts of topics, including flora, fauna, trekking and diving. The Researching Your Trip section of this chapter lists resources that will help you plan a thematic trip.

Ecotourism has become an extremely popular theme for trips to Central and South America, with many tour operators offering trips based on sustainable living and environmental practices. For details of ecotourism operators, see the Ecotourism section in the Issues & Attitudes chapter.

TREKKING

The Andean cordillera stretches from Venezuela to Chile – ample mountains to climb if that's your interest. Make sure you allow adequate time to adjust to the altitude before heading off and up. Also keep in mind that some of the climbs in this region are very strenuous or technical, so should not be undertaken by novices, though many treks are accessible to any reasonably fit person.

Central America and Mexico have peaks too, though nothing near the soaring heights of the Andes. In these locales, you'll probably be trekking in rainforests rather than along the valleys and ridges of snowcapped mountains (jungle trekking is also available in parts of the Amazon Basin). Jungle trekking is strenuous, and trekkers should be prepared. If you intend to make a holiday of trekking and camping, you might want to bring your own equipment as it may not be available locally or many be of inferior quality.

Mexico – Hikes in Barranca del Cobre (Copper Canyon) and Baja California are spectacular. Volcano hikes include Popocatépetl, Volcán Paricutín, Volcán Nevado and Volcán de Fuego de Colima. There are also more than 40 national parks that can be explored on foot.

Guatemala – The Petén region in northern Guatemala has it all for that jungle experience: virgin rainforest, monkeys, felines, tropical birds, plus big bugs and snakes. The ruins of Tikal are here and are alone worth the trip. Several volcanoes throughout the country, some active, also make good climbs.

Honduras – There are several national parks in Honduras with good hiking and wildlife viewing opportunities, including Capiro-Calentura, Cusuco, Pico Bonito and La Tigra.

El Salvador – With more than 25 extinct volcanoes, there is plenty of trekking to be done in El Salvador (but not many trails). There is also little tourist infrastructure here, but if challenging, independent travel is your goal, this may be the place for you.

Costa Rica – A hiker's dream, Costa Rica has an extensive and well developed network of national parks covering several geographical regions. From Volcán Arenal, which spews forth lava daily, and Cerro Chirripó, Costa Rica's loftiest peak at 3820m, to Parque Nacional Corcovado with its deep jungle, it's all here. You could spend months trekking and camping throughout Costa Rica.

Panama – Don't overlook Panama if you want a trekking adventure. Among its challenges is Volcán Barú, with seven craters; Cana, a bird lover's paradise and the most isolated area of Panama; and the rainforest at Soberanía.

Colombia – Trekking in Colombia is very risky due to the poor security situation for tourists, so you might opt for the Ecuadorian, Peruvian or Bolivian Andes instead. If things should settle down, however, two of Colombia's best mountain treks are in the Sierra Nevada del Cocuy and the Sierra Nevada de Santa Marta. You will need to bring all your own gear.

Venezuela – A network of 42 Venezuelan national parks offers good hiking, ranging in levels of difficulty. The Sierra Nevada de Mérida region is the best for hiking and mountain climbing.

Ecuador – A small country with intense biodiversity, you can climb Chimborazo (6310m) in the mountainous country south of Quito one day and be deep in the jungle to the east the next. There are many Andean peaks, volcanoes and *páramo* (high-altitude grassland) to explore throughout Ecuador. Gear can be rented in Quito, Cuenca and other large towns.

Peru – Mountaineering fans unite in Peru among peaks averaging between 3000 and 4000m high, with the highest, Huascarán, measuring 6768m. This peak is in the Huaraz region, the heart of Peruvian trekking country. May to September is the best time to trek in Peru, and gear is available for rent. Be sure to make the four or five day trek into the spectacular hidden Incan city of Machu Picchu.

Bolivia – The Bolivian Andes rival Nepal for trekking possibilities. You can follow ancient Incan roads into the dramatic Yungas region, take on the challenge of the remote Cordillera Quimsa Cruz and Cordillera de los Frailes, and perfect your snow-climbing techniques on the many peaks in the 6000m range. Parque Nacional Ulla-Ulla, along the Peruvian border, has good hikes. Some treks require guides and in some areas you'll be a curiosity (few foreigners make it to the heart of the Bolivian Andes).

Chile – Chilean national parks such as Torres del Paine, El Morado near Santiago and La Campana near Viña del Mar offer good trekking opportunities. Hikers visiting the southern hemisphere for the first time should look for a compensated needle compass like the Recta DP 10; northern hemisphere compasses are deceptive as an indicator of direction in far southern latitudes.

Argentina – Cerro Aconcagua (6962m) is South America's highest peak but is relatively straightforward for experienced mountaineers in peak physical condition. The Fitzroy Range (Cerro Fitzroy) in Parque Nacional Los Glaciares is another popular area, as are the mountains of Parque Nacional Nahuel Huapi, around Bariloche. Tierra del Fuego and the northern Andean region around Valle de Humahuaca are also popular.

Brazil – Along with superior Amazonian jungle treks that could occupy you for months, Brazil has challenging rock climbing opportunities, and within just 40 minutes of Rio de Janeiro are 350 documented climbs.

DIVING & SNORKELLING

The top three diving and snorkelling sites in Latin America are along the Belizean barrier reef, around the Bay Islands (Islas de la Bahía) off the coast of Honduras, and in the Galápagos Islands. These locales offer world-class diving and marine life viewing, some unlike any you'll see anywhere else.

Open-water scuba diving certification is available in the Galápagos for about US$400. Though this isn't too expensive and sounds very exotic, actually getting to the Galápagos will lighten your wallet by about US$1000. Still, many people get certification in the Galápagos because much of the fantastic wildlife, both marine and terrestrial, is found only here.

The Bay Islands are known for their affordable certification; a four day Professional Association of Diving Instructors (PADI) certification course costs around US$125 on Utila or US$195 on Roatán.

If you don a mask and poke your head below water just about anywhere along the Mexican or Central and South American coast, you're likely to see something, but unfortunately it might be no more than a Coke can! For superior snorkelling, try any of the above-mentioned locales, many parts of Coast Rica, the Caribbean coast of Panama and Nicaragua, and parts of coastal Venezuela.

Respecting the plants and animals you'll encounter while diving and snorkelling is imperative. Bring your own equipment if you plan an extensive diving or snorkelling trip; although rental gear is available at most places, nothing will compare with your own.

Mexico – Both coasts have good snorkelling and diving opportunities, although the visibility is generally better on the Caribbean side. There, divers favour Isla Mujeres, Playa del Carmen, Cozumel, Akumal and Xcalak. On the Pacific coast, Puerto Vallarta, Zihuatanejo, Acapulco and Huatulco are popular.

Belize – An underwater paradise awaits divers at Caye Caulker and Ambergris Caye, where Belize's 290km-long barrier reef is the second-longest in the world, after the Great Barrier Reef in Australia. Underwater visibility is up to 60m and some of the most exciting cave diving in the world is found here (you should only try this if you are an experienced diver).

Honduras – The coral reef of the Bay Islands of Utila, Roatán and Guanaja is an extension of Belize's barrier reef. The diving is superb and certification cheap, and more advanced divers can enjoy a variety of specialised diving opportunities.

Costa Rica – Good snorkelling spots include Manzanillo, Puerto Viejo and Cahuita on the Caribbean coast, and near Parque Nacional Manuel Antonio. Diving and certification opportunities on the Pacific coast can be found at Playa Hermosa, Playa del Coco and Playa Ocotal. Two boat dives will cost about US$60.

Nicaragua – The Corn Islands off Nicaragua's Caribbean coast offer excellent snorkelling. Near the coast of the big Corn Island, there's an old Spanish galleon in water shallow enough to be seen by snorkellers, and there are reefs full of marine life for exploring. You'll need your own gear.

Panama – Probably the best place in Panama for snorkelling and diving is Parque Nacional Marino Isla Bastimentos, in the Bocas del Toro Archípelago on the Caribbean coast of western Panama. Diving in the Panama Canal and exploring the sunken locomotive there is also possible.

Getting Hammered in the Sea of Cortez

In his book *The Fishes of New York*, Samuel Latham Mitchell tells us that during September, 1805, Joshua Turry of Long Island, New York, netted three hammerhead sharks, the largest of which was 11 feet long. 'On opening it, many detached parts of a man were found in his belly; these were collected and buried,' wrote Mitchell.

The man may have been dead before his rendezvous with the shark. Most sharks, hammerheads included, pose little threat to people. But the thought that a hammerhead *could* complement its usual diet of stingrays with a human being is something believed by all divers hoping to see one.

At least that's the case with the divers who seek out hammerhead sharks at El Bajo, literally the 'Deep Place', near La Paz, Mexico. Among the plethora of marine life here are scalloped hammerheads, which can grow to 4.5m. Within El Bajo, the place to find these massive sharks is the worn tip of a submerged extinct volcano known as the Sea Mount.

From boatside, the water above the Sea Mount is dark turquoise, and on a good day you can see the top of the undersea mountain 24m below. Scuba diving here, you will see schools of small fish when you enter the water and a sandy ocean bottom that appears to be stitched together with patches. As you descend, these patches become clear: they are in fact dark mounds of rock and coral rising off the ocean floor. And gracefully weaving between the piles are hammerheads prowling for stingrays.

There are no records of a scalloped hammerhead ever attacking anyone. But that fact is quickly forgotten when a few hammerheads sweep past. On a gorgeous day a few years ago, I found myself in just that position.

I was diving with a friend around the Sea Mount area. On the first of our four scheduled dives, we saw barracudas, two moray eels and many butterfly fish, but, alas, no hammerheads. It wasn't until our last dive that one appeared.

We were in front of five divers, swimming against a slight current that carried bits of grey crud kicked up by a recent storm, making the visibility awful. The sea floor appeared and disappeared as clouds of crud passed, and I was giving up hope of seeing a hammerhead when Rick pointed at something down and ahead.

There, gliding between masses of coral, was big shark with a broad T-head. In a moment it slipped out of sight, disappearing into a murky wall that we were quickly approaching. But just a beat after it vanished, a pair of even bigger hammerheads emerged from the same cloudy mass below. Then they, too, turned and disappeared.

We were running low on air when three more hammerheads appeared out of the greyness about 22m below us and moving towards us. At about 18m, two of the sharks cut to the right and vanished. The third, however, kept coming.

Several people had told me hammerheads are skittish around divers; the creatures don't like all the bubbles scuba tanks produce. By the time the big shark was within 5m of me, I'd taken to flapping my arms and making as many bubbles as I could.

To my extreme relief, the giant beast glided past, its motionless eye and rows of gnarled teeth practically in reach, but its appetite unwhetted by this weird creature in a skintight rubber suit.

In the days that followed, Rick and I snorkelled with sea lions, raced a school of fun-seeking dolphins in a rented boat, and partied with other travellers on one of the area's many secluded beaches. But what we'll remember most were those hammerheads, especially the one that came *so* close before turning and slipping back into the greyness of a stormy sea.

Scott Doggett
LP Author, USA

Venezuela – One of the most popular places for snorkelling and diving is Parque Nacional Morrocoy along Venezuela's north-west coast. Tours and equipment rental are available. The Archipiélago de los Roques is a 2211 sq km national park near Caracas, with beautiful beaches and coral reefs. The islands comprising Parque Nacional Mochima on Venezuela's Caribbean coast also have snorkelling opportunities.

Ecuador – In the Galápagos Islands, you can swim with penguin and sea lion colonies, check out hammerhead sharks, frolic with marine turtles and when you surface, observe birds and reptiles unique to these islands. It's expensive to get there, but worth it. The water is quite chilly (20°C or 68°F), very rough from September to November and visibility can be low. Snorkelling day trips are about US$10 per person (minimum four people) and a two-dive day trip is around US$75.

SURFING

With so much coastline comes waves, and Latin America has plenty. The Pacific coast of Central America has several internationally renowned surf breaks, including a perfect left-hand break in Costa Rica's Parque Nacional Santa Rosa. Several international surfing competitions are held in these parts, most notably at Zunzal in El Salvador.

In South America, Brazil is best known for surfing (though Brazilians can be possessive and aggressive in the water). Other surfing possibilities exist in Ecuador and Chile: work your way around the coast finding the rad breaks. If you're planning your trip around surfing, bring your own board. You may return with two: bargains are to be had in the Latino surf world. Wherever you end up, be very mindful of the riptides. For more information on surfing in Central America, visit Surf Reports at www.centralamerica.com/cr/surf or Surfline at www.surfline.com. For good photos and information (in Portuguese) on Brazilian breaks, visit CameraSurf Homepage at www.uol.com.br/camerasurf.

Mexico – Head to the Pacific coast breaks for some great summer surfing, and especially check out the stretch in Baja California between San José del Cabo and Cabo San Lucas (right at the bottom tip), Bahía de Matanchén, and Puerto Escondido's 'Mexican Pipeline' in Oaxaca State. There are many other breaks around Mazatlán, Ensenada, Manzanillo and Zihuatanejo.

Costa Rica – The left-hand break in Santa Rosa national park whips around a monstrous rock before sweeping onto shore. There's camping, and the road to the beach is closed to vehicles in the rainy season, when you could have the place to yourself. There are dozens of breaks throughout Costa Rica, including those at Tamarindo, Jacó, Quepos and Puerto Viejo. All these places are enormously popular, but there are many more off the beaten track.

El Salvador – The ever-popular La Libertad is a major surfies' hang-out, but you can also try Zunzal close by for some good waves. Both of these places can't really be surfed from March to October, when rocks are exposed and garbage washes up.

Nicaragua – Popular spots include Poneloya beach near León and Playa Popoyo in the department of Rivas, on the Pacific coast.

Panama – Again, the best breaks are on the Pacific coast. Try the easily accessible Playa El Palmar near San Carlos, Playa Venado at the southern end of the Península de Azuero, and the comparatively remote Santa Catalina further west, which can be reached by a long road turning off from Soná.

Brazil – Waves break all the way down the coast, but you'll find the best surfing in the south. Joaquina beach in Santa Catarina (host of the Brazilian championships the last two weeks in May), Saquarema in Río state, and Búzios and Itacoatiara in Niterói are the most popular. Conditions are best from May to August.

Chile – The Chilean coast has many breaks, most with dangerous riptides (use the buddy system in spots with particularly rough surf) and all with uncomfortably cold water. Bring a wetsuit and head to Arica, Iquique or Antofagasta in the Norte Grande. Pichilemu is another popular spot.

Ecuador – The breaks are not phenomenal here, but Ecuador's other attractions make it worth a stop. A cool place to catch some waves and hang out is Montañita, where the surf is up from February to June. Boards and gear can be rented, bought and sold here.

WHITE-WATER RAFTING & KAYAKING

Latin America truly has it all, and rafting and kayaking (river and sea) are fast becoming popular. Some of the best white-water rafting in the world in fact can be found in Chile, Peru and Argentina, which have all classes of rapids. Ecuador is developing a rafting industry, as is Guatemala and Honduras, while Costa Rica leads the pack in river adventure sports with many tour operators available. Kayaking is most popular in Chile.

Guatemala – The Lanquín and Cahabon rivers and the area around Lago de Izabal are the most popular for white-water rafting, and tours are offered by several companies. Different rivers are run at varying times, so you can raft year-round.

Honduras – White-water rafting is popular on the Río Cangrejal near La Ceiba, and several companies in La Ceiba offer rafting tours on this river. The rapids are Class III and IV. The Río Sico in Olancho is another possibility. Sea kayaking around the beautiful Bay Islands is an experience you won't soon forget. Equipment and guides are available.

Costa Rica – You can raft either the Río Reventazón or the Río Pacuare from San José as day trips. There are many tour operators to choose from. Sea kayaks are available for rent along the Pacific coast and are a good way to view wildlife.

Ecuador – South of Quito, good white-water rafting is possible on the Patate and Pastaza rivers near Baños. Beware of inexperienced guides here; several tourists died in 1998 when they were abandoned by their guide after he missed the pullout. Better rapids can be found further afield in the Oriente region. The Jatanyacu and Mishuallí rivers here are especially challenging.

Peru – In February, Class III rapids are running on the Río Cañete on Peru's southern coast, and both easier and harder runs are possible on Río Majes near Arequipa. In the same area, Río Colca is recommended only for the very experienced. In the hiking heartland of Huaraz in the north of the country, rafting is possible on the Río Santa during the rainy season (October to May).

Chile – The Maipo, Claro and Biobío rivers are hot spots for white-water rafting and kayaking, although hydroelectric development is seriously threatening the Biobío. Class V rapids exist on the Biobío, Futaleufú and others in the southern lakes district, and in Aisén with its islands, fjords and glaciers. Sea kayaking is becoming increasingly popular in and around the sheltered waters of Chiloé.

Argentina – The best white-water rafting is on the rivers that descend from the Andean divide, including the Río Mendoza and Río Diamante in the Cuyo region, the Río

Hua Hum and Río Meliquina near San Martín de los Andes, and the Limay and Manso rivers near Bariloche in Patagonia. Some of these are gentle Class II floats, but most of the rest are Class III, plus white-water.

WILDLIFE VIEWING & BIRDWATCHING

You may think yourself in the middle of a *National Geographic* spread during your Latin American adventure: there are so many diverse species dwelling in its forests, mountains and rivers that it's sometimes hard to believe it's all real. The wildlife viewing and birdwatching opportunities in Mexico, Central and South America are epic when you consider the area includes the Galápagos Islands, the Amazon rainforest and Patagonia, plus many other less known but just as spectacular spots.

A system of national parks, protected areas, wildlife refuges and biosphere reserves throughout the region facilitates independent wildlife viewing and birdwatching. However, it's worth considering an organised tour or two to increase your chances of seeing the rarer or more spectacular species. Many specialised books describing the animals and birds of the region are available to help you discern a macaw from a quetzal, a howler from a spider monkey, a peccary from a tapir and a marine iguana from a Jesus lizard.

Guatemala – It is especially easy to view all manner of jungle wildlife in the Petén region of northern Guatemala. Tikal, one of the most important Mayan sites, is also here, so you could plan an entire trip with this as your base. Birders favour the Biotopo del Quetzal reserve north of Guatemala City and the Bocas del Polochic, Guatemala's second largest freshwater wetland area.

Honduras – Birdwatching is especially good in Honduras, where there are hundreds of species, including toucans, quetzals (if you're lucky), macaws and parrots. Good viewing places are near the Copán ruins, Lago de Yojoa and the lagoon at Hacienda de Jaral, which is visited by thousands of migratory herons from November to May.

Costa Rica – What doesn't dwell in Costa Rica? About 200 species of mammals are recorded, nearly the same number of reptiles, about 850 bird species, 160 species of amphibians and 35,000 insect species. Head to Parque Nacional Corcovado to see scarlet macaws, monkeys, peccaries, sloths and snakes, and hear a feline or two crashing around the jungle floor. The seldom visited Parque Nacional Rincón de la Vieja has animals so unaccustomed to humans, they'll lurk around trying to figure you out.

Panama – There are 16 national parks in Panama. Within Parque Nacional Camino de Cruces, you may see titi monkeys, armadillos, iguanas and three-toed sloths. The Parque Nacional del Darién, a United Nations World Heritage Site and a Biosphere Reserve, is the largest tropical rainforest wilderness in Central America. At least 940 bird species have been recorded in Panama, and the elusive quetzal is more abundant in western Panama than anywhere else in the region.

Colombia – It's a shame travel in Colombia is so dangerous, because the country is packed with wildlife. Some 300 species of mammals call it home, along with ocelots, jaguars, peccaries, spectacled bears and tapirs. About 1550 bird species have been recorded. There are 34 national parks in Colombia.

Venezuela – Many of Venezuela's 42 national parks have been neglected as far as facilities and trails are concerned, but this provides a great opportunity for the adventurous wildlife fan. Three to four-day wildlife safaris are available to Los Llanos,

Venezuela's greatest repository of animals, particularly birds. Other good opportunities to see wildlife exist in the Delta del Orinoco and Cueva del Guácharo, a magnificent cave home to the unusual *guácharo* (oilbird).

The Guianas – Birders and wildlife enthusiasts should consider a trip to Guyana, French Guiana or Suriname to see the large, pristine tropical rainforest of the interior. Within the forest dwell jungle cats, monkeys, several types of frogs and butterflies. Possible bird sightings include harpy eagles, jabirus, macaws and scarlet ibises.

Brazil – Brazil ranks first in the world for its variety of primate and amphibian species and third for bird species. The superb places to go are the Amazon and the Pantanal, a vast alluvial plain bordering Bolivia and northern Paraguay. The latter is more diverse in terms of wildlife and has few people and no towns – a real challenge! You can go on a tour, drive or walk, which will often be your only option due to road wash-outs and lack of traffic. The dry season (April to October) is the best time to go and the birds are most plentiful from July to September. The Pantanal is also a sanctuary for giant river otters, anaconda and iguana, jaguar and cougar, among other animals.

Argentina – Excellent opportunities to view unique marine wildlife exist in coastal Patagonia and on the Falkland Islands (Islas Malvinas). Here you'll see sea lions, penguins, elephant seals and a plethora of birds.

Chile – Chile has a large network of well developed national parks akin to those you'd find in Europe or the USA. The rare Patagonian guanaco roams in southern Chile in the Parque Nacional Torres del Paine and endangered vicuñas live in the northern highlands, along with huge nesting colonies of flamingos.

Peru – The varied geography of Peru supports an amazing diversity of animals and birds. Marine wildlife and sea birds (Humboldt penguins, brown boobies, Incan terns and others) can be viewed from the Islas Ballestas and the Península de Paracas. For an Amazonian jungle experience, try to visit Parque Nacional Manu, which has more than 1000 bird species and 13 different types of monkey.

Ecuador – Darwin developed his theory of evolution in the Galápagos Islands and the animals here are so tame as to enable in-depth scientific observation. Here you can swim with sea lions and penguins, have a picnic with marine iguanas, watch red-footed and blue-footed boobies tend to their young and snorkel with sharks (which have never been known to attack a human swimmer). If you can't afford to get to the Galápagos, similar (though not the same!) wildlife viewing is available at Parque Nacional Machalilla on the coast. The Reserva Faunística Cuyabeno in the Oriente supports many jungle species and is well worth a look.

Bolivia – The Bolivian national park system is not the easiest to access, but that does mean fewer tourists and more animals. Try Parque Nacional Alto Madidi (for more than 1000 bird species), Parque Nacional Amboró, near Santa Cruz (for big animals like the rare spectacled bear, jaguars, capybaras and peccaries) and Parque Nacional Ulla-Ulla (for condors and a 2500-head vicuña colony).

ORCHIDS

The rainforests and cloud forest of Latin America harbour more than birds and wildlife; they are also home to wild plants. Orchids are the queen of the floral world, and some of the most flamboyant in the world grow in this region. Many of the thousands of species are unique to Central or South America (especially in the Amazon region), and if you are at all interested in native flora, don't pass up the opportunity to see these beauties in the wild. Mexico, Guatemala, Belize,

Panama, Venezuela, Peru, Colombia and Brazil all contain magnificent orchid habitats (see Specialist Guides in the Researching Your Trip section for some useful references).

LEARNING SPANISH OR PORTUGUESE

There are a number of Latin American cities with a reputation for good language schools. Usually, classes are combined with a homestay to promote language immersion. Other electives such as cooking, dance or literature may be offered. In this way, you learn a language while experiencing and participating in the culture of the country in which you're studying. Popular countries for learning Spanish include Mexico, Guatemala, Costa Rica, Ecuador and Argentina. Brazil has good Portuguese schools. There are other places, but it's most important that you find a program that's right for you. When choosing a school, consider the student-to-teacher ratio, hours of daily instruction, location, and other classes offered. The best information will come from alumni, so find out what other travellers have to say about the school you're considering. A terrific web site listing hundreds of Spanish schools in Latin America is *Learn Spanish* (www.studyspanish.com). It also has a free online tutorial.

Mexico – There is a long tradition of Spanish-language instruction in Mexico and you won't be disappointed with the range of options. Cities with public or private language schools include Mexico City, Guadalajara, Guanajuato, Cuernavaca, San Miguel de Allende, Morelia, Taxco, Oaxaca and Puerto Vallarta.

Guatemala – The current debate is whether it's better to study in Antigua or Quetzaltenango. Both have good schools, which is the important part. Antigua is more picturesque, but overflowing with tourists as a result. Quetzaltenango retains more of a Guatemalan feel; you can also study Mayan languages here. Antigua remains, however, the classic 'live with a family and study Spanish' town.

Costa Rica – San José has a slew of Spanish schools, so take time to find one that suits your needs. Instruction typically costs about US$300 a week, including a homestay with a Costa Rican family. Alternatively, you can study on the beach at La Dominical for about US$250 a week including accommodation, or near Monteverde if rainforest is more your scene. There are language schools in Heredia and Manuel Antonio as well.

Colombia – Two universities offer Spanish instruction: the Universidad Javeriana's Centro Latinoamericano in Bogotá offers regular one-year courses (260 hours, US$880) and three-week intensive courses (72 hours, US$370). The Universidad Nacional has seven-week courses (56 hours, US$280).

Brazil – You can arrange for Portuguese instruction in most large Brazilian cities, though Rio de Janeiro is by far the most popular place to study. Head to the Instituto Brazil Estados Unidos (IBEU) there for information on private tutors and language schools.

Ecuador – Quito is highly popular for language study and you'll find no shortage of schools. Costs average about US$5 an hour, depending on class size and the quality of the teacher. Literature, dancing and cooking classes are popular electives. You can also take classes in Cuenca or Otavalo, both prettier, slower towns than Quito.

Bolivia – A nascent language school industry is sprouting in Bolivia. You'll probably want to study in Cochabamba, a popular spot with travellers and where a private tutor charges about US$5 an hour.

Argentina – Probably the most expensive of the language locales, both in terms of the cost of living and the actual classes, Buenos Aires nonetheless has a good selection of schools; many people choose to study here despite the cost.

OTHER ACTIVITIES

If you can dream it, you can probably do it somewhere in Mexico, Central or South America. Just some of the options are skiing in Argentina and Chile, weaving lessons in Guatemala, archaeological digs in Costa Rica, samba lessons in Brazil, windsurfing in Honduras and cycling anywhere. The Researching Your Trip section in this chapter will help you plan a trip around a favourite activity.

Volunteer and paid work can also play a dynamic part in your trip; see the Work & Travel section in this chapter for tips on getting jobs.

When to Go

When you've saved enough money, that's when to go! But seriously, there are weather factors, festival seasons and times when every other traveller, local and foreign, is on the same beach as you. When you begin to plan your trip, consider the timing. Latin America covers such a large area that with a little forethought, you're bound to find a place where prices are affordable, crowds are thin and the weather is at least OK, if not ideal.

WEATHER

Weather talk is always tricky, especially when you're dealing with a landmass that straddles the equator, has massive mountain ranges and almost touches the South Pole. Still, there are weather tendencies that if taken into account should prevent you growing mouldy from damp or swooning from unrelenting heat.

The weather phenomenon known as El Niño is a serious concern for travellers to Latin America: the weather conditions it creates can knock out bridges and power, wash away hotels, chew up roads and flood towns. El Niño becomes especially capricious between November and February, and it can take months (or longer) for a place to recover. On top of this, the hurricane season hits Central America from June to November, so exactly when a place is recovering from the hurricanes, it's hit with El Niño. Some years are worse than others for both these phenomena.

Another factor to keep in mind is elevation. While Ecuador straddles the equator, has lowland temperatures reaching 25°C and receives nearly 450mm of rain in a month, it also contains highlands where it's 15°C and a drop of rain has yet to fall. The Andean countries, Mexico, Honduras, Guatemala and Nicaragua also fall into this alpine category.

Costa Rica, Belize, El Salvador, Panama and Venezuela are a little more consistent because they have fewer mountains. These countries have a distinct wet (winter) and a dry (summer) season, though these seasons vary slightly by region. The Guianas and Suriname on the north coast of South America fall into this category, as does most of Brazil. The following section divides the countries of Latin America into two broad weather categories: alpine and subtropical.

Subtropical Countries

Costa Rica, El Salvador, Panama, Belize and Venezuela have a wet season (winter) that runs from about April or May to November or December, and a dry season (summer) that starts around December and ends in April or May. These are not hard and fast time frames, however, and cheating on either side of the seasons can net you a trip with beautiful weather and few crowds.

The wet season is just that. On the coast especially you can expect rain more often than not, and sometimes hard for days in a row. Figure on serious humidity as well. The good news is that it doesn't rain as often inland and you might head there to dry off a bit. Winter temperatures in the lowland coastal regions average about 30 to 35°C, while inland they're cooler at an average of 26°C.

The summer dry season is the perfect time to travel in these countries – for you and everyone else. During this period, prices may rise, accommodation can become pinched, and tourist sights and transport will be crowded. Inland, it's dry and sunny, but you'll still face the possibility of rain on the coasts; it just won't rain as long or as hard. Mixing your itinerary between coastal and inland regions can help you follow perfect weather.

Closer to the equator, the Guianas and Suriname are super-hot and humid. In fact, the weather can be so uncomfortable it was one of the reasons the Spanish opted not to colonise here. Guyana has two rainy seasons, one from May to August and the other from November to January. Suriname gets drenched in December and January, and between April and July, while French Guiana's rains are from January to the beginning of June. By the time you get to French Guiana, you may want to cross over to Brazil, which has all manner of weather.

The Brazilian winter is from June to August. In the southern states of Rio Grande do Sul, Santa Catarina, Paraná and São Paulo, it's like a real winter, with average temperatures of 18°C and snow in spots. December to February is summer, when everyone is on vacation and travelling about is more difficult and expensive. Summer in Rio de Janeiro is brutally hot and humid with average temperatures of 40°C. On the north-east coast at the same time, it's pleasant and breezy. It rains inland during the summer, but only intermittently on the coast.

Paraguay and Uruguay are the most even-keeled countries weather-wise, with about 1500mm of rain falling evenly throughout the year.

Alpine Countries

Altitude has a great effect on weather, and those areas with peaks above 3500m average daily temperatures of about 10°C, although it's not always that cold. The general rule of thumb is that for each 1000m increase in altitude, the temperature drops 6°C. Even though there are technically wet and dry seasons in the alpine countries, it won't rain every day in the wet season and rain is unlikely to disturb travel plans. Countries with this type of alpine weather include Mexico, Honduras, Guatemala, Panama, Colombia, Ecuador, Peru, Bolivia, Chile and Argentina. The last two are special cases in that both altitude and latitude play a part in their weather. In fact Bolivia, Peru, Chile and Argentina boast snowcapped mountains *and* deserts. The latter two both claim territory in Tierra del Fuego and Patagonia, where weather can be inclement year-round.

For the most part, the Andes taper off into subtropical lowlands that are marked by heat, humidity and rain. Though there is no definitive pattern, it will be hotter here than in the highlands and it will rain more often. This occurs in Ecuador, Peru, Colombia and northern Bolivia. From December to April (coastal summer) the Ecuadorian, Colombian and Peruvian coast swelters and there's no controlling the heat and dust. April to December is generally dry, with a thick coastal fog that rarely lifts.

SPECIAL EVENTS

Holidays and festivals are a big deal in Latin America, and some people travel there specifically to witness special events. There are huge extravaganzas like Carnaval in Brazil, but there are also some more low-key, no less inspiring observances like the Mayan new year in Guatemala or Inti Raymi in Peru. While some people like to happen upon special events, these celebrations are almost guaranteed to provide a memorable experience, so if at all possible try to incorporate some Latin American holidays into your itinerary.

The downside to travel at these times is that people from all over the world, including the region you're visiting, flock to these celebrations. Rooms can be scarce, prices high and buses cramped to overflowing. The common wisdom is to book a room far in advance and arrive at least a couple of days before the beginning of the festival. Alternatively, consider visiting the event site on a day trip, hunkering down in a town further afield for the night. See the boxed text 'Major Festivals in Latin America' and the country profiles for descriptions of some of the region's more spectacular events.

TRAVEL PERIODS

When you get down to the nitty-gritty planning of arrival and departure dates, you'll have to take into consideration peak, off-peak and shoulder travel periods. Peak travel periods are the times when everyone wants to fly somewhere. These include, but are not limited to, Christmas and Hanukkah, New Year and Thanksgiving (in the USA). To complicate matters, your destination country will have its own peak periods. The entire Easter week throughout Latin America is known as Semana Santa; it is notoriously tough to get a room and travel about during this week. The same holds true for the period leading up to Brazil's Carnaval. Incoming flights will be expensive and heavily booked during these times.

In Central and South America, the peak seasons are December to January and March to April. The peak seasons for Mexico are July to August and

December to January. The shoulder period, when air fares are cheaper (but not as cheap as during off-peak), is from June to August for Central and South America and February to May for Mexico. For the budget-conscious, off-peak travel periods (February, May, and September to November) will net the

Major Festivals in Latin America

From sacred indigenous ceremonies in Peru to Carnaval in Rio, Latin America is chock-full of exciting festivals and observances. Try to wrangle at least one into your itinerary. Dates may vary from year to year because they are based on ancient calendars, or because local authorities alter the dates. Here is a selection of some of our favourite festivals in Latin America.

Rabin Ajau (Guatemala) – Held in Cobán in the Guatemalan highlands, Rabin Ajau is probably one of the most impressive festivals of indigenous traditions. From around 21 to 26 July, the Kekchi Indians of the region celebrate by wearing traditional costumes and dancing the sacred Paabanc.

Carnaval (Brazil) – Brazilians and visitors from all over the world let it all hang out during Carnaval. Carnaval takes over the entire month of February in the lead-up to Lent in Rio de Janeiro, the queen Carnaval city. Parades, dancing, music and good old debauchery abound.

Inti Raymi (Peru) – The 'sun festival' of Cuzco takes place on 24 June, when the streets are closed off for the huge celebration. The denouement is a re-enactment of the Inca winter solstice observance at Sacsayhuamán.

Los Diablos Danzantes (Venezuela) – Get your mojo working for the festival of the Devil Dancers, held on Corpus Christi (usually the ninth Thursday after Easter) in San Francisco de Yare, 60km south of Caracas. A fiery parade and devil-dancers cap off the festivities.

Día de Los Muertos (Mexico) – On November 2, Mexicans usher the souls of their dead back to earth in this festival called The Day of the Dead. Altars, offerings and graveside visits are designed to commune with those on the other side. The area around Pátzcuaro is especially colourful at this time, but the whole country comes alive.

Día de Nuestra Señora de Guadalupe (Mexico) – 12 December is the day of Mexico's patron saint, Guadalupe, who appeared to a Mexican Indian as the Virgin Mary in 1531. Festivities build momentum the week before and culminate with a huge procession and party at the Basílica de Guadalupe in Mexico City.

Festival of Yamor (Ecuador) – Otavalo's biggest shindig is held in the first two weeks of September (dates vary). The Queen of the Fiesta is a highlight, as are the fireworks, parades and all-round party atmosphere that seizes this highland town during the festival.

Chu'tillos, or the Fiesta de San Bartolomé (Bolivia) – This rocking festival takes place on the last weekend of August or the first in September in La Paz. Folk dancing and costumes, parades and exhibitions are staged by Bolivians from around the country. Musical and dance groups come from as far afield as China and the USA.

Festival Internacional de Música del Caribe (Colombia) – The second half of March is given over to the music of the Caribbean in the beautiful town of Cartagena. For three to four days, the Plaza de Toros hosts groups from Colombia and around the world to jam away.

Día del Tango (Argentina) – An informal event celebrated on 11 December, the birthday of the tango great Carlos Gardel. Hit Buenos Aires for tango events and a pilgrimage to the singer's grave. Also check out the Día de la Muerte de Carlos Gardel on 24 June, which has as many tango events but is celebrated on the date of the singer's death.

cheapest air fare; this can be nearly half the amount you'd pay during peak travel periods and getting the departure date you want should not be a problem.

Find out from a travel agent when the three periods fall for the country you want to visit. These travel periods may be referred to as the high and low seasons. Be flexible with your flight if possible – even one day's difference can save you quite a deal of money. For more information on air fares, see the Air section in the Tickets & Insurance chapter.

BAD TRAVEL TIMES

Travelling in peak periods through a popular country like Costa Rica or Peru can have its drawbacks. Prices are high, rooms are hard to come by and all the backpackers and tourists about may make you feel as if you never left home. There's a foreigner for nearly every stone at Machu Picchu in August, for example, and this may well detract from your experience of the place.

If the high season is the only time you can go, do so. Consider taking backdoor routes instead of the well travelled ones and try to visit smaller towns off the Gringo Trail. Chances are you'll stumble on an idyllic hamlet that tugs at your heart strings as you watch it recede from the bus window. If you want to see the major sites, advance reservations are highly recommended; or, arrive early in the morning to increase your chances of getting a room.

Locals like to travel too, and national holidays mean packed beaches teeming with families. All the other accessible natural wonders will also be overrun, so try to go further afield when a major holiday approaches. Buses will be crowded, some transportation stops running completely and stores may be closed during major observances like Semana Santa.

The hurricane season in Central America runs from June to November and while this needn't stop you, a particularly bad season might affect your travel plans. The same advice is true for El Niño, the weather phenomenon that can bring torrential rains and floods between November and February.

Researching Your Trip

Research can be a bit of drag, especially when you have a thousand other details to attend to, but focused reading, web exploration, film watching and discussion with travel experts and friends can greatly enhance your trip. This is particularly true if you're basing your trip on a particular theme (eg Mayan ruins, white-water rafting or surfing). Proper research can help you maximise your time away, prepare you for the quirks and rigours of different countries and ensure you get to experience most things on your wish list. Even if you're planning a rambling, extended stay in the region – allowing chance meetings and circumstance to dictate your path – minimal research is still necessary. You'll need to know the various border crossings between countries, visa requirements, the easiest and cheapest ways to get around, plus the health and safety risks.

GUIDEBOOKS

Guidebooks are an integral part of your travel toolkit. Landing in a strange city with hotel recommendations in hand and a list of restaurants to whet your appetite can help ease you into your new environment. A good guidebook will also provide highlights of a country, vocabulary lists, transport options and suggestions for exploring a culture in depth.

Visas and immunisations must be dealt with ahead of time, so don't wait until the last minute to get your guidebook. Taking care of the paperwork and shot requirements for your trip should be done at the earliest convenience.

If you're visiting several countries in a region, you don't need to buy a guidebook for each of those countries; this would be expensive and add way too much weight to your baggage. Instead, buy a regional guidebook that covers the area you're visiting (or most of it), or start with one individual guidebook and trade with other travellers on the road. Used guidebooks are usually for sale in most Gringo Trail locales.

Selecting a Guidebook

More people than ever are hitting the road and there is no shortage of travel guides out there. Lonely Planet is a major player in the guidebook market. Other top-selling brands for independent travellers are Footprint, Rough Guides, Moon and Let's Go.

Think carefully about which book to use. Ask your friends what they used on their trips, and browse before you buy or take out some books from the library. When assessing a guidebook, read the author's biography, check out the number of maps and their level of detail, peruse the photos, scrutinise the layout and organisation, and check the publication date. When comparing guidebooks, take a particular city or major sight and see how each conveys the hard facts, how informative the places to stay and eat entries are, the scope of the transport information and the tone of the writing. If you have particular activities in mind for your trip, see if they figure in the coverage. The number of references in the index will give you a good idea on this score.

How long you plan to spend in each country will help you decide what level of detail you'll need in a guidebook. For example, in Lonely Planet's *South America on a shoestring*, the Rio de Janeiro coverage is 22 pages; in its *Brazil* guide Rio is expanded to 53 pages; and the comprehensive *Rio de Janeiro* guide has 136 pages. If you're simply passing through Rio on your way to the Amazon, the shoestring guide will do, but you'll probably need the city guide if you're planning two weeks at Carnaval. As the books become more focused, the information is more exhaustive and sophisticated, with more recommendations, more maps and photos, and a greater, detailed discussion of historical, cultural and political issues.

This should get you started. At Lonely Planet we think we have the right combination of background and logistical information, with unbiased, insightful writing alongside excellent maps and evocative photos, all presented in an easy-to-use format. Our commitment at Lonely Planet is to produce guidebooks that provide the information and advice you need to design your dream trip, at your own level of adventure, comfort and speed. The travellers that do all the research and writing of our books are on the road now, living up to that commitment.

Complementary Guides

Along with the guidebook you'll use for everyday life on the road, you might also bring along a more general, cultural guide. Periplus, Odyssey and Insight publish these types of guides, with expansive information on religion, arts, architecture, history and other topics of cultural interest.

Specialist Guides

If you're interested in pursuing a particular activity, such as trekking, skiing or birdwatching, check out the specialised guides devoted to them.

Trekking There are many guidebooks dedicated to trekking in this part of the world. Lonely Planet's *Trekking in the Patagonian Andes* is great for detailed hiking information in Patagonia. Pick up *Bolivia – A Climbing Guide* by Yossi Brain if you're headed to that country. Bradt Publications (based in England) publishes a series of trekking guides including *Climbing & Hiking in Ecuador*, *Backpacking and Trekking in Peru & Bolivia*, *Backcountry Brazil* and *Backpacking in Chile & Argentina*. For Central America, try Bradt's *Backpacking in Central America*. Serious climbers wishing to ascend South America's tallest peak should pick up RJ Secor's climbing guide *Aconcagua*. If you're planning to head out to the Falkland Islands (Islas Malvinas), get a copy of *Walks and Climbs in the Falkland Islands* by Julian Fisher.

Birdwatching There are so many titles in this genre, you'll have to do some research to find out which one most appeals to you. Some suggestions are Meyer de Schauensee's *A Guide to the Birds of South America* and *A Guide to the Birds of Venezuela* (co-written with William Phelps); *South American Birds – A Photographic Aid to Identification* by John S Dunning is good for the Amazon, as is *Common Birds of Amazonian Ecuador* by Chris Canaday & Lou Jost; *A Field Guide to the Birds of Mexico and Central America* by LI Davis will be all you need for that region; and *A Field Guide to the Birds of the Galápagos* by Michael Harris will fascinate visitors to those islands. For birders going to the Falkland Islands there is Robin Woods' *Guide to Birds of the Falkland Islands*. If you're heading to Chile or Panama, try *Birds of Chile – A Field Guide* by Braulio Araya & Sharon Chester, or Robert S Ridgley & John A Gwynne's *A Guide to the Birds of Panama*, respectively.

Cycling For combining fun with transport, cycling is becoming more popular in Latin America and there are several books reflecting that trend. Try *Latin America by Bike – A Complete Touring Guide* by Walter Sienko for all of Central America except El Salvador; or *Latin America on Bicycle* by JP Panet, which covers Costa Rica, Guatemala and a handful of other countries.

A useful magazine is *Bicycling* (☎ 800-666-2806, www.bicyclingmagazine.com), 135 North Sixth St, Emmaus, PA 18098, USA, a leading monthly covering destinations, training, nutrition, touring, racing, equipment and clothing, maintenance and new technology. Also published by Rodale Press is *Mountain Bike* (www.mountainbike.com).

Diving & Snorkelling The Lonely Planet Pisces series covers many of the world's best dive and snorkelling spots, and relevant books include *Belize* and *Roatán & Honduras' Bay Islands*. The guides have detailed information on dive sites, marine life, tour operators, safety and conservation, history, weather, accommodation, transport, dining and money matters.

Surfing Surfing guides are woefully lacking for this part of the world. Garnering information from your local surf shop is worth a try, or write to *Surfer Magazine* (☎ 1-714-496-5922, www.surfermag.com), which has information on breaks around the world, equipment, clothing, courses and tours. It publishes *The Surf Report – Journal of World-wide Surfing Destinations*. Copies are about US$5 per destination. Send requests to PO Box 1028, Dana Point, CA 92629.

Orchids There are many books specialising in the thousands of orchid species that grow in Latin America. Be careful choosing one, though: there are so many of these flowers endemic to the region that some of the specialist guides are huge, heavy tomes. In-print orchid guides include *Orchids of Guatemala and Belize* by Oakes Ames & Stewart Donovan, *Field Guide to the Orchids of Costa Rica and Panama* by Robert L Dressler and *Orchids of Costa Rica* by Dora Emilia Mora de Retana. There are several excellent out-of-print books that may be worth tracking down: *Orchids of Brazil* by Jim & Barbara McQueen, *Ornamental Orchids of Colombia* by Pedro Ortiz Valdivieso, *Orchids of Venezuela* by GC Dunsterville & LA Garay and *An Introduction to the Orchids of Mexico* by Leon A Wiard.

Using Your Guidebook

A guidebook aims to do just that: to guide. Nothing contained within it will be the first and last word on a place. The writers bring their own experiences and perspective to the book and what interests them may leave you yawning. Also, the hard information in a guide – eg bus timetables, hotel listings and prices – tends to date quickly, so what was once a 5 pm bus may now be a 4 pm bus and long gone by the time you show up. Nothing is more accurate than your own research, so try to find out what time the bus leaves independently of what the book says.

You won't be the only one using a particular guidebook, and on the Gringo Trail you will find plenty of other travellers following the same itinerary from the same guidebook. In fact, the Gringo Trail has a tourist infrastructure that makes it easy to navigate, but if you want to veer off this well trodden path and discover the wilds of Latin America for yourself, see the Off the Beaten Track entry under Sightseeing in the While You're There chapter for some advice.

A guidebook is not sacred. Use pages for kindling, cannibalise it to lighten your load, swap or donate it to other travellers. If you want to keep it as a souvenir, send it home and move on.

MAPS

If you're travelling mainly by public transport, your guidebook's regional and city maps should be sufficient. However, if you aim to drive, ride a bicycle or motorcycle, climb mountains or run rivers, you will want more detailed maps. Try to purchase them before leaving home, as it may not be easy to buy what you need in Latin America. Indeed, some places have never even been mapped!

If you're after large-scale maps, skip those that show the whole continent, as they will lack the detail you're after. Instead, try to get individual country or regional maps. Lonely Planet produces detailed country maps, including its *Chile & Easter Island travel atlas*. The South American Explorers Club (www .samexplo.org) has an extensive catalogue of South American maps, including many topographical maps for Ecuador and Peru. Latin American Travel Consultants (www.amerispan.com/lata) has superb maps, as does International Travel Maps (www.nas.com/~travelmaps). Shops with a good map supply include:

Australia
  Mapland
  (☎ 03-9670 4383) 372 Little Bourke St, Melbourne, Vic 3000
  The Travel Bookshop
  (☎ 02-9241 3554) 20 Bridge St, Sydney, NSW 2001
  Nev Anderson Maps
  (☎ 02-9878 2809) 30 Fawcett St Ryde, NSW 2112

Canada
  World of Maps & Travel Books
  (☎ 613-724-6776, ✉ maps@magi.com, www.worldofmaps.com) 118 Holland Ave, Ottawa, Ontario K1Y 0X6

New Zealand
  Map World
  (☎ 03-374 5399, ✉ maps@mapworld.co.nz) PO Box 13-833, Christchurch
  Whitcoulls
  (☎ 09-356 5400) 210 Queen St, Auckland

UK
  Stanfords Map Centre
  (☎ 020-7836 1321) 12-14 Long Acre, London WC2E 9LP
  The Map Shop
  (☎ 06-846 3146) AT Atkinson & Partner, 15 High St, Upton-on-Severn, Worcestershire WR8 OHJ

USA
  US Library of Congress
  (☎ 202-707-5000; photocopies only – post-1968 maps can be searched for on www.loc.gov) Geography & Map Division, 101 Independence Ave, Washington, DC 20540

Hagstrom Map and Travel Center
(☎ 212-398-1222, www.hagstromstore.com) 57 West 43rd St, New York, NY 10036
Traveler's Bookstore
(☎ 212-664-0995) Time Warner Building, 22 East 52nd St, New York, NY 10019
Rand McNally — The Map & Travel Store
(☎ 212-758-7488, www.randmcnallystore.com) 150 East 52nd St, New York, NY 10022;
(☎ 310-556-2202) Century City Shopping Center, 10250 Santa Monica Blvd, Los Angeles, CA 90067;
(☎ 415-777-3131) 595 Market St, San Francisco, CA 94105-2803

TRAVEL AGENCIES

Chatting with travel consultants and perusing travel agency brochures are two free goldmines of information, especially if you find an agency that specialises in Latin America. Consulting a travel agent doesn't mean you have to go on an organised tour, it's just another research tool. Still, most agents work on commission, so don't take up too much of their time if you're not planning to book with them. You might consider buying your airline ticket from an agent though (see Buying from Travel Agents in the Tickets & Insurance chapter).

INTERNATIONAL TOURIST OFFICES

Very few Central or South American countries have overseas tourist offices, but consulates usually can provide some semblance of tourist information. Mexico is the obvious exception, with many overseas tourist offices, especially in the USA and Canada. To find those countries that do have offices overseas, go to *Tourism Offices Worldwide Directory* (www.towd.com), which has regularly updated links to tourist office sites.

NEWSPAPERS

Many of the larger western newspapers have decent weekly or monthly travel sections which advertise discounts, tours and package deals. You might also check out big city alternative newspapers (eg New York's *Village Voice* and San Francisco's *Bay Guardian*), which often have special travel sections and advertisements of interest to budget travellers.

Australia
Age (www.theage.com.au)
Australian (www.news.com.au)
Sydney Morning Herald (www.smh.com.au)

Canada
Globe & Mail (Toronto; www.theglobeandmail.com)
Vancouver Sun (www.vancouversun.com)

UK
Independent (www.independent.co.uk)
Southern Cross (www.southerncross.co.uk) – written for expat New Zealanders, Australians and South Africans in London
Time Out (www.timeout.com/london)
Times (www.the-times.co.uk)
TNT (www.tntmag.co.uk) – magazine for young Londoners, notable for its travel ads

USA

Chicago Tribune (www.chicagotribune.com)
LA Times (www.latimes.com)
New York Times (www.nytimes.com)
San Francisco Examiner (www.examiner.com)

MAGAZINES

Travel magazines are a good place to get an idea of what different destinations have to offer. Depending on the magazine's target market, there may be articles on individual destinations and activities, cuisine or shopping; pieces on adventure or exotic theme trips; articles on the economics of travelling, affordable destinations and cheap flights; columns on packing and health, travelling with kids and going it alone. Display and classified advertising can help you learn more about a destination and possibly to find a travel partner. Look for travel magazines that target your interests or destination and take a look at their e-zine if they have one. Some travel organisations also publish magazines, and the following are worth a look: STA's *Escape*, Intrepid Travel's *The Intrepid Traveller* and Trailfinder's *Trailfinder Magazine*.

Adventure Magazine
(☎ 800-846-8575) PO Box 461270, Escondido, CA 92046-1270, USA
(a full-colour glossy offering in-depth articles on adventure travel options and practical advice on doing it yourself)

Big World Magazine
(☎ 717-569-0217, ✉ orders@bigworld.com, www.bigworld.com) PO Box 8743, Lancaster, PA 17604-8743, USA
(no-frills approach offering the independent budget traveller a fresh look at the adventures and joys of travel)

Geographical Magazine
(☎ 020-7938 4011, ✉ geogmag@gn.apc.org, www.rgs.org/ed/8publgeo.html) 47c Kensington Court, London W8 5DA, England
(magazine of the Royal Geographical Society [UK], with a focus on cultural, anthropological and environmental issues; beautiful photographs, book and television reviews and some advertising for tour companies)

National Geographic
(☎ 1-800-647-5463, www.nationalgeographic.com) Box 98198, Washington, DC 20090-8198, USA
(the magazine of the US National Geographic Society with great photos and excellent background information)

National Geographic Traveler
(☎ 800-437-5521, www.nationalgeographic.com/media/traveler) PO Box 64026, Tampa, FL 33664-4026, USA
(practical information on getting to the places covered by *National Geographic*)

Outside
(☎ 800-678-1131, www.outsidemag.com) PO Box 54729, Boulder, CO 80322-4729, USA
(for travel by bike, skateboard, kayak or any other means that requires some physical effort; it has a US bias, but includes international destinations)

South American Explorer
(☎ 607-277-0488, www.samexplo.org) 126 Indian Creek Road, Ithaca, NY 14850, USA
(for Latin American travellers and enthusiasts; very informative, irreverent and with lots of classifieds)

Traveller Magazine
(☎ 020-7589 3315, ✆ mship@wexas.com, www.travelmag.co.uk) 45-49 Brompton Rd, Knightsbridge, London SW3 1DE, UK
(quarterly with an emphasis on anthropology, exploration and adventure travel, plus travellers health, book reviews, travel hot spots and advertising for UK-based tour operators)

Travel Unlimited
(http://travelunlimitedsc.com/main.htm) subscription by mail from PO Box 1058, Allston, Mass 02134, USA
(details of cheap air fares, special deals and courier options)

Wanderlust
(☎ 01753-620426) PO Box 1832, Windsor, Berkshire SL4 6YP, UK
(concise general travel information on both out-of-the-way and routine destinations; has heaps of ads for tours and tour companies)

BOOKS

Spend time at local bookshops and libraries to check out your travel destinations. Books are among the best tools for researching a region, whether you're interested in Incan or Mayan history or more recent developments. If you have access to Latin American literature in translation, you'll have hit the mother lode. From household names like Gabriel García Márquez to obscure, but equally brilliant craftsmen like Ignacio de Loyola Brandão, there are reams of great novels, short stories and everything in between by Latino authors.

Wanderlust is part of the human condition, and as long as folks have been touring Latin America, they've been writing about it. Travelogues are a fun and easy introduction to a region and also make good reading while on your trip. For those hungry for more in-depth dissections of a place, there are myriad speciality books available; enthusiasts of orchids, scuba diving, trekking, architecture, geology and probably any other hobby or pursuit you can imagine will be able to find books on the subject.

If analysis and nonfiction are more your bag, try out one of the many academic treatments of the region's politics, culture, religion and social movements. There are some very balanced and informative accounts available that can provide specific insights into the foreign cultures you plan to visit. For recommended reading lists, see the Books sections in the country profiles.

FILMS

Movies can give you an idea of the cultural and physical landscape you're likely to encounter during your travels. Western movies filmed on location in Latin America will help with the setting while home-grown products by Latino filmmakers will fill in some of the cultural blanks.

Western movies are often disingenuous regarding the country they're depicting: *Seven Years in Tibet* was filmed in Chile and part of *Independence Day* was shot in Colombia. On the flipside, films about Latin America can be frighteningly real. *The Panama Deception*, about the US invasion of that country, is one that comes to mind.

Brazil, Chile, Peru and Argentina have flourishing film industries, and other countries are working hard to catch up. To find films made by Latin Americans or filmed on location, go to the Internet Movie Database (www.imdb.com), and also see the Films sections in the country profiles.

USEFUL WEB SITES

The Internet makes it so easy to research your trip, and the following web sites can help you decide which countries to visit in Latin America. There are many more sites mentioned throughout this book with regards to health, maps, visa requirements and finding Internet cafes while you're on the road. For a full list, see the appendix 'Internet Addresses' at the back of the book.

Lonely Planet
www.lonelyplanet.com
(destination information, health advice, photographs, bulletin boards and links to all topics travel-related)

AmeriSpan/Latin American Travel Consultants Travel Resources
www.amerispan.com/resources/default.htm
(great links to sites on every Latin American country and decent trip advice)

British Foreign & Commonwealth Office
www.fco.gov.uk
(travel advisories written for Brits, but relevant for most travellers)

Green Travel Network
www.greentravel.com
(ecotourism focus with lots of trip reports, destination information and ideas)

Hiking & Walking Homepage
www.teleport.com/-walking/hiking.html
(excellent information on international trekking spots, tours and clubs)

Internet Guide to Hostelling
www.hostelling.com
(details of hostels across the world, with a good travellers news section)

Rain or Shine
www.rainorshine.com
(five-day weather forecasts for 800 cities around the world)

Travelocity
www.travelocity.com
(general travel information, bookings, equipment and links)

US State Department Travel Warnings & Consular Information Sheets
travel.state.gov/travel_warnings.html
(mildly paranoid warnings about world trouble spots written principally for American citizens)

World Events Calendar
travel.epicurious.com
(huge list of festivals, events and other festivities, which can be searched by theme, country or date)

World Tourism Organization
www.world-tourism.org/ows-doc/wtich.htm
(United Nations international organisation dealing with travel and tourism policy and development, with members in 138 countries representing local government, tourism associations, airlines, hotel groups and tour operators)

Language

You'll suffer far less travel stress if you have a couple of key foreign phrases up your sleeve (mostly these have to do with bathroom locations and departing buses). But travelling is more than getting to the bathroom in time and hopping on the right bus. Chatting to school kids, offering friendly words to the women at the market and being able to say 'pass the ball' during a pick-up game of hoops will go a long way towards enhancing your trip. Knowing a bit of the local language also helps you to meet people and learn about a culture in a way you wouldn't be able to if you couldn't communicate verbally.

You can't rely on English alone to get by in Latin America. In the big cities you may be able to get away with it, but outside of urban centres, people are probably going to speak only Spanish and possibly an indigenous language like Mayan Quiché. Luckily, Spanish is easy to learn. Portuguese and French are generally more difficult, but they're only spoken in Brazil and French Guiana respectively. Most travellers you run into will speak English, or within a group there will be some common languages in which you can all communicate laboriously.

LEARNING A LANGUAGE

Spanish is easy to pick up, and it's realistic to study at home for a couple of months and learn enough to serve you well on the road. If that seems like too much for you, committing a few pleasantries to memory ('Good morning', 'Pardon me', and 'Goodbye') is worth the reward of breaking the ice with locals. Better still, learning how to ask 'How much does this cost? and 'Where is the ...?' plus learning to count to 10 will make your life a lot easier. Most important, don't be afraid to try; it's amazing how even the botched, garbled delivery of a foreign phrase can garner respect and friendly overtures from strangers.

If you want to learn a language before you leave, get a textbook and tapes (for pronunciation). It takes commitment to learn a foreign language on your own, but if you're motivated, check out titles by Teach Yourself, Berlitz, Barrons and Routledge. If you want to learn Portuguese, make sure you get a Brazilian Portuguese course, as the form of the language spoke in Europe is not the same.

Make yourself a studying schedule and stick to it. Practise as often as you can and make flash cards so you can memorise the phrases you want to learn. Listening to Spanish or Portuguese music and watching television programs in the language you want to learn will help train your ear. Go to a Latino restaurant and practise on the staff.

Private lessons or classes are also worthwhile options. Local colleges may have night or extension classes, and community organisations often have foreign-language classes. Private teachers may advertise in local newspapers.

Don't forget that there are language classes offered all over Latin America and if you have the time, you might want to study in a country such as Guatemala or Ecuador. Often you can combine your language instruction with homestays, increasing your immersion in the language and culture. These arrangements are usually pretty affordable (see the Thematic Trips section earlier in this chapter for more information).

Phrasebooks

Phrasebooks should be small enough to fit in a coat pocket and have all the phrases written in both English and the local language. Lonely Planet publishes phrasebooks in Brazilian, Latin American Spanish and Quechua. A good guidebook will have a language section; this can be very useful for brushing up on the basics or supplying a word you need.

Work & Travel

Opportunities abound in Latin America for volunteer work, and many people take advantage of the cultural immersion and altruism volunteering affords; being a volunteer can expose you to a slice of local life that would otherwise remain hidden. Paying work is another story; it's usually hard to find and doesn't pay well. Still, if you have a specialised skill, including teaching English as a Second Language (ESL), you may be able to find work. A good place to start job hunting is in the classified advertisements of the *South American Explorer* magazine (see the Magazines section earlier for contact information). Another good publication that lists international job, living and research opportunities is *Transitions Abroad* (www.transabroad.com).

Researching work opportunities before you leave home is a good idea. Try to get the position before you leave, so that you and the organisation know what to expect, including the duties and compensation involved (if any). Talk to other people who have worked there, if possible. Some people like to land in a country and see what strikes their fancy. You may want to look for a job this way, but there are no guarantees.

ENGLISH TEACHING

There are opportunities for work in this field, but pay is low. Positions usually require a commitment of several months, which can be restricting, and most jobs are in big cities.

A university degree is almost a necessity and it will be easier to get a job if you have either a TESOL (Teaching English to Speakers of Other Languages) or TEFL (Teaching English as a Foreign Language) certificate. Advanced degrees also help, as does previous experience. See if there is a community or college program at home where you can teach English to recent immigrants to learn the ropes. In most countries you'll need a work visa to work overseas, although a lot of people teach English whether they have one or not. One great benefit of having a work visa is that you can stay in the country longer.

Mexico is probably your best shot for finding English-teaching jobs. Opportunities in Central America are in very short supply. Your best bets are Guatemala and Panama, although don't get your hopes up. Quito in Ecuador has some opportunities and you might check in with the South American Explorers Club there to see what's afoot. Generally you can expect very low pay in these countries; you may be able to make enough to live on, but that will be about it.

In Brazil you can expect to earn between US$5 and US$10 an hour as a private tutor. Finding pupils takes time, patience and determination, but you may get lucky and 'inherit' another teacher's pupils. It also helps to speak a bit of Portuguese, and you can expect many of your students to be businesspeople. Look under 'Professor de Ingles' in the classifieds or ask at the English schools. The pay is a bit better in Argentina – look in the *Buenos Aires Herald* classifieds.

Teaching Resources

Association of American Schools in South America
www.aassa.com
(places qualified teachers in private schools throughout the region)

Dave's ESL Café
www.pacificnet.net/~sperling/eslcafe.html
(chock-full of useful information, links and advice; includes a list of English-teaching jobs all over the world; strong on opportunities in Mexico)

TEFL Job Centre
www.jobs.edunet.com
(English-teaching positions all over the world, including some in Latin America)

English Expert Page
www.englishexpert.com
(good general information on teaching in Mexico and South America and some job listings)

International House
www.international-house.org
(good source of information on RSA Cambridge certification)

Job Registry Online Directory
www.edulink.com/JOBS_FILES_LIST/jobopenings.html
(all types of international teaching jobs listed by region and subject)

New World Teachers
www.goteach.com
(offers four-week training programs and job placement)

Teach English in Mexico
www.teach-english-mexico.com
(all the resources and information you'll need to land a teaching job in Mexico)

World Teach
www.igc.org/worldteach
(places volunteers to teach English and basic skills; tertiary qualifications required, but not specifically in education)

For good reading and research on teaching English in your travels, consult one or more of the following: *Teaching English Abroad – Talking Your Way Around the World!* (by Susan Griffith), *Work Abroad – The Complete Guide to Finding a Job Overseas* (compiled and published by Transitions Abroad), or *The Peace Corps and More – 175 Ways to Work, Study and Travel at Home & Abroad* (by Medea Benjamin & Miya Rodolfo-Sioson).

BOAT WORK

If you know boats, ships or are an inveterate sailor, you may be able to find work with foreign yachties: gringos who are sailing entirely or partway around the world. Visit yacht clubs along the Guatemalan and Costa Rican coasts, in Venezuela and in Ecuador or Peru, and see what you can drum up. Alternatively, there is sometimes casual work for deckhands in the Panama Canal. This is hard work and pays about US$50 for guiding a boat through the locks.

SERVICE JOBS

These are scarce, but bar jobs are possible to land in Santiago de Chile, especially in the numerous pubs along Avenida Suecia and General Holley, and in seasonally popular resorts like Chile's Pucón. You might try the Honduran Bay Islands for dive master positions. For information on dive masters licences and employment opportunities, go to the PADI web site (www.padi.com). In tourist towns throughout Latin America, you'll hear about jobs for tour leaders, hostel managers or shop workers; most places will want at least a three month commitment. There's recently been a huge boom in Internet cafes, so if you can hack, check into job opportunities there.

TRAVEL WRITING & PHOTOGRAPHY

You may be able to combine your work with pleasure by publishing articles or photos on the destinations you've visited. As you might imagine, competition in this field is stiff, but if you're dreaming about it, go for it. If you think you've an eye for travel photography, spend the money on good equipment (see the Camera section in the What to Bring chapter) and perhaps take a course in travel photography before you leave. At the very least you should consult a book on the subject to see what works. Don't get discouraged, and keep in mind that a stock photo library typically accepts fewer than 10 out of 100 images submitted. Remember to take slide shots, as they are the highest quality and the industry standard.

The same professional attitude should be taken with travel writing. Research your markets and make sure your material is appropriate. *Islands* magazine probably won't want an article on the colonial architecture of Buenos Aires, for instance. Send away for writer's guidelines before hitting the road. Very few publications pay for writers on assignment, especially if you're not already among their stable of scribes, so don't expect to pitch an idea on camping in Costa Rica and get a magazine to pay for it. If you're really serious about making a go of travel writing, check out the most recent edition of the excellent reference book, the *Writer's Market*.

VOLUNTEER WORK

Less than robust Latin American economies mean there are loads of volunteer jobs available. If you can afford to donate your time, you will be rewarded by an unparalleled travel experience that feels good and does good. Figure out what you'd like to do, where you'd like to go and work from there. Some programs provide room and board; find out what is included before signing on.

Research is important when looking for a volunteer position. For example, if you're applying to dig ditches in the Ecuadorian rainforest and you have a weak knee, this may not be the position for you. If you're tending to street children in São Paulo, but can't deal with anyone under the age of 10, reassess this particular opportunity. There are hundreds of organisations working in Latin America that offer volunteer positions. Consult a guidebook, hit the Internet and talk to other travellers about their experiences. The following are just some of the opportunities available:

Guatemala – There are many programs to help Quiché children in Quetzaltenango and Momostenango. Positions vary from teaching to tending organic gardens. There are several groups working with orphaned children in Guatemala City and there are two wildlife rescue stations: one in the north near Flores and a sea turtle hatchery near Monterrico.

Honduras – Volunteers are needed from April to June to help with giant leatherback turtles during their nesting period.

El Salvador – Volunteer positions can be arranged in many different fields by the Centro Internacional de Solidaridad; they require a three month commitment.

Nicaragua – An arm of Habitat for Humanity builds houses in Nicaragua and welcomes volunteers, as does the Nicaraguan organisation Movimiento Comunal Nicaraguense, which arranges community projects throughout the country.

Costa Rica – The Costa Rican national park system pays US$5 to US$10 a day to volunteers and requires a two month commitment. There are also volunteer reforestation and teaching opportunities here.

Panama – From protecting nesting sea turtles to patrolling national parks, there are many opportunities for volunteers interested in ecology. Short-term positions are available and room and board are usually offered.

Bolivia – There are a variety of volunteer positions in Bolivia, from environmental projects to working with street kids. Earthwatch has an ongoing program here.

Ecuador – The South American Explorers Club always has the inside tip on volunteer opportunities here. Scientists and other specially skilled folk may be able to land volunteer (or paid!) positions in the Galápagos Islands.

Brazil – The unfortunate reality of orphaned street kids in Brazil means there are lots of opportunities to volunteer with children's groups in the bigger cities.

Chile – Chile is very organised when it comes to volunteer work. Two publications to consult are *Directorio de Instituciones de Chile* (popularly known as the 'Guía Silber' after its publisher Silber Editores), a directory of political, labour, church, cultural and other institutions both official and nongovernmental; and the annual *Directorio de Organizaciones Miembros* published by Renace (Red Nacional de Acción Ecológica), a loosely affiliated network of environmental organisations throughout the country.

Peru – Head to the Lima office of the South American Explorers Club for information on current openings.

Following are some Internet resources to help you begin your research on volunteer opportunities.

AmeriSpan
www.amerispan.com/volunteer
(has a volunteer/internship program with opportunities for various skills in Ecuador and Peru)

Council on International Educational Exchange
www.ciee.org/vol
(has short-term projects in small communities)

Tx Serve
www.txserve.org/general/volopp2.html
(links to volunteer organisations in Latin America and elsewhere)

The following placement and aid organisations offer worldwide volunteer opportunities:

Australia
Australian Volunteers International
(☎ 03-9279 1788, www.ozvol.org.au) PO Box 350, Fitzroy, Vic 3065
Earthwatch Institute
(☎ 03-9682 6828, www.earthwatch.org/australia/html) 126 Bank St, South Melbourne, Vic 3205

New Zealand
Volunteer Service Abroad
(☎ 04-472 5759, www.tcol.co.uk/comorg/vsa.htm) PO Box 12-246, Wellington

UK
Earthwatch Institute
(☎ 01865-311 600, www.earthwatch.org/t/Toeuropehome.htm) 57 Woodstock Rd, Oxford OX2 6JH
International Voluntary Service
(☎ 0131-226 6722, www.ivsgbn.demon.co.uk) St John's Church Centre, Edinburgh EH2 4BJ
Voluntary Service Overseas
(VSO; ☎ 020-8780 2266, www.oneworld.org/vso) 317 Putney Bridge Rd, London SW15 2PN

USA
Earthwatch Institute
(☎ 800-776-0188, www.earthwatch.org) 680 Mt Auburn St, PO Box 9104, Watertown, MA 02272
Global Volunteers
(☎ 612-482-0915, www.globalvolunteers.org) 375 East Little Canada Rd, St Paul, MN 55117-1628
Peace Corps of the USA
(☎ 202-606-3970, www.peacecorps.gov) 1990 K St NW, Washington, DC 20526

MONEY MATTERS

Your air fare will be your greatest expense almost anywhere in the world you travel. This is true too for trips to Latin America, and particularly so for those coming from Australia or New Zealand. Still, a bonus to choosing Latin America as a destination is that once you've saved enough for your air fare, the rest is smooth financial sailing, as day-to-day expenses are relatively cheap. Some places are more expensive than others, of course, as are some itineraries: a ski trip to Argentina or a two week cruise in the Galápagos for instance, will set you back a couple of thousand dollars. On the other hand, a month-long trek through the Bolivian Andes could be the most affordable trip you ever take.

If you are starting from North America, you could travel overland, although overland trips have their own costs in terms of accommodation and food while you make your way down there. Still, you can save money on air fares and accommodation by travelling during off-peak periods. If you can only travel during the high season, increase your budget to reflect the higher prices.

Currency fluctuations can also effect the cost of your trip. For the latest currency information, go to Oanda online currency converter (www.oanda.com /converter/classic).

Once you have your air fare and trip money together, set some aside for an emergency. Some travellers pride themselves on living on the edge, getting the biggest bargain and squeezing the life out of every last penny. This approach has some benefits, but it also adds a lot of stress to what should be an enjoyable experience. Imagine how that stress skyrockets if something goes totally awry; be financially prepared in case something does.

The following sections provide advice and suggestions on budgeting a trip to Latin America. Remember, none of it is written in stone; there are always ways to spend more or less money, depending on your style and inclination while on the road.

Pretrip Expenses

You'll spend a good portion of your trip money before you even leave the ground. Air fare, equipment, immunisations, visas and travel insurance will all take a bite out of your budget. By all means, shop around for the best value, but don't cut corners on the important stuff. Buy your plane ticket from a reputable agent, get the yellow fever shot if you'll be deep in an affected area and make sure your equipment will stand up to the rigours of independent travel.

PLANE TICKETS

If you shop around for a decent deal, the following is what you can expect to pay for a return (round trip) ticket to Mexico City, Lima (Peru) on the western coast of South America, and Rio de Janeiro (Brazil) on the eastern coast:

from Australia & New Zealand:

Sydney/Auckland-Rio de Janeiro	A$1650 to A$2200
Sydney-Lima	A$1789 to A$2200
Sydney-Mexico City (via Los Angeles)	A$1950 to A$2300

from the UK:

London-Rio de Janeiro	£240 to £415
London-Lima	£285 to £400
London-Mexico City	£350 to £450

from Canada:

Toronto-Mexico City	US$230 to US$530

All other routes from Canada are cheapest through the USA.

from the USA:

Miami-Rio de Janeiro	US$795 to US$836
Los Angeles-Rio de Janeiro	US$886 to US$1050
Miami-Lima	US$400 to US$715
Los Angeles-Lima	US$600 to US$883
Miami-Mexico City	US$170 to US$540
Los Angeles-Mexico City	US$140 to US$450

With the Sydney/Auckland-Rio de Janeiro flight, visitors from Australia or New Zealand can stop in Santiago, Montevideo, Lima, La Paz and many other South American cities at no extra cost. Circle-Pacific (from A$1599) or Round-the-World fares (from A$1999) could work out to be a better deal, depending on your desired route (see the Tickets & Insurance chapter for information on these fares).

There are many resources for online air fare information, including the following:

Flight Info.Com (www.flifo.com)
Expedia (www.expedia.msn.com/daily/home/default.hts)
Travelocity (www.travelocity.com)
Preview Travel (www.previewtravel.com)

For more information on buying plane tickets, see the Tickets & Insurance chapter. For details on air fares within Latin America, see the Getting Around section in the While You're There chapter.

INSURANCE

Don't forego travel insurance, no matter how tempting it may be. Buy a good, used backpack instead of the fancy new one to save money instead. If you're lucky enough to have socialised health care, you may be covered while overseas, thereby saving on portions of an insurance package. Basic travel insurance packages usually include health, accidental death, baggage and cancellation insurance and are priced according to the length of the trip. Expect to pay around US$35 for a week, US$115 for a month, US$180 for two months and US$400 for six months. See the Tickets & Insurance chapter for more information on buying travel insurance.

VISAS

Visa regulations change periodically, so make sure you know which countries require them. In some countries, a tourist card issued upon arrival is sufficient; these typically cost less than US$10. Countries with visa requirements for some nationals include El Salvador, Nicaragua, Panama, Argentina, Uruguay, Paraguay, Chile and Venezuela. Brazil has the simplest visa schedule: if you're from a country that requires visas of Brazilian visitors, you'll need a visa when you visit Brazil. Visas can cost anywhere from US$10 (Panama) to US$40 (Venezuela). See the Passports & Visas chapter and the country profiles later in this book for more details.

IMMUNISATIONS

Depending on where you're going and how far off the beaten track you'll stray, prepare to be subjected to an armload of vaccinations. The whole battery of shots typically costs between US$150 and US$200, but that depends on where you live and what shots you had as a child. For more details, see the Health chapter.

EQUIPMENT

The amount of equipment you bring along depends on what you like to do and how you like to travel. How much you actually buy depends on what gear you already have and what you can beg, barter or borrow from friends and family. Travelling with friends can help lighten the load: splitting costs and sharing the carrying will save money and backpack space for everyone involved. Still, there is a good argument for being self-sufficient, so you may want to carry important equipment yourself. The following is a price list for gear you might want to take on your trip. Remember, these prices are for the items bought brand-new, so consider buying quality second-hand gear to save some money.

backpack	US$150 to US$300
camera (automatic)	US$50 to US$300
camera (SLR)	US$250 to US$800
hiking boots	US$80 to US$200
pocketknife	US$20 to US$50
sleeping bag	US$150 to US$250
tent	US$150 to US$250
torch (flashlight)	US$10 to US$20

AVERAGE PRETRIP EXPENSES FOR A TWO MONTH TRIP

The following figures are very rough examples to assist planning for your trip. Your actual expenses may vary quite a bit.

gear	US$490
immunisations	US$75
insurance	US$180
plane ticket (return)	US$900
visas	US$75
total	**US$1720**

Daily On-Road Costs

The major factors contributing to your on-road costs will be comfort level, how much and by what means you move around, and the cost of living in the country you visit. What one traveller considers frugal, another may find extravagant, so remember that all on-road costs are open to interpretation.

COMFORT LEVELS

'Anything you can do, I can do cheaper' is the anthem of some travellers. You'll know them when you see them; they're the ones who've made an art of finding dirt-cheap hotels, eat only from stalls in the market, travel on the slowest, lowest class of bus and never, ever buy souvenirs. In most Latin American countries, you can achieve this sort of trip on about US$10 a day, maybe even less. But do you want to?

Squeezing the life out of every cent can become tiring, and sometimes the principal gets in the way of practicality. If you're in Guayaquil, Ecuador for example, where there is 100% humidity and it's 40°C (109°F)in the shade, you'll suffer without a fan in your hotel room and earn no bragging rights because you saved a dollar and sweated out a night. There are no awards for travelling successfully on spare change. The point is to have fun, while experiencing new

---

Treating Yourself

Perhaps you've just been on a bus for the last 24 hours and you're so tired you can barely move. Maybe you've got a high fever and a raging case of diarrhoea. Or maybe you're just sick and tired of grotty guesthouse rooms and bad food. Whatever the case, there are times when you should forget about the money and give yourself a treat. Splurging on the occasional feast, comfy hotel room or cross-town taxi ride can make the difference between losing it or having a great trip. If you need a break, heed the call, even if it means digging deep into your budget and perhaps even cutting your trip short by a few days.

The perfect example of this is if you've been travelling in Bolivia and are feeling run-down after weeks of noisy dorm rooms, cheap food and 2nd class train journeys. Rather than continue and risk falling sick, pamper yourself – find a comfortable room in a nice hotel and chill out for a few days. Or, if you're really at the end of your tether, splurge on a ticket to Caracas and spend a week or two recuperating on a sunny Venezuelan island. In the long run, it's better to spend the money and stay well than to pinch pennies until you've run yourself into the ground.

The great thing about Latin America is that in most countries you can indulge yourself without blowing the bank. An excellent meal can be had in the restaurants of most top-flight hotels for less than US$15. An air-con room in a fine hotel can be had for around US$30, perhaps less, depending upon the place and time. And best of all, you can live in relative splendour on a beach for around US$10 a day.

All of which means you don't have to limit the occasional splurge to those times when you're feeling tired or sick. If you're not prepared to spend the money, how will you enjoy the experience? If you're aching to go on that rafting trip, desperate for that souvenir, or feel life just wouldn't be worth living if you never taste some 1st class Argentine steak, then go ahead and lash out – in most cases, you'll find it was worth it. Remember, with the low prices in Latin America, this may be one of the only chances you'll have in life to live like the jet set.

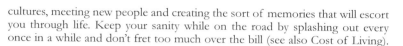

cultures, meeting new people and creating the sort of memories that will escort you through life. Keep your sanity while on the road by splashing out every once in a while and don't fret too much over the bill (see also Cost of Living).

MOVING VS STAYING PUT

Trains, planes and automobiles will erode your budget fast. If you're on a tight budget but have plenty of time, take buses instead. They can be slow, uncomfortable and unpredictable, but they're guaranteed to be the most interesting mode of transport. If time is a problem, look into flight passes that allow you to fly a certain number of legs within or between countries (see the Getting Around section of the While You're There chapter).

When planning your trip, try not to spread yourself too thin. If you have only a month, consider amending a proposed Venezuela to Chile itinerary to simply Bolivia and Peru; it's more enjoyable to see a lot of a few countries than to go crazy running from country to country and seeing little besides the airport, bus terminal and some seedy hotels. You can save money and aggravation by choosing a few destinations of particular appeal and staying put for several days or more. Travelling to many different places eats up both your budget and time.

COST OF LIVING

The cost of living varies widely in Latin America, and your budget should account for some wild swings in prices. If you're in Bolivia cruising happily along on US$15 a day, for example, and you decide to cross over to Argentina for a spell, you will need to spend about three times the money to eat, sleep and be merry. There are certain countries that are better to travel in than others in terms of budgeting, and if you aim to stay on the road as long as possible without much money, stick to these.

Generally, Mexico and Central America are cheaper than South America. Panama is the priciest of the Central American countries, but often you're still getting good value because although prices are higher, quality is better. Whereas you may budget US$15 to US$20 a day in the rest of Central America, in Panama (and in touristy parts of Belize and the Yucatán), US$25 to US$30 a day is more realistic.

South America falls into two basic cost categories: the US$10 and up countries and the minimum US$30 countries. Into the latter category fall Suriname, Brazil, Venezuela, Chile, Argentina and, to a lesser extent, Paraguay and Uruguay. If you're on any kind of tight budget, skip French Guiana: costs are comparable to metropolitan France, with US$50 per day being the rock-bottom figure. Peru, Ecuador, Colombia and Bolivia will go lighter on your wallet, and you can always cross into one of these countries if your budget is being stretched.

Latin American cities are pricier than rural areas and while you might pay US$10 for a decent room in Guatemala City, a clean bed in the countryside could be US$2. Camping is one of the best ways to conserve money. In many coastal places you can rent a hammock for the night and sling it under a tree.

All of the above costs assume you stay in cheap hotels or hostels, take public transportation, and eat set meals rather than from à la carte menus. You could spend double or triple these amounts, and if you require higher levels of comfort, such as air-conditioning or a private bathroom, you can count on spending even more. Inflation and fluctuating exchange rates have a direct effect on costs, so check newspapers or the Internet for the latest currency figures before you set off. See also the Money sections of the country profiles later in this book.

inexpensive	moderate	expensive
US$20/day	US$20-$40	US$50
Bolivia	Argentina	French Guiana
Costa Rica	Belize	Falkland Islands
Ecuador	Brazil	Galápagos Islands
El Salvador	Chile	
Guatemala	Colombia	
Guyana	Suriname	
Honduras	Venezuela	
Mexico		
Nicaragua		
Panama		
Paraguay		
Peru		
Uruguay		

SAVING MONEY ON THE ROAD

A trip cut short because of money problems can really get you down. The following are some ways to save cash on your travels:

- Eat what the locals eat. This is easy, because throughout Latin America there are 'set meals'. You can get two or three of these for the cost of a hamburger or pizza.
- Picnic and plan a day trip, shop at the market for bread, cheese, meats, fruits or whatever looks good and head out. Preparing your own food saves money, exposes you to new flavours and breaks the pattern of dependency that foreign travel sometimes creates. Alternatively, stay in a hostel that extends kitchen privileges and cook your own meals.
- Take a bus, the cheapest form of transport both in the city and the countryside. You'll have greater opportunities to meet locals, too.
- Shop in markets, whatever your needs are. Perhaps you need an extra bag for your souvenirs, or a pair of clean socks; the chances are you can find it in the local market and it will be cheaper than in a shop. The hunt is part of the fun.
- Ask for a discount, especially at hotels; they are remarkably willing to give discounts if business is slow. It doesn't hurt to ask (politely).
- Learning to bargain effectively can be entertaining and kind to your budget.
- Pack a tent and camp, to save lots of money in your travels. All you need is a flat patch of earth and permission, and you're camping for free. Otherwise, expect to pay around US$5 in established camp sites.

Carrying Your Money

The US dollar is the most convertible currency in Latin America. It's possible to change other currencies in major cities, but outside the capitals you'll inevitably need US dollars, either in cash or travellers cheques.

The three main choices for carrying money are cash, travellers cheques and credit and/or debit cards. For efficiency and safety, don't rely on just one method. Most experienced travellers carry a combination of all three (see the following sections).

Your money (and passport) should be kept hidden against your body and out of reach to others. There are all sorts of ways to carry money; a neck

Your Spending Power

Money is power, and this is never so evident as when travelling in Latin America. As a western traveller you will be regarded as having a bottomless well of resources at your disposal – whether or not this is actually the case – and your dealings with locals may well be coloured by this attitude. Hotel owners, tour operators, guides and others in the travel industry are legendary for the range and cleverness of their strategies to separate you from your hard-earned cash, but it's worth putting yourself in their place every now and again.

Most countries in the region lack the government-funded social security systems, charity-run support services and private philanthropy that we take for granted in western countries. It's often each person for themselves – if the individual doesn't earn any money, they're likely to starve, especially in the cities, where they might be separated from the family or village-based networks that would normally look after them during difficult times. It's a sad fact of life that many of Latin America's less educated and poorer people work very long hours, yet have very little in terms of personal possessions.

Compared with this, even the meanest western traveller looks wealthy. Your clothes, backpack, watch, personal stereo and constant spending on food, accommodation and souvenirs mark you as a person of wealth. The fact that you may have spent years saving for your trip, and are trying to minimise your expenses to stay on the road for as long as possible, is unlikely to register with locals. The mere fact that you can afford to travel at all places you in a different league.

The envy this can produce is often aggravated by the never-ending flow of tourists (who are often demanding, rude and heedless of local customs) and the changes that the travel industry works on local cultures, from inappropriate redevelopment to the breakdown of family and societal values.

So it pays to keep some sort of perspective on your financial dealings with locals while on the road. Being 'ripped off' can leave you feeling foolish and unworldly, especially if the amount is significant, but beware of adopting a siege mentality. Many travellers fall into a mind-set of never wanting to pay more than the local price for anything, but end up spending ridiculous amounts of time and effort trying to achieve this, to the detriment of their enjoyment of the country and its people.

Similarly, bargaining is part of the fun of travelling, but try not to be too niggardly, particularly with people running a small business or selling their wares at a market. Take a moment to work out just how much that extra 70 quetzales or five soles is really costing you. You're probably arguing over 10 or 20 cents – a paltry sum that you would never miss at home, but which could make a real difference to the life of the person you're dealing with.

In short, show a little panache and a trace of empathy for the other person's circumstances. They'll be happy with the transaction and you can travel on with a clear conscience.

pouch worn under your shirt or a money belt around your waist are the most popular options (see the Money Belt section in the What to Bring chapter for details). You'll need to have some money accessible in a small change purse or pouch. This can act as a decoy if you're robbed and means you won't have to dig into your money belt every time you take a bus or need a few coins for a snack. For more information on protecting your money from theft, see the Hazards & Safeguards section in the Issues & Attitudes chapter.

TRAVELLERS CHEQUES

Travellers cheques are still the most popular way to carry money, although not everyone is an advocate − you have to pay to get them, you have to pay to cash them and sometimes the exchange rate is lower than for cash. The biggest advantage to travellers cheques is that if they're stolen, they will be replaced within a few days by the issuing bank (if you have the correct documentation).

You must keep records of where you bought your cheques and where they were exchanged. Always maintain a separate list of the cheques' serial numbers and note how you spent each cheque along the way. If you can't produce records when you try to claim stolen cheques, the issuer may not replace them. Always keep the serial numbers, purchase record and spending record apart from the actual cheques (ie not in your money belt) so that they aren't stolen along with everything else.

The easiest brands to exchange in Latin America are American Express, Thomas Cook, Citibank and Visa. Smaller banks and companies also issue travellers cheques, but these are harder to change. Denominations of US$20 or US$50 are recommended because a little goes a long way in most Latin American countries, and exchanging US$100 could mean walking around with a huge wad of local currency.

CREDIT CARDS

Credit cards can be handy in emergencies, and some people use them for cash advances instead of walking around with a load of travellers cheques. This isn't always possible, however, and you shouldn't rely too heavily on a credit card. Indeed, cards will be useless in smaller Latin American towns. The best strategy is to have some travellers cheques, but to pay for big-ticket or splurge items with a credit card.

The amount you actually pay your credit card company will depend on when they bill you and the current exchange rate. It is entirely possible to check into a hotel costing US$75 a night, but find that by the time you arrive home, the currency has taken a dive and you are billed for only US$60. On the other hand, some cards require that you pay the amount in full at the end of each month − if you're in the middle of a lengthy trip and don't settle up, you'll be hit with serious penalty fees and/or interest. Some cards also charge a fee (usually around 2%) for international transactions; see if your company follows this policy. If it does, maybe it's time to consider changing credit card companies.

Depending on the country, credit cards can be used at automatic teller machines (ATMs) to withdraw cash (see the country profiles for details). Don't expect this to be the norm, however. Machines that can perform these transactions will have network icons displayed that should match one of the icons on the back of your card. For a list of ATMs worldwide that service Visa cards, go to www.visa.com/cgi-bin/vee/pd/atm/main.html?2+U; for Master-Card go to www.mastercard.com/atm.

Lastly, always double-check credit card receipts. Peruse the invoice when you get home and make sure what you bought is reflected accurately on the bill. Though uncommon, credit card fraud does happen, especially in Brazil (see Scams in the Issues & Attitudes chapter for more information).

DEBIT CARDS

Debit cards work just as they do at home except the ATM spits out local currency and the instructions are usually in a foreign language. In most big cities and tourist towns, you'll be able to use debit cards, especially MasterCard or Visa, and you should be able to find ATMs that take them; see the web sites listed under Credit Cards for a list of worldwide services. If you want to use ATMs, bring two cards in case one is lost or stolen, and keep an emergency number for your bank in a separate place.

The major problem with debit cards is that if your card is stolen and money is taken from your account, it's gone for good. When a credit card is stolen, however, you are only liable for a minimal amount or nothing at all.

CASH

Carrying around lots of cash is risky because if it's stolen or lost, *adios* as the locals say. For several reasons though, you will want to have some cash on you. Firstly, in some towns it's just not possible to change travellers cheques or use an ATM, but you can always find someone to change dollars. Secondly, border crossings present a tricky situation because you want to divest yourself of one currency (that of the country you're leaving) and buy another (that of your destination). Needless to say, you won't find any banks at border crossings, so you'll want to do this exercise in cash.

Many travellers like to carry a few hundred dollars in cash, kept in various spots, so if they're robbed they won't lose it all. Keeping some in a money belt and some stashed in a backpack frame or in a shoe usually works.

INTERNATIONAL MONEY TRANSFERS

Perhaps you're going on a long trip and don't want to carry all your budget on you, or you may have run out of money midway through your adventure. This is where international money transfers come in, whereby (with some lengthy paperwork) it's possible to have your home bank send money to a local bank. In Latin America, Western Union or American Express money transfers are the easiest way to go, although they are pricey (see the following section). Some countries are better than others to have money sent between banks.

RUNNING OUT OF MONEY

Falling short of money can happen to the best of us, so don't chastise yourself – but also don't wait until you're flat broke before doing something about it. Arranging for more money will usually incur some kinds of cost – if only getting back to a city where there are big banks – and if you can't at least do that, then you're in trouble. If you do find yourself penniless, you can try to sell some of your gear or borrow money from a friend or fellow traveller to tide you over.

If transferring money between banks is too complicated, expensive or time-consuming, search out a Western Union branch to get money sent direct to you from home. This is fast (usually less than 24 hours) and convenient. All you have to do is cajole someone at home to take money to a Western Union branch. There will be a fee of around 7% for this service. For more information, call Western Union (☎ 1-800-833833 in the UK or ☎ 1-800-325-6000 in the USA).

Another option if you're running out of cash is to try to find work. See the Work & Travel section in the Planning chapter for some pointers.

As an absolute last resort if you're stranded in a foreign country without a cent, go to your embassy and request repatriation. If repatriation is granted (don't count on it), you will be flown home and in many cases your passport will be confiscated until you repay the debt.

Changing Money

Changing money is one of those little errands you'll have to do every few days or weeks of your trip. The options for changing money are banks, *casas de cambio* (exchange houses), hotels and freelance moneychangers that work at border crossings and around banks.

Find out where the best place to change money is by consulting a guidebook or other travellers. In the few countries where there is a black market, the rates are no better than the bank's and may involve risk. In other countries, you wouldn't dream of changing money at a bank because you'll spend three hours in line getting a poor rate. Research the official exchange rate on the Internet or in a newspaper, and compare exchange rates and commission fees before committing to a place. Also, note the difference in rates between changing cash and travellers cheques, and if you're changing the latter, ask if the fee is per transaction or per cheque. Following are some more tips on changing money in Latin America:

- Casas de cambio and banks usually have the best rates, although the former are much faster, more convenient and may keep longer or weekend hours. You will find freelance moneychangers in the street (this is not usually a black market as such).

- Don't let anyone bully you into exchanging money. Feel free to shop around and tell aggressive moneychangers you're not changing money at the moment.

- Beware of scams by moneychangers. Unless you're in a bank or casa de cambio, there is always the possibility of getting scammed. Popular cons include the 'fixed' calculator or trading in old, outdated bills.

- Big cities have the best exchange rates, so change the money you'll need before heading out to the countryside.

- Try not to change a lot of money at borders, where rates are lower, but try to change just enough to get you on a bus to a major city.

- You'll be given a receipt to sign every time you change money in a bank or casa de cambio. If anything is amiss, you can terminate the transaction on the spot.
- You have to sign each travellers cheque in front of the person who's cashing it, so make sure that particular place accepts them. Otherwise, you could be stuck with worthless, signed cheques.
- Count and inspect the bills at the window where you're getting a cash advance or exchanging cash or travellers cheques to make sure you're not being short-changed. If you find a discrepancy once you step away from the window, it will be too late.
- If using a credit card or getting a cash advance, shop around for the best rates and lowest fees. Inspect the credit card slip carefully before you sign it, to make sure an extra zero wasn't added!
- Be extremely cautious and aware of your surroundings when changing money, even in a bank. This is one of those times when you'll have your money belt and your passport out in full view, which makes you vulnerable. Try to go with a friend when changing money, and make sure you have your passport, money and belt put away before you leave the counter.
- If you're just about to leave a country, don't change a large-denomination bill or travellers cheque, because you'll lose money when you reconvert it into the next country's currency or back into dollars.

Bargaining

Bargaining is one of those skills that takes minutes to learn but a lifetime to master and you'll definitely be practising among the professionals in Latin America. From hotel rooms and taxi rides to papayas and alpaca sweaters, you'll find opportunities galore to hone your bargaining skills. Don't get perturbed when you don't get the so-called local price; nine times out of 10 locals pay less simply because they're local. That's the way it is and there's something fundamentally egalitarian about it all, so just roll with it. Those foreigners complaining about the 13 extra cents they paid for a bunch of bananas are off-putting and embarrassing. If you're being shamelessly ripped off, that's altogether different and you should move on to another vendor if you think this is the case.

Most prices are negotiable in Latin America, though you'll find bargaining works better in rural areas than urban. In Chile, Argentina and Panama for instance, you'll have a hard time bargaining for anything outside of souvenirs at craft fairs. Meanwhile, taxi rides are completely open to discussion nearly everywhere else (though bus fares usually are not) and in Brazil you'll be expected to haggle over the price of a hotel room. Wherever you are, try to ask for a discount on your room if it's the low season. This doesn't mean that everything is negotiable: in supermarkets and regular shops you'll be expected to pay the marked price.

Bargaining techniques vary widely, but the best advice is to have fun. If you walk away annoyed or if the merchant gets insulted, you've flunked the bargaining test. Too many travellers feel constantly besieged and the victim of scams, and as a result haggle over small change in every little transaction. Remember that the people you're dealing with are trying to make a living and while they shouldn't rip you off, you shouldn't cut them off at the knees either. Basically, bargaining is successful when everyone gets a fair price and is satisfied.

To begin with, test your bargaining mettle at markets, where even the price of a piece of cheese will be open for debate, and from there work your way up to bargaining for accommodation. Ask other travellers what they have successfully bargained for, or just go for it; it will become quite clear what is open for negotiation and what is not. Don't push your luck, and don't bargain if you don't intend buying if your price is accepted – you will be wasting the time and energy of merchants who depend on sales for their livelihood.

Tipping

Generally, tipping will be up to you; the exceptions are porters at the airport, fancy restaurants (or those mostly patronised by foreigners) and guides on long Amazonian or Galápagos islands trips. If you receive bad service, try not to tip, as it will create a pattern of expectation that future travellers will have to live up to. Some restaurants will automatically add 10 or 20% service charge to the bill; there is no reason to tip again and the gratuity rate should be noted on the menu.

Typically, people in Latin America are struggling to make ends meet, so tips are appreciated. Good taxi drivers, children taking you to a hotel, and good waiters are all tipping candidates. If you're going to tip someone, do so directly rather than leaving it on a table or giving it to an intermediary. Often people will do things out of the kindness of their hearts, such as giving you a lift or inviting you to their home for tea. You can try to offer them a tip in these situations, but chances are they won't accept. See the boxed text 'It's Better to Give …' in the While You're There chapter for some gift-giving ideas.

Tips for Effective Bargaining

Your skill at bargaining can make a big difference in your daily expenses while on the road.

- Be polite, friendly and even playful when you bargain. Try not to think of the other person as an adversary.

- Do some research on what a reasonable price would be for the item in question. This is your best guarantee against being fleeced.

- Take your time. If you'll be in the area for a while, you could even stretch out a bargaining session over several days.

- Never quote the first price. Let the other person start and work from there. If the seller starts with an outrageous price, as taxi drivers are fond of doing, just walk away.

- If you're planning to make several purchases, buy everything at once to get a quantity discount. The more you buy, the more bargaining power you have. You can also pool your purchases with another traveller.

- Give reasons for asking for a lower price, eg everyone on the block is selling similar goods, or the item is flawed.

- Decide in advance the price you'd like to pay and the maximum price you will accept.

- Only bargain if you're serious about buying; if you are offered a fair price, accept it.

- The standard walking-away tactic is one of the best in the book, especially if you're close to the price you're willing to pay. You'll usually be called back to close the deal.

PASSPORTS & VISAS ▶▶

Passports

There are mountains of details to attend to, gear to buy and money to save for your trip, but before any of that matters, you'll have to get a passport. As a travel document, your passport is the most important: it's your main piece of identification, it holds visas and stamps that give you the legal right to be in a country and it contains emergency contact information if anything should go awry. Losing your passport doesn't herald the end of the world (or your trip), but it's a major pain in terms of time, money and energy to get it replaced. Carry your passport on you at all times, preferably in your money belt, and try not to part with it for long stretches of time, regardless of who requests it. Photocopy the front page and any other pages that have prearranged visas and carry them separately from your passport (see the Photocopies section at the end of this chapter).

IF YOU HAVE A PASSPORT

If you already have a passport, check the expiry date. Some countries will not admit you if your passport is due to expire in six months or less from when you arrive at the border. If you have a year or less on your passport, replace it before you leave to avoid any possible bureaucratic hassles down the road. Passports issued by most western governments are valid for 10 years; if you have at least a couple of years before your passport expires, you'll have the freedom to make work or personal commitments while you're on the road. Also check how many blank pages are left in your passport for those myriad stamps and visas that will adorn them. It would be unfortunate if you were caught short on passport pages miles from an embassy that could replenish them.

APPLYING FOR A PASSPORT

It takes some time to get a passport, so don't leave it to the last minute. Your passport is your key to the world and you'll have to show it to get visa applications (this can take from between three days to two weeks), pick up plane tickets and buy duty-free goods. Passport application requirements vary from country to country, but you should anticipate producing at least some of the following:

- Proof of citizenship, such as a birth, naturalisation or registration certificate.
- Two recent head-and-shoulder photos of you taken against a white background; signed and identified.
- Proof of identity is needed as someone must vouch for your identity on the application form and on your photographs. This can be either the holder of a current passport from your country who has known you for at least two years (but is unrelated to you) or a citizen of good standing such as a Justice of the Peace.

- Proof of any name change, such as a marriage or deed poll certificate.
- A fee, that will start at around A$125, C$60, NZ$80, UK£21 or US$65 for a standard adult passport of the minimum number of pages, issued within the usual processing time.

Issuing Periods & Rush Jobs

If all your supporting documentation is in order, you can expect to have your passport within two weeks. If you've left the process until the last moment or your passport is nowhere to be found and your departure is imminent, you may have to get a new one fast. Welcome to the process of 'expediting', where you'll pay dearly for a rushed passport job. You can get your passport expedited through the issuing agency or go to professionals who will take care of all the details for you, and the process will take at least two or three days. A search on the Internet or in the phonebook will give you plenty of leads on professional expeditors.

Issuing Agencies

The government agencies in charge of issuing passports in Australia, Canada, New Zealand, the UK and the USA are listed here (in many cases applications can be submitted to secondary agencies, such as post offices and banks):

Australia
Passports Australia, Department of Foreign Affairs & Trade
(☎ 13 1232, www.dfat.gov.au/passports/passports_faq_contents.html)

Canada
The Passport Office, Department of Foreign Affairs & International Trade
(☎ 1-800-567-6868, www.dfait-maeci.gc.ca/passport/paspr-2.htm)

New Zealand
The Passport Office, Department of Internal Affairs
(☎ 0800-22 5050, inform.dia.govt.nz/internal_affairs/businesses/doni_pro/fees.html)

UK
UK Passport Agency, The Home Office
(☎ 0870-521 0410, www.open.gov.uk/ukpass/ukpass.htm)

USA
Passport Services, the State Department
(☎ 1-900-225-5674, http://travel.state.gov/passport_services.html)

Dual Citizenship

You're a lucky person if you have two valid passports. Having the choice of different passports when entering a country means you can use the passport that will get you the cheaper or better visa. A second passport also allows you to use the one that will be better received by a particular country. For example, if you hold Canadian and Australian passports, you will need a visa for El Salvador if you use the Australian passport, but not with the

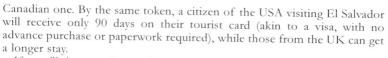

Canadian one. By the same token, a citizen of the USA visiting El Salvador will receive only 90 days on their tourist card (akin to a visa, with no advance purchase or paperwork required), while those from the UK can get a longer stay.

If you'll be travelling with two passports, don't advertise the fact. Certainly don't let border officials see you shuffling a stack of passports, and make sure you produce the same one you used to enter the country when you exit that country. It also a good policy to use the same passport when travelling through adjacent countries: if you entered Colombia on your Australian passport and then cross into Peru using your Canadian passport, the officials will wonder how you got there from the neighbouring countries.

Hostile Home Countries

In almost all cases, you should be well received throughout the region whatever your citizenship. If your passport and visas are in order, your arrival in a country and passage through customs should be perfunctory. There are however, lingering hostilities in some countries (especially in Central America) towards the USA. Assassination attempts by the CIA, the 1980s Iran-Contra affair and imperialist policies pursued by the USA in the region have understandably upset some. If you're uncomfortable arguing politics or stumble into an anti-American scenario, you may find things go more smoothly if you just say you're Canadian.

LOST OR STOLEN PASSPORTS

Obviously it's best to avoid losing your passport in the first place. Replacing a passport is a time-consuming hassle that costs money and energy, and the bureaucracy involved will try your patience.

There is quite a black market for stolen passports (and identities), so keep yours with you at all times (see Hazards & Safeguards in the Issues & Attitudes chapter for advice on keeping your valuables safe). If your passport is stolen, go to the nearest police station to file a report, then go to your embassy or consulate. If your country doesn't have diplomatic representation where you are, contact your embassy in the closest neighbouring country. The embassy staff can give you advice on what local authorities to notify.

If it's not possible for a new passport to be arranged before your visa is due to expire (eg if your passport is lost the day before you're due to fly home), you'll have to get a visa extension while you wait for your new passport to be issued.

You will need proper identification for the embassy to issue you with a new passport. A photocopy of the front page of your missing passport is preferable, but it could also be an old passport, a student ID card, a drivers licence or other identification with your photo on it. It will take a few days for your embassy to issue a new passport, and it probably won't be cheap.

Visas

Visas are stamps or paper inserts in your passport that allow you to enter a country and travel around for a certain length of time. Find out about visas during the research and planning stage of your trip. In some cases, you won't be able to apply for a visa until you have a plane ticket, so don't wait to book your flight until the day before you leave. Some countries require only tourist cards; these are forms issued on the plane or at the border and are very straightforward.

Mexico and all countries in Central and South America are open to visitors, but there are restrictions on the amount of time you can stay in different countries and where you can cross from one country to another. Border crossings may be grandiose affairs with big cement buildings or palm lean-tos with a man, a stamp pad and a sleeping dog. No matter how under-developed a crossing and whether you have your visa, you still must cross at designated borders to get the exit and entrance stamps that legally entitle you to be in the country.

HOME OR AWAY?

In many cases you'll have the option of obtaining visas in your home country. There are pros and cons to this strategy. Obtaining visas ahead of time locks you into an itinerary to some degree because all visas are time-sensitive. If you obtain a 30 day Brazilian visa at home, for example, but get side-tracked in Bolivia before you make it to Brazil and your visa expires, you're back to square one. If you want to set an itinerary and obtain all the visas you need for your trip beforehand, you will have to be very organised. If that's your style, go for it. Even so, you may not be able to get all the visas you need before you set off; Suriname may not have diplomatic representation in your country, for instance. See the Embassies sections in the country profiles later in this book for contact information for obtaining visas.

One Slip of the Pen

In July 1996 I made my first trip to South America, landing in Caracas. At the airport, the customs officer inspected my Swiss passport and stamped it, and I promptly caught a bus to the centre. It was a day later that I looked at my passport and discovered the officer had stamped 10 July 1995, not 10 July 1996 as the day of my arrival (and had made the same mistake on my tourist card).

What was I to do? In Venezuela, I was allowed to stay three months, so I was already illegally in the country nine months. I could speak little Spanish, and was alone in a large foreign city. I thought I could return to the airport and explain the mistake, go to the Swiss embassy and lose a week in Caracas with the authorities, or take a pen and change the '5' to a '6' ... so I did it, and instead of leaving Venezuela at the Colombian border, chose the safer Brazilian one.

The customs officer saw that something was wrong with my passport, but looked at the tourist card (a bit better counterfeited) and let me pass through.

The moral of this story is obvious – always inspect your passport immediately after an official has stamped it!

Johan, Switzerland

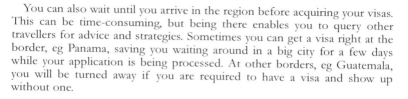

You can also wait until you arrive in the region before acquiring your visas. This can be time-consuming, but being there enables you to query other travellers for advice and strategies. Sometimes you can get a visa right at the border, eg Panama, saving you waiting around in a big city for a few days while your application is being processed. At other borders, eg Guatemala, you will be turned away if you are required to have a visa and show up without one.

PLANNING YOUR VISAS

Each country has different prices, lengths of stay and extension policies for visas. When you're planning your visas, the following tips are worth bearing in mind:

- Find out if there are different visa requirements for different modes of arrival. In Venezuela, for example, westerners do not need a visa if they arrive by air. Entering Venezuela overland is a different story and not only will you need a visa, but in some neighbouring countries (ie Colombia) it may be very difficult to get.

- Find out whether your visa is activated on entry or on issue. In some countries (eg El Salvador) visas are activated as soon as the stamp is in your passport, so if you linger before entering the country, you may not have much time left to explore once you arrive.

- Check how easy or difficult it is to extend your visa once you're in the country. If it's pretty straightforward, you may want to get a short-term visa at the border (if possible). If extensions seem convoluted, you might want to arrange a longer-stay visa from home.

- Consider whether you'll be entering and leaving a country more than once. If you fly into Brazil, plan to make a circuit of Argentina and Chile and then fly out of Brazil, this may effect your visa requirements.

- Be aware that if you overstay your visa in certain countries (eg Costa Rica and Panama), there is a whole procedure, sometimes complicated, for getting an exit permit. You must have this exit permit to be allowed to leave.

The Visa Requirements table in this section spells out who needs visas for where. For more information, see the country profiles. Visa requirements are subject to change without notice, so check with the embassy or consulate of the countries you intend to visit, or try the easy-to-use and generally accurate web site www2.travel.com.au/cgi-bin/clcgi?E=bevisreq, which prompts you for your home and destination country and tells you the visa requirements.

The Application Process

Don't expect efficient service when you line up to get your visas. Whatever the country, government offices tend to keep short hours, close on public holidays and employ the most dour staff. To make the process as smooth as possible, consider these tactics:

- Call ahead to find out the opening hours of the embassy, including whether they operate on weekends or holidays. If you're getting visas while in Latin America, it's important to find out if they close for lunch or a siesta. Also ask what you'll need in the way of documentation, photos, onward tickets and sufficient funds (sometimes required and asked for; see Other Paperwork), and what the visa will cost.

- Leave yourself a lot of time and be patient. Your visa may not be issued on your initial attempt.
- Get there as early as possible (before the masses arrive, preferably) and be prepared to stand in line. Bring a book, journal or stereo to pass the time. This is a good opportunity to write postcards!
- Have all your documents ready to show the agent; this includes your plane ticket and your arrival and departure dates. There's no need to dress up, but avoid showing up totally road-ragged either. Visas are a privilege, not a right, so a good demeanour and appearance can only help.
- Be punctual when picking up your visa and inspect all the details (dates, length of stay etc) before leaving the window.

Photographs

You'll need plenty of passport-size photos for all the required visas, whether you apply for them at home or on the road. Some countries require two or three photos for a visa application and not all cities have photobooths for this purpose, or if they do they can be very expensive. A tip to remember with these photos is that black and white ones nearly always look better than colour.

VISA REQUIREMENTS IN CENTRAL & SOUTH AMERICA

destination	Aust	Can	NZ	UK	USA
Argentina	–	–	–	–	–
Belize	–	–	–	–	–
Brazil	✓	✓	✓	–	–
Chile	–	–	–	–	–
Colombia	–	–	–	–	–
Costa Rica	–	–	–	–	–
Ecuador	–	–	–	–	–
El Salvador	–	–	–	–	–
Falkland Is	–	–	–	–	–
French Guiana	–	–	–	–	–
Guyana	–	–	–	–	–
Honduras	–	–	–	–	–
Mexico	–	–	–	–	–
Nicaragua	✓	✓	✓	–	–
Panama	–	–	–	–	–
Paraguay	✓	✓	✓	–	–
Peru	–	–	–	–	–
Suriname	–	–	–	✓	–
Uruguay	–	–	–	–	–
Venezuela	–	–	–	–	–

Other Paperwork
ONWARD TICKETS

Before granting you entry, many countries require that you show an onward ticket as proof that you'll eventually leave. Some destinations, such as Panama and Venezuela, are particularly strict about this requirement and you won't be permitted to board a plane without showing an onward plane or bus ticket. If you're asked to produce an onward ticket at an overland border crossing and can't, you may be turned away. Try showing the border officials some 'sufficient funds' in this case and promise to buy a bus ticket.

SUFFICIENT FUNDS

As well as onward tickets, some countries will ask you to show 'sufficient funds' so they can be assured you won't try to work during your travels or otherwise freeload on their economy. It's not clear what constitutes sufficient funds, but flashing a wad of travellers cheques or a credit card usually does the trick.

DOCUMENTS FOR MINORS

Certain countries require auxiliary documentation if you are under 18 years of age (20 in the case of Paraguay) and travelling without your parents. Requirements for minors are particularly strict in Mexico and you should be aware of what extra paperwork, often notarised, that you'll need. See the country profiles for details on travelling minors.

HOSTELLING INTERNATIONAL CARD

Becoming a member of Hostelling International (HI) is not expensive and the discounts it may provide you in some countries – eg Argentina, Brazil, Chile and Uruguay, where hotels are relatively expensive – may be worth it. Membership is around US$25 a year; visit the official HI web site (www.iyhf.org) for more information. Though there are accredited hostels in other Latin American countries, they are still pricier than other accommodation options, discounts or not.

INTERNATIONAL STUDENT CARD

The International Student Identity Card (ISIC) is recognised almost everywhere *but* Latin America. One of the reasons is that the cards are too easy to forge, and fakes have been circulating in recent years. Still, in countries like Mexico, Argentina or Chile an ISIC card may get you discounts on entry fees to museum and archaeological sites. Some cards also carry automatic travel insurance, or it can be purchased by card-holders at low prices. The ISIC card is available only to full-time students, no matter what age, and is issued by accredited travel agencies (such as STA Travel) through the International Student Travel Confederation (ISTC; www.isic.org/index.htm), based in Copenhagen, Denmark. You'll need proof of your full-time student status.

Other cards such as the International Youth Travel Card (IYTC; also issued by ISTC) and the GO 25 International Youth Travel Card (also known as the

GO 25 Card) will be even less useful than an ISIC card. Still, if you have one, try for a discount – you never know; they also serve as secondary pieces of photo identification and may provide travel insurance.

INTERNATIONAL TEACHER CARD

If you teach full-time at a recognised school, you'll qualify for an International Teacher Identity Card (ITIC). Also issued by the ISTC, it provides discounts similar to the student cards. For details on this card, visit the ISTC web page (www.isic.org/index.htm).

INTERNATIONAL DRIVING PERMIT

If you intend to drive in Latin America, you will need an International Driving Permit (IDP). There is another type of driving permit called the Inter-American Driving Permit, which is the only permit recognised by Uruguay (in theory). You'll want the IDP. These are administered by automobile associations in your home country only. Occasionally a web site will claim to offer IDPs, but these are usually fake and expensive – a bad combination, especially considering the real things are affordable and a breeze to obtain.

To get an IDP, you have to be over 18 years of age and hold a valid driving licence from your home country. You'll need a couple of passport photographs and must pay a nominal fee. Check with your automobile association about the IDP conditions; some are only valid for a year, while others are valid for cars, but not for motorcycles.

Some countries require an IDP and others do not. Even if the country you're visiting does require one, bring along your driving licence from your home country. Following is contact information for some automobile associations:

American Automobile Association
(☎ 1-888-859-5161, www.aaa.com/vacation/idp.html)

Australian Automobile Association
(☎ 02-6247 7311, www.aaa.asn.au – for links to the state-based automobile associations that issue IDPs)

British Automobile Association
(☎ 0990-500 600, www.theaa.co.uk/membership/offers/idp.html)

Canadian Automobile Association
(☎ 613-247-0117 ext 2025, www.caa.ca/CAAInternet/travelservices/frames14.htm)

New Zealand Automobile Association
(☎ 0800-500 444, www.aa.org.nz)

NAME CARDS

Name cards or business cards with your name, telephone number, home and email addresses may seem excessive, but they really come in handy when you're meeting lots of people on the road with whom you'd like to stay in touch.

Offset printers are ubiquitous in Latin America, and you can get a stack of cards made up very inexpensively. Business cards are also useful in official encounters, good or bad, because they carry a lot of weight with bureaucrats. If you're looking for work in your travels, cards are indispensable.

YELLOW FEVER VACCINATION CERTIFICATE

You will need to show a Yellow Fever Vaccination Certificate if you're coming from an infected area. In the western hemisphere, yellow fever areas include almost all of tropical South America. Border officials will ask to see your certificate, which is given to you after you get your shot. See the Health chapter and the country profiles for details on which countries require yellow fever immunisations.

DOCUMENTATION

Before you leave home, make two copies of all your important travel documents. This includes the front page of your passport and any visa stamps, plane tickets, travel insurance information, travellers cheques receipts and serial numbers, International Driving Permit, birth and marriage certificates (if you're bringing them) and credit cards. Keep one set of copies stashed in your luggage (keeping the originals on your person) and give the other set to a friend or family member at home. Having copies will make replacing lost or stolen items much easier, especially if you have to deal with local bureaucrats.

A more effective way to store vital travel documents such as passport details and travellers cheques numbers is to use Lonely Planet's eKno travel vault. You can access these details by using a password at cybercafes around the world. It's free to join eKno (www.ekno.lonelyplanet.com) and free to use the travel vault.

Your Ticket

AIR

Most visitors to Mexico and beyond arrive by air. The sooner you buy your ticket the better; good deals on fares are usually easier to swing weeks or months before your departure date. Although very good discounts are available on tickets the airline is trying to unload at the last possible second, there are some serious problems with these. Firstly, you probably won't get the route or departure dates you want. Secondly, if it's really the last moment, you may not have time to arrange immunisations, visas or travel insurance. Lastly, holding out until the end for a cheap ticket can always backfire if there are none available. In this case you'll have to settle for a full-priced fare or delay your departure while you scramble around for an appropriate flight.

Airlines

All sorts of people with all sorts of budgets fly to different corners of the world, and there are airlines and levels of service to fit almost anyone's style. There are big fancy carriers with movies, food and state-of-the-art facilities like United Airlines, KLM and British Airways. At the other end of the scale are regional or local airlines flying reconditioned planes from the former USSR. Local airlines can be decent, but older planes do carry a higher safety risk, offer lower levels of comfort and are less reliable overall. As well, cancellations and delays are more likely with these outfits. Luckily, in the airline business there is a middle ground. Here is where you're likely to find deals, a modicum of comfort and an acceptable level of reliability at a decent price. Healthy national airlines like Brazil's Varig and AeroMexico are good examples.

Travel agents can outline airline, flight and ticket options for you, as can individual airlines' web sites. Some things to think about are the type and age of the planes they're flying; stopovers or plane changes involved in your proposed route; frequent flier programs; payment and booking options; and the policies for cancelled or altered tickets. The following web sites can help you sort these questions out:

AeroContinente (http://200.4.197.130/Acerca-in.htm)
Aerolineas Argentinas (www.aerolineas.com.ar)
AeroMexico (www.aeromexico.com)
Air France (www.airfrance.fr)
Air New Zealand (www.airnz.com)
Alitalia (www.alitalia.com/english/index.html)
American Airlines (www.americanair.com)
Ansett Australia (www.ansett.com.au)
Avensa (www.avensa.com)
Avianca (www.avianca.com.co)

British Airways (www.british-airways.com)
Canadian Airlines (www.cdnair.ca)
Continental Airlines (www.flycontinental.com)
Guyana Airways (www.turq.com/guyana/guyanair)
Iberia (www.iberia.com)
LanChile (www.lanchile.cl)
Lauda Air (www.laudaair.com)
Lloyd Aéreo Boliviano (www.labairlines.com)
Lufthansa Airlines (www.lufthansa.com)
Mexicana Airlines (www.mexicana.com)
Qantas Airways (www.qantas.com)
United Airlines (www.ual.com)
Varig (www.varig.com.bra)

A consortium of five Central American airlines is united under the Grupo Taca banner and can be accessed at www.grupotaca.com. The individual contact information for these airlines is:

Aviateca (Guatemala)
  (☎ 800-327-9832)

COPA (Panama)
  (☎ 800-359-2672, www.copair.com)

LACSA (Costa Rica)
  (☎ 800-225-2272)

Nica (Nicaragua)
  (☎ 800-831-6422)

TACA (El Salvador)
  (☎ 800-535-8780)

Partnerships Which airline you settle on is likely to effect your route, because not all carriers fly to the same destinations. In fact, airlines are a bit tyrannical about their routes and the competition is very stiff between carriers attempting to broaden the number of destinations they maintain. To do this, many airlines form partnerships and reciprocal arrangements so they can have access to each other's routes. This permits the airlines to offer more destination options and is particularly beneficial for special fares such as Round-the-World (RTW) tickets. If you choose one airline to fly you throughout the region, you will almost certainly be flying some of the legs with that airline's partners, so research those carriers beforehand as well.

Frequent Flier Programs Most airlines have frequent flier programs that let you redeem accumulated miles or kilometres for free plane tickets and other benefits. Points are accumulated primarily by flying with the airline and its partners, but can also be garnered through affiliated car rental agencies, credit cards and even long-distance phone companies.

The specifics of frequent flier programs differ, and you may want to check out the finer points before signing up. Some programs require that you use your points within five years; with others, there is no expiry date. Some allow you to transfer points between family members, and most have free enrolment, though a few may charge a small fee to join. Once you're in a program, you'll be tempted to fly that particular airline or its partners to rack up points. However, you might decide to save cash on your ticket by flying with another carrier altogether.

Generally, you earn one point for every one you fly, so you'll want to sign up with the airline that is going to take you the furthest on your trip. Keep in mind that if it is a carrier from your home country, you can use your points at home at a later date.

There are all kinds of restrictions regarding redemption of a frequent flier ticket. For example, there are only so many seats on each flight allocated for these tickets, so book your flight well in advance. There are also significant blackout dates, which means you won't be able to use a frequent flier ticket anywhere near a holiday.

Keep your frequent flier information with your other travel documents; you'll need to cite your membership number each time you buy a ticket or use a service that earns you points.

Tickets & Restrictions

There are many types of tickets available, and they all have some type of restriction. The myriad restrictions and rules can get quite convoluted, but here are some of the most common:

- Financial penalties may be incurred for cancellation or changes to your ticket once you've purchased it (most travel insurance policies will protect you against unavoidable cancellations).
- Directional restrictions apply to some tickets, eg most Round-the-World tickets will only let you travel in one direction.
- Minimum or maximum stay limits may apply, such as a minimum stay of two weeks and a maximum of 12 months.
- Some tickets are refundable only at the travel agency where you bought it, which will do you no good once you're on the road.
- Some fares may have seasonal limits, meaning they are available during off-peak or shoulder periods only (see When to Go in the Planning chapter for details).
- You may have a limited number of stopovers or a certain amount of time that you can spend at a stopover destination, known as a stop-off.

The basic ticket is either a one-way or return (round trip) ticket between two destinations. There are usually three flight classes offered by the airlines: 1st class (coded F), business class (coded J) and economy class (coded Y). Once you start to hunt, the restrictions get more complicated and exhaustive as the ticket price drops. Some of the most common deals are discussed in the following sections.

Discount Return Tickets If you plan to visit only one area or country, then a good old-fashioned return ticket will probably work for you. If you can get a discounted ticket to a Central American hub like Guatemala City or San José

(Costa Rica) or to a South American hub like Rio de Janeiro, Lima or Caracas, you can visit other countries on your itinerary through a combination of internal flights, trains and buses. This only works if you have ample time and don't want to cover great distances beyond the city you flew into. To squeeze the most out of a return ticket, see if you can include stop-offs en route to your final destination city. Stop-offs are sometimes for as long as a few weeks, and allow you to explore an area before continuing onto your ultimate destination. An example is a London-Quito fare with a stop-off at Curacáo, allowing you a little Caribbean beach vacation before heading into the wilds of Ecuador. Alternatively, you can get an open return ticket that flies into and out of the same city, but has no fixed return date; these can be expensive.

Open-Jaw Tickets These are return tickets that allow you to fly into one city and out from another. These tickets save a lot of time and backtracking, but are more expensive. Still, if you want to see a lot of a region, these tickets are the answer. For instance, you can buy an open-jaw ticket that arrives in Santiago de Chile, but departs from Bogotá, Colombia, thus sparing you the return trip to Chile.

One-Way Tickets These are almost always more expensive (sometimes frighteningly so) than return tickets, but can be useful if you have no idea when or if (!) you'll return home. Having the freedom to go wherever you like can open up a whole new world to you. The downside to one-way tickets is that some countries (eg Colombia, Venezuela and Panama) require an onward ticket before they'll grant you a visa or tourist card. Often you can show sufficient funds – usually a wad of travellers cheques a or credit card will do – in lieu of an onward ticket and you'll be granted a visa. This isn't foolproof, however, and some places can be stubborn on the onward ticket issue. Airlines are particularly difficult when it comes to onward tickets, and may ask you to show one before boarding the plane. For example, airlines in Costa Rica and Panama will not sell you a one-way ticket to Colombia unless you have an onward ticket.

Round-the-World Tickets If you plan to travel to more than one continent, or if you're coming from New Zealand or Australia, a Round-the-World (RTW) ticket is a good deal. This type of fare gives you a limited time period (eg 12 months) in which to make your way around the world. These tickets have a certain number of stop-offs, and you can increase the number of stop-offs by paying a fee for each extra stop. The big catch is that you can only travel in one direction, with no backtracking. Also, you can only fly on the routes serviced by the airline and its partners that issued the ticket. However, these tickets are such a bargain overall (you just couldn't get near the price of a RTW if you bought all the legs separately) that paying for a flight to an extra destination not serviced by your airline is tolerable. An RTW ticket will also rack up the frequent flier points, although these tickets accumulate points at a lower rate than one-way or return fares.

Circle-Pacific Fares Consider a Circle-Pacific fare if you're coming from the USA, Australia or New Zealand and want to visit Easter Island off the coast of Chile. This is usually a very expensive side trip, but Circle Pacific tickets ostensibly offer Easter Island as a stop-off, saving you some money. These fares are offered by LanChile, the Chilean national airline, in conjunction with its partners. From the USA, the Circle-Pacific flight could leave from Los Angeles and stop in Hawaii, Japan, Australia, New Zealand, Papeete (Tahiti), Easter Island and Santiago before returning to the USA. These tickets are offered by Singapore Airlines in conjunction with Aerolíneas Argentinas and cost US$289. From Australia (A$1599 for 45 days) or New Zealand (NZ$1899 for 45 days) the route is from Sydney or Auckland to Papeete, Easter Island and Santiago, with a free onward flight to either Buenos Aires or Rio.

Discover South America Fares These are special fares offered by Qantas and Air New Zealand; they can be a great deal and have moderate flexibility. Qantas offers a 'Discover South America' fare leaving from Sydney or Melbourne and going to Buenos Aires, with connections to Lima, Santiago, Rio, La Paz or Santa Cruz at little or no extra cost. This fare costs A$1449 for a 35 day stay and A$1640 for up to 45 days in the low season. Air New Zealand has a 'Visit South America' fare that is good for three months and permits two stops in South America and one in the USA before returning to Auckland. There are open-jaw and backtrack options with this ticket so you can custom-design your itinerary; the low season cost is NZ$2986.

Group Tickets Airlines offer volume discounts and if you can organise a group, you may save a huge amount on your air fare. Groups can be arranged by a travel agent that buys a block of tickets to get lower fares; there is no obligation to travel with the group once you arrive at your destination. There are usually inflexible and numerous restrictions, and you may not be able to change your dates or stay longer than 60 days. Discuss details in full with a travel agent before committing to this kind of ticket.

APEX Tickets Advance Purchase Excursion (APEX) tickets are inflexible, but can offer excellent discounts. These fares must be purchased at least two to three weeks prior to departure, you cannot stop off and there are usually minimum and maximum stay requirements. You also must fix departure and return dates, and there is a penalty if you want to change those dates. Still, these can be good if you have to be home by a certain date. If you're uncertain of your return date, APEX one-way tickets are a better choice.

Student, Teacher & Youth Fares If you have a teacher, student or youth card, you may be eligible for up to a 25% discount on your fare (see Other Paperwork in the Passports & Visas chapter for details on these cards). Some airlines will also require a letter from your school. Discounts of this sort are usually only available on regular economy class fares.

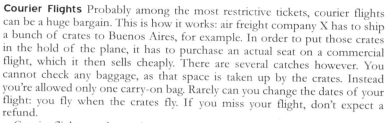

Courier Flights Probably among the most restrictive tickets, courier flights can be a huge bargain. This is how it works: air freight company X has to ship a bunch of crates to Buenos Aires, for example. In order to put those crates in the hold of the plane, it has to purchase an actual seat on a commercial flight, which it then sells cheaply. There are several catches however. You cannot check any baggage, as that space is taken up by the crates. Instead you're allowed only one carry-on bag. Rarely can you change the dates of your flight: you fly when the crates fly. If you miss your flight, don't expect a refund.

Courier flights can be a pain to arrange, but you'll be amazed at the discount. There aren't that many courier tickets available, so try to arrange it at least a month or two in advance. Your preferred route may not be offered either, but major cities such as New York, Los Angeles and London have regular courier flights to South America.

There are several major courier services that specialise in these flights. Some are like memberships that collect fees and have limited enrolment, while others are free. Some of the larger outfits (all US-based) are the Air Courier Association (☎ 1-800-822-0888, www.aircourier.org), Air Courier International (☎ 1-800-682-6593) and the International Association of Air Travel Couriers (☎ 561-582-8320, www.courier.org/index.html).

Tickets to Avoid

Back-to-Front Tickets These are return tickets purchased in your destination city rather than your home city. If you live in Paris, for example, where tickets are fairly expensive, and want to fly to Caracas, where tickets are fairly cheap, you could theoretically buy the ticket by phone or on the Internet and have a friend in Caracas send it to you in France. Unfortunately, this isn't as clever as it seems, for the airlines have computers that tell them where the ticket was purchased; if you try to check-in at Orly, and the airline computer says the ticket was bought in Caracas, you won't be allowed to board. If you do buy tickets over the web or by phone, make sure you don't violate the back-to-front rules, as shifty types do sell airline tickets using this scam.

Second-Hand Tickets Gone are the days when you could buy someone else's ticket or frequent flier points cheaply and get away with it. Still, you will see postings on electronic and youth hostel bulletin boards, and occasional newspaper advertisements for unused tickets.

The price might be tempting, but in this case, it's not worth it. Second-hand tickets very rarely work because the name on the ticket must match the name on the passport of the person trying to check in. Some folks selling used tickets will try to talk you into it, reasoning that they can check in for you and then give you the boarding pass. This is a bad idea for a lot of reasons, not the least of which is that immigration officials will most likely try to match the boarding pass with your passport. Once they see the names don't match, you won't be allowed to board.

If you legally change your name after you've purchased a plane ticket, make sure you have official documents proving that the old and new you are the same person. These can include a birth, marriage or divorce certificate, an old passport or a deed poll certificate.

Buying Your Ticket

Before you rush out and buy your ticket, decide what type of trip you're after and where you want to go (see What Kind of Trip? in the Planning Chapter for some ideas). If you plan to take an organised tour, the plane ticket will be included in the package price and so won't be a factor. If you want to travel independently, the two elements with the greatest impact on the cost and type of plane ticket you purchase will be where you want to go and how long you want to be away.

Buying from Airlines Buying your ticket directly from an airline is an option, although you probably won't get a discount because fares offered directly to the public are full-price. However, the airlines dump difficult-to-sell tickets on travel agents, who in turn sell them at a discounted price to travellers. Unless you need a flight at the last second, purchase your ticket through a source other than the airline.

Buying from Travel Agents There are numerous travel agents to choose from, but they all fall into two categories: bonded and unbonded. The first is your normal travel agency that is 'bonded' to a national association that makes sure its members live up to certain ethical standards, including selling guaranteed tickets that will be fully refunded if the agency goes into bankruptcy before you've taken your trip. The second type are called 'consolidators' in the USA and 'bucket shops' in the UK. These are not bonded and you run some risk of losing your money if the company goes belly-up before you get your ticket. However, the savings on these tickets will be substantial because they work in high volume. Tickets from unbonded agencies are on regular, commercial airlines.

To minimise the risk if buying from an unbonded agent, use a credit card; if the company goes under, your credit card company will probably cover the loss. If you pay in cash, make sure you pick up the ticket in person. Do not pay up-front and agree to pick it up later or have it mailed to you. Once you have the ticket, call the airline and confirm that there's a booking in your name.

This is advice developed from old hands who learned the hard way, but don't let these precautions put you off unbonded agencies; there are many reputable companies who have been in business, successfully, for years. Travel sections in major papers and free weeklies in big cities carry a slew of advertisements for these companies. Look for ones that specialise in Latin America. One worth trying is eXito (☎ 1-800-655-4053, fax 510-655-4566, www.exitotravel.com), 1212 Broadway, Suite 910, Oakland, CA 94612.

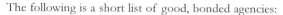

The following is a short list of good, bonded agencies:

Australia
  STA Travel
  (☎ 1300-360 960, www.sta-travel.com)
  Flight Centre
  (☎ 13 1600, www.flightcentre.com)

Canada
  Travel CUTS
  (☎ 1-800-667-2887, www.travelcuts.com)

New Zealand
  STA Travel
  (☎ 0800-100 677, www.sta-travel.com)

UK
  Trailfinders
  (☎ 020-7938 3366, www.trailfinder.com)
  STA Travel
  (☎ 020-7581 4132, www.sta-travel.com)

USA
  Council Travel
  (☎ 1-800-226-8624, www.counciltravel.com)
  STA Travel
  (☎ 1-800-781-4040, www.sta-travel.com)

Buying Online There are some serious deals floating in cyberspace, but you have to be an Internet junkie to take advantage of them. The real bargains go fast and the time you spend tracking them down may be time better spent doing other research. Remember that travel agents get paid to find air fares, and they can probably get a cheap fare for you in half the time it will take you on the Net.

Even if you don't buy online, the Net is a great way to find out what a ticket will cost and will help you make informed decisions at a travel agency. Try these sites:

  Expedia (expedia.msn.com/daily/home/default.hts)
  Flight Info.Com (www.flifo.com)
  Preview.Travel (www.previewtravel.com)
  Travelocity (www.travelocity.com)

Getting a Good Deal Start your research by checking out the travel sections of major newspapers, magazines and free weeklies (see Researching Your Trip in the Planning chapter for some useful titles). Also call the major airlines or visit their web sites to find out which carriers fly which routes. Once you've done this and looked at the web sites mentioned in the Buying Online section, you'll have a decent idea of the bargains available and the restrictions and conditions they carry.

To get the best deal, try to buy your ticket as far in advance as possible, preferably three months before you depart, when there are still seats available and you can satisfy any advance purchase restrictions. This will also allow plenty of time for getting visas and immunisations (see the Passports & Visas and Health chapters for more information).

Check out some travel agencies, preferably those that specialise in Latin America, and try to find an experienced agent with a travel philosophy akin to your own. Finding a good deal among all the travel options out there takes a skilled and creative agent, and it's OK to shop around for one you like. Here's some basic advice on tracking down a cheap fare:

- Decide if you're willing to take a roundabout route. Some of the cheapest fares involve stopovers and plane changes in different countries. This can be very tiring, and while some people insist on direct flights, if you want a rock-bottom fare, this is the way to go. If you're willing to do this, let your travel agent know so they can organise the flights.
- Be flexible with your departure dates. If you plan to start a trip in the peak season, consider delaying or bringing it forward so you depart in the shoulder period. If your schedule allows you to drastically shift your dates so that you leave during the off-peak season, even better.
- Be prepared to alter your itinerary if a deal presents itself. But, if you're set on visiting a destination for which there is no deal, think about flying to somewhere cheaper close by and purchasing a separate sector flight or travelling overland to where you want to be.
- If you're flying to a destination that is serviced by more than one daily flight, see if flying overnight (called a 'red eye') lowers the fare. Flights that arrive late at night in your destination country can also be cheap, as this is an unpopular time to land.

Once you have all these parameters set, get a quote from a travel agent and then call or visit several other agencies to see if they'll beat that price. Airlines have preferred agents and so not all the same deals are available to all agents; shopping around works. Inquire as to the payment options; some tickets do not have to be paid in full until six weeks before departure (giving you more time to save), while others require a nonrefundable deposit.

Your Arrival Time Though arriving at night can lower your fare, there are some drawbacks. Firstly, it can be intimidating to arrive in a strange country after hours. Secondly, the logistics can be a nightmare: you have to clear immigration and customs, change money and somehow get to the city centre and a hotel when lots of services are closed. Experienced travellers may opt to spend the night at the airport if they arrive really late, but this doesn't appeal to everyone and few airports in Latin America are open 24 hours.

Your First Night
Even if you tend to leave everything to fate, going where the wind blows, make an exception on your first night in Latin America and research, or book, a hotel. Life will be a lot easier if you don't have to traipse around looking for accommodation while dealing with a new time zone, language and currency. You should have no problem finding clusters of hostels where travellers hang

out. Study your guidebook on your flight and kill time by choosing the neighbourhood where you want to stay; work out how to get there from the airport; and pick a few promising hotels. When you land, go to your first choice, check it out and rent a room if you like it. Otherwise, move on to candidate number two. This little bit of preparation will ameliorate some of the stress associated with jumping headlong into a new world.

You may want to make a hotel reservation from home for that first night. If it's late, buses may not be running, budget accommodation could be closed (not all have night porters) and pickings could be slim. Expect to spend a minimum of about US$30 for a prebooked hotel; this may be worth it, particularly if you're travelling alone.

Bikes & Surfboards

If you'll be travelling with a bike, surfboard, kayak or other such equipment, you have to let the airline know beforehand. With enough advance notice, it shouldn't be a problem. Some airlines will charge a nominal fee to accommodate your extra baggage and the packing materials needed to transport it safely (usually around US$10). When you reconfirm your ticket, remind the airline of your additional baggage and get to the airport earlier than the required check-in time so you can pack it and check it in before the rush. It will travel better if it's not the last piece packed into the plane's hold.

Bikes Most airlines won't make you take your bike apart if there's room in the hold. They will, however, charge you for shipping (sometimes upwards of US$100 each way!) and it may be subject to space availability. They'll also require you to loosen the handlebar nut so you can turn the handles 90° and remove any attachments like lights or panniers. If you are concerned about damage to your bike, consider wrapping it in bubblewrap or purchasing a bike box to protect it from scratches and dents. Some airlines may allow you to check a bike into the airplane's hold in lieu of a piece of luggage – it's worth a try!

Surfboards It's not a good idea to send your board into a plane's hold unprotected. A decent travel bag with extra padding will cost around US$200 to US$300. A professional model can hold up to three boards, so look into splitting the cost of a bag if you're travelling with surfing friends. Bubblewrap can add an extra layer of protection from the bumps inflicted by airport baggage staff.

Other Considerations

Travel agents can arrange a wide variety of services above and beyond booking a plane ticket. They may be able to reserve a specific seat if you're travelling with a child, or if you're prone to sickness or extra tall. They can also help with hotels, rental cars, tours and the like (see the Takeoff chapter for further discussion of these issues and advice for disabled travellers).

Travel agents also provide other services, including currency exchange, visa procurement, immunisation arrangements and issuing travellers cheques, although you should be able to do these things yourself, thus saving money and learning the ropes in the process.

One thing travel agents can't help you with is the antismoking policies now followed by most airlines. If you want to smoke en route, try flying with the Latin American national airlines, some of which still permit smoking on board.

LAND
Train

Train travel may sound hopelessly romantic, but in much of Latin America, it's just hopeless. You could fly to Mexico or travel overland from the USA and try to wend your way south to Central America by train, but you'd probably grow old doing it. You'd also probably lose money on nonrefundable tickets that went unused due to strikes, floods, derailments and track repairs. Travelling overland is best done by bus and car, with a few boat trips thrown in.

Bus

Buses are ubiquitous in Latin America, and travelling overland through Mexico and Central America by bus and then flying on to South America is a popular trip. Overland is the way to go if you want to experience Latino culture up close and personal and spend some time appreciating the varied, beautiful landscapes. Sketch out a tentative route and consult a travel agent to see what works (remembering that travelling overland from Panama to Colombia is extremely difficult). If you plan particularly well or have a wide-open schedule, you can hop off the bus and explore cities that look too good to pass by. Overland travel is perhaps the most exciting way to go, but it's also the most time-consuming and can be expensive. Research is important because you'll have to plan for various visas, border crossings and currencies (see the Your Route section in the Planning chapter for more information on overland travel through the region).

Car & Motorcycle

It's possible to travel in your own vehicle overland from the USA, through Mexico to Central America and beyond. The cost and legwork involved are substantial, however, and travellers wishing to drive through Latin America should do their research. Unleaded gas is rare and the paperwork involved at borders could bury you. Since there is no road connecting Panama and Colombia, vehicles have to be shipped around the Darién Gap.

SEA

Choices for travelling to Latin America by sea are limited and pricey. There are a few cruise ships that sail between the USA and Europe, but they are much more expensive than flying. Houston, New Orleans, Hamburg and Amsterdam are among a few of the departure points for cargo ships to South American ports. These are also expensive. For more information on cruise ships, consult the *OAG Cruise & Ferry Guide* published by Reed Travel Group in the UK.

Travel Insurance

Though it's tempting to save money by ignoring insurance, a travel insurance policy is a must. Depending on the breadth of your policy, it can pay for medical costs resulting from sickness or injury, reimburse you for lost or stolen luggage or tickets, protect you from cancellation penalties on tickets and tours, and fly you home in case of serious illness (or even death).

Health care in Latin America runs the gamut from superior to 'Take this shot of rum while I amputate your leg' (see Medical Services in the Health chapter for how to avoid the latter). If you fall seriously ill or have a major injury while on the road, you may have to be flown home or to a nearby country with topnotch hospitals. If you are treated in Latin America, it's important to keep all receipts and copies of your medical reports, preferably in your native language, for insurance purposes. For the same reason, you will need a police report to claim stolen property on your insurance.

If you have a medical insurance policy at home, whether administered privately or by the government, check to see if it can be used internationally. You may also be automatically covered under your International Student Identity Card (ISIC), GO 25 Card or an International Teachers Identity Card (ITIC). Ask where you purchased your card (for details see the Other Paperwork section in the Passports & Visas chapter).

Travel insurance policies are offered by travel agencies, regular insurance agencies, student travel organisations and some credit card companies. Investigate the options − some are really cheap, but that's because there's minimal coverage. Have a good look at the small print and know what your policy does and does not cover. Here are some insurance buying tips:

- Once you have your departure date and itinerary, it's time to get your policy. Some 'pre-existing conditions' won't be covered by your insurance if you weren't a policy holder when the condition started. For instance, if an airline experiences cancellations due to a two month labour strike and you've only held your policy for a week, you may not be covered.

- Credit cards are getting into the travel insurance business. You may be eligible for benefits as a card-holder, or if you purchase plane tickets with a credit card you could be reimbursed for cancelled flights. Policies vary; ask your credit card company what it offers.

- See what the conditions are if you stay beyond your anticipated return date and how easy it is to extend your policy. If you'll be travelling with a partner or friend, see if there is a cheaper family policy available.

- See what the maximum coverage is on worldly goods. Most policies have a ceiling that they'll pay out for lost and stolen items; if you're travelling with a lot of computer or camera equipment, this could effect your policy choice.

- Most policies charge an 'excess', a predetermined amount you have to pay for each claim. Depending on what you have, it may be cheaper and easier for you to pay the replacement cost out of your own pocket. Find out how much excess your policy charges.

- Find out if your policy reimburses you or pays the provider directly. If it's the former, you have to pay out of pocket, save all documentation, file a claim and wait for a reimbursement. In the case of medical treatment, some policies require you to call (reverse charges) a centre or doctor in your home country to get an assessment before Latin American doctors can treat you.

- If you have a pre-existing medical condition, tell your insurance company straight out rather than obfuscate in the hopes of getting a cheaper policy. That way, if something happens down the road, it can't refuse to honour your claims.

- Some policies specifically exclude 'dangerous activities'. These can include motor-cycling, scuba diving and trekking. Motorcycle licences acquired locally may not be recognised by your policy. Finally, make sure your coverage includes ambulance rides and plane flights if you have to be flown from a remote area or home altogether.

HEALTH

Travel in Latin America can expose you to plenty of health hazards, but as long as you are up to date with your immunisations and take some basic preventive measures, including against malaria where necessary, you will be pretty unlucky to get anything more serious than a bout of diarrhoea.

Before You Go
INFORMATION SOURCES

Part of your preparation for this trip should be to get up-to-date information and advice on the health risks at your destination and the precautions you can take to stay healthy on the road. You can get this information from your family doctor, travel health clinics or national and state health departments. The Internet is also a great reference source.

Specialist travel health clinics are probably the best places to go for immunisations and advice, although they are often more expensive than going to your health department or family doctor. Some clinics provide specific travel health briefs (usually for a fee) by mail, phone or fax, which you can then take to your doctor. Most clinics also sell health-related travel essentials such as insect repellent, mosquito nets, and needle and syringe kits.

UK
British Airways Travel Clinics
(☎ 01276-685040, www.britishairways.com/travelqa/fyi/health/health.html) (countrywide network of clinics – plus three in South Africa – and you don't need to be travelling on British Airways to use them)

Hospital for Tropical Diseases Travel Clinic
(☎ 020-7388 9600, health line ☎ 0839-337733) Mortimer Market Centre, Capper St, London WC1E

Liverpool School of Tropical Medicine Travel Clinic
(☎ 0151-708 9393, health line ☎ 0906-708 8807) Pembroke Place, Liverpool L3 5QA

Malaria Healthline
(☎ 0891-600 350)
(recorded information on malaria risks and avoidance from the Malaria Reference Laboratory at the London School of Hygiene & Tropical Medicine)

MASTA (Medical Advisory Services for Travellers)
(health line ☎ 0891-224 100) at the London School of Hygiene & Tropical Medicine, Keppel St, London WC1E 7BR

Nomad Travellers Store & Medical Centre
(☎ 020-8889 7014, health line ☎ 09068-633414, @ nomad.travstore@virgin.net) 3-4 Wellington Terrace, Turnpike Lane, London N8 0PX

USA & Canada

To find a travel health clinic in your area, you could call your state health department, or try one of the following:

Centers for Disease Control & Prevention in Atlanta, Georgia

(☎ 888-232-3228, fax 888-232-3299)

(the central source of travel health information in North America. The CDC has phone travel health information lines, and can advise you on travel medicine providers in your area. The CDC publishes an excellent booklet, *Health Information for International Travel* – ☎ 202-512-1800 or order it from the Superintendent of Documents, US Government Printing Office, Washington, DC)

American Society of Tropical Medicine & Hygiene

(☎ 847-480-9592, fax 480-9282, www.astmh.org) 60 Revere Drive, Suite 500, Northbrook, IL 60062

(can provide a comprehensive list of travel health providers in your area)

International Society of Travel Medicine

(☎ 770-736-7060, www.istm.org) PO Box 871089, Stone Mountain, GA 30087 (will provide a list of ISTM member clinics)

Health Canada

(www.hc-sc.gc.ca/hpb/lcdc/osh)

(the Travel Medicine Program of this government department provides information on disease outbreaks, immunisations and general health advice for travellers, more detailed information on tropical diseases, plus information on travel medicine clinics)

The US Department of State Citizen's Emergency Center has travel advisories on a recording (☎ 202-647-5225). Take a record of the number with you, as these advisories can provide US citizens with access to medical advice and assistance over the phone if you are in an emergency situation overseas.

Australia & New Zealand

The Travellers Medical and Vaccination Centre has a network of clinics in most major cities – use the phonebook to find your nearest clinic or check out its web site (www.tmvc.com.au). It can provide an online personalised travel health report (for a fee) via the web.

Internet Resources

These two authoritative web sites are the first point of call for the latest on travel health issues:

WHO

www.who.ch

(official site of the World Health Organization, this has all the information you'll ever need, including disease distribution maps and all the latest health recommendations for international travel. The section that's probably going to be most useful to you is at www.who.int/emc – it has disease outbreak news and health advice for travellers)

CDC

www.cdc.gov

(official site of the US Centers for Disease Control & Prevention, this includes disease outbreak news and disease risks according to destination)

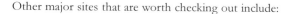
Other major sites that are worth checking out include:

MASTA
www.masta.org
(this highly recommended site of the Medical Advisory Services for Travellers is easy to use and provides concise readable information on all the important issues. It also has useful links, including to the Foreign and Commonwealth Office for advice on safe travel)

Medical College of Wisconsin Travelers Clinic
www.intmed.mcw/travel.html
(has useful information on all the usual travel health issues, and a comprehensive list of links to a variety of other travel health information sites – browse till you drop)

Shorelands
www.tripprep.com
(this well organised site is easy to navigate and has lots of good general travel health information, as well as handy country profiles, including US State Department travel advisory information)

Travel Health Information Service
www.travelhealth.com
(this chatty site, run by US-based Dr Stephen Blythe, is easy to navigate and has loads of good information and links)

Travellers Medical and Vaccination Centre
www.tmvc.com.au
(this Australian-based site has lots of useful information, including disease outbreak news and good sections on travelling while pregnant and with children)

Books

If you're looking for a guide to take on the road, Lonely Planet's *Healthy Travel Central & South America* is a handy pocket size and packed with useful information.

IMMUNISATIONS

Immunisations help protect you from some diseases you may be at risk of catching on your travels. It's best to make your first appointment for advice on immunisations about six to eight weeks before you go. This is because you usually need to wait one to two weeks after a booster or the last dose of a course before you're fully protected, and some courses may need to be given over a period of several weeks. For example, a full course of rabies vaccine takes a month. See the 'Immunisations Details' table for more information on timing.

Don't panic if you have left it to the last minute. Immunisation schedules can be rushed if necessary and most vaccinations you'll need for Latin America can be given together two weeks, or even one week, before you go. Just bear in mind that you won't be as well protected for the first week or two of your trip as if you'd had them earlier.

You'll need to get individual advice on which immunisations to have, as this depends on various factors, including your destination, the length and type of trip, any medical conditions you have, which ones you've had in the past, and any allergies you have. Some shots are not suitable for everyone, especially if you have a medical condition that weakens your immune system, and some shots can provoke allergic reactions in susceptible people. Immunisations in pregnancy or children also need special considerations.

Whatever your travel plans, you'll need to be up to date with your 'routine' immunisations, including tetanus (often given together with diphtheria), polio and some 'childhood illnesses'. In addition, you'll probably need some of the following immunisations.

Cholera

Immunisation against this diarrhoeal disease is no longer generally recommended because it only provides short-lived and poor protection, and travellers are at very low risk of getting cholera. However, some border officials

Immunisations Details

If you're an adult, you will probably have had the full course of some of these immunisations before, usually as a child. With most immunisations, it takes two to three weeks to build up maximum protection. There are currently no immunisations available for travellers diarrhoea, dengue fever or malaria.

vaccine	full course	booster	comments
tetanus, usually given with diphtheria	three doses given at monthly intervals (usually in childhood)	every 10 years	full course usually given in childhood
polio	three doses given at monthly intervals (usually in childhood)	every 10 years; usually given orally	full course usually given in childhood
hepatitis A vaccine	single dose	booster at six to 12 months	gives good protection for at least 12 months; with booster, protects for more than 10 years
hepatitis immunoglobulin	A single injection; needs to be given as close to travel as possible	gives protection only for two to six months, depending on dose	because it's a blood product there's a theoretical risk of HIV and hepatitis B or C
typhoid	single injection, or three or four oral doses	injection: every three years; oral: every one to five years	the old injectable vaccine was notorious for producing unpleasant side effects, but the new one causes few side effects
hepatitis B	two doses one month apart plus a third dose six months later	three to five years	more rapid courses are available if necessary
rabies (pre-exposure)	three doses over one month; booster at six to 12 months	two to three years	may be worth considering in some situations – see the main text for details
yellow fever	two doses over one month	three years	gives very good protection; certificate is valid 10 days after the injection
BCG (for tuberculosis)	single dose	protected for life; no booster required	often given in childhood, so you may already be protected

in Latin America may demand to see a certificate of immunisation before allowing you across the border, even though this is contrary to international law. Your best bet is to discuss this issue with your travel health clinic or doctor before you go. You may be able to get a certificate of exemption or some other form of relevant documentation to carry with you just in case.

Hepatitis A

All travellers to Latin America should be protected against this common viral infection of the liver. Protection is either with hepatitis A vaccine or immuno-globulin. Although it may be more expensive, the vaccine is recommended as it gives good protection for at least a year (longer if you have a booster). Immuno-globulin needs to be given as close as possible to your departure date. It protects you for a limited time and carries a theoretical possibility of blood-borne diseases like HIV, although this is a minuscule risk in most western countries.

A combined hepatitis A and typhoid vaccine has recently become available – good news if you're not keen on needles (see the Typhoid entry later).

Hepatitis B

Protection against this serious liver infection is recommended for long-term travellers to Latin America (and elsewhere). It is also recommended if you're going to be working as a medic or nurse in Latin America or if needle sharing or sexual contact with a local person is a possibility. This immunisation is given routinely to children in some countries, including Australia and the USA, so you may already be protected. If you need both hepatitis A and B immunisations, a combined vaccine is available.

Meningococcal Meningitis

There are occasional outbreaks of this serious brain infection in some areas of Latin America, eg around São Paulo in Brazil, but immunisation for travellers is not generally recommended.

Malaria – Did You Know ...

Some facts to ponder are:

- Malaria is spread by mosquitoes.
- Malaria is a potentially fatal disease.
- Malaria is becoming more common and more difficult to treat (because of drug resistance).
- Most cases of malaria in travellers occur in people who didn't take antimalarials or who didn't take them as recommended.
- Most malaria deaths in travellers occur because the diagnosis is delayed or missed.
- Malaria is particularly dangerous in children and pregnant women.
- Malaria can be transmitted by transfusion of blood and other blood products, by needle-sharing among intravenous drug users and from mother to foetus.

Rabies

With rabies, you have the choice of either having the immunisation before you go, or if you are bitten by a potentially rabid animal. If you have a pretrip immunisation, you will need to have a course of three injections over a month, which gives you some (but not complete) protection against the disease. If you then get bitten by a suspect animal, you will still need to have two boosters to prevent rabies developing.

Rabies vaccination is generally recommended if you will be travelling through Latin America for more than three months or if you will be handling animals. Children are at particular risk of being bitten, so they may need to be vaccinated even if you're going for a short time; discuss this with your doctor or a travel health clinic.

Tuberculosis

You may already have had this immunisation as a child (although not US travellers). In any case, you probably won't need it unless you're going to be living with local people for three months or longer. Although TB is common worldwide, short-term travellers are at very small risk of the disease.

Typhoid

You'll need a vaccination against typhoid if you're travelling in Latin America for longer than two weeks. Typhoid vaccination is available as an injection or as tablets (oral form), although you may find availability of the oral form limited. The old injectable typhoid vaccine can produce some pretty unpleasant reactions (eg fever, chills, headache) but the new injection causes few side effects. However, the oral form can sometimes give you an intestinal upset.

Yellow Fever

Proof of immunisation against yellow fever is a statutory requirement for entry into all Latin American countries if you are coming from a yellow-fever infected country in South America or the African continent. In addition, immunisation is medically recommended if you are planning to visit rural areas of infected countries in South America (see the map). In 1996, two travellers died after contracting yellow fever in the Brazilian jungle.

YELLOW FEVER

0   1000   2000 km

Map data supplied by World Health Organization

■ Areas with yellow fever   □ Areas with no yellow fever

MALARIA PREVENTION

If you're going to a malarial area in Latin America, it's vital you take steps to prevent this potentially fatal disease. If you're going to a malarial area:

- Get the latest information on risks and drug resistance from a reliable information source (see the Information Sources section at the beginning of this chapter for some useful pointers).
- Take suitable malaria preventive drugs or carry malaria treatment with you if appropriate, and discuss this with your doctor or a travel health clinic before you go.
- Take steps to avoid insect bites (see the Insect Bites section later in this chapter). This is even more important now that malarial parasites have become resistant to many commonly used antimalarial drugs.
- You need to know a little bit about the symptoms and signs of malaria and what to do if you think you have it. Information is readily available from any of the information resources listed earlier in this chapter.

Malaria Preventive Drugs

Medical recommendations change all the time, so you need to get the latest advice from your doctor or a travel health clinic before you go (at least a month before). The main options are currently chloroquine (with or without proguanil), mefloquine or doxycycline. For some low-risk malarial areas (eg some parts of Mexico), you may not need to take malaria pills, but instead you may be advised to carry emergency malaria treatment to use if you think you may have malaria.

You need to start taking malaria pills before you leave: a month before for chloroquine; two to three weeks for mefloquine; and a few days for doxycycline. This enables them to reach maximum protective levels in your body before you arrive at your destination. It also gives any side effects a chance to show themselves. Minor side effects are common with all the drugs, but if you get major side effects that make you unsure about continuing the drug, you should get advice on changing to a medication that suits you better.

Emergency Treatment

If you're going to a high-risk malarial area without access to medical care you'll need to take treatment doses of medication with you to use in an emergency. You have to use a different malaria drug for treatment than the one you are taking to prevent

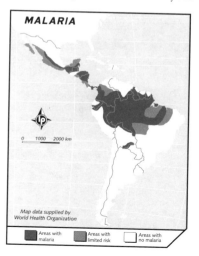

MALARIA

0   1000   2000 km

Map data supplied by World Health Organization

Areas with malaria | Areas with limited risk | Areas with no malaria

malaria. You should also consider taking a malaria diagnosis kit with you in this situation – these are available from major travel health clinics. Discuss these issues with your doctor before you go, as you need to be clear about when to use emergency treatment and what to do if problems arise. Emergency treatment is a first-aid measure only, to tide you over while you seek medical help.

TRAVEL INSURANCE

However lucky (or poor) you're feeling, you don't want to be without travel insurance. Medical treatment, at least in the public sector, may cost less in many countries in Latin America but evacuation from a remote area is always frighteningly expensive. For more details, see the Tickets & Insurance chapter earlier in the book.

PRETRAVEL CHECK-UPS

If you're going to be away for more than about six months or you're going to a remote area, a medical check-up is a good idea to make sure there are no problems waiting to happen. If you've had any niggling problems, now is the time to get them checked out. This goes for your teeth too – make sure you get a dental check-up before you go, to prevent problems arising when you are far from reliable help.

Remember to get any prescription medicines you need from your doctor before you go. If you take any medicines regularly, you'll need to take sufficient supplies with you, as well as a record of your prescription. If you are going to be travelling to remote areas, you might want to discuss taking emergency treatment for diarrhoea or chest infections with you, which you will need to get on prescription.

Afraid to Take Your Medicine?

Mefloquine is one of the most effective antimalarials available, but it's also one of the most controversial, and there has been much discussion in the media and among travellers about its side effects. These range from common side effects such as sleep disturbance (especially vivid dreams) to uncommon but more serious effects such as panic attacks, hallucinations and fits. Many people who take mefloquine do not, however, have any problems. Perhaps it's simply a case of bad news travelling faster than good.

You can get information on mefloquine and alternative antimalarials from travel health clinics, your doctor or the web sites listed under Information Sources earlier in this chapter. For a discussion of the issues surrounding mefloquine, try www.travelhealth.com/mefloqui .htm or www.geocities.com/TheTropics/6913/lariam.htm. Or you could visit Lariam Action USA's web site at www.suggskelly.com/lariam.

The bottom line is that the risk of death or severe illness is much greater if you don't take antimalarials. If you cannot or would prefer not to take mefloquine, there are other options, such as chloroquine (with or without proguanil), or doxycycline, which may be better than taking nothing at all.

If you wear contact lenses, you may want to talk to your optometrist about hygiene and other issues on the road. It's a good idea to take a plentiful supply of any cleaning solutions you use. If you wear glasses, consider taking a replacement pair, and take a copy of your prescription with you, in case you need to have a pair made up while you are away.

MEDICAL KIT

A medical kit is an essential piece of equipment you should take on your trip. For information on what to include in a medical kit, see the Equipment section in the What to Bring chapter.

FIRST-AID COURSE

Everyone should be familiar with basic first-aid techniques, but it is even more important if you are going to places where you cannot rely on rapid-response emergency services. If you're going to be spending time in remote areas more than a day or so away from medical help, you should seriously consider doing at least a basic first-aid course before you leave. Contact your local first-aid organisation for details of courses available. More specialist training in outdoor survival skills is generally offered by organisations concerned with wilderness activities such as mountaineering, trekking and white-water rafting.

TRAVELLERS WITH SPECIAL NEEDS

You don't have to be able-bodied or in perfect health to travel, but make sure you know what to expect and be prepared to take extra precautions. A short trip to a country with well developed medical services may not present you with any major difficulties, but you may want to think more carefully about longer trips, especially to remote areas.

Whatever your plans, you'll need to get advice from your doctor or specialist on problems you may encounter when you're travelling and what to do about them. Take with you a written summary of your medical problems and any treatment you are currently on or have received in the past – you may need to ask your doctor for this before you go.

Health Documents

When you're travelling, it's a good idea to keep the following information on you at all times, in case of emergency:

- travel insurance hotline number
- serial number of your travel insurance policy
- contact details of your nearest embassy
- US State Department Citizen's Emergency Center number (US citizens only)
- vaccination certificate (if necessary) or any official record of your vaccinations
- summary of any important medical conditions you have
- contact details of your doctor back home
- copy of the prescription for any medication you take regularly
- details of any serious allergies
- blood group
- prescription for glasses or contact lenses
- if you are a diabetic, a letter from your doctor explaining why you need to carry needles and syringes (for customs)

Check that your travel health insurance covers you for pre-existing illnesses. Remember that medical facilities in rural areas of most countries in Latin America are usually extremely limited, and emergency rescue may take some time to organise.

Everyday Health

Before you go, find out what precautions you can take to ensure you stay as healthy as possible while you are away. Only a few travel-related illnesses, and none of the more common problems like sunburn, diarrhoea and infected cuts, are preventable by immunisation.

SUN

Getting burnt by the sun is probably the main hazard you'll face in Latin America, especially if you are going to a high-altitude Andean area. Over-exposure to the sun has well known long-term consequences (such as skin cancer) as well as painful short-term consequences (sunburn), so it's worth taking steps to avoid getting fried. Cover up and wear a hat to protect your face and neck from sunburn. Take high-protection factor sunscreen with you, and use it on exposed areas. You will probably be able to get sunscreen at most tourist destinations, but it's usually expensive and you may not be able to get the highest-protection factors. You'll also need to protect your eyes with UV-blocking sunglasses (wraparounds are a good idea). The sun is generally at its fiercest between 11 am and 3 pm, so it makes sense to spend this time resting in the shade or indoors.

HEAT

Remember to give yourself a chance to get used to the heat. You're probably going to feel hot and easily exhausted for about a week after you first arrive in a hot climate. After this, your body will have made adjustments to cope with

Pandora's Box

In Latin America you'll find that many medicines are sold without prescription and often much more cheaply. Even controlled medicines such as some tranquillisers are often available without prescription. Because medicines tend to be considerably cheaper over the border, many Americans regularly cross the border into Mexico to buy them. In Latin America, medicines are not seen as something special but as a commodity like any other. Most local people self-treat with medicines bought from the pharmacy as a matter of course. Often pharmacists are the main source of treatment advice for the majority of people, especially in rural areas. Although this set-up can sound very convenient for you as a traveller, it's not quite as good as it seems. Local pharmacists are not necessarily medically trained, and may recommend inappropriate treatment. In malarial areas, for example, potentially toxic anti-malarial drugs may be recommended for any fever, and antibiotics tend to be readily used for many ailments, often inappropriately. With less control over medicines, it is easier for counterfeit drugs to be passed off, as well.

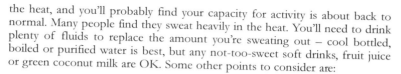

the heat, and you'll probably find your capacity for activity is about back to normal. Many people find they sweat heavily in the heat. You'll need to drink plenty of fluids to replace the amount you're sweating out – cool bottled, boiled or purified water is best, but any not-too-sweet soft drinks, fruit juice or green coconut milk are OK. Some other points to consider are:

- Because your feet swell in the heat, especially at first, take footwear that is a little too big rather than small; blisters and chafing can easily become infected.
- Help your body out by not doing too much during the heat of the day, and avoid large heavy meals and excess alcohol during the hottest part of the day.
- Avoid prickly heat and fungal infections (both common in hot climates) by washing regularly (but avoid over-using soap, which makes it worse) and drying yourself carefully.
- Learn to recognise the symptoms of heat exhaustion and heatstroke, which are the most serious consequences of heat exposure.

Heat Exhaustion & Heatstroke

Heat can cause a range of conditions from heat cramps and fainting to heat exhaustion and potentially fatal heatstroke. Even if you don't feel too bad, heat and dehydration can affect your physical performance and mental judgement.

In a hot climate you can lose an astonishing 2L of sweat in an hour, more if you're doing strenuous physical activity. Sweat contains water and salts, which you need to replace, so drink a lot more than you would in a cool climate, even when you have acclimatised. An adult needs to drink about 3L of fluid a day in a hot climate, or 5L or more if doing a strenuous activity such as trekking or cycling. Take a water bottle with you everywhere, and drink from it frequently.

Prolonged exposure to high temperatures and inadequate fluid intake can cause heat exhaustion and, more seriously, heatstroke. Symptoms of heat exhaustion are headache, dizziness, nausea and feeling weak and exhausted. You may get muscle aches or cramps. If you notice these symptoms in yourself or your travel companions, rest in a cool environment and drink lots of fluids.

With heatstroke, sweating stops and body temperature rises dangerously, which can be fatal. Symptoms include severe, throbbing headaches, confusion and lack of coordination. This is an emergency situation.

FOOD

It's generally agreed that contaminated food, not water, is the most common source of gut troubles in travellers. The impressive list of diseases you can get in this way includes most forms of diarrhoea, including dysentery, hepatitis A and E and typhoid (not common in travellers generally but relatively more common if you're travelling in Mexico).

You can get sick from food anywhere, but it's more likely when you're travelling. Problems with safe waste disposal countries mean that cooking utensils and hands are more likely to be contaminated with disease-causing microorganisms, mainly from faeces. Travelling can mean you're eating out three meals a day for perhaps weeks on end, relying on other people to prepare your food safely. Most countries in Latin America don't have enforceable food safety standards.

You can build up immunity to some diarrhoeal diseases, but you can't build up immunity to many of the more serious diseases (like dysentery or food poisoning) or to parasites (like hookworm), so it's worth taking a few precautions to minimise your risks.

- Heating kills germs, so food that's served piping-hot is likely to be safer than lukewarm or cold food, especially if it's been sitting around; note that freezing doesn't kill germs.
- Fruit and vegetables are difficult to clean (and may be contaminated where they are grown), but they should be safe if they're peeled or cooked.
- Well cooked meat and seafood should be OK; raw or lightly cooked meat and seafood can be a source of parasites in many areas.
- Bread, tortillas and cakes are usually safe, although it's best to avoid cream-filled goodies if you can, as bugs like salmonella love cream.
- Your stomach's natural defences can cope with small amounts of contaminated foods. If you're not sure about something, don't pig out on it!
- Avoid unpasteurised milk, although powdered or UHT milk should be OK.
- If you can, choose popular, clean-looking eating places.

Street food can be risky as vendors are unlikely to have high food hygiene standards, but you can minimise the risks by choosing freshly cooked, hot food that hasn't been handled by the vendor after cooking.

If you're on a long trip, or you're budgeting hard, you'll need to take care that your diet is balanced and that you don't lose a huge amount of weight. Consider taking multivitamins with you in case you get run-down.

WATER

Although you can generally rely on tap water in developed countries to be safe, this is not always true of countries in Latin America. Check your travel guidebook or travel health clinic for information on the reliability of water supplies at your destination, and also see the Health sections of the country profiles later in this book. If you're not sure if the water is safe, it's best to assume the worst. Never assume that water from rivers, streams or lakes is safe, as even in relatively unpopulated areas it can be contaminated by animals or trekkers.

Avoid drinking unboiled tap water and don't brush your teeth in it. Ice is only as safe as the water it's made from, so it's best to avoid this too.

How you deal with the water issue depends on where you are and what sort of travelling you're doing. Drinking bottled water is one obvious option, and it's generally widely available in Latin America. As a general rule, it's best to stick to major brands of bottled water, preferably with serrated tops; always check the seal carefully.

However, the cost of bottled water can add up over a long trip, especially if you're travelling in hot climates, and there's a very real concern over the environmental and aesthetic effects of millions of discarded plastic bottles. If you're trekking or travelling off the beaten track, bottled water is a less practical option anyway.

The simplest and most effective way to make water safe to drink is to boil it, which kills all disease-causing bugs. You just need to bring it to a rolling boil for a minute or two and then let it cool.

If boiling doesn't sound like a practical option, it's easy to disinfect clear water with chemicals. Chlorine and iodine are the chemicals most widely used. Both are available in tablet form, and iodine is also available as a liquid (or tincture; add five drops of 2% tincture of iodine to every litre of water) or as crystals you can make up into a liquid.

Water purifiers are the third choice. These devices usually combine a simple filter with chemical purification and some means of neutralising the chemicals. While it may seem like a big outlay, it's possibly worth the expense, especially if you are planning a long trip in remote areas. Always have a back-up method of water purification with you as well.

PERSONAL HYGIENE

Many diseases you may be at risk of catching on your travels can be avoided by maintaining good personal hygiene, eg always wash your hands before you eat and after using the toilet. This is particularly important if you're eating with your hands. Short fingernails are easier to keep clean than long ones. Some travellers like to take their own utensils (plastic cup, bowl, spoon) for street food or eating meals on trains. Try to remember to keep your hands away from your mouth and eyes, especially on public transport, as you can introduce infection in this way.

DIARRHOEA

This is a great conversation-starter in travellers circles – and sometimes a stopper too. Although the risks vary with your destination, the fact is that diarrhoea affects about 50% of travellers to developing countries. Even if it's relatively mild, you're probably going to feel a tad sorry for yourself for a day or so as it passes through your system, so it's worth building a few rest days into your travel schedule to allow for this. Taking basic precautions with food and drink and paying attention to your personal hygiene are the most important preventive strategies.

If you get it, diarrhoea usually strikes about the third day after you arrive and lasts about three to five days. It's caused by a range of factors, including jet lag, new food, a new lifestyle and new bugs. It can come back again in the second week, although you do build up immunity to some of the causes. Symptoms are diarrhoea without blood, mild fever, some nausea and stomach cramps.

The most important aspects of treatment are to prevent dehydration by replacing lost fluid, and to rest. You can drink most liquids, except alcohol, very sugary drinks or dairy products. Oral rehydration sachets can be useful but aren't essential if you're young and otherwise healthy. If you feel like eating, starchy foods like potatoes, plain rice or tortillas or bread are thought to help fluid replacement.

Antidiarrhoeals ('stoppers' or 'blockers') are of limited use as they prevent your system from clearing out the toxin and can make certain types of diarrhoea worse, although they can be useful as a temporary stopping measure, eg if you have to go on a long bus journey. They should be avoided in children.

Although most episodes of travellers diarrhoea clear up in a few days without any treatment, sometimes you can get a more serious illness, for which you need medical help and probably a course of antibiotics. If you're going to a remote area, you may want to consider taking antibiotics for self-treating diarrhoea. Signs of serious illness include profuse diarrhoea and vomiting that make you unable to replace the fluid lost, a high fever, blood in your faeces and severe cramps. Persistent diarrhoea that won't go away after a week also needs medical attention.

INSECT BITES

These are the scourge of travellers to Latin America, especially if you're going to tropical or jungle areas, and you'll probably find they're a popular conversation topic too. Everyone has an opinion on the best way to avoid bites and how to stop the itch if you do get bitten. Although the bites can seem bad enough in themselves, their main importance is that several serious tropical diseases can be transmitted in this way – see the boxed text for more details.

Most mosquitoes are night-biters, but some (such as the one that transmits dengue) bite mainly during the day. Some tips on how not to get bitten are:

- Cover up with long-sleeved tops and long trousers or skirt; light-coloured clothing is thought to be less attractive to mosquitoes than dark colours.
- Use insect repellents on any exposed areas; if you're using sunscreen or other lotions, apply insect repellent last, and reapply after swimming if necessary.
- Sleep in a screened room or under a mosquito net; always cover children's beds or cots with mosquito nets; air-conditioned rooms are usually insect-free zones.
- Remember there are day-biting mosquitoes, and avoid shady conditions in the late afternoon or taking an afternoon siesta without the protection of a mosquito net.
- Spray your room or tent with an insect spray before you retire for the night to get rid of any lurking insects.
- Consider using electric insecticide vaporisers or mosquito coils (which you burn). You will need a power socket for a vaporiser, and both are less effective if you have a fan going.

Insects & the Diseases They Transmit

Immunisations are currently not available against any of the diseases listed except yellow fever. Don't allow yourself to get bitten, and you won't catch any of these diseases.

mosquitoes – malaria, dengue fever, filariasis, yellow fever
sandflies – leishmaniasis, sandfly fever, bartonellosis
triatomine bugs – Chagas' disease
blackflies – river blindness
ticks – typhus, tick fevers
fleas – plague

There are many insect repellent products on the market, but the most effective are those containing the compound DEET (diethyltoluamide) – check the label or ask your pharmacist to tell you which brands contain DEET. Some major brands include Autan, Rid, Doom, Jungle Formula, Off and Repel. Remember to try a test dose before you leave to check for allergy or skin irritation.

There have been concerns about the safety of DEET, but it's generally agreed that these are largely unfounded. For children, however, it's best to err on the cautious side – always follow the dosing instructions carefully, and choose a lower-strength long-acting cream.

Permethrin is an effective insecticide that can be applied to clothes and mosquito nets, but not to skin. If you're planning on trekking through tick-infested areas (rainforests, scrubland, pastures), consider treating your clothes, particularly trousers and socks, with permethrin before you go.

You may prefer to use one of the new lemon eucalyptus-based natural products, which have been shown to be an effective alternative to DEET, with similar action times (although DEET is probably still your best bet in high-risk areas). Other natural repellents include citronella and pyrethrum, but these tend to be less effective and to have a short action (up to an hour), making them less practical to use.

EFFECTS OF ALTITUDE

The Andes are one of the world's greatest mountain ranges, and many of the top tourist destinations in South America are at significantly high altitude. As you gain altitude, there is less oxygen in the atmosphere. With time, your body is able to adapt to the lower oxygen concentration with various physiological changes. However, until it does, you will feel the effects, especially if you fly straight to a high altitude.

Symptoms of mild altitude sickness are common when you first arrive at altitude and include headache, nausea and loss of appetite, difficulty sleeping and lack of energy. They usually respond to rest and simple painkillers. A small proportion of people can get more severe symptoms, including severe breathing difficulties and swelling of the brain – these are medical emergencies.

The best treatment for Acute Mountain Sickness (AMS) is descent, and the golden rule is never to continue to ascend if you have any symptoms of AMS. If mild symptoms persist or get worse, you must descend.

The Kiss of Death

The distinctive kissing bug, also known as the triatomine, cone-nose or assassin bug, also has many local names, including *chinchas* (Mexico), *barbeiro* (Brazil), *chipo* (Venezuela) and *vinchuna* (Argentina). Its main claim to fame (apart from its great names) is that it transmits a serious parasitic infection in Latin America called Chagas' disease, which is a major public health problem, and can be fatal (though the disease is very rare in travellers).

These bugs are usually black or brown, with patterns in red, orange or yellow on their thorax and abdomen. They occur in tropical areas of Latin America, and live in dark crevices in the walls of dwellings, coming out at night to feed on the blood of humans and other animals. Bites aren't usually itchy unless you become sensitised to them. In heavily infested households, blood loss due to bug bites can be significant. You are probably going to be at most risk of bites if you stay overnight in huts in rural areas (eg if you are trekking). Use insect repellent and sleep under a mosquito net if possible.

The best way to prevent AMS is to ascend slowly. Drugs such as acetazolamide (trade name Diamox) are sometimes used to prevent AMS, although this is controversial. The most important point to remember is that taking drugs is no substitute for proper acclimatisation.

If you're going to a high-altitude destination, make sure you find out about the effects of altitude and what to do about them. You can get advice on preventing AMS from a travel health clinic, expedition organisers, or read up about it in your guidebook or one of the travel health guides listed earlier. Two authoritative web sites with information about AMS and other altitude-related problems are www.princeton.edu/~oa/altitude.html and www.gorge.net/hamg/AMS.html.

Hypothermia

The higher you go, the colder it gets, even in the tropics. The Southern Cone countries have a temperate climate with very cold winters, so be prepared.

Creepy Crawlies of the Jungle

If the South American jungle conjures up images of deadly creatures and carnivorous fish, you can be reassured that you are far more likely to be attacked by tiny critters like mosquitoes (that can transmit serious disease) and leeches (common and a nuisance but not dangerous) than from any other wildlife hazards. Having said that, Latin America does have its fair share of dangerous creatures that you should at least be aware of and take steps to avoid.

Vampire bats are found in many forested areas but hardly live up to their reputation. These small creatures don't suck blood; instead they make a small nick in the skin and lap up the blood as it comes out. They feed off animals mainly (and are therefore considered a great pest by livestock raisers), but if you are spending the night in the forest, you could be at risk, so always sleep under a net (essential to keep the mosquitoes away, too). The main danger with vampire bats is that they can transmit rabies in their saliva.

Tarantulas are large, hairy and scary-looking spiders, but they are not aggressive and bites are no more dangerous than an insect sting. They are said to make very good pets. Of more concern are the deadly black widow spider and the banana spider, but you are fairly unlikely to come across them.

Anacondas and boa constrictors are similarly the stuff of nightmares, but in reality pose little if any risk to travellers. Latin America does have some dangerous venomous snakes, including the infamous bushmaster and fer de lance. Sensible precautions are to wear strong shoes and thick socks when you are walking through overgrown areas (never wear open shoes; apart from the risk of snake bite, there are leeches and mosquitoes, and you run the risk of cuts and scratches). Give snakes plenty of warning of your arrival.

Venomous scorpions are a risk in some areas, especially in Mexico, but you should be able to avoid them with some sensible precautions.

Piranhas are notorious flesh-eating freshwater fish that occur in some South American rivers. Although you should avoid getting in the water with a shoal of hungry piranhas, you will be relieved to know that their danger is somewhat overrated. There are various marine hazards to be aware of, including venomous jellyfish, stingrays and venomous fish. If you are planning to do any water sports, it's probably sensible to find out about these and other hazards so that you can avoid them.

Make sure you take adequate layers of clothing and appropriate equipment if you are planning on sleeping out. The weather can be very unpredictable, so always be prepared for the worst possible weather, even if you're just on a half-day trip or planning to cross the mountains on your way somewhere.

CUTS & SCRATCHES

You need to take more care of these than you would normally. Dust, dirt, lack of washing facilities and hot, humid conditions all make infection of any break in the skin more likely when you're travelling. Take care to prevent injury and insect bites. Keep any skin breaks as clean as possible.

ACCIDENTS & INJURY

Accidents and injury, not tropical diseases, are the leading cause of death in travellers. In addition, accidents are the main reason for needing a blood transfusion or other medical treatment, with all the potential problems that this entails, including infection with HIV, hepatitis B and C and Chagas' disease. Make sure you are aware of the risks, and take care to avoid them. The Latino temperament and a lack of resources in some countries make road traffic accidents a real possibility throughout the region, so take some precautions. Some basic safety tips are:

- Drinking and driving is best avoided wherever you are.
- Use a seat belt if possible.
- If you're riding a motorcycle or moped, wear a helmet and protective clothing.
- Hire cars from reputable firms.
- If you're driving, try not to speed, and avoid travelling at night.

Latin America's magnificent coastline is a major drawcard for tourists, but drowning is a common cause of death in travellers, especially children and

Needles & Injections

Due to scanty resources and insufficiently rigorous sterilisation procedures, injections and blood transfusions in many less developed countries can carry infection risks, including HIV/AIDS, malaria, hepatitis B (or C) or, in Latin America, Chagas' disease.

Assuming that you are basically healthy, not pregnant and take sensible precautions to avoid accidents, it's very unlikely that you would need a blood transfusion while travelling. This is yet another reason why it's essential to have a good travel and health insurance policy. However, in the worst-case scenario, fear of HIV or other infection should not discourage treatment for serious medical conditions.

To minimise the risk from injections, avoid them if you have any doubts about standards of hygiene. Ask if there is a tablet you can take instead. If you do need an injection, ask to see the syringe unwrapped in front of you. If you will be travelling for extended periods, or in remote areas, also consider carrying sterile needles and syringes with you. You can get packs from most travel health clinics.

young adults. Even strong swimmers can get taken by unexpectedly strong currents, particularly those on the Pacific coast. Try to follow these safety rules:

- Avoid alcohol when swimming.
- Beware of strong currents; check the local situation and don't swim alone.
- Don't dive into shallow water.

SAFE SEX

While it's true that sexually transmitted infections (STIs), including HIV/ AIDS and hepatitis B, are a risk anywhere if you're having casual sex, it seems that you're more likely to throw caution to the wind when you are away from home, and are therefore more at risk. Opportunities for casual sex tend to be greater while you're travelling. Added to this, levels of STIs in the countries you are visiting may be higher than at home.

Avoiding casual sex altogether is the safest option; otherwise, remember to use a condom. Condoms are available in most Latin American countries, but you may prefer to take a familiar, reliable brand with you. Rubber condoms disintegrate in the heat, so take care to store them deep in your pack and to check them carefully before use.

ALCOHOL & DRUGS

Be wary of local brews, especially distilled spirits, as they may contain undesirable additives or methanol, a highly toxic form of alcohol which can cause permanent blindness.

If you decide to use drugs, be aware there's no guarantee of quality, and locally available drugs can be unexpectedly strong or mixed with other harmful substances. Overdose is always a risk – never take drugs when you're on your own.

Women's Health

BEFORE YOU GO

Some issues you might want to discuss with your doctor before you go include: how travel will affect your method of contraception or hormone replacement therapy; the possibility of taking emergency contraception (the 'morning after pill') with you; stopping your periods temporarily; or taking emergency treatment for cystitis or thrush with you, if you are prone to these.

If you are on the oral contraceptive pill, the timing of pill-taking can be tricky if you're crossing time zones, and diarrhoea, vomiting and the anti-biotics used to treat common infections can all reduce the effectiveness of the pill, so this is worth bearing in mind. Take a plentiful supply of your medication with you, as it may be difficult to get your brand. In some countries, oral contraceptives may not be readily available. The International Planned Parenthood Federation (☎ 020-7487 7913, www.ippf.org), Regent's College, Inner Circle, Regent's Park, London NW1 4NS, can provide information on the availability of contraception and local attitudes towards birth control and termination of pregnancy in various countries in Latin America.

If you're planning on travelling while you're pregnant, you'll definitely want to discuss this with your doctor as early as possible.

EVERYDAY HEALTH

You may find that your periods stop altogether when you're away – a result of the physical and mental stresses of travelling (but have a pregnancy test done if you think you may be pregnant). However, you're just as likely to find that travelling brings on the worst period of your life, at the most inconvenient time. If you suffer from premenstrual stress (PMS) be prepared for it to be worse while you are away and take plentiful supplies of any painkiller or other remedy you find helpful.

Hot weather and limited washing facilities make thrush (yeast infection) more likely when you're travelling. If you know you are prone to thrush, it's worth taking a supply of medication with you.

Get any symptoms like an abnormal vaginal discharge or genital sores checked out as soon as possible. Some STIs don't cause any symptoms, even though they can cause long-term fertility and other problems, so if you have unprotected intercourse while you're away, be sure to have a check-up when you return home.

Medical Services

In general, you will be able to find reasonable to good medical care for most common travel illnesses and injuries in most large towns in Latin America. Less developed countries in the region tend to have more basic services and supplies may be in shortage, so evacuation is often the best option if you have anything serious in one of these countries. Services in rural areas throughout the region tend to be much more limited.

You will generally find both public and private services available in most large towns. Public hospitals and clinics are often free or charge only a minimal rate, but tend to be overstretched and you'll probably end up queuing for ages. They're probably best avoided as a rule, unless they are a specialist centre or affiliated to a university. Private clinics or hospitals are generally better, but they can be expensive – not an issue if you are covered by insurance, which you should be. Don't expect it to be exactly the same as back home – cultural differences impact on the doctor-patient relationship too. For specific country information on medical services, see the Health sections in the country profiles.

You will generally have to pay upfront for a consultation and any treatment. If you have insurance, your insurance company may be able to guarantee payment and so you may not have to pay upfront, but don't rely on this – keep an emergency stash with you, and ask for and keep any receipts. Medical evacuation is always hugely expensive, which makes insurance an absolute necessity for travellers.

If you need to get medical help while you are away, your embassy or travel insurance hotline should be able to provide you with names of local doctors. Upmarket hotels can often recommend a doctor, and may even have a doctor attached to the staff. Alternatively, you could consider joining an organisation like the International Association for Medical Assistance to Travellers (☎ 519-836 0102, www.sentex.net), 40 Regal Rd, Guelph, Ontario N1K 1B5, Canada. This is a nonprofit organisation (it welcomes donations) which can provide you with a list of reliable doctors in the countries you're planning to visit. Members of the South American Explorers Club (www .samexplo.org) can get a list of doctors, dentists and homoeopaths in Quito and Lima.

Medical Problems

Here's a rundown of some of the main diseases that occur in the region. For more in-depth information on any of these problems, try any of the information sources listed at the beginning of this chapter. Just remember that you are much more likely to get a bout of diarrhoea, an infected insect bite or a cold than most of these scary-sounding diseases.

CHAGAS' DISEASE

Also known as American trypanosomiasis, this parasitic disease is unique to Latin America. Although it's a significant public health problem in the region, it's very rare in travellers. The disease is transmitted through the bites of a distinctive bug known as cone-nose, kissing or assassin bugs, as well as many local names. Chagas' disease has two stages: an early flu-like illness, and the more serious long-term stage due to damage to various internal organs that may be fatal. Specific drug treatment is available for Chagas' disease, and is effective in the early phase.

CHOLERA

This serious diarrhoeal illness receives much publicity but, as a rule, is unlikely to affect travellers. Cholera is spread through contaminated food and water, and usually affects the poorest of the poor in developing countries. The best prevention is to take care with food and water. Dehydration is the main risk, and the mainstay of treatment is fluid replacement.

DENGUE FEVER

This viral disease is transmitted by day-biting mosquitoes, and is on the increase in tropical areas worldwide, including Latin America. Symptoms are fever, headache and severe joint and muscle pains (hence its old name, 'breakbone fever'). Simple dengue can sometimes progress to a more severe form, known as dengue haemorrhagic fever, but this is extremely rare in travellers. There is no specific treatment for dengue. Aspirin should be avoided, as it increases the risk of haemorrhaging. The best prevention is to avoid mosquito bites at all times.

FILARIASIS

This is a mosquito-transmitted parasitic infection found in many parts of Latin America, but it is extremely rare in travellers. Possible symptoms include fever, pain and swelling of the lymph glands; inflammation of lymph drainage

A Lesson Learned

On my first trip to Mexico, I travelled by bus and train, crossing the California/Mexico border at Mexicali, and aiming for Mazatlán. On the bus I met a family who were going to Navojoa, and we got on so well that they invited me to stay. I spent a few magical days with them at Navojoa. I learnt how to make flour tortillas by hand, enjoyed walks around the town, and relished every little thing that was so different from where I came from.

The bliss ended when, one morning, I got a bad cramp in my stomach and had to run to the toilet many times. The pain became so bad I was screaming, and before long I had a fever so high so I was delirious. I lay on the bed and in the confusion of my mind saw the bed on fire, with flames leaping around me. I saw a gentle white light up in one corner of the ceiling, waiting. I wanted to go with the light. Then I fell into a deep sleep.

Someone from the family had gone to find transport, and the next thing I knew they were pulling and dragging me off the bed and into the cab of an old dusty pick-up truck.

At the doctor's office, they laid me down on the table, and the doctor gave me a big horse shot in the bum. He asked what I'd been eating and drinking. Especially he asked me if I had drunk any tap water, at any time. No. What about coffee? Oh, yes, I'd had coffee with the family. What I didn't realise was that you have to boil water vigourously for several minutes to kill all the germs. No-one ever does that just to make coffee.

I was sick and weak for a couple of days, but after taking some pills prescribed by the doctor, I soon felt good enough to travel. Finally I reached Mazatlán. Not long after, I got another fever. There was no severe and sudden onset, and there were no stomach cramps – it was just a fever. I lay in bed for days, in semiconsciousness. Sometimes it was daylight outside, sometimes it was dark. I lay there and listened to all the sounds of the barrio, the women sweeping the sidewalks in front of their houses, the people calling across the narrow street to one another, roosters crowing, music coming from somewhere down the block, children playing. Sometimes I smelled tortillas cooking, sometimes I enjoyed the stillness of the night.

By the time I got over that fever, I looked like a walking skeleton. But I was well again. Friends in Mazatlán encouraged me to visit Puerto Vallarta, which I had often heard of. In Puerto Vallarta I was strong at first, but then I found myself feeling weaker every day. A friend took me to a doctor. Before I knew what he was doing, the doctor stuck out his finger and poked me in the stomach, right at the bottom of my sternum. The pain was unbelievable! I almost fell off my chair! The doctor said, 'Ah ha! You have hepatitis!'

The kind of hepatitis I had was type A. It comes from contaminated food or water. Fortunately, it does not do permanent damage.

Eventually I became well, and managed to get home to California. Even though I had been so sick there, I was in love with Mexico.

One of the most important things I learned after that trip was how to take care of my health. I read everything I could find about how to stay healthy while travelling in tropical climates – about garlic, and lime juice, and iodine drops for purifying water. And in all the many years I've travelled to Mexico since, I'm happy to say that I've never had those health problems again.

Nancy Keller
LP Author, USA

areas; swelling of a limb or the scrotum; skin rashes; and blindness. Treatment is available to eliminate the parasites from the body, but some of the damage already caused may not be reversible. Medical advice should be obtained promptly if the infection is suspected.

HEPATITIS A

This common infection is transmitted through contaminated food and drinking water. Make sure you are immunised against it. Take basic food and water precautions. Symptoms are fever, sometimes intestinal symptoms, and jaundice (yellowing of the skin and whites of the eyes). It can leave you feeling weak for some time after, but has no other long-term effects.

HEPATITIS B

This viral infection of the liver is spread through contact with infected blood, blood products or body fluids, eg through sexual contact, unsterilised needles and blood transfusions, or contact with blood via breaks in the skin. Other risk situations include having a shave, tattoo or body piercing with contaminated equipment. The best prevention is to avoid risk situations. The symptoms are similar to hepatitis A but are more severe, and the disease can lead to long-term problems such as chronic liver damage, liver cancer or a long-term carrier state.

HIV/AIDS

You're at risk wherever you go if you don't take measures to protect yourself. HIV infection is being increasingly seen with in the heterosexual community in Latin America. Rates of infection are high in some parts of the region, including urban areas of Brazil and parts of Central America.

INTESTINAL WORMS

These parasites are common mainly in rural, tropical areas. The different worms have different ways of infecting people. Some may be ingested in food such as undercooked meat (eg tapeworms) and some enter through your skin (eg hookworms). Taking care with what you eat, especially avoiding under-cooked meat, and wearing shoes is the best preventive measure against intestinal worms. Symptoms are often vague and infestations may not show up for some time, and although they are generally not serious, if left untreated some can cause severe health problems later.

LEISHMANIASIS

This parasitic disease is transmitted by sandflies. Travellers can occasionally get the skin form of the disease, which usually heals up without special treatment. Prevention is through avoiding sandfly bites.

MALARIA

Malaria is a parasitic disease carried by infected mosquitoes. It is a major risk to travellers in some parts of Latin America (see the Malaria Zones map earlier).

Prevention is important, and consists of avoiding mosquito bites and taking antimalarial tablets. Symptoms can be nonspecific and include fever, chills and sweating, headache, diarrhoea and abdominal pains or just a vague feeling of ill-health. Without treatment malaria can rapidly become more serious and can be fatal, but if treatment is started promptly, most people recover.

MENINGOCOCCAL MENINGITIS

Outbreaks of meningococcal meningitis occur periodically in parts of Latin America. A fever, severe headache, sensitivity to light and neck stiffness which prevents forward bending of the head are the first symptoms; sometimes there is also a rash. Immunisation is not usually recommended except in special circumstances.

RABIES

Rabies exists throughout Latin America, and pretravel immunisation may be recommended in some circumstances. Practically any warm-blooded animal can be infected, although infected dogs, rodents and bats are probably the greatest risk to you as a traveller in Latin America. Once symptoms have appeared, death is inevitable, but the onset of symptoms can be prevented by a course of injections with the rabies vaccine, which you need whether or not you have been immunised previously. Avoid contact with animals.

RIVER BLINDNESS

This parasitic disease occurs in parts of tropical Latin America. It is transmitted by the bite of a small blackfly which lives and breeds around rivers. It causes an itchy rash and severe infections can cause eye damage. It's very unlikely to affect travellers.

SCHISTOSOMIASIS (BILHARZIA)

This parasitic disease is a risk to you in a few parts of Latin America, including parts of Brazil, Suriname and Guyana. It's caused by a tiny worm that lives in freshwater snails for part of its life cycle and in humans for the second part. It can cause an itchy rash several hours after swimming (swimmer's itch), but it mainly causes long-term problems in your bowel or bladder. Schistosomiasis can be treated but it's best not to get infected in the first place. In risk areas, you'll need to take care to avoid swimming, paddling, crossing streams and doing water sports in fresh water. If you do get wet, dry off quickly, as the disease-causing worms can't survive long out of water.

TETANUS

This disease is caused by a germ which lives in soil and in the faeces of horses and other animals. It enters the body via breaks in the skin. The first symptom may be discomfort in swallowing, or stiffening of the jaw and neck; this is followed by painful convulsions of the jaw and whole body. The disease can be fatal. It can be prevented by vaccination.

TUBERCULOSIS

Although tuberculosis (TB) is a major and growing problem in Latin America, the risk to short-term travellers is very low unless you will be living in close contact with locals. TB is a bacterial infection usually transmitted from person to person by coughing but which may be transmitted through consumption of unpasteurised milk. Milk that has been boiled is safe to drink, and the souring of milk to make yoghurt or cheese also kills the bacilli.

TYPHOID

This vaccine-preventable disease is transmitted through contaminated food and water, and is a risk where hygiene standards are low. Symptoms are initially similar to flu, with headache, aches and pains and a fever. Abdominal pain, vomiting and either diarrhoea or constipation can occur. Serious complications such as pneumonia, perforated bowel or meningitis may develop. It can be effectively treated, but medical help must be sought.

TYPHUS

There are several varieties of typhus, which can be spread by ticks, lice and mites. The different varieties all cause a similar disease but differ in severity. There are no vaccines against any form of typhus, but they all respond rapidly to appropriate antibiotic treatment, without any long-term effects.

YELLOW FEVER

This viral disease is spread by mosquito bites and is mainly a risk in rural, jungle areas. It's unlikely to affect travellers, and the vaccination is considered to be 100% effective.

When You Return

If you were away for a short time only and had no serious health problems, there's probably no need to get a medical check-up when you return, unless you develop symptoms. If you become sick in the weeks following your trip, be sure to tell your doctor that you have been away, which countries you have visited and any antimalarials you may have been taking. Remember: you need to keep taking antimalarials for four weeks after you leave a malarial area.

If you've been on a long trip or are concerned that you may have been exposed to a disease, such as schistosomiasis or an STI, a check-up is advisable. See also the Coming Home chapter for a discussion of post-holiday blues.

WHAT TO BRING

Getting all your gear together for your trip will be fun, but it won't come cheap, especially if you're starting from scratch. There are strategies for stretching your savings, but buying inferior equipment is not one of them. You don't want a leaky tent in Guyana's rainy season or a backpack that falls apart halfway to Machu Picchu. Depending on your departure city, duty-free shops may be a great place for bargains. Items like cameras, personal stereos and cigarettes can usually be had comparatively cheaply in these shops (see Duty-Free Allowances in the Takeoff chapter for more details).

This chapter discusses what you'll need to bring on your trip and how to pack it. Money-saving tips and advice on recording your trip are also covered.

Equipment
BACKPACKS

You'll be living out of your backpack: heaving it onto buses, digging into its depths every day and unpacking and repacking it often. Comfort and handling are two important components of a backpack, so research what works for you. Backpacks are not cheap, but you get what you pay for and a well made, quality backpack will last for years, escorting you through many miles of adventure.

Today's backpacks are light, comfortable and waterproof. Most good packs are constructed of nearly indestructible materials, and they come in men's and women's models that adjust to particular back and body shapes. There are two basic pack designs you'll want to consider – the toploader and the travel pack.

Toploaders

As the name suggests, these packs load from the top. They are durable, watertight packs designed to hold a lot of weight and stay on your back comfortably for extended periods of time. If you go for a toploader, get one with a zipper compartment on the front bottom section of the pack so you can reach the stuff in the nether regions without having to take everything out from the top. Campers, hikers and rafters will probably want a toploader design, while those staying in hostels for good portions of their trip will probably prefer a travel pack.

Travel Packs

These packs win out for their simplicity and accessibility. A zipper running all the way around the top and sides of the pack gives you easy access to the main compartment and makes packing a breeze (see the Packing section later in this chapter for some advice). Another excellent feature of travel packs is the zippered compartment in the back that lets you stow the harness and straps when you're throwing your pack on the roof of a bus, in the trunk of a taxi or overhead on a train. Side handles (also stowable) can be used to carry the pack like a suitcase in crowds, tight spaces or any other place where having a big bulky item on your back just won't work. Travel packs are also easier to lock than toploaders.

Buying a Pack

Don't buy a generic pack to save money. Instead go for a second-hand, name-brand pack or wait for a big sale – right after Christmas or at the end of summer are good times. Some camping shops have sections where used, quality equipment can be bought cheaply. Ask around about second-hand gear, as it's out there.

Some recommended brands include Macpac (www.macpac.com.nz), Karrimor (www.karrimor.com.uk), REI (www.rei.com) and Lowe Alpine Packs & Apparel (www.lowealpine.com). These companies make comfortable, durable packs that will stay dry in inclement weather and can withstand serious travelling. Prepare to spend US$150 at the very least for a new pack, but don't be shocked if you see price tags into the thousands (this is how the other half hikes!). Take advantage of salespeople when you're shopping. If they don't know how a pack should fit or the difference between designs, move on to someone who does. Consider the following when looking for a pack:

Capacity – Bigger isn't always better and that's true for packs. In fact, erring on the small side will force you to pack lighter. You can always send things home during your trip to free up space. Don't get caught up in how long your trip is, but focus on what you'll be doing. For a general three month trip, we've found a 60L pack will suffice to carry your clothes, equipment and purchases. Campers, however, will need a bigger pack, as they'll be carrying a sleeping bag and tent at the very least.

Fabric & stitching – Look for strong fabric, preferably waterproof but at least water resistant, with double stitching at the seams and weight-bearing spots. The zippers should also be strong. If you're checking out a pack and it seems lightweight, move up to a more expensive model.

Straps & Padding – You don't want to be carrying a pack that digs painfully into your hips or shoulders. This won't happen with quality packs because they will be well padded at the shoulders and hips and have extra padding down the back. The waist belt is the most important, as the majority of weight should ride on your hips, not your shoulders or back.

Fitting – Always try on a pack before you buy it. Manoeuvre the internal frame to fit the shape and size of your back (salespeople can be helpful with fitting). Make sure the pack isn't too tall or too wide, prohibiting your mobility. Remember that there are separate models for men and women, the shape of which effects the pack's centre of gravity. Get one that's right for you.

Versatility – Packs with several compartments can make life on the road much easier. Bottom compartments are good for dirty laundry or sleeping bags and will shield more perishable items in the top compartment. Front and side pockets are useful for everyday items like toiletries, torch (flashlight), journal, insect spray, reading material and maps. Many packs have day-packs that zip off (see Day-packs). Loops are good for attaching a sleeping bag, sweater, poncho or tent to the outside of your pack. You can also hang wet shoes from them.

Securing Your Pack

Pack theft occurs in Latin America, but perhaps not as frequently as people would have you believe. Still, it's a good idea to secure your pack, if only as a deterrent. Most packs have double zippers on the main compartments that can be secured together with a padlock. If not, find a strong place in the fabric and punch two holes, thread a small lock through the holes and attach the zipper fastener. To prevent your entire pack being stolen, bring a light chain so you can secure your pack to the overhead luggage rack on long bus or train rides.

DAY-PACKS

Day-packs are indispensable for independent travel. Whether you're on the bus, touring the museums, going on a picnic or to the beach, your day-pack will hold all the stuff you'll need. This can be a lot, and will include snacks, camera, water bottle, guidebook, camera, sunblock and so on. Versatility and comfort are the catch words here, so make sure the straps are amply padded, there are several zippered compartments and it's of a durable fabric.

Some companies sell backpacks with detachable polyps they market as day-packs. Unfortunately, these are usually too small to be of much use; carrying around an overstuffed day-pack will strain your back, shoulders and patience.

If you do go with a detachable day-pack, remember to empty it of fragile items before reattaching it to your main pack, and lock it down when you hit the road.

MONEY BELT

How you hold your money and documents is one of the most important (and debatable) travel strategies. You'll be walking around with cash, travellers cheques, credit and debit cards, a passport and plane tickets almost every day. That's a lot of booty and to protect it, you should wear a money belt or pouch hidden beneath your clothing. Carrying a bumbag, purse or other easy-to-snatch bag is not a bright idea.

The most common money belts are worn either around your neck or waist and always under your clothing. They're not easy to get at, so you'll want a change purse to hold your daily spending money. Whether you go with a waist or neck model is up to you, but be aware that the strap of neck pouches can almost always be seen where your shirt collar ends.

Think about materials when choosing a money belt. Velcro has become all the rage, which is a shame: you can hear foreigners miles away trying to discretely rip into their money pouches. Plastic is sweaty and sticky, and leather is heavy and holds in perspiration. Cotton is a good middle ground because it can be washed and is fairly comfortable. Unfortunately, it's not very durable. Put your documents and plane ticket in a plastic bag if you use a cotton money belt; otherwise, your sweat will deteriorate the paper.

Make sure the straps and clasps are secure on your money belt. If you go for a neck pouch, thread a metal guitar string through the strap so it can't be cut. You might also want to invest in a waterproof, plastic container that holds your money and passport while you indulge in water sports. You can get creative with how you carry your money, but use your common sense. Splitting it up is a good idea, and you can stuff cash in your shoes, under your hat, in a bra or anywhere else not easily accessible to twitchy hands. Some travellers sew secret pockets into the inside of their clothing to keep money safe; you can also buy ready-to-wear travel clothing with hidden pockets.

MEDICAL KIT

You can buy prepackaged first-aid kits from travel shops, pharmacies and camping goods shops, or you can put one together yourself, which will be much cheaper. Start with a waterproof, crush-proof container like a clear plastic box or zippered pouch. Consider including the following items in your kit (decanting whatever you can into smaller containers) and consult a pharmacist for brands sold in your country:

Antibiotics or any other regular medication — Antibiotics are useful if you're travelling well off the beaten track, but they must be prescribed and you should carry the prescription of these (and any other regular medication you use) with you. If you are allergic to commonly prescribed antibiotics such as penicillin or sulfa drugs, carry this information with you when travelling.

Antifungal cream or powder — For fungal skin infections and thrush.

Antihistamine — Useful as a decongestant for colds; for allergies, such as hay fever; to ease the itch from insect bites or stings; and to prevent motion sickness. Antihistamines may cause sedation and interact with alcohol, so take care when using them.

Antiseptic (such as povidone-iodine) — For cuts and grazes.

Aspirin or paracetamol (acetaminophen in the USA) — For pain or fever.

Bandages, Band-Aids (plasters) & other wound dressings — For minor injuries.

Calamine lotion, sting relief spray or aloe vera — To ease irritation from sunburn and insect bites or stings.

Cold and flu tablets, throat lozenges & nasal decongestant

Insect repellent, sunscreen, lip balm & eye drops

Loperamide or diphenoxylate — 'Blockers' for diarrhoea; prochlorperazine or metaclopramide for nausea and vomiting.

Multivitamins — For long trips, when dietary vitamin intake may be inadequate.

Rehydration mixture — To prevent dehydration, eg due to severe diarrhoea; particularly important when travelling with children, but is recommended for everyone.

Scissors, tweezers & a thermometer (note that mercury thermometers are prohibited by airlines).

Syringes & needles — In case you need injections in remote areas, which may have medical hygiene problems. Ask your doctor for a note explaining why you have them.

Water purification tablets or iodine (see also Everyday Health in the Health chapter).

OTHER USEFUL EQUIPMENT

The following are travel essentials you'll want to have along:

Address Book — To keep in touch with friends and family back home and to collect addresses from people you meet on the road. This doesn't have to be a book per se;

it can be a computer printout pasted to the back of your journal or handwritten on the back pages of your guidebook.

Alarm clock – Early buses, trains and flights are common; don't miss them for lack of an alarm. Travel alarm clocks are compact and light. Alarm clocks in Latin America are cheap, but you'll get better quality at home.

Baby wipes or moist towelettes – From axle grease to leaking sunblock, use these to clean almost everything that oozes or dribbles onto you or your gear.

Batteries – Put new batteries in all your equipment before you leave. You can bring spares or buy them on the road.

Contraceptives – Bring condoms with you. They're available in Latin America, but quality will vary (always check the expiry date). If you're on the pill, bring as many months' supply as you'll need. Depo Provera is available over the counter in one-month injections in some countries. Talk to your health-care provider and see the Health chapter for more information.

Cotton swabs or Q-tips – For cleaning ears, electronics or other sensitive areas.

Eye-wear – Good sunglasses are essential to protect you from powerful rays; try to get a pair with a UV coating – inferior sunglasses can be worse for your eyes than none at all. If you wear corrective lenses or contacts, bring your prescription and an extra pair. Cleaning solution, an extra case and lens wipes are a good idea, too.

Padlocks & a chain – Locks are good for securing your pack and locking hotel room doors. Chains can be used to lash packs to roof racks on buses and overhead racks on trains.

Passport photos – You'll need these for any visas you have to get along the way; each visa application will require two or three photos.

Pocketknife – A day probably won't go by without you whipping out your pocketknife. Swiss army knives (or one of similar quality) are recommended. Look for ones with tweezers, scissors, a decent blade and bottle opener.

Sunscreen – The sun is very powerful in Latin America, especially in the Andes, so use a good sunblock (SPF 15 or better) with moisturiser, and a lip balm with sunscreen.

Tampons & pads – You can get these in the big cities, but don't depend on it. It's better to have your own supply.

Toilet paper – You'll be surprised at the scarcity of toilet paper on the road; you'll be glad not to be caught short.

Torch (flashlight) – For searching the depths of your pack, getting to your hotel room late at night, finding the bathroom out the back or in the event of a blackout, you'll want a torch. MagLites are powerful and come in a variety of sizes. Camping stores also sell headlamps that are like miners lights that you wear around your head, thereby freeing up your hands.

Toiletries – You can get almost anything in the larger towns and cities, but if you use something particular, bring it with you.

Towel – Yes, bring your own. Most hotels won't supply towels and even if they do, there's a good chance they'll be stinky, scratchy or both. Quick-drying travel towels made of chamois or microfibres are easy to pack and lightweight. Sarongs are good for towelling off and using as a beach cover or blanket.

Travel guides, maps & phrasebooks – For more on these, see Researching Your Trip in the Planning chapter.

Water bottle – You can purchase bottled water and reuse the container, but it won't last as long as a camping model. It also won't be as practical for purifying water on a regular basis and you won't be able to attach it to your pack from the loop.

Ziploc baggies – Any and all sizes are recommended to keep food separated from clothes, insect spray from toothbrush and soggy socks away from everything else.

Nonessential Equipment

The following items are hardly essential, but choose a few and life on the road can be far more enjoyable:

Bandannas/kerchiefs – Wiping sweat from your brow, mopping up spilt coffee and blowing your nose are but a few suggestions for these versatile items.

Binoculars – These are a real bonus item, especially if you anticipate doing any wildlife viewing; check out the mini-models available.

Books – Every trip has dull moments, but a good book can turn those times around. Take one or two good reads and swap them with other travellers or at a used-books shop.

Camping gear – If you plan to camp a lot, bring your own equipment – a sleeping bag, tent, stove and cooking gear are essential. Camping can save you money, but unless you want to do a lot of it, don't lug around the extra weight. Rental gear is available at the most popular camping spots, eg Machu Picchu (Peru) and Tikal (Guatemala).

Candles – These are good for atmosphere anywhere, plus illumination during blackouts or while camping.

Compass – If you know how to read one and plan on trekking and camping often, take a compass for orienteering.

> ### Floss It
>
> For the cost of a crummy cigar, you can buy a vacation-saving item. It's called dental floss, and its uses are innumerable. Got a fishhook but no line? Four words: green waxed dental floss. Need to secure a mosquito net? Reach for the dental floss. Forgot to pack a clothesline? You're in luck if you've packed dental floss. Tear in your jeans, rip in your pack? A little dental floss and a sewing needle, and life goes on.
>
> Dental floss comes in 50m and 100m lengths and is sold in nifty little cases complete with in-built cutters. It's cheap, it's light, it's strong and it's outrageously useful. Some say dental floss can even remove decay-causing material from between teeth and upper gums. Now in cinnamon, mint and grape flavours. No kidding.
>
> *Scott Doggett,*
> *LP Author, USA*

Electronic translator – Some people complement phrasebooks with these gadgets that hold thousands of foreign words.

Food – A small cache of your favourite food from home, properly packaged and stored, can offer comfort and nutrition.

Games – Chess, cards, checkers, backgammon, Scrabble … whatever your gaming preference, there's probably a travel version. Games can help shorten long bus rides and ease introductions to strangers.

Gifts – Small presents for new friends and homestay families are discussed in the boxed text 'It's Better to Give …' in the Accommodation section of the While You're There Chapter.

Glue stick – For stamps with no glue and affixing labels, tickets and other items in your journal, this will come in handy.

Inflatable or travel pillow – For long trips and for the rocks that pass for pillows in lots of Latin American hotel rooms.

Mosquito Net – If you plan to stay on the tourist circuit most of the time, don't bother with a net; because they'll be supplied much of the time. But, if trekking and jumping on jungle buses is on your itinerary, carry your own net – when that scorpion bounces off your net inches from your nose, you'll be glad you did!

Personal stereo/radio – These can help pass time (but they also cut you off from your surroundings). Those with recording functions are useful for making tapes of festivals, friends or jungle noise. Short-wave radios are great for keeping you informed.

Plug – Rarely are you supplied with a plug for a sink or tub. Bring a double-sided rubber or plastic plug, or simply stop the drain with a sock.

Sewing kit – Pack a couple of needles, some thread, safety pins and a few buttons, and you can fix anything from the seat of your pants to a pair of sunglasses.

Sleeping bag/sleeping sheet – A sleeping bag is always a tough call, because it takes up so much space. You may opt for a sleeping sheet instead. This is two sheets sewn together that you slip between. Stick to cotton or silk and you have lightweight, easy-to-wash bedding. The Andes, Central American highlands, Patagonia and Tierra del Fuego can get very cold. If any of these destinations is on your itinerary, try to squeeze in a sleeping bag, as you'll definitely need one.

Travel journal & pens – Even if you don't fancy yourself a writer, you'll want to record and remember certain experiences, dates, destinations and people. See the Recording Your Trip section later in this chapter.

Washing line – Rest assured, you will be hand-washing clothes and a line will make this chore easier. There are inexpensive models with suction cups, hooks or both on each end. Get the kind that holds clothes without clips.

Washing detergent – You can get your clothes washed by someone else, but the technique is brutal. Liquid detergent is versatile but rare in Latin America; bringing a bit of your own can go a long way.

Specialised Equipment

Special equipment for snorkelling, diving, surfing, mountain climbing or rafting can be rented at sites catering to those activities, such as the Bay Islands

Lessons from Mary Poppins

On a sunny day in London or New York, it's rare to see anyone walking around with an open umbrella but up until the 1920s the parasol was a popular accessory. In fact, next to the spacesuit, the umbrella may be one of the greatest tools ever designed to protect the body from the elements, especially the rays of the sun. In many parts of the world, women and (wise) elderly men have not yet abandoned the umbrella to the whims of progress. The informed Latin American traveller will find it indispensable while walking, waiting by the roadside, riding in boats and even, for the acrobatically inclined, on bicycles. An umbrella is cooler than a hat and may be more elegant to boot. Besides the obvious benefits of keeping out the heat and ultraviolet rays, walking in the sunshine with this ingenious device gives the bearer a semblance of dignity and poise (one of the umbrella's original functions, after all, was to designate rank for royalty), qualities that may otherwise be lacking in one's life on the road.

Marie Cambon
LP Author, Canada

in Honduras, the Belizean reef and at Brazilian breaks. Equipment can be old, inferior or both in Latin America, so you may want to bring your own gear if you're keen on certain activities. Enthusiasts of more unusual activities, eg spelunking, should definitely bring their own equipment.

Clothing

Choosing what clothes to take will take more thought than you might expect. A lot depends on where you're going and what you'll do once you get there. For example, if mountains and beaches are on your itinerary, you'll have to bring clothes for both hot and cold climates. This is a pain, but it can be done without weighing yourself down with two completely separate sets of clothing.

A rule of thumb is: don't take anything you can't live without, because clothes tend to get trashed, traded or donated while travelling. Also, pack the same amount for two months as for two weeks. Clothes are cheap in Latin America and certain areas are renowned for quality ponchos, sweaters and hats, so if you need to buy any clothes en route, you can.

DAY-TO-DAY

Comfort is your number one priority in daily wear; shirts, shorts, skirts, pants, underwear and socks should be made of natural fabrics. Cotton, silk, linen or any blend of these travel well. Synthetic fabrics like rayon, nylon and lycra are lighter and wrinkle less than natural fabrics, but they don't breathe and you'll be uncomfortably sweaty and sticky. There are a lot of lightweight, quick-drying, comfortable travel clothes made of hi-tech synthetic fabrics on the market these days, which are great if you can afford them.

Below are some clothing suggestions for hot and cold climates. It's worth bringing something presentable for special occasions or encounters with officialdom such as customs and border crossings.

For some tips on what not to wear in Latin America, see the boxed text 'Dressing Appropriately' in this chapter.

KEEPING COOL

In hot climates, you'll want lightweight, roomy clothing that breathes. Light colours are cooler, but dark clothes look clean longer. Sarongs are great travel wear because they can function as a skirt, dress, towel, sheet or sun shade. Unfortunately, men wearing sarongs in public in Latin American will be treated as curiosities (at best).

Avoid denim, as it's heavy, hot and takes too long to dry. Cotton trousers or long skirts are much more practical and comfortable in tropical conditions. Two-in-one pants that unzip to become shorts are popular and functional. A couple of short-sleeved shirts are a good idea, though the less skin you show, the better for both health and cultural reasons. Long-sleeved shirts and long pants protect you from the sun and mosquitoes, which can carry diseases such as malaria and yellow fever. Outside of beach towns in Latin America, shorts and tank tops are not appropriate, especially for women.

Wide-brimmed hats are recommended over caps because they shield your ears and neck from the sun. The best Panama hats are made and sold in Ecuador; these are the ultimate travel hats, as they can roll up to pass through a ring. You should bring some kind of swimwear, though it doesn't have to be a suit – a pair of shorts and a tank top can double up for women and regular old shorts will work for guys.

KEEPING WARM

Warmer clothes are a must for the Andes, Patagonia and the highlands in Central America. Layers work wonders here because the weather can change quickly from hot to cold to nasty. The golden rule with layers is you can always take some off, but if you have none to put on, well, you're out of luck. A mix of natural and hi-tech synthetic layers will keep you warm in all situations. Hi-tech clothing is not cheap, but it's amazingly effective against wind, rain or snow (see Specialised Clothing).

Whether you go natural, hi-tech or a combination of both, your layers should start with long underwear (or a silk T-shirt), followed by a T-shirt, a long-sleeved shirt, a sweater and jacket. Silk is an amazing natural fibre that keeps you warm or cool and dries super-fast; wear it if you can. Warm, clean socks are imperative, and you may want to wear a woollen pair over cotton ones. Sweaty, wool socks next to your skin is not a good idea, but the wool over cotton combination will keep you warm.

Dressing Appropriately

Latin America is pretty strict about its dress codes, especially as they pertain to women. Shorts, tank tops and (gasp!) bikini tops are definitely out everywhere except the beach. Travellers should check out what locals are wearing to get an idea of what will be acceptable. Shorts are generally not worn in the city, and you may feel uncomfortable in this kind of casual attire.

Across Latin America, folks do their best to be well turned out, regardless of their socio-economic position, and travellers flouting local dress codes may be perceived as demonstrating insufficient respect for these social mores. For women, the more skin you show, the more attention you're going to get. Like it or not, you'll be seen as promiscuous and fair game if you are showing any leg, let alone cleavage. Wearing revealing clothing also reinforces the widely held belief that all western women are 'easy'.

Men who wear shorts in public won't be taken seriously, as shorts are the young boy's uniform in many countries. This is particularly the case when dealing with officialdom. Men and women should take care to be as covered as possible when entering churches or cathedrals. In the same vein, it's considered seriously bogus to wear indigenous clothing while you're in that country; Guatemala comes to mind here.

In short, it's easy to save yourself hassle, ignominy and possible hazard simply by dressing appropriately. Don't wear figure-hugging clothes, always cover your arms and legs, and keep the plunging necklines, bikinis and bare chests for tourist towns and beaches. Apart from making good practical sense, you'll be showing a level of respect for local cultures that will make your trip more fulfilling and will go some way to lessening resentment against travellers as a whole. Never forget that you're a visitor in someone else's country.

Rain is a serious consideration, and you should know the difference between waterproof and water resistant. If your jacket is of the latter classification it won't do much good in a tropical downpour; bring a raincoat too. Gloves and a hat are useful and warm, and alpaca ones are sold throughout the Andean nations. Always remember to bring sunblock, sunglasses and a hat into the mountains because the sun, though not hot, can be fierce.

SPECIALISED CLOTHING

Much specialised clothing, eg for trekking or cycling, is made from hi-tech synthetic fabrics. Polartec and Goretex are probably the best known, but there are others. Goretex and similar synthetics are lightweight fabrics designed to keep you warm and dry while letting your sweat escape as you move around. There are whole Goretex suits available with matching tops and trousers, but most people can manage with just the top, and layer other clothing on their legs.

Why Backpackers wear Hiking Boots in Bars

I liked wearing boots. I thought they were cool, they made me look taller, and I could wear odd socks without anyone noticing. So naturally I took my boots with me – the brown ones for around town, the black ones for going out at night, and an expensive pair of brand-name hiking boots for serious walking. Then I added a few changes of jeans, some shirts, a thin sweater, two thick sweaters, a warm jacket, a waterproof jacket, a sleeping bag, camera, books and so on. I could barely walk with all this stuff in my backpack, but I knew that everything I had was essential.

In less than two weeks I was near crippled from walking the streets in leather-soled boots, and my pack was no lighter – in fact it was getting heavier. It was time to redefine my idea of 'essential'. By that stage my bag was filled mostly with unwashed clothing, and I realised I was travelling the world with 15kg of dirty laundry. Worse still, it was obvious that the few remaining clean garments were completely useless. Facing the fact that I was in little danger of eating in a fancy restaurant, I sent my good shirts home by surface mail.

A sweater has been defined as a garment a child wears when its mother feels chilly, and by extension it's something a traveller packs when they're going somewhere cold. But a thick sweater is not a great travel accessory – it's bulky, hard to wash, and just not versatile enough. If the weather is really cold, you should be wearing every garment you have, and your bag will be almost empty. But you can't wear two thick sweaters at once, or even a thick one and a thin one. Don't tell your mother, but one thin sweater is enough.

There's an important packing principle here – everything you carry should be mutually compatible. If you can't wear shirt A with jacket B, leave one of them at home. That's why the footwear is so problematic – you can only wear one pair at a time. But shoes and boots are bulky in your bag, and expensive to pack and post home, which is why my calf-length brown boots were ultimately abandoned on a lonely train station, standing straight but empty, as I walked away in my black boots, now too scuffed to wear in the classy nightspots I wasn't going to anyway. And what about the brand-name hiking boots? I'd bought them in Australia, but they were made in Taiwan for an American company. They didn't last a week.

So if you're planning a trip that includes trekking as well as some nightlife, or if you'll be walking city streets as well as strolling on beaches, you'll need something versatile from the ankles down. You'll have to decide which is more difficult – dancing in hiking boots or climbing a volcano in high heels.

James Lyon
LP Author, Australia

Polartec or polar fleece is another synthetic fabric worth checking out. There are different classifications of fleece, with some spectacular wind-blocking grades, and they get more expensive as the quality and protection increase. Fleece is lightweight and can be worn in both cooler and warmer climes, but it becomes terribly soggy in rain.

FOOTWEAR

Along with sleeping bags and mosquito nets, shoes are a packing conundrum. Rubber-soled sandals are useful in some circumstances and worthless in others. They're good for the beach, walking around town and wearing in showers, but they're bad in the jungle, on long treks and in inclement weather. They don't offer great arch support and insects will nip at your feet incessantly. Still, they're compact, can tolerate wetness and are justifiably squeezed into most packs. At the very least, buy a pair of cheap thongs (flip flops) in a local market for showering; not only will these protect you from fungal infections, they'll spare you having to deal with someone's stray hairs floating across your toes.

If you plan on trekking quite a bit, a quality pair of leather hiking boots is a good investment. Break them in before you set out on your trip. An in-between choice is a pair of lightweight boots or walking shoes made from synthetic materials. They won't be as durable as leather, but they'll be more comfortable.

Sneakers, the versatile footwear of the masses, are also a possibility. Consider a canvas pair, as they can get wet and dry fairly fast. Most shoes are heavy and unwieldy, so try to limit them to a couple of pairs.

Packing
BACKPACK

When you start collecting items to pack, remember that weight and bulk are equally important. A half-empty pack weighing as much as a small car will be as hard to manage as a light pack that won't fit through your front door. Don't stuff your pack full to bursting before you leave; you'll want some space for the souvenirs you collect on the road, plus your pack will never be as organised and compact as it was the night before your trip. Here's some advice on packing your backpack:

- Even if you leave your packing until the night before you depart, allow enough time for a trial run. See what works where and how much you can comfortably carry. Take the pack out for a while in your area. If it's too

Clothing Checklist

- light jacket
- long pants/skirts/dress
- long-sleeved shirts
- sarong
- shoes/boots/sandals/thongs (flip flops)
- shorts (can double as swimwear)
- short-sleeved shirt
- socks/underpants/bras
- something presentable
- specialist clothing, such as hat, gloves, thermals, woollen socks
- sweater
- swimwear
- waterproof jacket
- wide-brimmed hat

heavy or unbalanced, repack it and rethink that extra book you threw in. Some veteran travellers insist on packing at the last possible moment to keep their packs light, but they're usually the ones borrowing your towel in the shared bathroom!

- Pack your heaviest items as close to your spine as possible, preferably in the centre and top portions of the pack. This will prevent the pack pulling backwards at your shoulders, maximise the strengths of the design and provide the most comfortable position for long-distance walking.

- Assign spots in your pack for different items (books on one side, underwear on the other) and always try to pack them in that vicinity. This allows you to access things easier, especially in the dark.

- Items that you'll be using more often should be the most accessible, either at the top, in a side pocket or a zippered compartment.

- Expect your pack to be thrown, jostled and thrashed about on planes, buses and trains. You'll probably also sit on it pretty often and should pack appropriately to protect anything fragile. Wrapping T-shirts around delicate items and burying them among clothes and stuffing items in your shoes are two good protection strategies.

- Make the most of any compartments. Putting your sleeping bag, dirty clothes or other soft items in the bottom compartment will provide a soft, protective layer for other more fragile items. These items are also relatively light, allowing you to store heavier items higher in the pack.

- Plastic bags are very handy for separating wet and dry things and for storing anything that might leak, eg toothpaste and insect repellent.

DAY-PACK

It won't take you long to figure out what you'll need to carry in your day-pack. One bathroom experience without toilet paper will make it clear in a hurry! Other items may include:

- book, journal, pen, postcards, aerogram
- camera and film
- guidebook, phrasebook and map
- hat
- personal stereo
- moist towelettes
- pocketknife
- sunscreen, lip balm and insect repellent
- sweater or light jacket
- water bottle

Also see Carry-On Luggage in the Takeoff chapter for ideas on what to bring on planes, buses and trains.

Recording Your Trip
CAMERA

At first glance, it may seem strange that some people opt to travel without a camera. However, there's some logic behind it. Cameras are expensive and a liability on the road, where anything can be stolen, lost or damaged. Cameras

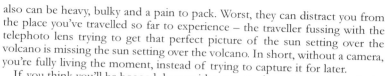

also can be heavy, bulky and a pain to pack. Worst, they can distract you from the place you've travelled so far to experience – the traveller fussing with the telephoto lens trying to get that perfect picture of the sun setting over the volcano is missing the sun setting over the volcano. In short, without a camera, you're fully living the moment, instead of trying to capture it for later.

If you think you'll be bogged down with a camera, leave it at home and take advantage of postcards, photo books and your own memories of a place. You could also arrange for other travellers to send you copies of their pictures. In some Latin American cities you can buy disposable cameras, which may be the right choice for you.

If you're travelling with a friend or partner, discuss sharing a camera. After all, for the most part you'll be taking similar shots. While you may disagree on photo composition and who should be taking the pictures, being prepared to compromise and bringing along lots of film should sort things out.

The camera you decide to bring should reflect the types of photos you want to take. If you want to sell your photos (see Work & Travel in the Planning chapter for some tips) or are after high-quality, artistic shots, go for a single-lens reflex (SLR) camera. If, however, you'd just like to take photos of friends and places for your own memories and to share with folks back home, an automatic point-and-shoot camera will suffice. If you like the quality photos of an SLR and the convenience of a point-and-shoot, you might consider getting a good, compact camera with a built-in zoom lens.

Remember that although SLR cameras take great pictures, their attachments are unusually heavy and bulky. This will affect how you pack and carry your camera gear. Special camera waist pouches are favoured by some travellers using SLRs. These cameras are also expensive. A good SLR and a few lenses can cost upwards of US$1000, and when you're travelling with something that expensive, you fret.

For more camera photography information, go to Photo.net (www photo .net/photo).

SLR Cameras

The best aspect of SLR cameras is that you're in control. Put the camera on the manual setting and use the internal light meter, and you can compose photos in ways that you can't with a point-and-shoot camera. Most SLR cameras also have an automatic setting for when you just want to take photos quickly. Manual or automatic, SLRs let you switch between a variety of lenses and filters and so broaden your options. Most SLR camera bodies or frames are metal and can take a beating. There are lightweight plastic bodies out there, but they're significantly more sensitive. An SLR will also require the following:

Lenses – Zooms can save you space and weight; in most events, a 24-100mm and an 80-200mm should suffice. If you like fixed lenses, you'll need three or four to accommodate the same situations.

UV (skylight) filters for all your lenses – These will sharpen your photographs by screening out ultraviolet rays and protect your lenses.

Camera case – This protects your camera and allows you to keep it outside your back-pack.

Spare camera batteries – You may be able to buy these in the bigger cities, but you may not find them in rural areas; don't let your camera die for lack of juice.

Lens paper – Bring your own from home and make sure it's the lint-free kind.

Silica gel packets – These keep moisture from collecting on your film and equipment.

Point-and-Shoot Cameras

Affordable, light and easy to use, point-and-shoot cameras will be just the thing for most travellers. They also make portraits easier and less obtrusive to take because they focus almost instantly. These cameras range from disposable to fancy. Visit your local camera shop to explore the options and get advice from professionals. While you're there, pick up a camera case, silica gel packets to protect your camera and gear from moisture, some lens paper and extra film.

There are several point-and-shoot cameras on the market that take pictures in three formats: classic (4x6), high definition (4x7) and panoramic (4x10). These can be very handy, especially if you're planning to photograph some sweeping Latin American vistas. These cameras take a special kind of film called Advantix, and while you can usually get it in large cities, you may want to bring a stash from home.

Digital Cameras

These are fast becoming all the rage as prices drop and camera technology becomes more sophisticated. These essentially store photos on a mini-hard drive within the camera. Digital cameras work without conventional film and you can erase photos you don't like. Unfortunately, unless you're travelling with a super laptop, it will be difficult (if not impossible) to download the photos, which you must do if you want to take more photos once the memory is used up. For shorter trips, a digital camera may be great.

Film

You'll be surprised at how easy it is to buy film in Latin America. Still, that doesn't mean the kind you want will be available (slide film is especially hard to find) and if it is, it may be of substandard quality. It's not uncommon to buy film that has an expired use-by date or that has been stored improperly, so that your pictures come out like junk. Bring at least a few rolls of film from home and stock up in the bigger cities on the road.

Film comes in slide or print, colour or black and white, and fast or slow speeds. If you have any desire to try and sell your photos, take slides. Print film is cheaper, easier to view, and cheaper to develop than slides, so most people prefer prints. Black and white film versus colour is a style question, with the former being more artistic and the latter being more realistic. Take at least a couple of rolls of black and white if you want to experiment. Speed depends on the lighting conditions and action in your photos. For example, 100 ASA is good for landscapes in bright daylight, but it probably won't work for a shot of your friends in the bar. A happy medium is 400 ASA, which works in most conditions with the help of a flash.

Take care how you store film, as sunlight and heat can adversely effect it. Store it in a cool, dry place and consider sending it home if you don't get it developed on the road.

Try not to leave film in your baggage at airports, as the high-powered x-ray machines used to check luggage can damage it. The carry-on luggage detectors, however, are at low enough levels that they shouldn't affect your film. You can always hand-check your film if you're concerned. Just let the airport staff know and take your film out and hand it to them. If you're really concerned, there are lead-lined film bags that you can purchase specifically for this purpose.

Developing Film

You should get film developed as soon as you can because it deteriorates over time. Some people prefer to develop their film on the road while others wait until they get home. You can also send rolls home in prestamped mail envelopes and have the developed pictures sent to your permanent address. While Latin American developers are usually OK, there are no guarantees and you should ask other travellers for recommendations. Alternatively, put in only one roll of film to be developed and see how it comes out. Pictures that sit in your pack for several weeks or months probably won't weather well, so consider sending them home.

Photo Etiquette

See the Photo Etiquette section under Avoiding Offence in the Issues & Attitudes chapter for tips on photography etiquette in Latin America.

VIDEO

Videotape of your travels provides a great sensory trip down memory lane, and hopefully all your friends and family will clamour to see it. Whereas video equipment was once heavy and unwieldy, there are now compact, hand-held video units that allow you to easily and discreetly take videos on your travels. Increasingly affordable, they still require extra gear like plug converters, film, and a transformer so you can recharge the battery. If videotaping on the road appeals to you, keep the following in mind:

• Mountains, sunsets, and pristine beaches are decent video subjects, but sometimes the mundane (a woman cutting meat at the market or shoeshiners in the park) can be as interesting and shed more light on a culture. Don't overlook everyday subjects in your quest for the spectacular.

• The great advantage of video is that it moves and flows, allowing you to meander up a river in a canoe, passing villages and capturing life's vibrancy in a way still photography can't.

• Be patient and still when you film and try to shoot long takes. Use the stabiliser on your camera (if it has one) when taking video on bumpy rides.

- Video cameras have sensitive microphones and can pick up sounds you didn't even hear while you were filming. This can be good in intimate situations, bad if there is a lot of background noise that is deafening on tape.
- Keep in mind people's aversion to being photographed and observe the same photography etiquette as you would with a still camera. Pointing a video camera in someone's face is rude and can be frightening. Always get a person's permission before you tape them.

TRAVEL JOURNAL

Even if you hate to write, there will be people, places, anecdotes, dates and details from your trip that you will want to remember. This is where a journal comes in. Journals record all the memories you want to revisit, but they're also a testimony to who you were during that trip and at that particular time of your life. The dimensions and complexity of your character will not be so well represented in video or photos as they will in your journal. If you have any desire to sell your writing, your journal can serve as a springboard and a well of ideas for future articles (see Work & Travel in the Planning chapter for some advice on travel writing).

Travel journals are a large chunk of the blank book market. Lonely Planet has one out, and you may want one specifically for travel.

CASSETTE RECORDINGS

Cassette tapes allow you to send long, meandering letters to family and friends back home without suffering from writers cramp or block; just press record and start talking. Tapes also provide an aural record of your trip that can bring back memories faster than any photo; the eerie call of the oripendula or the trills of Andean flutes, the bus drivers shouting out your destination in a rapid-fire staccato with a loopy finish or the explosions of a New Year's fireworks show with the marching band playing in the background, will all serve to ignite the ashes of your memory.

NICHE TRAVELLERS ▶▶

There are some groups of travellers who face particular issues when travelling, variously due to age, sexual preference, disability or family responsibilities. This chapter has a look at some of the issues each group faces and suggests some strategies to maximise their travel experiences.

Senior Travellers

Seniors in reasonably good health and with a modicum of travel experience should definitely consider Latin America for a holiday. Bathroom facilities and public transportation will be more rustic than you are used to at home, but the hospitality of the region will more than compensate for any minor discomforts. The one major difficulty will be long bus rides on unpaved roads; uncomfortable for everyone! If your itinerary involves this type of overland travel, consider breaking up the ride into two or three legs. In Latin America, older people are generally accorded the respect they're due and travelling seniors will probably receive a similar encouraging welcome.

DISCOUNTS

Discounts are few and far between in Latin America. Still, it's worth checking out travel bargains offered by organisations dedicated to seniors. These include the American Association of Retired Persons (AARP; ☎ 800-424-3410, www.aarp.org), 601 E St NW, Washington, DC 20049, which represents people over 50 (non-US residents can get one-year memberships for US$10); Grand Circle Travel (☎ 617-350-7500, 1-800-350-7500), 347 Congress St, Boston, MA 02210, which distributes a useful free booklet,

Tips for Senior Travellers

- Travel as lightly as possible. You can buy almost anything you need on the road.
- Research your trip thoroughly. A good guidebook will have a special section for senior travellers listing the difficulties and facilities of the country you intend to visit. The Internet is still a little short on information for seniors, but see what you can find.
- Keep the weather in mind when planning your trip. The extremes of hot and cold you may encounter can be debilitating, so try to travel during a period of moderate weather.
- Try to do most of your sightseeing and local travel during off-peak periods, as negotiating streets and public transport during busy times can be a nightmare.
- Be prepared for long bus journeys. Bring a pillow if you have a bad back and find out if there are toilets on board.
- Bring medications you need from home.
- Be flexible. If you find that your original itinerary was too ambitious, don't be afraid to change it.
- You may want to start your travels in a country that is easier to travel around, such as Argentina or Venezuela, before tackling a country like Nicaragua.
- Don't be afraid to give things a try. You'll be surprised what you can do in Latin America, and a little effort and enthusiasm can go a long way.

Going Abroad – 101 Tips for Mature Travelers; and the USA's National Council of Senior Citizens (☎ 301-578-8800), 8403 Colesville Rd, Silver Spring, MD 20910 USA, which gives access to discount information and travel-related advice.

HEALTH CONSIDERATIONS

Travelling in Latin America can be taxing on the body, and you should assess your overall health and fitness before venturing there. Getting a physical checkup and seeking a doctor's advice prior to your departure is a good idea. A doctor can recommend immunisation programs and depending on where your trip takes you, vaccinations may play an important role in a healthy trip. Unless you're passing from a plane to an air-conditioned tour bus to a private car, you'll be doing a lot of walking in your travels. To prepare for this, you might incorporate walks into your daily routine before you leave. A comfortable pair of walking shoes is essential. Load up on any prescription medications you may be taking so you have enough to last through your trip, and always carry copies of the prescriptions with you, to explain your medications to customs officials.

Gay & Lesbian Travellers

On the whole, Latin America is a pitifully unwelcoming place for gay men, although lesbians have it a bit better. In some countries (eg Ecuador and Nicaragua), homosexuality is illegal and harassment of gays does occur here and elsewhere; Guatemala and Panama are particularly homophobic. Misinformation about homosexuality in general and AIDS in particular has made Latin America that much more inhospitable for homosexuals. Even Costa Rica, which boasts tolerance and promotes tours for gays and lesbians, has experienced violent protests against homosexuals visiting from abroad.

But there is some good news (sort of). Lesbians are less maligned than gay men, if only because it doesn't occur to the macho Latino mind that some women don't prefer men! Gay women travelling together should have few, if any, problems. Some destinations are more tolerant than others, and the big Brazilian cities (particularly Rio) are nonstop parties for all sexual orientations and flavours. Santiago, Buenos Aires, Mexico City and Acapulco are also good cities for getting 'out' and about. Underground gay scenes exist in other countries, but you'll have to ferret them out. There is usually at least one gay bar in every city, which makes meeting people easy. In rural Latin America, gay men will have to retreat deep into the closet, so you'll have to decide whether you're prepared to make this sort of compromise.

LAWS & TOLERANCE

Ecuador and Nicaragua are the only countries with anti-gay laws, but tolerance is low throughout most Latin America. Public displays of affection outside of the major cities mentioned above will not be tolerated, and gay men (and possibly women) could find themselves the target of verbal or physical abuse. Discretion is definitely the rule, and getting a room with a double bed for yourself and your lover probably won't happen – a call for creativity if nothing else.

RESOURCES

If you want to visit Latin America, do some research beforehand so you'll know the tolerant places to go. Good guidebooks list gay-friendly places. In addition, check out the *Women's Traveller*, with listings for lesbians, and *The Damron Address Book* for men, both published annually by Damron Company (☎ 415-255-0404, 800-462-6654) PO Box 422458, San Francisco, CA 94142-2458, USA. Gay Scape (www.gayscape.com) is a great search engine to browse by country.

More information on gay-friendly travel in Latin America can be obtained through the US or Australian offices of the International Gay & Lesbian Travel Association (IGTLA; in the USA ☎ 954-776-2626 and in Australia ☎ 02-9818-6669, www.IGLTA.org). It can provide a list of travel agents and tour operators specialising in Latin American destinations. A gay-friendly tour might be the best solution for homosexual men wishing to check out this part of the world. If you're interested in visiting Costa Rica, you may want to get *Pura Vida – Gay & Lesbian Costa Rica* by Joseph Itiel.

Travellers with a Disability

Disabled travellers will find Latin America a challenge, to say the least. For the most part, little to no accommodation is designed for physically challenged folks, no matter what your impairment. Wheelchair ramps and accessible bathrooms are a novelty, Braille signs and telephones for the sight and hearing-impaired don't exist, and public transportation is very hard to navigate. The situation is better in the Southern Cone countries (Chile, Argentina, Paraguay and Uruguay), and Brazilian cities are making progress where access is concerned, but less developed nations and rural areas have no infrastructure for disabled travellers.

Still, if you want to get off the beaten track in Latin America, go for it. Although it's easier if you're with a partner who understands and can help with your particular needs, the hospitality and courtesy of the locals will quickly become apparent if you're travelling alone. Everyone will try to help you, whether you want it or not! Many countries in Latin America are so cheap, it's not beyond the realm of possibility for you to hire a car and driver or an assistant to help you get around.

ACCESSIBILITY

The more developed the country, the better access will be, though don't expect even the best facilities to come close to what you're used to at home. Argentina, Chile and Brazil will present the most options for disabled travellers. Outside of the cities in those countries and throughout the rest of the region, a little creativity will be called for. You may want to ask your airline about accessibility features at the airport in which you'll be arriving so you know what to expect when you land.

Public transportation will be extremely difficult if you're in a wheelchair, but not insurmountable. Arrive for bus and train departures early so you get the best seat choice and can stow your baggage while working out how to get on and off safely. Navigating hectic, crowded streets will be a nuisance, so consider attaching a flexible pole with a flag to the back of your chair so both cars and pedestrians can easily see you coming. You might collect the flags of the countries you've visited or fly the colours of your home country. Public bathrooms can be very cramped, and for men are often just a trough running along a wall. Use your hotel bathroom as early and often as possible before venturing out, minimising your need for public facilities.

Accommodation is not always accessible in Latin America, but fortunately the Spanish colonisers left an architectural legacy of the interior garden and courtyard. Many cheap and mid-range hotels are laid out around a ground floor courtyard, off which are individual rooms. These are often, incidentally, wheelchair accessible

Tips for Travellers with Disabilities

- Research the specific challenges and facilities for disabled travellers in the country you'd like to visit. A good guidebook will have a section on travel for people with disabilities and will give contact numbers for local organisations that can assist. The Internet is useful for researching your trip.

- Consider travelling with a companion who can help with day-to-day affairs and arrange for assistance if necessary.

- Consider travelling to one of Latin America's more accessible countries, such as Chile, before tackling a more challenging one like Peru.

- Don't be afraid to ask locals for assistance. People are usually more than willing to help out. If someone is particularly helpful, give them a tip.

- Don't be afraid to try new things. You'd be surprised what you can do with a little imagination and improvisation.

- Don't feel that you have to travel as a part of a group tour. It is quite possible to travel independently and this can be far more rewarding.

- Consider hiring a private car for sightseeing. You may want to hire a personal assistant for some parts of your travels.

- Ask for ground floor rooms in hotels — few have elevators.

RESOURCES

There are many resources for disabled travellers, offering both general and Latin American-specific advice. Organisations in the USA include Mobility International USA (☎ 541-343-1284, www.miusa.org) PO Box 10767, Eugene, OR 97440; Access Foundation (☎ 516-887-5798) PO Box 356, Malverne, NY 11565; and the Society for the Advancement of Travel for the Handicapped (SATH; ☎ 718-858-5483, sath.org/index.html) 26 Court St, Brooklyn, NY 11242.

Publications you may find useful are *Abilities* magazine (☎ 416-766-9188, fax 762-8716) PO Box 527, Station P, Toronto, Ontario, Canada M5S 2T1, which has a column called 'Accessible Planet', offering advice on foreign travel for people with disabilities. Also worth a look is *Nothing Ventured — Disabled People Travel the World*, edited by Alison Walsh (Rough Guides).

There are interesting, informative Internet sites for disabled travellers, including the Global Access web site (www.geocities.com/Paris/1052), which has good tips and personal accounts of Latin American travel; and the Access-Able Travel Source homepage (www.access-able.com), with good general advice on travelling for people with disabilities. Accessible Journeys (www.disabilitytravel.com) offers interesting trips to Latin America, including for independent travellers.

In Australia there is the National Information Communication Awareness Network (NICAN; ☎ 02-6285 3713, fax 6285 3714, www.nican.com.au) PO Box 407, Curtin, ACT 2605 for information; and in the UK try the Royal Association for Disability & Rehabilitation (RADAR; ☎ 020-7250 3222, fax 250 0212, www.radar.org.uk) 12 City Forum, 250 City Rd, London EC1V 8AF, England. This organisation publishes three information booklets (costing UK£2 each) addressing planning, insurance, useful organisations, accommodation, transportation and equipment for disabled travellers.

Travelling with Children

Taking the kids on an outing to the supermarket can be difficult enough, let alone in a foreign country. Still, there are strategies for successfully travelling with children. You'll find that the natural curiosity and extroversion that kids have in great supply can open a lot of doors for you in Latin America. Your main concerns will be familiar: boredom on long rides, health issues, availability of things particular to small children, like nappies (diapers) and baby food and, of course, keeping them entertained.

Typically, children are adored in Latin America, and you'll find that they will provide a natural introduction to the people and customs of the region as locals shower them with affection. In some countries and well off the beaten track, travelling with children is an anomaly, but anywhere your itinerary takes you, you'll be treated with friendly curiosity. On the road, children will rarely want for playmates, and their interpretation of foreign cultures can be very endearing indeed. Travelling with a child is a special opportunity; who knows, your whole family could become addicted to travel and to Latin America.

Tips for Travel with Children

- Consider travelling in an easier country like Argentina before heading to a difficult one like Bolivia. This will give you an idea of how your kids (and you!) hold up to the stresses.

- In some countries, you may need to bring your own supplies of nappies (diapers), baby bottles and baby food.

- Bring your children's favourite toys and games to keep them amused.

- While clothes are readily available, good-quality shoes in your child's size may not be, so bring these from home.

- Travel on buses is not recommended, as children quickly grow restless with no room to move about. You might consider taking taxis or hired cars instead.

- Be careful about what your children eat, as they are particularly vulnerable to food-borne illnesses.

- Bring plenty of sunscreen, and wide-brimmed hats.

- Make sure your child is fully immunised for the countries you plan to visit.

- If your children are old enough, get them international student ID cards so you can take advantage of student benefits (see Other Paperwork in the Passports & Visas chapter for details on cards).

CHILD-FRIENDLY PLACES

All Latin American countries are child-friendly. Luckily, almost all towns and cities have parks and playgrounds and the wildlife in parts of Latin America will pique the interest of children of all ages. If you can afford a tour of the Amazon or Galápagos Islands for instance, you and your children will experience a memorable other world. Beaches, mountains, rivers and all the activities specific to these natural wonders should be entertainment enough, though the ruins in the Yucatán, Guatemala and Peru, though spectacular, will have most children yawning uncontrollably.

RESOURCES

There are several web sites related to travelling with children, but most address health concerns and not much else. The Travellers Medical and Vaccination Centre site (www.tmvc.com.au/info7.html) and the Travel Health Information Service (www.travelhealth.com/kids.htm) are two good places to start. Guidebooks generally have a section on travelling with children, but the whole story is covered in Lonely Planet's *Travel with Children* by Maureen Wheeler.

TAKEOFF ▶▶

You've got your plane ticket and visas, your travellers cheques and immunisations, you're still nursing a headache from your wild bon voyage party and you're ready to go. Before you burst onto the Latin American travel scene, however, you'll have to withstand a long, perhaps excruciatingly boring, plane flight. This chapter explores strategies for dealing with long flights, discusses customs and immigration and suggests ways to make airport navigation, flight confirmation and other nitty-gritty travel minutiae easier.

Before You Fly

The following suggestions need to be considered well before you fly.

SPECIAL NEEDS & REQUESTS

If you have any special needs, eg you're shipping a surfboard, chaperoning children, or travelling in a wheelchair, let the airline know as far in advance as possible so they can deal with your request. Ideally, this would be when you book your ticket. Remind the airline early and often of your situation; when you reconfirm your ticket and when you check in are good opportunities. Most airlines are very helpful in accommodating passengers, but if you're getting the cold shoulder about your special needs, try a different carrier. Special meals are reserved for those with specific dietary needs and you just have to ask for one.

Most modern international airports are equipped with ramps, wheelchair accessible toilets and telephones. The airport in which you arrive will be a different story, however, and you'll want to inquire about accessibility (see Travellers with a Disability in the Niche Travellers chapter). Aircraft toilets can be a challenge if you have a physical disability, so it's worth discussing this with the airline beforehand. Seeing eye dogs must travel in a special pressurised compartment with other animals and may be subject to quarantine requirements (up to six months upon entering or leaving rabies-free countries such as the UK, Japan and Australia). Hearing-impaired passengers can have airport and in-flight announcements written down.

If you are travelling with children, ask about discounts; if they don't take up a seat, children under two usually fly free or for 10% of the standard fare, but are given no baggage allowance. Children aged two to 12 are eligible for substantial discounts and can check in baggage. Skycots should be supplied upon request and hold children up to 10kg. Pushchairs (strollers) are usually allowed on board if they fold to fit in an overhead compartment.

RECONFIRMING YOUR FLIGHT

Most airlines require reconfirmation 72 hours before your flight, but it's best to reconfirm twice. Call four to five days ahead of your departure date and then again 72 hours before your flight. This is especially important if you're flying a national airline because these carriers tend to book flights full to bursting.

You may receive a reconfirmation number when you call to confirm your flight. Write this down in a safe place! This code is yours alone and will expedite a refund claim if you are bumped from your flight (see the Glossary at the back of this book for explanations of air travel terms). You can sometimes make a seat selection at the time you reconfirm, although if you want a seat in an exit row you must wait until you check-in (see Best Seats later in this chapter). Reconfirmation time is when you should remind the airline of any special need you may have.

CARRY-ON LUGGAGE

Your carry-on luggage should contain all breakable or perishable items and everything you'll need to make your flight as enjoyable as possible. Airlines impose size and weight limits on carry-on luggage, but most day-packs will pass the test. Some veteran travellers pack so light and tight, they can bring their main pack and their day-packs as carry-on baggage. This prevents any loss or damage to your checked baggage. Here are some suggestions for what to bring on board with you, both to ensure your flight is fun and make life easier if you arrive at your destination but your pack doesn't:

- Passport, money, plane tickets, insurance papers and other identification should be on you always, preferably in your money belt.
- Fragile electronic gear including your camera, alarm clock, or personal stereo.
- Photographic film. Exposed or unexposed, carry your film with you, as checked baggage sometimes receives higher doses of radiation than carry-on luggage.
- A change of clothes, a few pairs of underwear and toiletries. These will be very handy if your pack doesn't arrive when you do.
- Bottled water is handy as the recirculated air in airplane cabins is very dehydrating, and you can't rely on the cabin crew at every turn. Moisturiser can relieve dry skin.
- Blankets are supposed to be available on flights, but that isn't always the case; bring something warm like a sweater to wrap around you in case the cabin is too cool.
- Bring some food, as airplane food is notoriously bad and, even if it's passable, you'll want to snack during the flight.
- Medication that you take regularly, whether you'll need it during the flight or not, should be with you. Also aspirin or paracetamol for headaches.
- Earplugs to help you sleep among general cabin noise.
- Games, guidebook, novel and journal can all help pass the time on a long flight.
- Pens for filling out customs and immigration forms.

DUTY-FREE ALLOWANCES

Most countries impose a limit of 200 cigarettes (or the equivalent in tobacco) and 2L of alcohol, although these limits can vary. If you bring in more than the permissible limit, you'll have to pay duty (import tax).

It is illegal to travel with firearms and ammunition, illegal drugs, and fireworks. Don't even think of flying with any of these items, as jail is a very real possibility if you're caught. Drugs are a particularly contentious point in this part of the world, and you can expect no mercy if you're caught carrying illegal narcotics.

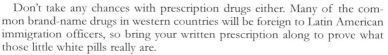

Don't take any chances with prescription drugs either. Many of the common brand-name drugs in western countries will be foreign to Latin American immigration officers, so bring your written prescription along to prove what those little white pills really are.

Countries with strong agricultural sectors, eg Chile, will not permit you entry if you're carrying fruits and vegetables. These can carry bugs, fungus or flies that devastate crops unaccustomed to foreign vermin. It is also unlawful to fly with certain kinds of gas typically used in camping stoves, so empty your canister beforehand. You may have to declare any expensive electronics like personal computers, cameras (still and video) and stereos so officials can be sure you won't try and sell them once you arrive in their country. The amount of money you're carrying and an onward ticket might also be required; see Immigration in the Touchdown chapter.

Buying Duty-Free

Once you've gone through the customs and immigration rigmarole in your home country, you'll have the opportunity for some bargain shopping the airport duty-free shop. The best bargains are tobacco and liquor; stock up on your favourite brands that may not be available where you're going, but remember not to exceed the limit of what you can import. Perfume, electronics and cosmetics are also for sale in these shops and on board the plane duty-free.

Departure Day

A lot of the following may seem obvious, but you'd be surprised what you can forget in the frenzied moments leading up to departure. Use the following as checklist on the day you're leaving, and you'll be spared that fate.

DRESSING FOR YOUR DESTINATION

When dressing for the flight, keep your destination climate in mind and wear comfortable clothes. It's probably easier to go from a cool climate to a warm one, as you can just shed layers before and during the flight (but keep one warm layer for the plane cabin or if you're arriving at night). If you're going from hot to cold, bring a change of clothes and change in the plane or airport bathroom. If it will be really cold, try to take your jacket in your carry-on luggage.

BEING ON TIME

Running late for an international flight can be very stressful and may affect your plans adversely. Latecomers can get bumped from their flight, have their checked baggage left on the tarmac for lack of room in the hold, or they may get the absolute worst seat on the plane. Traffic jams on feeder roads into airports account for a lot of tardy travellers. If at all possible, take a train to the airport. If you must arrive by car or bus, leave plenty of time to get to the airport. The standard airport arrival time is two hours before the scheduled departure. This may seem like overkill, but it really takes that long to check in all the passengers and their baggage.

NAVIGATING THE AIRPORT

Swarming with anxious people trying to reach their departure gate through a maze of luggage and other travellers, airports can be confusing. Signs should point you to your airline; otherwise, stop someone to ask them directions (this may be your last opportunity to do so in your native language!). Airports have plenty of information desks and large maps that say 'You Are Here' – use them.

READY MONEY

In a perfect world, travellers would have a pocketful of the local currency when they touch down at the airport. Unfortunately, except for the Mexican peso, it is not possible to obtain Latin American currencies before you arrive (see Changing Money in the Money Matters chapter for more information). If you're travelling to Mexico, go to a bank or change enough money at the airport on the day of your flight to cover transportation, food and accommodation for your first night. For other countries, you'll have to wait until you get there to change money. This shouldn't be a problem, as the banks and *casas de cambio* (exchange houses) are usually open for foreign flights.

CHECK-IN

Once you're at the airport, you need to find the departures terminal and check-in counter for your airline. Make sure all your bags have identification tags with your name, address, home phone number and a number where you're going, if possible. Don't leave anything like a sleeping bag strapped to the outside of your pack, as there is a good chance it will become separated. Tag your sleeping bag and check it in separately.

Make sure all zippers and pockets are securely closed on your pack, put anything that may leak (like toothpaste) in a plastic bag and transfer fragile electronics to your day-pack. If your pack has seen better days, ask airline staff for a plastic bag to protect it and make it easier to identify at baggage claim. Your baggage will be weighed and the agent will fix destination tags to it (make sure they're filled out correctly and that each bag has a tag). If you have to change planes, inquire about what happens with your baggage during the stopover. Sometimes the airlines transfer the bags and sometimes you have to claim them from one flight and recheck them for the next.

Flight Day Checklist

- Make sure you've reconfirmed your flight (better late than never).
- Make sure you have your house key for when you return.
- Turn off the gas and electricity in your home.

Check that you have the following essentials:

- address book
- backpack
- camera
- day-pack
- medications you might need
- money belt (with all your credit cards, travellers cheques, cash)
- passport
- plane ticket
- visas you've already received
- wallet

You'll be asked for your plane ticket and your passport at check-in. This is when you'll choose a seat, and you can remind the agent of any special meal arrangements you've made. Once all these details are in order, you're given a boarding pass, to which your baggage claim should be attached and away you go!

Best Seats

The best seats in economy class are probably the exit row seats, which are usually over a wing and afford great amounts of legroom. There are certain responsibilities that come with these seats if there is an emergency, and not everyone can sit here (eg children or foreign-language speakers).

The next best seats are on the aisle because you can stretch your legs easily and get up without disturbing your neighbours. Some people prefer window seats because there may be a view. These seats go fast because no one wants to end up in the middle. If this happens to you, and you end up caught between annoying passengers, think positively and wander the cabin in search of potential travel mates.

INSPECTION & IMMIGRATION

Departure inspections are cursory; you'll be asked to walk through a metal detector while your carry-on luggage is passed through an x-ray machine. Primarily they'll be looking for flammable gases, aerosol cans and weapons. It's best to stow your pocketknife in your checked baggage to avoid any hassles with inspection officials over a little old Swiss army unit.

Immigration is usually just as perfunctory; your passport will be inspected and you'll be waved through. Sometimes you'll get a departure stamp (but don't get your hopes up).

Surviving the Flight

Air travel does not have to be the frightening or boring experience some people make it out to be. This section suggests some ways to make your flight reasonably enjoyable and seemingly shorter. For items that can help you enjoy your flight, see Carry-On Luggage earlier in this chapter.

ALCOHOL

Some flights can be like sky-high parties where complimentary booze flows freely and travellers whoop it up in pretrip revelry. Beware, however, of the way altitude and alcohol mix: you'll get tipsier faster and the dry cabin air will dehydrate you more dramatically than normal. Also, depending on how much you drink and the length of your flight, you'll either arrive at your destination hungover or drunk, both terrible options.

SMOKING

You're out of luck on almost all flights if you smoke. Try the national airlines, which may not have antismoking policies on all flights. Alternatively, you can get a flight with a stopover. If you're on a nonsmoking flight, bring lots of chewing gum, sleep a lot and try to stay off the liquor. At least for the duration of the flight, some travellers also resort to nicotine gum, inhalers and other products designed to help people quit smoking.

SLEEP

Some people sleep on planes effortlessly and arrive at their destination fresh as a rose. Then there's the rest of the world. If you're not able to sleep, bring lots of snacks, games, a good book and a guidebook to pass the time. Fine-tuning your itinerary is a constructive way to eat up some hours. Plan on watching the in-flight movie and try to meet some new people or study your phrasebook. Sleeping pills are not advisable because there's a good chance they'll leave you disoriented or still sleepy when you arrive, making the details of negotiating a foreign city even more difficult to handle.

THE BEST MEALS

Best meals in terms of airplane food may be the quintessential contradiction in terms. But there is some decent plane food around, and airlines are constantly trying to improve their 'menus' in an effort to win over passengers. Requesting vegetarian or vegan meals can net you some good vittles, while some people request Hindu or kosher meals, and these can be quite delicious. Special meals must be requested in advance, but if you see a special meal go unclaimed on your flight, ask for it. No matter how you feel about airline food, try to bring along some home-cooked snacks, sandwiches or appetisers for your flight.

TRANSIT BREAKS

Take advantage of long stopovers to write postcards, take a nap or get a decent meal. Some airports expand on the normal amenities and you may be able to take a shower, shoot pool, or play video games. Sorting events are always showing in airport bars. Inquire at the information desk regarding stopover diversions or entertain yourself; it's all good practise for when you hit the road in earnest.

Fear of Flying

If you've flown before and found the experience frightening, or have never flown and are afraid to, you should take some sensible steps to make the flight as painless as possible. If you are absolutely terrified of flying, do not try to overcome your fear by yourself but get some appropriate counselling. If your fear is a little more mild, psyche yourself up before boarding. Make sure you ask for the seat where you are most comfortable. Some people find sitting in aisle seats more reassuring than window seats, or vice versa.

Attempting to drown your fears in alcohol is not a good idea, as the dehydration that will result will merely replace your unpleasant mental condition with an unpleasant physical one. If you need something to calm your nerves, ask your doctor to prescribe a mild tranquilliser.

Finally, there is no need to worry about turbulence during your flight. Planes can withstand infinitely more stress than most people imagine. It may feel horrible, but you've got more to fear from the mystery meat in your dinner than from the shaking of the wings.

TOUCHDOWN

Imagine you've just endured 16 hours of crying babies, a string of bad movies featuring talking animals, a couple of servings of what is generously referred to as food and now everyone is speaking Spanish at a fast pace. What you need at this point is a friendly face, a nice soak in a tub and a cosy bed, but what you get is baggage claim, customs and immigration, currency exchange and a wickedly strange city all functioning in a foreign language.

Welcome to a new world! Try not to let first arrival jitters and all the details of landing and entering a foreign country overwhelm you. Drink in the sights, sounds and smells as much as you can – never again will this be virgin territory, and sometime down the road you'll revisit these memories with affection and a laugh or two. Navigating your way from airplane to your first night's accommodation isn't always trouble-free, but if it were too easy, it wouldn't be the adventure it promises to be.

Immigration

The immigration drill is pretty much the same for all Latin American countries and starts with the customs form you are given and fill out on the plane (see Duty-Free Allowances in the Takeoff chapter for information on declaring items at customs). These forms are typically in Spanish and English. Usually you'll also be given an embarkation/disembarkation card; the disembarkation card goes to the immigration officer upon arrival. In countries where you'll be issued a tourist card, you'll have to fill out a short form describing the purpose and length of your visit as well.

Once your paperwork is in order, immigration should be straightforward and quick. Don't expect leniency if you don't have an appropriate visa or if your passport is due to expire; immigration officers can and will put you on the next flight home. Research what paperwork you'll need long before you're due to leave. Keep in mind that while most visas must be acquired beforehand, tourist cards are issued on arrival. You may also be asked to show a Yellow Fever Vaccination Certificate, sufficient funds or an onward ticket in some countries. (See the Passports & Visa chapter and the country profiles for details.)

Once you hand your passport to the immigration officer, you may be asked some simple questions such as how long you'll be staying and the reason for your visit. Tell the truth and keep it simple – just call it tourism and be done with it. If you're required to show any other supporting documents, the immigration officer will ask for them; hand them over with a smile and you'll soon be on your way.

Dressing neatly can facilitate your passage through immigration. The long-haired traveller in tie-dyed overalls and Birkenstocks is more likely to be scrutinised then the one in jeans, sneakers and a clean shirt. Though dressing 'straight' is no guarantee that you'll breeze through the formalities, it makes it more probable.

BAGGAGE COLLECTION

Once you've passed through immigration, it's on to the baggage claim carousel. Once you've retrieved your pack, head over to customs. In some Latin American countries there may be drug-sniffing dogs snorting at the baggage or military personnel patrolling the area with big machine guns. The guns are especially disconcerting, but don't worry, they won't train them on you – just try not to stare.

There is always the chance that your baggage will not materialise on the conveyor belt. If this happens, go directly to the baggage office or grab the first airline representative you see. You'll have to fill out a form describing your pack and it's contents; keep a copy and get a phone number for the airline's lost baggage office. You'll probably have to call the airline periodically to find out if your pack has arrived and return to the airport when it (finally) does, perhaps several days later.

If you have a decent travel insurance policy (see the Tickets & Insurance chapter), you may be eligible for compensation for each day you're without your pack. This will allow you to buy clothes and any gear that you need until you're reunited with your luggage. Depending on your policy, it can be up to US$200 a day, but you'll have to save receipts and make a claim upon your return home. As well, the carrier may offer its own compensation for your troubles, which can be in the form of cash or free airline tickets. Inquire about compensation if your bag doesn't arrive when you do.

CUSTOMS

There are usually two lanes in customs, one for items to declare and the other for no items to declare. The customs official will ask for your passport and customs declaration form, and you may be asked to open your bags. This is usually just a formality, but if they don't like the look of you or are just having a bad day, they may make a more extensive search of your belongings or even your body. It's wise to be polite with customs officials.

Latin American countries do not play games when it comes to drugs, and even paraphernalia can land you in big trouble. Triple-check your pack if there's any chance something illegal may be lurking in a hidden pocket from previous travels.

On Your Way

Once your passport is stamped and your luggage clears customs, it's time to change money. Within the airport terminal are banks and *casas de cambio* (exchange houses), and they'll probably be open when you arrive. In the remote possibility that they're closed, don't panic. First see if there's an ATM. If not, go to the taxi stand. Taxi drivers are more than willing to take US dollars, and you should set aside a few small bills for this purpose. You'll pay more for the ride than you would in local currency, but at least you won't be stuck at the airport. Once you're at your hotel, explain the situation; most places will understand and either wait until you can change money the next day, or accept US dollars. If you arrive at noon, banks may be closed for lunch or siesta, so just wait until they reopen.

Always be aware of your surroundings when changing money. If you buy local currency at the airport, only get enough to see you into town, pay for a hotel room and a meal or two. The exchange rate at the airport is usually lower than you'll get in the city centre, so you'll want to do your major money-changing the next day. Get a mixture of large and small bills and some coins, too, in case you have to use a phone. Keep your exchange receipts, as you may be asked to show them when you exit the country. For more money tips, see Changing Money in the Money Matters chapter.

LEFT LUGGAGE

Most airports have a left-luggage service where you can store baggage you won't need until later in your trip. For example, if you arrive in Guatemala but won't be scuba diving until you fly out to Belize three weeks later, you may want to leave your gear at the airport, retrieving it before your flight. This is rarely a cheap option, however, and many hostels in Latin America offer their guests secure baggage storage either free or for a nominal fee.

GETTING INTO TOWN

Your guidebook should have information on how to get to the city centre. Usually your choices will be a taxi, bus or occasionally a subway, and you can get more information at booths in the airport. Beware of booths that are pushing their own agenda and trying to steer you to their hotel, taxi service or shuttle bus.

Read the airport transportation section of your guidebook carefully; know your options and their approximate cost. In some countries, the bus from the airport is very straightforward, comfortable and cheap, in which case you might take it. In other places, the bus could be a nightmare and you'll be better off opting for a taxi. A lot of travellers prefer to take a taxi from the airport to their hotel because it's door-to-door service and they don't have to worry about pickpockets or having exact change. If you're travelling alone and planning on taking a taxi, try to hook up with some other travellers to minimise your costs.

There will be crowds of touts and taxi driver waiting outside the terminal. It's best to have an idea of a hotel and address you'd like to go to – and make sure your money and documents are securely in your money belt, and that your pack is zipped up and comfortably on you back.

It's likely you will be shouted at and jostled as everyone clamours for your tourist dollar, but don't intimidated. The taxi drivers at the airport will try to overcharge you. Even in countries where meters are the norm, drivers will try to get away with not using them and you'll have to bargain for your fare. Always agree on a fare beforehand and stick to it. Note the agreed figure on a piece of paper as insurance. Some countries regulate prices for taxi rides, and these prices should be posted at the airport taxi stand. Don't worry too much about whether you're being ripped off on your first night – you'll have plenty of time ahead to master the art of bargaining. Resign yourself to paying a few extra dollars, chalk it up to experience and get on your way to exploring the country you've worked so hard to visit.

Your First Night

It's best if you have an inkling about where you're going to spend your first night. Some travellers like to pick two or three choices beforehand, while others just head for a general area with lots of hostels and see what looks good. If you go with one of these strategies rather than reserving a hotel room from home (see Your First Night in the Tickets & Insurance chapter), head for the section of town with lots of accommodation options in a relatively small area. Often called a 'travellers ghetto', these neighbourhoods give you lots of choices and provide back-ups if the place you had your heart set on is out of business or full for the night.

Backpacker hang-outs in Latin America include the Centro Histórico in Mexico City; the New Town in Quito, Ecuador; all of Antigua and Panajachel in Guatemala; and around the Plaza de Armas in Lima, Peru. All of these cities are chock-full of hostels catering to backpackers, and you just have to wander into a few that look good, check out a room or two and choose the one you like best. If you're travelling with a friend, one of you can guard the baggage while the other looks at rooms.

Always look at a room first, and don't feel obligated to take something you don't like. There is almost always another option. Sometimes a hostel will have different quality rooms, and it's worth asking to see what else they have to offer. See the Accommodation section in the While You're There chapter for advice on choosing a room.

Once you've found an acceptable room, try to bargain. In certain cities at different times of year this will be easier than others, but in some places they won't know the word discount no matter how perfect your Spanish or Portuguese. If there are other travellers loitering about, find out what they're paying so you know the going rate. Expect to pay more on your first night and plan to hunt down a better, cheaper room the next day when you have a greater understanding of the lay of the land.

If you haven't a clue where to stay on your first night, use the resources at the airport. An information booth, other travellers, even taxi drivers will all have suggestions. There may even be hotel representatives at the airport. In the case of taxi drivers and hotel representatives, however, be prepared to pay a commission, either to the person directly or in the form of an inflated room price. As long as you're safe and reasonably comfortable in your room, don't worry too much about it. You can always find the accommodation of your choice the next day.

If none of the above works and it's late at night and you're stranded in a foreign airport, you basically have two choices. You can stay in the airport overnight (some have 24-hour cafes) or get a room at the airport hotel. The former will be uncomfortable and the latter expensive, but either is preferable to stumbling around in a strange city with a big pack on your back.

Coping with Jet Lag

Some travellers, either due to their departure point or their body's temperament, will suffer no untoward effects from jet lag. Other folk, however, will be nodding off at noon, confused about the date and generally disoriented.

Jet lag is the result of the miscommunication between your body clock (which is still ticking to the night and day cycle of your home country) and the actual clock of your destination country (which runs on a completely different night and day cycle). It can take a few days for the two cycles to synchronise. Until then, you may be bright-eyed at 3 am and exhausted at lunchtime. You can try to adjust your waking and sleeping hours a couple of days before you leave home, but this is difficult and not always worth the hassle. Instead, try getting into the local rhythm as soon as you arrive by sleeping at night and waking at a normal hour. The longer you observe your body clock by napping during the day and staying awake at night, the longer it will take to shake the jet lag.

Some travellers take sleeping pills on their first night, while others have reported very successful results from taking melatonin (available at health-food stores). Meditating or a good book may also lull you to sleep. Here are some more tips for beating jet lag:

- Avoid alcohol on the plane and during your first few days in the country. There's nothing like a straight-up hangover with a jet lag chaser to put you in a foul mood and further disrupt your body clock.

- Try to be well rested if you're arriving during the day or dead tired if it's at night.

- See if you can get a flight that minimises how much sleep you lose; if you're on a 12 hour flight that arrives at noon, you'll have to try to stay up until night to adjust to local time. That same flight that arrives at midnight will usher you straight into bed and your body clock will adjust faster.

- Eat light, and avoid fatty or greasy foods that will slow you down and contribute to the jet lag syndrome.

ISSUES & ATTITUDES

One of the best things about foreign countries is the, well, foreignness they have about them. This chapter addresses just that, with advice on tempering culture shock, avoiding offence, and protecting yourself and your gear from thieves, scam artists and other petty criminals. This chapter wouldn't be complete without a discussion of ecotourism, an issue that has taken Latin America by storm. Stash the information in this chapter away in an accessible corner of your brain because you'll want to haul it out once your adventure is afoot.

Culture Shock

Even the most experienced travellers suffer culture shock in one form or another, you won't be the first or last to lurch away from a Latin American scene stunned and shocked. Keep in mind that culture shock does abate with time and exposure, so don't let a disconcerting scene put you off the region. The day-to-day reality in foreign countries can lead to culture shock, and the following section provides some advice for adjusting.

Loosely defined, culture shock is the disoriented feeling you get from all the strange, antithetical and perhaps offensive behaviour and customs you experience in a new country. Little will be what you're used to, from the pollution and dangerously crowded buses to the exotic foods and very short beds, and there will be something new at every turn challenging your perceptions. Some people just shut down in the midst of it all, but if you look at culture shock as an inevitable part of travelling to which you have to adjust slowly but surely, you'll be able to handle the peculiarity of it all with aplomb and humour.

The extent to which you feel culture shock will depend on your previous travel experience, language skills and what you learned to expect before you left home. Culture shock and homesickness often go hand in hand because the confusion you feel over a foreign culture evokes a desire for the familiar. Everyone gets pangs of homesickness and it's OK to indulge those fantasies of hot showers, good beer or whatever else you may miss about home once in a while.

Culture shock can also manifest itself as anxiety, depression, lethargy, insomnia or feelings of impotence, isolation or paranoia. All these symptoms can make some people withdraw and it's not uncommon to hear stories of travellers who were scared to leave their hotel room. Eventually, however, almost all do venture out and end up having the time of their lives.

It's entirely natural that struggling with a new language and culture should give rise to feelings of anxiety. Ease into it; there's no good reason to try that fried guinea pig on your first day! Being well rested will help you ease into and even appreciate your new surroundings: if you're just off the plane and exhausted, culture shock has a much more fertile breeding ground. Leave heavy-duty sightseeing or off-the-wall attractions until you've had a few days to adjust.

Culture shock comes in waves, though not everyone experiences them in the same order or at all. The first wave is known as the honeymoon stage, when you're enthralled and excited by everything around you and even the drunk passed out on the cathedral steps is intriguing. Eventually, this euphoria wears off and you're ushered into the disintegration stage. At this point culture shock can be dangerous because you're no longer infatuated with the new culture, but are perturbed and possibly repulsed by it. Every little thing gets on your nerves. If you feel this happening, set a realistic goal to get out of town or to the beach or some other placid environment that you can enjoy. Focus on what you really like about the culture you're experiencing and remember that travelling means taking the bad with the good.

Luckily, disintegration is followed by the reintegration stage. You won't be back on the honeymoon (which wasn't realistic anyway) and you may have negative feelings still about this new culture, but with a few positive thoughts and experiences, you'll have your wings and be on your way to the autonomous stage. This is typified by a more confident, relaxed attitude where you set about to explore the country and culture with new and realistic travel goals. At last, the feelings you had been hoping for become a reality and you swing into the interdependence stage. In this stage, culture shock has cycled through to become cultural appreciation and you begin to develop an emotional attachment to your new surroundings.

To ameliorate the initial stages of culture shock, do some research before you leave home. Read travelogues and history books, peruse maps, cruise the web and most important, talk to other travellers who have been where you're going. For more specific suggestions, see Researching Your Trip in the Planning chapter.

POVERTY & BEGGING

In both the quantity and quality, poverty is one of the most shocking and saddening parts of travelling in Latin America. Although some countries may be better off than others on the whole, there are pockets of poverty in every country and even if you want

Tips on Dealing with Culture Shock

- Travel from 'easy' countries (eg Argentina, Chile, Belize, Costa Rica, Panama or French Guiana) to 'harder' ones (eg Guatemala, El Salvador, Colombia or Peru).

- Know what to expect by doing some research before you get there.

- Travelling alone will be harder than travelling with a friend or partner who can lend support and familiarity in strange circumstances.

- Call home and send emails frequently to keep you in touch with your 'real' life.

- Chat with other travellers and expats. They've all experienced culture shock and can offer perspective and advice.

- Don't fall into the trap of comparing your home country with your host one. Of course they are different, so try to think in terms of differences, not better and worse.

- If it's too stressful or peculiar where you find yourself, move on to somewhere more comfortable. This may be within a country, from the isolated mountains of Peru to Cuzco where there are plenty of foreigners and amenities, for example. Alternatively, you may elect to leave Peru all together.

to turn a blind eye, you won't be able to avoid it in your travels. This section deals with the abject poor, homeless and beggars you're likely to encounter. Though you'll probably still be overwhelmed (it's very hard to fully prepare for the poverty you'll be faced with), develop a philosophy and policy for dealing with the poor and try to stick to it; you won't be able to help everyone even if you try, and knowing this may help you cope.

Wherever you go in Latin American cities, you'll be asked for money. Whether or not you give to beggars is a personal issue, but there are three basic schools of thought. One is that giving poor people a few cents is the least you can do, as such a small amount makes nearly no difference to you, but will to them. The catch with this is where does it end? This is especially problematic if you're in a severely economically depressed city (eg Mexico City or Lima) and you're being solicited for money on every corner. Further, some people believe this perpetuates the problem by encouraging beggars to continue to beg. The second philosophy is that you shouldn't give any money to anyone, but you will see real suffering on your travels, and to deny everyone borders on the inhumane.

The last school of thought is a middle-of-the-road approach where you assess requests for money on a case by case basis. Musicians and the disabled may deserve something, for example, and you may make it a policy to give hungry families food. If you can't fathom who really deserves alms, watch the locals. They know who is genuinely hungry and who is hustling (beware of anyone that turns down food) and it's not uncommon to see people who are badly off giving to the worse off. Real charity like that should put it all in perspective for you.

Donations

Another way to cope with the poverty you'll experience is to donate to local aid organisations. This can be in the form of money, gear or even time as anything that makes a difference will be welcomed. International aid organisations like Oxfam International (www.oxfaminternational.org), which deals with hunger or Habitat for Humanity (www.habitat.org), which builds housing, can always use donations.

Depending on the scene and your state of mind, children can be particularly annoying or endearing when they're pestering you for something. The ubiquitous request for pens, gum or candy will at some point grate on your nerves. But don't be surprised if every so often a little cherub tugs at your skirt, stares up at you with soft angel eyes and you're forking over gum by the handful. For all the other times, tell the kids you haven't got any, but bring along pens, notebooks and other supplies that you can donate to a local school, ensuring they'll go to good use.

You may feel besieged by the amount of people asking you for money and other items. Poverty is endemic in Latin America and many people see foreign travellers as rich. Compared to them, you are rich, no matter how low you are on the economic food chain back home. If the poverty really gets you down, volunteer with a local group working to ameliorate it. More ideas on volunteering are discussed in Work & Travel in the Planning chapter.

Avoiding Offence

With a decent amount of courtesy and the advice that this section provides, you will avoid putting the proverbial foot in your mouth as regards committing offences. What is considered offensive in one setting may not be in another, so getting a feel for the differences will help avoid embarrassment. Countries with large indigenous populations, such as Bolivia and Guatemala, follow a stricter code of conduct than less traditional areas. Keep in mind that Latin American indigenous populations have been exploited since Columbus. Understandably, they don't take to outsiders quickly and this wariness sometimes manifests itself as wariness; you should be low-key in these situations. Once people have a chance to warm to you, you'll experience some of the greatest hospitality on earth.

For the most part, unacceptable behaviour in Latin America focuses on two things – clothing and rudeness. For more information on taboo behaviour in specific countries, consult the society and conduct sections of your guidebooks.

DRESSING APPROPRIATELY

Showing a lot of skin and dressing in dirty, shabby clothing are two of the easiest ways to offend people throughout Latin America. If you're not at the beach, pool or gym, bathing suits, tank tops and to some extent shorts are unacceptable.

This attire is entirely appropriate if you're hanging out in a beach town surfing the days away, and even the locals will be wearing shorts and tank tops in this situation. But no matter how hot it may be, these clothes don't transfer to the cities. Loose-fitting, cotton clothing is more the norm and women should favour long skirts. Generally, the more skin you show, the more attention you'll get. Wearing conservative clothing is especially important if you plan to visit churches. Check out what the locals are wearing if you're in doubt.

Latin American beaches are not the French Riviera – topless and nude bathing are out. The only possible

---

Latin American Do's & Don'ts

The following rules generally apply throughout Latin America. While you will find exceptions to every rule, you'll never go wrong by being too cautious:

Do's

- Dress discreetly. This is the most important rule to observe (see the boxed text 'Dressing Appropriately' in the What to Bring chapter for details).
- Observe proper etiquette in churches (see Avoiding Offence in this chapter).
- Bring a gift if invited to someone's home. This is particularly important if you're at a homestay.
- Ask for permission before taking someone's photo.
- Greet people on the bus, in shops and along country roads. Hello and how are you? are customary openers.

Don'ts

- Don't engage in public displays of affection.
- Don't lose your temper, especially when dealing with authority figures. This will generally get you nowhere and may lead to serious problems.
- Don't take photos of military personnel or installations.

exceptions are some beaches in Brazil, but it's wise to follow the locals' lead if you don't want to be harassed. Last, there is an unspoken understanding about appropriating indigenous clothing while you're still in that country. In Guatemala, for example, it is considered in poor taste to wear the beautifully woven *huipiles* (blouses) the country is known for. Buy them, cherish them, but wait until you're out of Guatemala to wear them.

Most Latin Americans make every effort to dress as well as they can. Even if their closet only holds one set of clothes, you can bet that set is turned out clean and pressed every day. Even the less fortunate strive to dress themselves and their families in well mended, neat clothes. It is unfathomable therefore that rich people (having the luxury to travel automatically puts you in this category) would choose to wear grubby, torn clothing. Frankly, many see this as disrespectful, both to yourself and your host country. Budget travel is not suited to stylish, new clothing, but leave the torn jeans and grungy shirts at home and bring clothing that's in good condition.

POLITENESS & CIVILITY

In all imaginable circumstances, from getting on the bus to buying avocados at the market, Latin Americans greet each other with at least *Buenos días* (Good morning) and may throw in a *¿Cómo está?* (How are you?) for good measure. You should do the same. Greetings break the ice, signify friendly intentions and get a conversation or business matter rolling. In small towns, when you pass someone on the road, hitch a ride or approach a stranger for directions, greetings are important and you'll find yourself doing it naturally after a time. It is important to know how to say please, thank you, good morning/afternoon/evening and excuse me in the language of the countries you'll be visiting (see Learning a Language in the Planning chapter for more details).

In traditional societies, women are not accustomed to speaking to foreign men. Men travelling in indigenous communities and needing help or directions should go into a store or approach another man for the information. This will spare everyone an awkward moment.

Often what is acceptable is shaped by history – here's two specific instances to be aware of. First, Simón Bolívar, the hero who almost single-handedly liberated South America from Spain, was Venezuelan. Known as 'El Libertador', Bolívar is revered in Venezuela and the many statues and monuments to him should be respected; this means not sitting on them, crossing the Plaza Bolívar with heavy parcels or defacing them. Second, some queer turn of events in recent years led to a rumour that foreign women were coming to Guatemala and kidnapping children for their organs. Panic spread wildly and mob violence against foreign women occurred in rare instances. Women viewed as overly friendly towards Guatemalan children will be considered suspect in some areas.

Photo Etiquette

Politeness also extends to photography and video etiquette. It is considered very bad form to stick a camera in someone's face and start snapping away; ask

Holiday Romances

If you've seen Julie Delpy and Ethan Hawke killing time in Vienna in the film *Before Sunrise*, you might well be planning a holiday romance yourself. And while losing yourself in the arms of a mysterious lover at the same time as losing yourself on the streets of a strange city has enormous romantic appeal, there are a few things to consider. If you're going to be spontaneous these days, it's important to plan. And there's more to consider than just the price of a bottle of red wine and the easy spread of sexually transmitted diseases.

Lots of travellers, and especially those travelling alone, set out with the intention of seeing a bit of love action while away from home. But few contemplate the variety of motivations and enormous list of repercussions such play might carry with it.

Many travellers find part-time love with other travellers. This is hardly surprising; you're unlikely to find a native Frenchman in a Paris youth hostel. You might even hook up with someone you've just met in order to cut costs on a day-trip or taxi fare, then end up beginning a beautiful — if necessarily short — friendship. People travel with different itineraries, and after a couple of days in the City of Lights, you'll be off to the French Riviera to catch a tan and he'll be heading to Somalia to unload grain for the Red Cross. Now if you never really liked him anyway — maybe you've just always wanted to kiss a Welsh guy — there's no problems. Unless he likes you. Or unless you start to miss him. Or unless he's stolen your day pack. The liberation of travel is quickly eclipsed by affairs of the heart, and where that troublesome organ is concerned, all other care can fly out the bus window.

Breaking up is hard to do. It's almost inevitable, though, when travelling. And the longer you drag out travel together, the harder the parting is likely to be. It's important to remember that although you may share intimate secrets with your new pal, you probably won't tell them everything, and they'll keep things from you too. They might have a partner they're planning to return to, they might be homesick for the Vladivostok coast or they might simply be after some quick, disposable sex. If you're just after sexual experience and conquest, you might be in luck. But all can end in disaster if the people you meet have more serious intentions, attach stronger cultural importance to physical relationships or if you plunge headlong into love. If anyone's going to get hurt, the best advice is to skip the encounter and head to Hong Kong as you'd planned.

If you're looking to hook up with a local in a new country, many of the same pleasures and risks can be expected. Again, discovering your intended partner's expectations is the first step to carnal bliss. Are they aware of your travel plans? Are they aware that you need to marry a local in order to stay? Are they aware of the 'Love Checklist' in your back pocket with a gap next to 'Spain'? Are you aware of local customs and expectations of a sexual partner? A night of passion is all well and good, but you don't want to wake up the next morning buried to your waist and being force-fed raw lobster in the first of a 12-step marriage ceremony. As with new relationships at home, establishing the ground rules is the best way to avoid nasty or upsetting confusion.

If sex (always safe sex) is one of the reasons you're travelling, remember that it carries different connotations in different cultures. Learn a little about where you are before heading for someone's pants. There are plenty of girls on the road looking for a little short-term affection and plenty of guys at their local bar who'd love to show a traveller their etchings, which means there's no need to take advantage of someone who is playing by different rules.

There is, of course, a chance that you may actually find the love of your life on the road. My parents met while my mother was on holidays. But their blossoming relationship meant that my father-to-be had to pack his bags, leave his job, family and friends and chase her half way around the world. Not everyone is happy to throw it all away just to give it a go with someone they've just met. Are you?

John Ryan
Lonely Planet, Melbourne

before you shoot. Often you will be required to compensate your subject with a dollar or a small gift. Use your judgement in these situations. Usually if it's a friendly exchange between two strangers, there will be no need for payment. In touristy areas, however, locals will ask for money before, during and after having their picture taken. In some societies, cameras are seen as a kind of soul snatcher and you will run into people who are adamant about not having their picture taken. If this happens, move on. Follow these rules of photo etiquette and you should be fine:

- You are not at a zoo, so don't treat your subjects that way. Long lenses allow you to take portraits from a distance, so use these if you have them.

- Asking permission to take photos can result in wooden images. To promote candid, spontaneous pictures, take two of your subject or disarm them with humour.

- In religious buildings or during rites, make absolutely sure it's OK to take photographs *before* snapping away. In most churches, photography is not permitted, but it's worth asking.

- Always be as inconspicuous as possible, particularly during religious processions. Take care that the sound of your shutter or the light of your flash won't disturb the participants.

- People may request copies of the pictures you've taken of them. After all, they may never have seen a photo of themselves. Only agree to do this if you intend to follow through.

- Don't take photos of military personnel or installations. Exercise extreme caution when photographing anyone in a uniform or with a gun.

Women Travellers

Though men have been sexually harassed while travelling, women are much more likely targets. Two women travelling together or a woman alone in Latin America may experience unwanted sexual advances or insulting and disrespectful comments and behaviour. Being prepared for this eventuality and exploring your options before something happens can be empowering and help you deal with any uncomfortable overtures thrown your way.

Machismo, that myth which stereotypes men as strong and women as dependent and fragile, is alive and well in Latin America. Some places are worse than others (traditional societies are typically better) and liquor heightens the megalomania. As a woman travelling alone, you can expect to hear wolf whistles and other obviously sexist sound effects; ignoring these usually works. If someone is making derogatory comments about you and ignoring them doesn't work, try to let the offenders know with a look or comment that you understand what they're saying, you don't appreciate it, and they better not push their luck. Be assertive, but not antagonistic.

Invasive behaviour is another story and looks won't be enough if a man tries to grope you on a crowded bus. If this happens, you'll have to assess what response will work best given the situation and the culture. You can try to move away. If this is not practical, make a bit of a scene, announcing in a loud voice that a strange man is touching you in a disrespectful way. Public embarrassment is very effective if spoken in the local language, but people will get the picture even if you say it in your own. Pointing and wagging a finger can get your point across as well. The other strategy is to confront the person directly, looking him in the eye and telling him to stop his offending behaviour.

Western women are considered 'easy' by most Latin American men. This is largely due to Hollywood movies and porn magazines; if you're travelling alone you will definitely be considered fair game. Minimise your troubles by dressing conservatively, don't hang out in bars until the wee hours getting drunk, and don't encourage overtures you have no intention of entertaining. (For more on appropriate behaviour and clothing, see Avoiding Offence earlier in this chapter.) Take all the normal precautions, such as avoiding dark places and lone stretches of beach, and always keep a little extra money on you in case you want to catch a taxi back to your lodging. Wearing a wedding ring can help deflect unwanted attention.

Most important, be confident and assertive when you travel. Assertive and aggressive are not the same thing and the point is not to antagonise people, but to have them respect your boundaries. With clear boundaries and a confident step, you will have an awesome, hassle-free adventure.

Lone Travel

I've met many people who have asked me if I'm afraid to travel alone. Most recently in Creel, Mexico a young woman told me she would be bored if she was travelling alone. Bored! I can't remember a time when I have felt bored. Maybe when I was a child, but not since then.

If I'm doing some serious travelling, travelling alone is the way I like to go. I love the freedom of it. And oddly enough, I've often found that I have more interaction with other people when I'm travelling alone than when I am with a partner, especially with locals. I don't know how many times local people have invited me to party with them, come to their home, share a meal or just a good conversation. Travelling with a companion tends to be more insular – you spend more time with the person you're travelling with, and meet less people.

Just because you leave home alone doesn't mean that you have to stay alone. There are so many opportunities for combining with other people, for short trips or long ones, once you get out on the road. Starting off alone gives you the chance to meet like-minded travellers along the way, to travel together for a while, and then take off on your own again whenever you want to.

Sometimes I've been actually afraid to travel alone in certain places. When that has happened, I've joined up with other travellers. In Managua, Nicaragua I met Sonja, a beautiful, well educated young Egyptian-Swiss woman who, like me, wanted to travel throughout Nicaragua but was afraid to go alone (this was just after the civil war). We combined forces and both got to see Nicaragua, knowing we each had a partner to watch our back. Travelling with my companion for a while broke the ice, and the scary feeling of travelling in Nicaragua at that time. Later, when I felt more at home there, I was able to travel alone without being afraid.

Sometimes people feel sorry for me because I travel alone so much, thinking they'd be lonely, afraid or even bored. But I wouldn't trade it for anything. The feeling of freedom to do whatever I feel like, whenever I want to is its greatest appeal.

Nancy Keller
LP Author, USA

Ecotourism

Depending on whom you ask, ecotourism is the greatest blessing or most heinous curse visited upon Latin America. In theory, ecotourism refers to travel that provides the widest exposure to a host environment, while having minimal impact on the environment and providing sustainable development for the local population. Ecotourism is a contentious issue because it involves many conflicting interests. In an oversimplified example, imagine a government has designated a portion of rainforest as a national park, but the forest lying outside the boundaries is cut down to make room for a guesthouse. Now you have a protected rainforest, but at what cost?

Several organisations have tried to sort out the issues by developing guidelines for responsible ecotourism travel. Among these are Conservation International's Ecotravel Center (www.ecotour.org/ecotour.htm), the Ecotourism Association of Australia (www.wttc.org) and Tourism Concern (www.gn.apc .org/tourismconcern). These web sites contain general information on ecotourism and lists of recommended tour operators. Another good resource is Planeta.com (www2.planeta.com/mader).

ECOTOURISM GUIDELINES

- Don't leave garbage behind you. If you're in the jungle for five days, plan to cart out whatever trash you create.
- Take nothing away with you. Just because it seems there are plenty of orchids or coral, does not mean there's enough for you or anyone else to take some as a souvenir.
- Know what specific problems a region faces so you can make informed cultural and environmental decisions.
- Research which local and international conservation groups are working in a country and support their efforts.
- Buy locally produced goods and promote local businesses, particularly those involved in conservation projects.
- Never buy products or souvenirs that come from endangered species.
- If practical, use environmentally friendly transportation or walk.
- Don't go off marked trails; use designated camping sites.
- Potable water is particularly important, so don't pollute the sources! Use established toilets or go at least 50m from lakes or rivers.
- Minimise your energy consumption.
- Produce as little garbage as possible. Eschew overpackaged goods, use recyclable containers, and wash out plastic bags and reuse them.

It will be hard to follow all of these guidelines all of the time, but if each traveller follows some of them, we'll all be better off.

One particularly important aspect of ecotourism is patronising only those guides and tour operators who are truly practising and promoting environmentally friendly activities. Too often, 'green' travel means greedy for the US dollar, not protecting the rainforest canopy. There are many good, respectable ecotourism outfits out there; see the above web sites or consult your guidebook.

Ecotourism that involves visits to isolated indigenous communities also draws criticism. These communities can be negatively affected by exposure to outsiders, especially organised tour groups. If one of these trips is on your itinerary, make absolutely sure the guide has the consent of the community you'll be visiting. It's probably best if the guide is a member of that community, can speak the language and interpret the culture accurately.

Hazards & Safeguards

Don't believe the hype when it comes to safety and independent budget travel: remember the media only makes a big deal when something goes awry. Indeed, there are places in Latin America that are probably safer than your home country. Most of the crimes targeting travellers are petty theft and with some savvy tips for protecting your valuables (see Money Carrying Options in the Money chapter) you'll have little stress in this regard.

The one exception is Mexico, which has experienced a rapid increase in crime as a result of its economic crisis in the early 1990s; you should know some strategies for protecting your valuables here. Natural hazards, including earthquakes, volcanic eruptions, hurricanes or diseases, and dangers like terrorism, kidnapping and political coups, will in most cases have little consequence for your trip. Don't be reckless, heed advice about potential dangers and you should have little to worry about except simple twists of fate that are out of your control. Also make sure you have decent travel insurance covering medical and baggage loss or theft (see the Tickets & Insurance chapter for details).

Know the hot spots in the countries you plan to visit before you leave home so you have an idea of what to expect. Guidebooks are a good place to start. For the latest information, consult newspapers, magazines and the Internet before you depart. There are helpful web sites listed in the Researching Your Trip section of the Planning chapter.

THEFT

No matter where you are in Latin America, getting your gear stolen is a possibility. There are certain areas with bigger theft problems than others, but you should be conscientious throughout your trip to thwart criminal overtures, from locals and foreigners alike. Unfortunately, there are travellers out there looking to pick up some extra gear or money free of charge. If you are robbed in Latin America, go to the police station immediately and file a robbery report. This probably won't get you much action towards retrieving your belongings, but a report is necessary for insurance claims. Here are some tips for keeping everything safe:

- Always keep your money belt and its contents (passport, travellers cheques, plane tickets, insurance papers etc) on you, preferably beneath your clothing. If your hotel has a safety deposit box, you can leave your belt in there (get a receipt) while you sightsee. When you're sleeping it should be under your pillow.
- Keep photocopies of all your important documents separate from your money belt.

- When at the beach and enjoying water sports, carry your documents and money in a waterproof container that you carry on you while swimming or diving. Alternatively, you can put them in the hotel safe, or share looking after them with a group of friends.

- If you're being robbed, the best course of action is to fork over whatever they want. None of it is worth your life.

- When sitting at a restaurant or bar, do not sling your pack on the back of a chair. Either put it on the floor with your foot resting on top or hook a chair or stool leg around the strap so someone can't snatch it. At least have your bag touching you in some way so you can feel if someone interferes with it.

- A small padlock or combination lock will be useful for locking your hostel door and securing the zippers on your pack.

- Pack slashing is a concern. To keep those blades away from your pack, always keep moving. Even when you're standing waiting for traffic lights, move around a little bit. Be aware of your surroundings. A thief will choose a tired, dazed traveller over an alert one every time.

The Pickpocket's Hand

One morning Sonja and I were riding a bus in Nicaragua, from Managua to León. I was sitting on a seat, and Sonja was standing in the aisle beside me, the bus being extremely crowded.

Slowly and carefully, a man standing behind her slid his fingers into her jeans pocket, the tiny little pocket in the right front where she kept her daily money. He slid his fingers into her pocket so slowly and gently that she never felt a thing. He did not look at her – his face was looking absently around the bus, as if he was just one more bored bus rider.

I was amazed to be seeing this, right at eye level, just a few inches in front of my face. I just kept watching as his fingers slid deeper into her pocket. Finally I realised I should stop him before he actually got her money into his grasp. So I reached up, took hold of his hand, and pulled it out of her pocket.

'Look what this man was doing!' I told Sonja. 'His hand was inside your pocket!' I held up his hand – the evidence!

Sonja looked doubtful, because she had not felt anything at all, and her dubiousness was helped along by the would-be pickpocket, who instantly started protesting with the utmost sincerity, to me, to Sonja and to the occupants of the bus in general. His protests were so heart-rending, against my simple statement of fact that his hand had been inside her pocket, that I think Sonja actually believed him more than me.

Later, I told a Nicaraguan man about this incident. He said I was lucky I didn't get hurt. He pulled up his shirt and showed me a knife scar over his ribs – a souvenir, he said, of the time he had tried to help a young female tourist who was being robbed in Managua. He told me that no Nicaraguan would interfere in a robbery, as I had, because it was very dangerous to do so.

Another time, I wasn't so lucky. In Managua, as I was getting onto a local city bus, there was a terrible crush of passengers struggling to get in the door. It happened frequently that there could be a swarm of passengers trying to board a bus, but this jostling press of people seemed past the point of ridiculousness.

When I finally managed to get on the bus and sit down, I no longer had my coin purse in my skirt pocket. I don't know how they managed to get it out – I was wearing a very deep pocket that I had sewn into my full skirt, covered by a long shirt hanging over my hips. But they got it.

After that, I went back to using my Mexican system – I got a handkerchief and sewed myself a pocket that I could attach to the inside of my clothes, with safety pins.

Nancy Keller
LP Author, USA

- For long-distance bus rides, stow your pack yourself. Usually it will go on the roof or in a compartment in the back or alongside the bus. If you have a choice, put your pack in one of the side compartments and take a seat on that side so you can see what is happening when the bus stops. If your pack goes in a compartment, make sure it locks or lock your pack down yourself.

- Maximise your choices by arriving early for buses. Your pack can either go above you on the bus, under your seat or sometimes up by the driver. If you do arrive early and your pack is put on the roof or in a compartment, don't get on the bus and zonk out for the 45 minutes before you're due to leave. Hang outside and keep an eye on your pack.

- If you want to be less conspicuous, buy a big rice or grain sack at the market. These are what locals use to carry around big loads and they'll hold most backpacks very conveniently for throwing on the roof of a bus.

- Be as discreet as possible with your cash, passport, camera and every other valuable. Don't wear flashy jewellery and try to keep your money belt hidden.

- Don't accept food, drinks or cigarettes from strangers. Thieves sometimes inject these items with a tasteless, odourless drug that can disorient you, knock you out or kill you. In the meantime, they rob you of everything you have. If someone is pressuring you to take food or drinks, claim you have allergies or stomach problems.

- Unload your baggage before paying a taxi driver.

- Don't tell strangers in which room or hotel you're staying. This makes it too easy for them to tail you and rob you.

- Pickpockets often work in teams and while one is spilling soda on your shoe or bumping into you by way of distraction, his cohort is robbing you blind. If you get bumped, jostled or otherwise engaged, be alert and do a mental check of your belongings. Remember that men, women and children can be thieves.

- If you're planning a night of partying and drinking, leave your valuables in the hotel safety deposit box. If there's no safety deposit box, consider having drinks closer to home, such as in the hostel garden or courtyard.

- If you're taking a shower and you're unsure as to the security of your room, either slap a padlock on the door or take your pack to the shower with you.

- Don't walk around unfamiliar areas at night or alone. If things start to get sketchy, hail a taxi or jump on a bus.

- Be cautious with unregistered taxis and their drivers. Be aware of the route you want to take (consulting a map if necessary) and don't fall asleep in the back.

- Bus stations, train depots and crowded markets are the milieu of thieves. Be extra alert in these situations and never leave your bag unattended. Wear your day-pack in front and your main pack on your back, keeping your hands free.

- Highway robberies occur in certain countries, almost always at night. Avoid taking night buses if possible, though if you must, go on the fastest, most direct one.

SCAMS

Scam artists are working all through Latin America and hundreds of travellers write to us every year to report the latest con. In response, crooks are always adapting their scams, transporting them across borders and generally devising new ways to rip off the unsuspecting. Talk to other travellers about the newest scams on the street. Some scams target the greedy. If your first thought is, 'This is too good to be true!', then it probably is. More often in Latin America, travellers are victimised during their search for a dream adventure, signing up for tours that don't exist, for example. Women are particular targets, but everyone will benefit from knowing the latest scams.

- Impersonating a police officer is an easy way for petty criminals to intimidate foreign tourists into handing over some money. In Ecuador, the current trend is for thieves to pose as drug enforcement officers. They show you an official-looking document and tell you they're collecting money from foreigners to stem the drug trade. A variation on this theme is the 'police officer' who asks to see your passport and upon inspecting it informs you that a trip to the police station is necessary. He'll hail a taxi, you'll both get in and you'll be fleeced or the fake cop will confiscate your belongings as evidence. A different form of this scam involves another 'traveller' who readily complies with all the 'police officer' requests, adding an air of legitimacy to the proceedings. Don't be fooled – this 'traveller' is in on it. If you are stopped on the street, the officer should be in uniform and willing to produce identification when you request it.

Oiling the Wheels

To get a seat on the morning plane, I'd been reliably informed, I would have to bribe the booking clerk. Of course the word 'bribe' wasn't used – it never is. There are a thousand euphemisms for this very simple transaction. In Brazil, if a cop starts talking about buying some beers, it's not an invitation to the nearest bar, but an indication of how much money he wants. If he starts talking about his four kids and their school fees, you could be in big trouble.

But the next flight was in three days time, the tiny booking office was packed, and I was on a tight schedule. So the next question was ... How much? This is a question you shouldn't ask out loud.

The amount depends to some extent on what you expect the other party to provide – whether you want a visa extension, release from prison, or a multimillion dollar contract. Mercifully, most minor officials just want to supplement their meagre salary, and they don't bleed every case for all it's worth. Higher officials require larger amounts, partly because they can do bigger favours, but mostly because they aspire to higher standards of living. Officials of any kind can be greatly offended if they're offered a bribe and it's too small.

It was worth a lot to me to avoid three days in that Brazilian backwater, but my reliable local informant had told me that US$20 would be enough. A bribe is said to 'oil the wheels' of the bureaucratic machine, and the clerk spent an hour demonstrating how slowly the wheels moved without oil. While I waited, I double-checked that I had a crisp greenback in a discreetly conspicuous location. Bribes are usually payable in cash, and you should have the correct amount ready; if you inadvertently flash 500 pesos along with your drivers licence, a cop is unlikely to be happy with a 50 peso pay-off.

When I finally reached the ticket counter, it was an anticlimax. The clerk read my mind, the US$20 disappeared, and the boarding pass was in my hand.

It's easy. Everyone does it. Every day, in every walk of life, people choose between delay, inefficiency and frustration, or the quick, easy, and corrupt alternative. Sensible tourists will avoid unnecessary contact with Latin American officialdom, but those who breach byzantine traffic regulations, use remote border crossings, or need to file a police report may be asked to make a contribution. If you victimised, have some sympathy for Latin America's poorest, least powerful people, who must endure inconvenience and indignity because they don't have the dollars to oil the wheels – the people who didn't get a seat on the morning plane.

James Lyon
LP Author, Australia

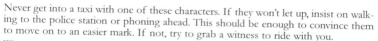

Never get into a taxi with one of these characters. If they won't let up, insist on walking to the police station or phoning ahead. This should be enough to convince them to move on to an easier mark. If not, try to grab a witness to ride with you.

- Women in particular should be aware of shady men posing as tour guides. The intent of these criminals is far beyond relieving you of cash and valuables. In the worse-case scenario, you take a tour with them and they drug you, rape you and leave you for dead. There have been credible reports of this sort coming out of Rurrenabaque, Bolivia specifically. Only sign up with reputable tour agencies that employ licensed guides. Each country has different requirements for accrediting guides, but if you ask to see a guide's licence and he doesn't show it to you, move on; do not be swayed by whatever story is offered as to why the licence can't be produced. Travelling to very remote areas is best done with a larger tour group. Get recommendations from other travellers.

- Smuggling is a very straightforward con where someone approaches or befriends you and asks you to take a package to their brother, cousin or uncle in whatever country you happen to be going to. Payment is promised upon delivery of the package. Then, you either get busted at customs by an official in on the scam and you're expected to pay him off, or you deliver the goods and never get paid. This con is a lot harder to detect when the person asking you to carry the package is a friend. As a policy, you should never agree to carry packages across borders for anyone.

- Real estate and business scams are popular with Panamanian and Costa Rican con men who see foreigners as an easy mark. You wouldn't enter into a business or real estate deal at home without having a lawyer peruse the pertinent documents, so don't do it abroad. If it's a legitimate deal, the players will have no problem with you consulting a lawyer.

NATURAL DISASTERS & WILD ANIMALS

Unpredictable forces of nature are perhaps more dangerous than crime because they are hard to prepare for and impossible to deter. Mexico and Central and South America cover a huge area and host all sorts of natural disasters including flash floods, earthquakes, hurricanes and volcanic eruptions. Add to this dangerous wild animals such as snakes, poisonous insects, large, belligerent mammals and sea creatures and it can seem like a pretty scary place. However, the percentage of travellers that are anywhere near these occurrences or in direct contact with dangerous wildlife is extremely small. Take precautions, follow your common sense and conduct some research and you're extremely unlikely to be part of that percentage.

Hurricanes – June to November is the hurricane season on the Central American coast. Unless you're caught in the middle of one, you have little to worry about. With hurricanes you get plenty of advance warning, so if one is approaching the coast, move inland to higher ground. Transportation systems can be disrupted for a time after a hurricane hits, so you may have to adjust your itinerary. Hurricanes often knock down power lines and damage potable water supplies; stockpile food and water if a hurricane is moving in. It's worth researching whether Central America is experiencing a particularly bad hurricane season during your proposed travel time. A good place for all your hurricane research needs is the FEMA Tropical Storm Watch web site (www.fema.gov/fema/trop.htm), which has the latest news and forecasts.

Rip tides – At least 160 people die every year in Costa Rica from rip tides and you should be very aware of these powerful currents that seemingly sweep you out to sea. In fact, rip tides don't kill people; swimmers caught in rip tides panic and drown. If you find yourself in a rip tide (you'll know it because the harder you try to swim in, the faster you'll be swept out), don't thrash about trying to fight your way through it. Relax, float, take some deep breaths and let the rip take you out past the breakers. These currents won't take you out to sea and once you float out of it, you can then swim in to shore at a 45° angle. Mentally, it is difficult to grasp that you have to go further out to sea to get back in, but that's the way it works. Hailing a nearby swimmer with a floatable device like a surfboard also works, but only if they're willing to rescue you. Often, you can see rip tides from the shore because they come in at odd angles, creating perpendicular waves. Ask about local conditions before swimming.

Volcanoes – Latin America is a hotbed of geothermic action: there are active volcanoes in Mexico, Costa Rica, Guatemala, Nicaragua, El Salvador, Bolivia, Chile, Colombia and Ecuador. Check with local authorities as to how active particular volcanoes are. If a large eruption threatens, don't stand around checking it out.

Earthquakes – Latin America sits on several terrestrial and submarine tectonic plates that get frisky every once in a while, causing great devastation. If a big one hits, the safest place to be (aside from the other side of the world) is in a doorway or under a sturdy table. Don't go outside as you risk being hit by falling debris or collapsing buildings. Fires and tsunamis can follow earthquakes, so remain alert after the shaking has stopped. Earthquakes can damage buildings and threaten water and food supplies. Check with authorities before heading into an area recently hit by a quake.

Floods – The weather phenomenon known as El Niño periodically rocks Latin America with floods and other attendant disasters. El Niño hangs around from November to about March and if it's been a particularly bad year roads may be destroyed, accommodation razed and travel difficult. Floods often follow other disasters such as earthquakes and hurricanes as well. You will usually have enough advance notice to get out of the area in this case.

Dangerous animals – If you're trekking off the trodden path, you may meet up with some unwelcome creatures. These can include irate peccaries in Costa Rica, sharks in Ecuador, scorpions in Brazil, jaguars in Suriname and the Guianas, crocodiles in Venezuela and deadly snakes just about anywhere. Add to this list bedbugs, lice, leeches, ticks, chiggers and all sorts of other parasitic bugs and you get the idea. The chances of being attacked by a wild animal are very slim indeed, though you'll want to take appropriate precautions.

DRUGS

You probably already know that extraordinary quantities of illegal drugs are grown, processed and shipped throughout Latin America in an effort to satisfy the worldwide demand for more potent and frequent highs. From common farmers to presidents of nations, drugs are part of the shadow culture in many of these countries and you do not want to be involved. If you're caught with illegal drugs or even with drugs that are legal in one country (eg coca leaves in Peru) and illegal in another (eg Brazil), you are bound for jail, and it could cost you a lot of money to get out (if you do get out). You'd be surprised how many gringos are sitting out middle age in Latin American jails.

Trying to buy drugs is one of the most ignorant travel moves you can make. Locals will set you up and knock you down; it's just way too easy. Either you'll be buying from an undercover cop or you'll be buying from a dealer in the employ of the cops. Bribing your way out of a drug possession or (even worse) smuggling charge will cost you plenty. Another popular drug-related scam involves a stranger coming over and chatting you up. Once the stranger departs, the police approach you and demand money to not arrest you for talking to that 'drug dealer' who is nowhere to be seen. A variation on this theme is having drugs planted on you and then having to bribe the police to let you go.

Other travellers or locals may try to use you as a 'mule' to carry drugs or other illegal items across international borders. People may approach you with a mule opportunity or they may just hide parcels of drugs in your pack. Do not accept packages from anyone and check your bag carefully before boarding planes or crossing borders.

For information on the health risks associated with drug use, see the Drugs & Alcohol section in the Health chapter.

OTHER HAZARDS

There are plenty of other potential hazards, but you're unlikely to encounter them if you keep your head on straight, do some research and observe simple precautions. Still, we'd be remiss if we didn't mention just a few more things:

Guerrilla activity – Internal political turmoil is practically a cottage industry in Latin America and though things have quietened down a bit, there are still hot spots. Mexico and Colombia experience flare-ups and insurgent groups are still operating in Peru and Guatemala. Colombian guerrilla groups have begun to target foreigners, so you'll want to research the current situation before heading there; use extreme caution and don't get too far off the beaten track. In other countries, you should have no problems with insurgent activity.

Bus hold-ups – There are certain routes favoured by bandits who ambush buses and then rob the passengers. These robberies usually occur on long-haul, night-time buses, so travel during the day whenever possible and avoid the dangerous routes. If you are ambushed, hand everything over. Nothing material is worth your life.

Riots & transport stoppages – Most Latin American economies are less than healthy, and fluctuations in world prices and markets can hit these nations hard. Currency devaluation and austerity measures like gasoline price hikes and wage freezes can send people to the streets protesting, sometimes violently. Labour strikes and transportation disruptions are not uncommon and can affect travel. Keep abreast of economic developments in the countries you plan to visit and adjust your itinerary accordingly if riots are afoot.

Traffic accidents – Buses go over cliffs, pedestrians get hit crossing the street and taxis smash into each other in a race to get through intersections. Be very aware in cities about traffic lights, pedestrian crossings, and stop signs and how drivers respond, if at all, to these attempts to regulate their driving. Too often it's a free-for-all, with foreign backpackers at the bottom of the heap. Look both ways and be careful when stepping into the street! Drunk driving is a chronic problem in some countries and the idea that alcohol and vehicular machinery don't mix is not an integral part of the Latino sensibility. Don't ever ride with a drunk driver.

ANNOYANCES

Here's another book idea, for there are so many annoyances that listing them would mean penning a tome. Here are the leaders:

Shoeshine boys – You can't imagine how much you'll be pestered to have your shoes shined. If you are wearing leather footwear, it will sparkle because eventually, you have to give in. The shoeshine boys are like a trickle of water eroding a canyon.

Noise – It's not only noise, it's deafening and it's everywhere. In the market, at hotels, in restaurants and in the room next door. Silence is simply not appreciated in this part of the world and you'll be lucky to find any. Create some by wearing earplugs; wadded up toilet paper or cigarette filters work too.

Pollution – Buses burping diesel, locals throwing trash out windows, and open gutters can be nauseating, but there isn't much you can do about it. In some cities (eg Mexico City, Lima and Guayaquil), air pollution can be particularly bad and aggravating to sinuses, asthma, eyes and throat. Move to the country or the beach if the fumes are choking you or wear a kerchief or surgical mask around your mouth and nose.

Sneezing openly – Watch when someone goes to sneeze because mucous may be flying your way. Handkerchiefs and covering one's nose and mouth are not customary, so sneezing people let the airborne germs run wild.

Toilet issues – Toilet seats are a novelty in the less developed areas of Latin America and you should take care not to fall in. Plumbing is rarely what you're used to at home and the wastebasket by the toilet is for used paper, tampons and sanitary pads. In short, nothing can go into a toilet except human waste – the rest goes in the little pink basket in the corner. This can get unsanitary and downright gross in heavily trafficked communal toilets, so check out the shared bathroom before agreeing to rent a room.

IF YOU DO GET INTO TROUBLE ...

If something goes horribly wrong during your trip, shake off the shock as quickly as you can so you'll be able to assess your options. Making decisions and being proactive on your own behalf will go a long way towards restoring your balance and psychological wellbeing. Enlist other travellers or bystanders in your time of need; don't be too proud, we all need help occasionally and this may be that time for you. People will meet the challenge, with complete strangers offering to help you out.

If you have been the victim of a crime, including a robbery, go immediately to the police and file a report. Lost passports, insurance claims and stolen travellers cheques all require police reports so go to the local precinct first. Don't expect the criminal to be caught, but file the report for your own peace of mind and insurance purposes.

If your passport is lost or stolen, you'll have to visit your embassy or consulate directly after the police. Your embassy can issue a new passport, advise you on local laws, refer you to a translator, doctor or lawyer and contact family back home in case of an emergency. It will not lend you money, bail you out of jail or pay for your flight home (except in extraordinary circumstances).

WHILE YOU'RE THERE ▶▶

Between the glory and tragedy in life lies the mundane, and travelling is no exception. When you're not scaling mountaintops, running wild rapids and making exciting new friends, you will have to perform some tedious daily chores. Providing food, transportation, shelter and entertainment for yourself every day is no easy task, but there are ways to make it easier and even enjoyable. This section sheds light on finding good accommodation and meals, plus advice on getting around efficiently.

Accommodation

Unless you hole up in the local travellers guesthouse for six weeks, accommodation will be your most pressing daily concern. Obviously, you'll stay more than one night in hostels you like, but there will still be a lot of room-hunting in your travels. There are some really terrifying 'hotels' in Latin America (drug runners and lice are only half the story) but there are many more places that are clean, cheap and lovely. Following is advice on how to tell the difference between these two extremes, and how to settle in comfortably and securely once you're handed the key.

TYPES OF ACCOMMODATION

From rustic to regal, Latin America has all types of accommodation. You'll find cosmopolitan five-star hotels, luxurious resorts and secluded hideaways for top-end jet-setters. There are also campgrounds, hammocks on the beach and refuges tucked deep within national parks. Then there's everything in between, where you will be amazed at how the quality jumps when you spend just a few extra dollars. Not only do your options become cleaner and more comfortable, you get more amenities (like a private bathroom) or more atmosphere, like a patio amid lush gardens. In Tegucigalpa, Honduras for example, you can get a cot in a box for around US$2 and be serenaded by skittering cockroaches, or you can spend US$4 for a modern room with a private bath and take your breakfast in the hotel cafe downstairs. If you spend US$8, you're truly living the high life and can expect a room with bath, telephone, cable TV, free coffee, the works. Keep in mind that Tegucigalpa is the Honduran capital; things will get considerably cheaper once you're out exploring the countryside.

Although searching for a room can be tiresome and tiring, try to drum up the extra energy to find a place you'll enjoy, rather than staying in the conveniently located but generic hotel next to the bus terminal (unless you have a very early bus). A great hotel room can make all the difference to your attitude, experiences and memory of a place. If these types of rooms are not available or finding one is not practical, get out and explore, returning just to sleep, pack up and move on.

Guesthouses

Called *hospedajes* or *casas de huéspedes* (guesthouses), these are ubiquitous and cheap throughout Mexico and Central and South America, and you'll probably be staying in them a lot. These can be family homes in which a few rooms have been converted to accommodate paying guests or whole buildings designed specifically for this purpose. If you're anywhere near the Gringo Trail, folks at hospedajes will be knowledgeable in the ways of tourists, often speak foreign languages and may offer services like locked luggage compartments, safety deposit boxes, laundry, and perhaps fax, phone and email. These are good places to hook up with other travellers, as there is usually a common room or restaurant.

Although the entrance areas and garden may be delightful, don't expect anything fancy in the room itself: a bed, table and chair, and maybe a sink or fan if you're lucky. In a concession to foreign customs, hospedajes may have rooms with private bathrooms, but you will pay more for these. Normally, you will share a shower and toilet down the hall with several other guests. Things to look for include cleanliness, a window that opens, a firm bed (they can be

'Real' Travellers

Spend enough time on the road and you'll definitely run into a few 'real' travellers. These are people who think they've been everywhere there is to go, done everything there is to do, and seen everything there is to see. More importantly, they like to think they did it the right way (read: the hard way). The problem with 'real' travellers (who invariably seem to be men) is that not only do they insist on boring you with their tales of derring-do, but they tend to look down their noses at other travellers.

If you tell them you're going, say, to Quetzaltenango in Guatemala, they'll say you shouldn't bother – the place was good 10 years ago, but it's a total bust today. They know a better hidden indigenous village in El Salvador that you can only get to by mule. Of course they won't tell you where it is, because that would ruin the spot. Likewise, if you say you're staying near Puno on the Peruvian shores of Lake Titicaca, they'll tell you the place is strictly for tourists, a 'real' traveller wouldn't go near there. They know a much better place in the middle of the lake where the rent is free, everyone plays an instrument and the fish grow on trees. Again, they can't tell you where it is since that would attract the wrong sort of people.

You'll find that 'real' travellers like to think of themselves as Stanley or Livingston types pushing out alone into untrammelled wilderness, where no westerner has been before (an unlikely situation these days). Oddly enough, the only place you seem to meet 'real' travellers is in the travellers ghettos, like Ecuador's New Town or Antigua in Guatemala. Of course, they're only passing through – they wouldn't dream of spending too much time in such places.

The point is that your trip need not be a gruelling test of survival. Nor is it a competition to find the last untouched spot in the country. If that's what you're after, fine. But there's nothing wrong with seeing the famous sights of a region (along with everyone else) or treating yourself to some luxury. And don't let yourself be intimidated or belittled by these people; if you find that you can't stand the company of a 'real' traveller any longer, try telling them that you eat mostly at McDonald's, insist on air-con wherever you stay and wouldn't dream of travelling anything but 1st class. More than likely they'll quickly lose interest in you.

Adapted from Chris Rowthorn
LP Author, USA

quite saggy and lumpy in this part of the world), decent lighting (flourescents are far too popular), and proximity to the communal bathroom (which can be a good or bad thing depending on circumstances). Prices vary widely throughout the region, but you can expect to pay between US$3 and US$10 for accommodation like this. Solo travellers will pay almost as much as two, as there isn't much price difference between a single and double room.

Hotels

Hotel terms and distinctions get blurry as you cross borders, and anything from a brothel to an Intercontinental installation can be called a hotel. This section refers to cheap to mid-range hotels that are tailored more for local businesspeople and middle-class families than for foreign tourists. Still, these hotels can be a great bargain for travellers, and in mid-sized cities with few attractions they may be your only option. Clean, comfortable and safe are the hallmarks of this accommodation. Don't expect anything luxurious.

Hotels usually have different types of rooms with different amenities, and are priced accordingly. Basic rooms will have a fan and a shared bathroom, while the more upscale could have air-conditioning, cable TV, a private bathroom and telephone. Usually, the cheapest type of hotel room will suffice.

Hotel rooms also come in different sizes. You will have the choice of a single, double, triple and sometimes a quad or even bigger in hotels that accommodate families — common in beach towns where locals vacation. Singles and doubles are often one and the same, both equipped with a double bed. For this reason, solo travellers pay almost the same as two people. There are also doubles with two single beds. Triples, quads and larger rooms typically have a number of twin beds spread throughout a big room.

In the budget and mid-range brackets, hotels will cost anywhere from US$10 to US$20 in the cheaper countries, but expect to pay closer to US$30 in popular tourist areas and more developed nations such as Argentina and Chile. It pays to shop around both between and within hotels. One hotel similar in price and facade to its neighbour may offer dungeon-like rooms and surly employees, while next door there are light and airy rooms with a family atmosphere. If you like the hotel but not the room you're shown, ask to see another. This is perfectly acceptable and you might even specify what it is you're after: perhaps something cheaper, bigger or with a window is available.

Most Latin Americans are Catholic, and sometimes unmarried couples are turned away from hotels. This can be discouraging, but there isn't much you can do other than to move on to a different hotel or town altogether if the other accommodation options aren't appealing.

Some of the cheapest hotels in Latin America are actually brothels, and these can be good budget options if the location isn't too seedy. On the plus side, the communal shower is rarely used and it will be like having your own private bath. On the downside, there is a lot of foot traffic and it may be hard to sleep. These places typically rent rooms by the hour, so they may be reluctant to let a room for the entire night. If you do get a room for the night, make sure the sheets are clean. Solo women travellers may not feel comfortable staying in these hotels.

Hostels

Again, this term is bandied about when referring to many types of accommodation in Latin America, but here it refers to the youth hostels familiar to many budget travellers. *Albergues juveniles* (youth hostels) are rarely the cheapest option in this part of the world and with so many other budget choices, you probably won't stay in these very often. They usually offer beds in shared dormitory rooms or private rooms. The former share a communal bathroom, while the latter may have a private facility. A bed at a youth hostel is rarely the cheapest lodging available. Still, they typically have services and conveniences attractive to travellers, such as email, fax and telephone, bulletin boards, laundry and a restaurant. Your room may come with free breakfast, so ask, but if you'd rather forage for your own morning meal, ask for a lower room rate. Theft can be a problem in any communal rooming situation, so mind your stuff. For information on the Hostelling International (HI) card, see the Other Paperwork section in the Passports & Visas chapter.

Homestays

Staying with a local family is a great way to immerse yourself in the culture and language of your host country. There are organisations that arrange homestays, or you can wait for chance (sometimes known as desperation!) to intervene: you're stuck at the end of a track with nowhere to go and a family invites you into their home. Homestays can be fantastic, but beware of the pitfalls. Privacy will be very hard to come by and you will have to be on your best behaviour most of the time. Then there are families who treat you badly, use you as a maid or try to pair you off with their daughter. For every depressing homestay story though, there is one about the wonders of a local family, the emotional bonds everyone formed and the cultural appreciation gained by the foreign visitor. Check your guidebooks for homestay options,

It's Better to Give ...

It's common practice to offer a gift when staying with a local family (a homestay) during your travels. After all, you're basically getting a free – or very cheap – room and board, simply because the family is eager to meet foreign visitors. A thoughtful gift will go a long way towards showing your gratitude and will make your stay more rewarding and memorable for both you and your hosts. The best gift is something unique to your own country that is difficult or impossible to obtain in your host's country. Unfortunately, the things which best fit this description are often heavy or bulky – just imagine carting several bottles of your country's best wine around Latin America in your backpack. More probably, you'll have to improvise. Consider lighter, more compact items such as postage stamps, sports cards, phonecards, picture books or even coins. Of course, these go over best with the kids. In most parts of Latin America, adults will appreciate music cassettes, liquor (surprise!) and big league sports paraphernalia.

inquire at Spanish schools (see the Thematic Trips and Learning a Language sections in the Planning chapter) and check with local tourist offices.

Hammocks & Cabañas

On the beach and in other natural settings throughout Latin America, you can rent hammocks for the night or bring your own to sling between two trees. Usually the space to hang your hammock will be under a thatched-roof or lean-to type structure called a *palapa*. Hammock space can be an organised affair run by the proprietors of an adjacent guesthouse, or you could just approach a restaurant or family and inquire if hanging your hammock nearby is OK. Expect to pay between US$2 and US$5 for a rental hammock and space. Prices will be higher depending on where you are and the season.

Another accommodation option on the beach and occasionally in the forest are cabañas, or bungalows. These can be dirt-floor, thatched-roof arrangements or lovely bamboo honeymoon suites with private bath, mosquito netting and a balcony overlooking the grandeur of it all. Obviously, prices will reflect the type of amenities involved, but a basic beach cabaña should cost between US$5 and US$10.

Camping

Now you're talking! Camping is the best way to control your costs, while getting close to some real nature and wildlife. Having your roof and kitchen on your back frees up a whole range of options for exploring Latin America that fixed accommodation just can't offer. In certain countries (eg El Salvador), locals have never seen a tent and camping will be a challenge, as there are few campgrounds. Still, you can usually get permission from a local landowner to pitch camp for a nominal fee. In other places (eg Costa Rica, Argentina, Brazil and Chile), campgrounds are developed and have all the usual amenities. Camping does present certain security problems and carrying all that gear can be a trial, especially in the jungle. If you're keen to camp in Latin America, see Trekking in the Specialist Guides section in the Planning chapter for resources that can help you plan a successful trip.

Other Accommodation

There are so many places to lay your head for the night, you'll have to choose what you like best. The above options don't even begin to paint the whole picture. Other choices may include:

Refugios – These are cabins within national park boundaries where you can rent a bunk and cook your meals in a communal kitchen. Sometimes they are designed for backpackers, but more remote refugios are primarily for park employees; if there's a bunk, you can usually rent it. If you're doing a particularly long trek through a national park, food staples may be provided at cabins further afield.

Jungle lodges – Resorts by any other name, lodges are buried in remote rainforest and are usually only accessible by plane or boat. You'll find these almost anywhere there is reasonably dense jungle. All meals and lodging are included, although activities like guided hikes may cost extra. Some of these outfits are for rich folks who want to say they visited the Amazon, and cost at least US$150 a day. Others are genuine ecotourism projects that use only local materials and labour, conserve energy and resources and may have volunteer opportunities; these typically cost around US$40 a day.

Apartments – In some cities it's possible to rent short-stay apartments, and these can be a very good deal if you're in a group. Apartments have everything you'd expect: bathroom, bedrooms, kitchen and common area.

B&Bs, posadas & inns – This accommodation goes by different names throughout the region, but is usually lovely and costs around US$15 to US$30 per person. Often inns will be converted colonial houses and have amenities and charm to spare. Open courtyards, gardens, private balconies, patios, tasteful furniture, and romantic lighting and accents all contribute to the palatable atmosphere of Latin American inns. These make a good splurge when you need a rest from the Gringo Trail.

Casas de familia – Literally 'family houses', these can be a cheap and fun way to get the atmosphere of a homestay, but without the restrictions. In these houses, families rent rooms to tourists and will share laundry, kitchen and parking facilities with you. These are popular in Chile, Ecuador, Peru and Argentina, and cost from US$6 to US$12.

Motels – You'll find motels along major roads like the Panamerican and Interamericana highways. These rooms are good if you're on the road, but if you have the time and energy, you may want to find something with a little more character. In Brazil, motels are completely different and you can bet they have lots of character, as they're for short-stay couples. Rooms typically have mirrors on the ceiling and a vibrating bed.

FINDING THE RIGHT PLACE

Summoning up the energy to find any room – let alone a decent one – after a 13 hour crowded bus ride or while carrying a load on your back through a polluted, hot city will test anyone's mettle at some time or another. Still, a good night's sleep in a clean, comfortable room is a key to maintaining your mental and physical stamina while on the road. With a few tips and some practise, you'll have the room search down to a science, freeing up time to explore, relax and enjoy.

Other travellers and an up-to-date guidebook are the best places to start in your search for accommodation, and how reliable the recommendations are will become clear once you visit a few places. If the guidebook is inaccurate or doesn't correctly reflect your tastes or budget, ditch it and switch; there are many places to buy used guidebooks in the major cities, or trade with another traveller. Bulletin boards and English-language newspapers are other ways to discover hotels that haven't made it into the guidebooks or become trendy with the backpacking set.

Occasionally, taxi drivers will take you to a hotel. They may assume that you want a very fancy or expensive hotel, or take you to such a place because their commission will be larger. If you are stuck for a hotel recommendation and you decide to go with a taxi driver, make it very clear what you are looking for and how much you are willing to pay. In smaller towns, children may converge on you when you alight from the bus, offering to lead you to a hotel. You are expected to give them a small tip. In big cities, there are usually clusters of guesthouses catering to backpackers. Head to these 'backpackers ghettos' if you don't know where you want to stay.

The most effective tool you have for finding a good room is the ability to walk away from a place that doesn't suit your needs. With this strategy another, better room will miraculously become available in the same hotel, the price will drop dramatically on the room you just saw (making it worth your while) or you'll head to a different hotel and get a feel for what's available. Settling for the first room you see, unless you're bone-tired or there are other mitigating circumstances, is usually not the best policy. (Although spending half the day on a wild goose chase for a room isn't recommended either.) Searching for rooms is easier in pairs because one person can hunt while the other sits in a cafe with the bags.

Arriving in town before noon or as early in the morning as possible is a good idea because it broadens your options. Locals and foreigners who know the best places head there first, and rooms may go fast. If all the hotels in one area are full, head to another part of town. In the worst scenario, you may have to leave for another town altogether, or dent your budget by staying in a hotel of higher calibre and price.

Inspecting the Room

Do not rent a room without checking it out first. This is standard operating procedure; it would be pure folly to shell out money for something unseen. If you don't like the room you're shown, ask to see another. This can sometimes lead to a considerable upgrade. Things can get touchy if you're shown a couple of rooms but decline to stay at that hotel. Some proprietors will be insulted and even ask you to explain why you won't stay there. Remain polite and be reasonably honest, and they may try to accommodate your requests. Keep in mind that you never really know what a room has to offer until you spend a night, so the following are just guidelines:

Cleanliness – Look closely at the sheets and pillows to see if they're clean. If you can, peek at the mattress to see if any bugs are in evidence. Bedspreads are washed very infrequently, so look at them too. Check out the bathroom and shower. Notice if the toilet is clean and if the wastebasket for used toilet paper is empty.

Comfort – Sit on the bed and bounce a couple of times. Is it firm enough or lumpy? Does it sag in the middle or slope to one side? Some mattresses are cheap foam and will not provide a good night's sleep. How does the room or hotel smell? In Latin America kerosene is often used as a cleanser. This is very off-putting and you'll know it when you smell it.

Condition – Check that the light turns on, that the windows open, the water pressure in the shower is reasonable, and the fan or air-conditioning works. Water on the coast may be brackish, so run the taps.

Safety – Spend some time inspecting the window and door latches. Can you use your padlock if you want to? Can you lock the room from the inside? Windows – especially those that lead to balconies or fire escapes – should be lockable. Check that there is a way to escape in case of a fire.

Quiet – If the room is above a disco, near the lobby or faces the common area, there may be any combination of music, television noise or partying.

Holes – Holes in the walls or ceiling are sometimes used as peepholes to spy on guests, so plug them up if you can or move to another place. Some travellers have reported the use of mirrors to spy on guests.

Screens/mosquito net – Check that these are in good condition, to ensure you are not at risk of being bitten by mosquitoes while you are sleeping.

Useful items – An ashtray, garbage pail, or place you can hook up your clothes line are all handy.

Negotiating a Rate

When you're quoted a price, repeat it back and find out if there is any tax or surcharge involved. Make sure you find out if the price is per person or for the entire room. If there is a cafe or restaurant attached to the hotel, always ask if breakfast is included; complimentary breakfast may be standard and they're just neglecting to mention it or it may get thrown in during negotiations. Some places will ask you to pay upfront every day even if you plan to stay a while. This is fine, but get a receipt. In other places, you will settle the bill when you're ready to leave. In either case, you may want to write down the price you're quoted so as to avoid any problems later.

Depending on the country and season, the price may be open for negotiation. Even in places where there are posted rates, you may be able to bargain and it never hurts to try (for tips on bargaining, see the Money Matters chapter). The two best opportunities to negotiate for a room are in the low season and when you intend to stay more than three days. Ask if they have a cheaper room to get the discussion rolling. Walking away is surprisingly effective, and when they see you heading for the door, a lower price may be forthcoming. In the high season or classic tourist spots like Cancún in the Yucatán, hotels won't negotiate.

Checking In

At almost every hotel you'll be required to fill in a form with your pertinent information. This will include passport number, length of stay, occupation and the like. You may have to show your passport, but be on guard if you're asked to part with it, and request an explanation. If it seems reasonable, give them a photocopy, but not your actual passport, as it may get lost, stolen or sold. Offer other photo identification such as a youth or student card if they're adamant. If they want your passport as security against your unpaid bill, offer to leave a cash deposit and get a signed receipt. If they will take nothing short of your actual passport, get a signed receipt with a note about the visas contained in it.

In many hotels in Latin America, you are required to leave the key at the front desk, whether you're just stepping out for a minute or the whole day, to ensure you don't make copies of the key. While this is legitimate most of the time, some places are less than scrupulous and you may not want to leave the key with them. In this case, try to play ignorant and just walk out with the key in your pocket. If you really don't trust the place, take all your valuables with you.

Security

Keeping all your valuables safe may take some creativity. If the hotel you're staying in seems trustworthy (consult your guidebook and other travellers for leads) and it has a safety deposit box, use it to store your documents and travellers cheques. Get a signed receipt detailing everything you leave in the box and its value; keep out some spending money.

Not every hotel has a safety deposit box, and you may be in a city or area where hiding your valuables in your room is a better risk than carrying it around. Use your best judgement. Some ideas for stashing valuables include putting them in a plastic bag and storing them in the toilet tank, or taping them behind a picture or under the bed frame. If you're not sure if your room is secure, use your own lock.

You should lock your door from the inside before you go to bed. Make sure you can unlock the door quickly in case of fire. Locking your door from the inside will prevent late-night thieves or drunk revellers from coming into your room. If your door doesn't lock from the inside, place a chair in front of it or hang something from the doorknob that will make a racket if the door is opened; a tin cup or flashlight works well.

BATHROOMS & TOILETS

Bathrooms and toilets can be a particular shock in Latin America, and it's worth knowing what you could be in for.

Showers & Baths

If you're on a strict budget, most of your bathing experiences will be in shared facilities, though a few extra dollars will usually get you a room with a private bath anywhere in Latin America. Some places only have cold water, some turn on hot water for certain hours of the day, while other places have hot water round the clock. In the last case, this probably means the shower is equipped with one of the niftiest, yet scariest mechanisms of Latin American devising: the electric water heater. Hot water whenever you want or need it is a good idea. Exposed electrical wires, live current and running water are a decidedly bad idea. Most of the time, electric heaters are a treat because you can toggle between cold, luke-warm and hot settings to have a delicious shower. You should always wear rubber or plastic thongs (flip flops) when using one of these contraptions, as this will ground you in case of electrical shock. If the mechanism looks at all dicey, leave it off and brave the icy water or skip showering altogether. Public baths and bathing are rare in this part of the world, though languishing in hot springs for therapeutic purposes is common. Follow local customs regarding nudity in these situations.

Toilets

Except in the most rustic accommodation, squatting over a hole won't be necessary in Latin America, as indoor plumbing has become the norm. Still, that plumbing leaves a lot to be desired and nowhere in the region should you throw paper or anything else in the toilet unless it specifically says it's OK to do so. Signs posted near toilets will read something like: 'Please: gringo, no paper in the bowl!', or conversely: 'Put paper in toilet for hygiene, thank you'. Wastepaper baskets are supplied for discarding used toilet paper. When there is no receptacle, there will be piles of the stuff at your feet. Most guesthouses will make efforts to empty the baskets regularly, but this isn't always the case. Check the communal bathroom before you rent a room.

Never assume because there is a toilet that there is paper, since usually there isn't. You should always have your own stash. Sometimes there is a person posted at the door of public restrooms selling squares of paper. Whether you need them or not, you're expected to pay to use the bathroom. Public toilets may be few and far between, but most restaurants and bars will let you use their bathroom if you ask politely. Established bus terminals typically have decent bathrooms. More rudimentary bus stations may have a trough for men to urinate, but not much else. Here are some more tips:

- In all of Latin America, use facilities when you get the chance – you don't know when you'll next have the opportunity.
- If you're hiking or camping, try to use established toilets. Otherwise, go at least 50m from a water source or trail, and burn or bury both your waste and toilet paper.
- Public urination for men is fairly common in Latin America, though on long bus rides you'll see men, women and children squatting at an impromptu pit stop. Ankle-length skirts are handy here.
- If you're in a city and need a bathroom, international fast-food chains are the places to go. You'll look completely in place heading in and out and the bathrooms are usually clean.
- In some countries, *baño* refers to the place where you bathe, while *servicio* refers to the toilet.

Food

According to the old saying, when you get tired of rice and beans, switch to beans and rice. While there is some spectacular food in Latin America, you're going to be living on staples a lot of the time. Most of it is more interesting than just beans and rice, however, and you should make an effort to search out food that will challenge your palette. Fried guinea pig in the Andes and fried ants in Colombia are ambitious goals to shoot for.

Markets are good places to familiarise yourself with foodstuffs, especially among the rows of unidentifiable fruits and vegetables. In many countries, these fruits and vegies are blended into juices and shakes and are a refreshing, vitamin-packed introduction to regional flavours. Street food is popular and a good way to sample local cooking on the cheap. Many illnesses are blamed on improper or unhygienic preparation of such food, however, so you should use your judgement when eating on the street (see Everyday Health in the Health chapter for information on food and waterborne diseases). Don't be afraid to try new things, especially local specialities – you don't have to know the word for the delicious-looking morsel on your neighbour's plate, just point.

LOCAL FOOD

Eating local dishes is cheap and expands your horizons. Food is one of the easiest introductions to a new culture and you should embrace it. Of course there will be times when you crave a hamburger and you can indulge that whim, but the bulk of your day-to-day eating will be local. And once in a blue moon you may go hungry because while you thought you'd ordered soup, you ended up with a plate of pig's feet. Roll with it and just put it down to experience!

Thorough guidebooks will have sections on a country's cuisine and eating customs, and information on ordering food. The very best books will have a bilingual list of dishes, with descriptions, that you can consult in a restaurant. The vocabulary section of the book should have simple phrases useful in restaurants such as 'I am a vegetarian' or 'What do you recommend?' See the Ordering Meals section later in this chapter for more details. Remember that guidebooks only offer suggestions and you should not hesitate to branch out and find restaurants not included in your guidebook.

Almost everywhere in Latin America, you will find 'set meals' that are filling and dirt cheap. *Comida corrida* or *plato del día* in Mexico and Central America, *el menú* in Ecuador and *prato do dia* in Brazil – whatever you call it, it's a heaping pile of food usually served in the middle of the day for a dollar or two. Sometimes it's prefaced by soup and punctuated with a dessert, but the main course is set and consists of a starch (yucca, plantain or, most likely, rice), beans and a fish or meat dish. Look for cheap eateries crammed with local office workers at lunchtime and you'll have discovered the place for a good set meal.

Ask staff at your guesthouse or other travellers for restaurant suggestions. Friendly strangers on the street can also have good advice on where to eat. Make it clear to locals that you're interested in local food, or you may be directed to a KFC. Expats are a good source for food and drinks tips as well.

Places to Eat

From the swank restaurant in the five star hotel to the open-air beach restaurant, there is no shortage of eateries in this part of the world. In some countries you'll eat a roasted chicken at a sidewalk table in the city for lunch and be at the beach hand-picking your fish for dinner. Here are some of the types of places you'll probably eat at your travels:

Comedores – Literally 'dining rooms', these are basic, local eateries where you'll find cheap set meals and sometimes à la carte menu items as well.

Chifas – There will be many a night when these ubiquitous Chinese food restaurants save you from a growling belly. Chinese labour was imported to Latin America in the wake of slavery, and the prevalence of Chinese restaurants here reflects that. Chifas are typified by large portions and many vegetarian options.

Street vendors – From snacks to drinks, and from fruit to entire meals, street food is always cheap and can be good. Be careful of ill-prepared street food; it's best to patronise a busy vendor.

Hotels – Fairly cheap hotels usually have cheap eats and fancy hotels can be a treat when you're feeling a bit ragged. Look for ones with a buffet style menu or cheap set meals.

Markets & Self-Catering

Markets are the heartbeat of a country, and you'll learn a lot about a culture by visiting the local *mercado*. Latin American markets are divided into sections (eg meats over here, spices over there, cheeses someplace else) and there's always a dining section. Here rough benches or stools are lined up in front of a counter. You can usually see what each stall is serving for the day; for safety's sake, look for clean stalls and stay away from meat dishes, as meat is rarely refrigerated properly at the market. Steer clear also of stalls that leave food out waiting to serve it (see Everyday Health in the Health chapter for more details).

Plan a picnic and shop in the market to get a taste of local produce. You can buy cheap utensils, plates and almost anything else you'll need for preparing a meal at the market. Cheese, bread, fruits and nuts are good starters. Cooking for yourself is a great way to cut costs and make new friends by inviting them over for a meal. Try to stay in a hostel or family house that extends kitchen privileges. Campers will want to have their own stove, though other basic cooking gear is for sale at bargain prices in local markets.

Vegetarians in Latin America

Eating well (or at all) in Latin America will depend on the strictness of your vegetarian diet. Problems arise the further off the beaten track you roam, and if you forego fish or meat by-products such as bullion. On the more popular tourist routes there are vegetarian restaurants galore and you should have no problem finding them with the help of a good guidebook. Awareness about vegetarian diets and the benefits of certain local grains (eg quinoa) and proteins (soya) is on the rise; if you explain your dietary preferences, someone will at least make an attempt to whip something up. It may too often be rice, beans and eggs, so vitamin supplements or your own periodic trips to the market for nuts, fruit and grains should be incorporated into your travels to avoid deficiencies. Vegans will face tougher hurdles than vegetarians and should anticipate doing a lot of their own cooking while on the road.

Ordering Meals

You could eat only at western-style restaurants or the places where someone speaks English, but eventually the scents wafting from a food cart will be too intoxicating to ignore any longer. You'll face the vendor who doesn't speak a word of English and have to figure out how to get that delicious-looking morsel from his brazier into your hand. Here are some tips for ordering in challenging food situations:

- Point at what you want. Food is easy because you can see it before you commit. Point to it, hand over a bit of cash (see what the locals are paying first) and it's yours.
- In restaurants, pointing works too. Look at what other people are having, and if it looks appetising, point at it.
- Use your guidebook. The writers have been there, ordering the goat's-head soup when what they wanted was a fried steak. A good book will have a list of dishes in both English and the local language.

- Learn a few important phrases from your guidebook, including 'What do you recommend?', 'Is there a set meal today?' or 'Can I take this to go?'. Memorise the names of some dishes.

- Ask at your guesthouse for restaurant recommendations and names of local dishes. You may learn the best place to get a secret speciality. Write this information down.

- Leaving food on your plate can be touchy and in some cases insulting. Still, if health or other concerns dictate you shouldn't eat it, ask if you can take it to go.

- Find out what things cost before ordering. Sometimes prices aren't listed, and you don't want to learn that the terrible meal you just ate cost four times what you expected.

WESTERN FOOD

There will come a time, no matter how you try to ward it off, when you can't stomach another plate of rice and beans. Whereas food in Latin America is filling and hot sauces and chillies can add a lot of zing, your palette will need a change of pace every so often. Some people crave a big green salad, for others it's pizza or omelettes. You'll find there's a travellers prejudice about chowing down at Pizza Hut or McDonald's, as though you're not fit for the road if you eat in these places. Ironically, this bias doesn't extend to the many restaurants catering to foreign backpackers in travellers ghettos, where you can get bacon, eggs, bagels and a cup of Earl Grey for breakfast, and the most popular item on the dinner menu is a vegie burger with Swiss cheese. You are travelling to have fun and if that means eating a Big Mac with fries every once in a while, go for it and the critics be damned.

Fast food is fairly common in Latin America, though a few countries are still spared McDonald's. KFC is everywhere, which is somewhat peculiar because throughout the region you can get delicious chicken roasted over an open fire for low prices. Western-style fast-food restaurants are usually not inexpensive; you can expect to pay double or even triple what you'd pay for a local set meal.

Larger cities have restaurants specialising in cuisine from Italy, France, Japan and just about anywhere else. These places can be very expensive, so check out the prices before sitting down. A selection of international cuisine will be available in destinations popular with backpackers. In these towns, guesthouses often have small restaurants serving pizzas, pasta, sandwiches, hamburgers and the like. You may want to eat here just for the convenience, but you'll usually pay for it. These places are good for breakfast, especially if it's included in the price of the room.

Drinks

Even the drinks are exotic when you're on the road, and Latin America has a wealth of delicious and bizarre potables. Experiment with your drink choices and don't be shy about asking what's in particular concoctions; this will allow you to try and replicate them at home.

WATER

To increase your chances of staying healthy while on the road, don't drink the water. In Argentina and Chile it's OK to drink tap water, but elsewhere you'll want to buy bottled water or purify drinking water yourself (see Everyday Health in the Health chapter for more information). Bottled water, both carbonated and still, is widely available and cheap. In areas where the water supply is really suspect, you may opt to brush your teeth with bottled water and skip any vegetables or fruits you haven't washed or peeled yourself. Also be wary of ice.

COFFEE

Even though some of the best coffee in the world is grown in Latin America, most of it is exported and only the dregs are available locally. Instant coffee is very popular as a result. In most places, you can get a cup of percolated coffee but it may take some time to figure out how to order it. Coffee culture differs in individual countries and you may have to do some investigative work, pointing and discussing before a waiter will understand that you want a cup of drip coffee with milk.

SOFT DRINKS

There is no shortage of sodas in Latin America, from the multinational brands like Coca-Cola, Sprite and Fanta to national brands like Inca Kola in Peru and Bimbo in Ecuador. Throughout Latin America, soft drinks come in bottles, which are more expensive than the liquid they contain. Rarely can you take a bottle with you, so you have to drink it there. Alternatively, for taking away, drinks can be decanted into a plastic bag and a straw inserted.

FRUIT DRINKS

These are fresh, cheap and widely available in Latin America, so take advantage of them. Fruit drinks can come straight up, mixed with water or whipped up with milk. If they have water in them, make sure it's purified water. This can be a concern if you're buying fruit drinks from a street or market vendor.

ALCOHOLIC BEVERAGES

You won't have trouble finding a beer when you want one. Each country has national breweries and while some can be light and watery, Mexican beers like Negro Modelo will hit the dark beer spot. You'll be able to get imports in cities and tourist destinations, but not elsewhere. Wine is fantastic and cheap in Argentina, and Chile also has world-renowned wines. Elsewhere wine is scarce and expensive. Hard liquor and local moonshine is usually available wherever you go.

Sightseeing

Sightseeing styles follow many beats, and you'll develop your own rhythm once you're comfortable in a new destination. Some people like to map out a daily sightseeing schedule in an effort to squeeze it all in, while others prefer to wander around and stumble across sights in their travels. Most likely you'll be somewhere between the two. Don't feel like you have to sightsee everyday; if it's too hot or your energy is sapped, relax with a good book and write some postcards. You'll need this time out every once in a while.

If you only have a short time in a place that has many attractions, do some planning. Over drinks the night before or after dinner with a cup of coffee are good ways to unwind from the day's activities while planning the next. Check out your guidebook, solicit input from other travellers and locals, and plan an itinerary giving your top spots priority. If you're travelling with friends, compromises will have to be hammered out as each person's interests vie for dominance. Splitting up for the day sometimes works if a consensus can't be reached. Guesthouses and local travel agencies catering to backpackers often have day tours designed to see area highlights. This can be a good alternative if logistics for getting to a sight are convoluted, or if you want to split off from your travelling companions for the day.

You might consider hiring a guide or driver to maximise a day's sightseeing opportunities. This is a good way to cover significant distances, while getting local insight into an area. If you are with a group, you'll find this very affordable in many spots in Latin America. If you're travelling solo, try to hook up with other independent travellers interested in checking out the same sights and hire a guide and driver.

OFF THE BEATEN TRACK

Getting off the Gringo Trail takes a bit of effort, as the track has been well tramped by many decades of independent travellers making their way around Latin America. From Playa del Carmen on Mexico's Yucatán Peninsula to Punta Arenas in Patagonia, foreign backpackers have been there and done that. They'll be there when you're there too and it's all too easy to stick only to the Gringo Trail. You can speak English, eat like you do at home and have cultural experiences no more stimulating than watching the local women wash their clothes in the river below your guesthouse. If this starts happening, think of all the money you spent on your air fare, get on a bus and go see the country you've worked so hard to get to.

Better yet, go someplace the bus doesn't go. Try trekking in, hiring a canoe, or get off at the end of the line and flagging down a car or horse. Opportunities abound in Latin America because there is so much wilderness. The Chaco frontier of the Southern Cone, the Amazonian rainforest, the mysterious indigenous communities tucked away in Central America: if you set out to explore, you will be rewarded with inspiring sights, sounds and experiences. You'll have to work to get to these places and others more remote, and few people make the effort. Tourist infrastructure, from roads to hotels, are in short supply in the Latin American wilds, so be prepared for a challenge.

The easiest way to step off the beaten track is to go someplace not listed in the guidebooks or hop on a rickety bus without knowing the final destination. Nervous and excited, you'll have no idea if there will be hotels and restaurants at the other end or if the place is even worth a visit. Maybe it was purposely left out of the guidebook! But you will be guaranteed to see and experience a way of life, with friendly, curious locals checking you out, that is just not possible in the cities or travellers ghettos.

Another way to get off the beaten path is to visit countries less popular with the backpacking set. Usually these are the places with few tourist services or that are recovering from violence or unrest. Though Colombia is one such place, it's not recommended because foreigners are targets for kidnapping and murder, so cross Colombia off your list until things cool down. Rather, check out safer destinations with less infrastructure like El Salvador, Nicaragua, Panama, Bolivia or the Guianas, if you want to blaze your own trail.

Fewer crowds and lower prices make travelling in the off season another attractive proposition. If you want to minimise your gringo interaction while on the road, plan your trip for this time, but also realise that you could experience the worst weather the region has to offer. Still, a deserted Machu Picchu in a thunderstorm may be more your speed than tourists swarming over every bit of the ruins on a bright sunny day.

Jumping on a bus to an unknown destination may not be your style, or you may want to build up to it. You can get your feet wet off the beaten track by visiting an outlying suburb from your base city as a day trip.

Off-Road Travel

Travelling isn't really the right word to describe making your way around hidden Guatemala without a guidebook. Groping might be more appropriate, and my travelling buddy and I did lots of that after we caught wind of a 'backdoor route' to the Tikal ruins. We weren't even thinking about guerrillas, though it should have crossed our minds considering how remote we were.

We took buses until there were no more to take, and trucks until they ran out too, and ended up stranded on a dirt track where a motorised vehicle hadn't been seen for a week. It wasn't long before the village children started peeking out of their mud huts to get a look at two very dirty and unmistakably lost foreign people standing by the side of the road. After about 45 minutes of contemplating our options, the sky opened in a fury. Rain as hard as hail pelted us and the foraging pig nearby. We ran to an abandoned hut and stood under the thatched eaves in a failed attempt to stay dry.

After a few minutes we were drenched. While we checked out the kids across the way and they us, a young woman in traditional Mayan clothes ran towards us. She spoke no Spanish, but with a series of hand signals indicated we should come to her house. We accepted gratefully. Eventually the rain stopped and we met everyone in the village, as even the elders couldn't ignore their curiosity for long and came out one by one to meet us. Everyone spoke a Mayan dialect, so we had to find other ways to communicate. My travelling partner's clarinet was a wonder to all the young Mayans, who we surmised had never heard one before. Scores of villagers packed into the small hut and stared fascinated at the popcorn we popped on their wood stove in the centre of the room. For a lack of lids, popcorn flew around wildly, but it was a delight to introduce them to a new by-product of one of their daily staples.

Finally, all the villagers returned to their own homes and the matriarch insisted we take her bed for the night, though we flatly refused. After some vehement hand gestures, we came to understand she wouldn't take no for an answer. She built and stoked an open fire in the middle of the hut and bid us goodnight. We never did make it to Tikal, but my time with the Mayan family in the village for which I have no name will stay with me forever.

Conner Gorry
LP Author, USA

Hazards

Don't let naivety be your downfall once you've summoned the courage to get off the beaten track; there are some real dangers in remote regions and you'll benefit from being aware of them. Armed insurgents can be a problem in Mexico, Guatemala, Peru and, especially, Colombia. In fact, if Colombia is on your itinerary, we strongly suggest you do not veer from the tourist trail, as violent attacks on foreigners are a growing concern. Unexploded landmines in countries recovering from civil war (eg El Salvador) mean you should consult local authorities before traipsing off.

If you're going into very remote areas, you'll need the equipment and expertise to handle certain situations. Foreign language skills are the key. You may want to hire a guide if you don't speak the language or if the area is particularly difficult to navigate, such as the overland crossing from Panama to Colombia. Notifying your embassy of your itinerary is a good idea. If you go missing, it will be able to provide help and notify family and friends back home. Camping is a great way to get away from the travellers ghettos, but presents its own hazards. No matter how isolated you may feel, never assume there is no human habitation nearby. Be especially careful in drug-producing regions, as traffickers will not think twice before reducing you to just a memory. For more information on dangers while on the road, see Hazards & Safeguards in the Issues & Attitudes chapter.

Shopping

Shopping is a good way to hone bargaining skills, check out markets, meet locals and pick up some fantastic souvenirs. There are exquisite handcrafts for sale in Latin America, but there is a lot of awful kitsch as well. Your choices will depend on your style and sense of humour, but regardless of your taste, if you want special souvenirs, you'll find them in Latin America.

There are two basic categories of souvenirs for sale: those produced for tourists and those produced for locals. Tourist crafts will cost more, but you'll probably have a broader range of choices. Still, the quality of the goods won't be any better, so you'll save money and have more fun shopping in local shops and markets than in the souvenir malls sprinkled throughout big cities. Bargaining is also more prevalent in local shops and markets, so you'll be able to strike deals by negotiating and buying several items from the same merchant (see Bargaining in the Money Matters chapter for haggling tips). Also bear in mind that when you buy in markets, more profit usually goes directly to the artisan.

Shopping around and consulting your guidebook for advice will help you to discern between good and shoddy workmanship. Buying pre-Columbian art in Latin America is not for the novice, as you may be ripped off or buy fakes. It is also illegal in many countries to import or export pre-Columbian antiquities regardless of their authenticity. To be safe, stick to clothing, jewellery, musical instruments, folk art and day-to-day items unavailable at home (eg *mate bombillas*, or Mexican hot chocolate stirrers).

One of the biggest pains about shopping is toting around all that loot. If possible, do your shopping as near to the end of your trip as is practical. Still, if you're starting in Peru and finishing in Mexico, you may not want to pass up that handmade alpaca sweater for sale on the shores of Lake Titicaca. In this case, buy the sweater, wear it until you get to warmer climes and then post it home along with any other souvenirs you've accumulated along the way (for more details on sending things home, see the Staying in Touch chapter). Another option is to keep your goods in the luggage storage of a trustworthy guesthouse, returning later to collect your things.

Some places in Latin America are better for souvenirs than others. The textiles in Guatemala are hard to surpass in beauty, while the silversmiths of Mexico are superior to just about anywhere else. Here's some general advice for shopping in Latin America:

Good Souvenirs

Argentina – leatherwork, *mate* paraphernalia and woollen clothing
Bolivia – woollen clothing and musical instruments
Brazil – music cassettes, wooden sculptures, ceramic figurines and hammocks
Colombia – jewellery, ceramics and hammocks
Costa Rica – coffee, leather wallets and purses, and wood items such as jewellery boxes
Ecuador – Panama hats, ponchos, woollen sweaters, hats and vests, leather items and bread figurines
El Salvador – hammocks and knick-knacks inspired by the artist Fernando Llort
Guatemala – any textiles such as *hupiles* (woven, white, embroidered dresses from the Mayan regions), tablecloths, skirts or blankets
Honduras – woodcrafts and musical instruments, woven baskets and ceramics
Mexico – blankets, pottery, yarn paintings, masks and leatherwork
Nicaragua – *junco* woven mates, ceramics, painted gourds and molas (Kuna Indian embroidery), wooden masks and lace dresses
Panama – *molas* (Kuna Indian embroidery), wooden masks and lace dresses
Peru – alpaca sweaters, ponchos, weavings and carved gourds

• Markets are the best places to shop, and some are world renowned. Guidebooks often list the best markets and you should try to visit them if only for the experience.

• Try to price different items that appeal to you before buying. Browse at shops and markets to get an idea of price ranges and ask other travellers what they've been paying. Being an informed shopper will help you save money.

• Always attend to the shipping yourself even if a shop promises shipping and handling in the price.

• The export of artefacts and antiquities is strictly controlled and you may need documentation for replicas. Many western countries also control the import of pre-Columbian artefacts, so be prepared for some serious questions at customs if you've bought any antiques or artefacts.

• Textiles can vary in quality according to the design, weave, dyes and technique used in creating them. A good guidebook will tell you what to look for. Do a little research before shopping.

• Ceramics should be bought at the end of your trip and carried on the plane.

• Big-time shoppers should remember that there is a baggage limit on your plane flight and if you exceed it, you'll have to pay a fee. Also consider what can be easily carried and stored in the tight spaces of a plane.

Getting Around

There are so many transport choices in Latin America you'll have to learn new lingo just to keep it all straight. You'll need to know a *triciclo* from a *buseta* and a *ranchera* from a *colectivo*. It's not unusual to have to take a combination of transport to get somewhere, and canoes, ferries, motorboats, trucks, buses, trains and planes will all figure into your travel plans. You may even experience a donkey ride or two. Many travel horror stories involve public transport in some way. Still, that hair-raising bus ride across an Andean pass with the mountains soaring above your right shoulder and a cliff dropping 100m to your left will stay with you forever. There are many dangerous rides in Latin America, but the greatest way to see the landscape is by local transport.

Different countries favour different types of transport; your options will largely depend on the geography and infrastructure of where you travel. Parts of the Amazon are only penetrable by boat and even more remote areas are accessible on foot alone.

In most of Latin America, however, you will have the choice of bus, plane or truck to get around. Taxis or private cars are also a possibility, though trains are not. For the most part, trains in Latin America either do not run, or run off the tracks, and there are only very specific routes practical for travel (see the 'Great Latin American Train Trips' boxed text). Factors to consider when deciding upon mode of travel are safety, efficiency, cost, comfort and schedule. For example, you can take a plane or a local boat to the popular Honduran Bay Island of Roatán. While the former is more expensive, the latter could find you frighteningly overcrowded in a listing boat without life jackets and locals vomiting *arroz con pollo* at your feet.

Don't be lulled into the common myth that nothing runs on time and everyone is slow in this part of the world. For every bus that leaves 15 minutes late, there's one that will leave early either because the bus is full, the driver has a date or the bridge is about to close for the day. The best policy when dealing with public transport is to arrive early. On popular bus routes, there will be several daily departures and you can basically just show up at the terminal to hop on one going to your destination. Ferries and planes are different, however, and you'll want to leave yourself plenty of time before you're due to depart.

Research the transport situation in the countries you plan to visit to figure out the smartest, quickest and most enjoyable way to go. The Internet and your guidebook are good resources (see Researching Your Trip in the Planning chapter for pointers). Talking to other travellers and local authorities once you're in the country will give you the best idea of current conditions and options.

AIR

Though some travellers refuse to travel by air for budget reasons or because it's too disconnected from the landscape and culture, air travel can be cheap and efficient within Latin America. Regional and national airlines are (for the most part) safe and cover extensive areas. Often you can get passes that permit you several stops in the region. These can be a real bargain.

Flying can save you a lot of time, which in many travel scenarios is dearer than money. A 20 hour, 250km bus ride on a pocked jungle road may not be how you want to spend your holiday. In the same vein, guides, private transport, food and other assorted costs involved in travelling over the Darién Gap from Panama to Colombia, make it cheaper to just hop on a flight.

Air travel allows you to get to remote areas quickly. In some travellers circles, this is a bad thing, but if there's an airstrip in a wilderness location there will be flights and this can save you a lot of time. For example, it can take five to six days by boat to get to São Gabriel da Cochoeira in the Brazilian Amazon, but you can fly there in just three hours.

You do sacrifice opportunity and adventure by flying, however, and if you have the time and the sense of adventure, overland travel is truly the way to go. Be prepared for mishaps, missed connections and mistakes if you travel by surface transport. Overland is always hard, often rudimentary and rarely comfortable. Some people prefer to travel overland to a destination and then fly out if they're feeling too bedraggled.

Air Travel Tips

- Ask your travel agent if you can add regional or internal flights to your international flight. For example, the Circle Pacific fares offered by LanChile from Sydney or Auckland allow you to add a free flight to Buenos Aires or Rio once you're on the South American continent. Other airlines offer similar deals, so it's worth it inquiring.

- Regional air passes can provide big discounts within certain routes. The Mayan Airpass (also known as the Visit Central America Program) is one such deal, affording you cut-rate fares on up to 10 flight segments. Similarly, the Mercosur pass allows you to travel to cities on almost any carrier between Brazil, Paraguay, Argentina and Uruguay. Check restrictions on all air passes, as some have to be bought outside the region, some are mileage-based and others have time limitations. The following countries have air passes for use within their borders: Argentina, Bolivia, Brazil, Chile, Colombia, Peru and Venezuela.

- Always ask for discounts when purchasing a fare. If you're a student or senior or you're travelling during the off season, there's a chance the airline or travel agency may have special offers on certain flights.

- Ask about cancellation policies and penalties for changing your ticket.

- In some countries (eg Ecuador) there is a two-tiered price system, with foreigners paying substantially more than nationals.

- Confirming (and reconfirming) your flight is imperative. Airlines will use any reason and sometimes none at all to bump you from a flight. If language is a problem, ask at your guesthouse or hotel if they'll reconfirm your flight. They're usually happy to do it (if they have a phone!).

- It's often cheaper to buy your ticket from a travel agency than the airline, though this isn't always the case. Shop around and don't hand over any money until you have your ticket in hand.

- Be at the airport several hours early, as boarding passes may be meted out on a first-come, first-served basis. Also, some airlines like to depart early.

- Be prepared for delays or cancellations. Cancellations may be due to weather and you should consult your guidebook regarding the best flying times. In Peru, for example, afternoon clouds make flying after 4 pm impossible in some areas, even though a regular 5 pm flight is scheduled!

- Aerial sightseeing is a distinct possibility in the Andes and Amazon regions, so research which side of the plane to sit on for good views.

- There may not be seat assignments on domestic flights, in which case there is a mad dash to the boarding gate long before departure time and then a line until you leave. When the doors are opened onto the tarmac, everyone runs at top speed towards the plane to get the best seats. You'll get the hang of it.

- Don't check in your luggage unless you have to; there's too much margin for error.

BUS

You'll probably spend most of your travel time and money on buses, and this will be an experience in itself. Buses in Latin America range from super-fast and comfortable 1st class coaches with videos and meal service to converted flatbed trucks with wooden seats.

Unless you plan really well and have money to spare, you'll often be on uncomfortable buses that have no shock absorbers and are driven by a cigar-smoking maniac listening to Whitney Houston at full volume. Meanwhile, you'll have to share your small seat with a phlegmatic old lady who keeps falling asleep on your shoulder. The good news is that buses are so cheap and ubiquitous, you can usually get off one and on to another if any of the above-mentioned conditions threatens to drive you insane. As a general rule, budget on a dollar an hour for bus trips, though that can fluctuate wildly depending on where you are and the type of bus service you choose. If you're taking buses between countries, it may be cheaper to take a bus to the border and change to another bus rather than travelling on one bus all the way through.

There are different bus classes and types of service (the choices in Mexico can be dizzying) and it pays to know what type of bus you'll be taking. Usually, there are direct, semi-direct and local (sometimes called regular) buses. Direct is typically nonstop, though it may involve a few predetermined stops along the way. Semi-direct has stops, but not nearly as many as local, which stops for anybody, anywhere and is essentially door-to-door service. On local buses you may have chickens, pigs, bushels of bananas, bicycles and other sundry baggage along for the ride. The local bus can be long-distance and refers to the number of stops, not the distance it covers. The class of bus refers to the amenities it offers, such as reclining seats, videos, air-conditioning and snacks.

But wait, there's more! *Busetas* or *colectivos* refer to minivans that cram as many as 20 people and their baggage into a very small space and zip around as fast as they can on predetermined routes. These are uncomfortable, but cheap and efficient. Throughout Latin America you can usually just stand by the side of the road and hail a bus going in your direction. Shuttle buses between tourist spots are becoming increasingly popular, serving routes such as Guatemala City to Antigua, or San Pedro Sula to the Copán ruins in Honduras. Bus terminals are usually centrally located, though different companies may use different terminals. Ask around or consult your guidebook before setting off to a terminal and make sure you know where your bus will be leaving from.

Bus Travel Tips

- Before you buy your ticket, ascertain the class and type of bus you'll be on and ask about the approximate length of the trip.
- Buy your ticket beforehand, even a day early, if possible. If there are no tickets available at the terminal, try a travel agent.
- Choose a seat towards the front, as these are the least bumpy. If seats aren't assigned, arrive early to get the best seat (towards the back and over the wheel hub are the worst). Make sure the window near your seat opens.
- Arrive early in case the driver decides to take off ahead of schedule and especially if there are no assigned seats.
- If you a travelling duo, have one person deal with the baggage while the other snags two good seats.
- Before your trip, empty your bladder and buy some snacks for the ride. In most of Latin America, hordes of food sellers jump on the bus at bridges, lights and in small towns. Still, it's good to have your own food stash.
- Keep an eye on your luggage until the bus is ready to leave.
- Have some earplugs handy for the inevitable loud music and crying babies that will serenade you during the ride.
- Before the ride, transfer anything valuable or fragile from your backpack to your daypack.
- Don't ride on the roof unless you have no other choice; hang on tight and watch for low-hanging branches.

Get to the Frontier Early

This was my first trip to Central America. It was a relief to reach the Honduran frontier, as the road to the border had been unpaved and horribly potholed. Copán was near and it was nice not to be bounced around like a pinball, as I had been for the past five hours. The camioneta (pick-up truck) stopped at the border, where the guard waved everyone onward but me.

I was the only foreigner on the camioneta, and I'd not seen another traveller since leaving Lago de Atitlán in Guatemala a week earlier. The guard motioned for me to go inside a hut. As he carried a rifle, I complied, wondering a little anxiously what he wanted. Did they always have such formalities just to stamp your passport?

It was hot and humid in the hut, and the fan didn't work. The guard motioned for me to sit down. He asked where I was from and what I thought of his country. I replied simply that I was looking forward to visiting Copán. Pleasantly surprised that I spoke Spanish, he produced a deck of cards and started dealing. We played basic five card draw poker, until eventually he asked for my passport, staring at it for a while and saying he didn't see many 'Norteamericanos' out here. I responded with how happy I was to visit his country, because I didn't know anyone else who had visited Honduras.

After an hour, he wished me well in my visit and returned my passport. We shook hands and, greatly relieved, I boarded the next camioneta heading to Copán.

Jeff Rothman
LP Author, USA

- If you're a woman travelling alone, try to sit next to other women or children.

- Try not to take night buses if at all possible. Certain routes are favoured by robbers who ambush the bus and fleece the passengers. Consult your guidebook and local authorities for dangerous routes.

- Keep your camera and money belt out of sight. Loop a day-pack strap around your foot so someone can't snatch it.

- In parts of Latin America, especially near borders, you'll be subject to identification checks on buses. Sometimes an armed official boards the bus and sometimes you have to get off, go to a checkpoint and show your passport. It's all very routine if your papers are in order and the bus waits for you.

- Bring a personal stereo, book, knitting, journal, games or anything else that will keep you entertained on long trips.

- If you have to vomit and sticking your head out the window is not an option, do it in a plastic bag (preferably not clear).

CAR & MOTORCYCLE
Renting

Renting a car in Latin America is not cheap, but it allows you the freedom to make your own schedule and reach remote areas. To mitigate the costs of a rental car, try to get a group together and use local, rather than international rental agencies. Ask about deals, and try to be flexible, as some discounts are only offered on specific days or cars. Getting a car with unlimited kilometres built into the deal will be your best bet.

Most countries require an International Driver's Permit, and 25 is usually the minimum age for renting a car. You may have to produce a credit card or leave a large cash deposit in order to rent. If it's the latter, get a signed receipt. Many agencies will require you to take out additional vehicle insurance and all parties should be very clear on what this covers, who is liable and for how much in the case of theft or accident. Get it in writing. Motorcycle rental is less common, though it is possible. There are certain hazards associated with driving in Latin America, including crooked policemen demanding bribes, indecipherable road signs, drunk drivers and bandits. Consult your guidebook on the particular driving dangers in the countries you'll be visiting. A few suggestions for driving on your travels are:

- If you want to drive, get an International Driver's Permit from an automobile association in your home country (see Other Paperwork in the Passports & Visas chapter).

- If you rent a car, check it for damage, cosmetic and otherwise, before you drive away. Note any dents, scratches or defects on the car and have them verified by the rental agent, who should sign and date a receipt describing any damage. Make sure everything works and that there is a spare tyre and a jack.

- Learn the basic rules of the road before setting out. A guidebook should discuss the rudiments; the rental agency may provide a list of road signs in English. Sometimes signs are listed on maps.

- Secure parking can be a problem, and in many places street parking will not be safe. Look for hotels listed in your guidebook with parking facilities. Sometimes this is simply the hotel courtyard or lobby, but it's safe.

- Theft is a real problem with private vehicles. Never leave the car unlocked and never leave anything in the car or trunk. Make sure your rental insurance covers all or partial theft; you don't want to have to pay for a new set of tyres for the rental car if that's all the thief swipes.

- Keep a list of the rental agency's offices and phone numbers with your rental agreement. Many of the bigger companies have 24-hour emergency numbers, which is helpful if you break down.

13 Topes

'*Uno*,' says Ernesto as we approach the first *tope* of the town. A tope, or Mexican speed bump, aims to slow all vehicles to the speed of a mule. The little Chevy rental car bumps over it at a gentle 8km/h. Ker-runch ... ker-runch. It feels like the doors will fall off.

I'm giving Ernesto a lift to Tampico, and he's warned me there are a record 13 topes as the highway passes through this sweaty pueblo. Topes can be hard to spot at night, but Ernesto knows every one.

The Chevy has good acceleration, but as soon as we're into top gear again we come up behind an overloaded semitrailer, droning along at 20km/h. The semi flashes its left indicator − the driver is telling me it's 'safe' to overtake, so I edge the Chevy over to have a look wondering whether to use my left indicator to show I'm planning to overtake.

The big sedan behind doesn't hesitate − it blasts past the Chevy *and* the semi at about 120km/h. We both brake hard.

'*Dos*,' says Ernesto.

The semi slows to a crawl, and one by one, its many axles thump over the second tope, with our Chevy right behind.

We're stuck behind the truck for the next three topes, while Ernesto explains, with resignation, how it's come to this − it's because most drivers exceed the speed limit if they can, not because they are reckless by nature, but because the posted limits are so low that nobody can treat them seriously.

At the sixth tope, the semi slows and I pull out alongside it, bashing over the speed bump. Sure, there are cars coming the other way, but they all have to slow down for the tope, and some even drive right off the road to get around the obstruction. Topes can be useful!

Safely past the truck, we crash across a tope every 100m through the middle of town. Then we're behind the big, fast sedan which has been following a lumbering petrol tanker for a painfully slow 2km. The topes become more widely spaced as we leave town, and the sedan goes for it, accelerating to 80km/h to pass the tanker, on the outside of a blind corner.

'*Un hombre valiente!*' says Ernesto.

I'm not sure if the sedan driver is 'a brave man', or simply one made suicidal by sheer frustration, but Ernesto sees him like a matador, unflinching in the face of death. We both see red as the tanker hits the brakes.

'*Doce*,' says Ernesto.

We bounce over the bump and I give the Chevy everything, desperate to overtake the tanker before it winds up to an unpassable 80km/h on the open road. The Chevy just squeezes past as a deluxe bus charges towards us. Suddenly the bus slows, as if it were wounded.

'*Trece!*' says Ernesto.

I slam on the brakes, but we still hit the 13th tope at axle-smashing, vertebrae-crushing speed. I apologise for my bad driving, but Ernesto says I drive very well.

Of course I'm pleased.

'Sure,' he says, 'You drive like a Mexican.'

James Lyon
LP Author, Australia

- Pay attention when you're having petrol pumped by an attendant. There are many scams in this realm.
- Try to get a spare key, in case you lock yourself out or lose the key.
- Whether you're renting a motorcycle or riding your own, wear a helmet and protective clothing.
- Get the most detailed maps you can; roads may be poorly marked or there may be no signs at all.
- Never drink and drive.

Buying

Buying a car may seem like a good idea if you want to explore an area extensively, but there are a lot of strings attached. In Central America, the cost of buying a car is prohibitive – you can buy the same car in the USA for a quarter of the cost you'll pay in Central America. Indeed, travellers once subsidised their trips by selling cars in Central America that they'd driven down from the States. In South America, cars are cheaper, but the bureaucracy will drive you mad. Argentina, Chile and Brazil are the best countries to buy cars. Make sure the title is clean, and get a notarised document authorising your use of the car.

Bringing Your Own Vehicle

Shipping your car to South America is an option, though you have to be really crazy about your vehicle to do this: it's not cheap and there is a lot of paperwork. From North America, it is generally cheaper to ship from the east coast than the west. There are many companies specialising in shipping cars and it pays to shop around; look in the phonebook under 'Automobile Transporters'. Expect to pay at least US$1500 to get your car from an eastern US port to Guayaquil (Ecuador) or Barranquilla (Colombia). Alternatively, you can drive your car through Central America and ship it from Panama across the Darién Gap to Colombia. This is costly and difficult, but can be done.

BICYCLE TOURING

Bicycling overland is becoming more popular than ever, with cyclists making odyssey trips from North America, through Mexico, Central and South America with the final goal of Tierra del Fuego. It's definitely advisable to bring your own bike, preferably a model that can handle all terrains; the Andean nations will require a mountain bike, while the Southern Cone countries have many beautifully paved roads. There are several good routes, ranging from what could be called the gringo bike trail to dirt tracks recommended only for the hardy. A good place to start your research is the Sierra Club's *The Bike Touring Manual* by Rob van de Plas. Other good resources include *Latin America on Bicycle* by JP Panet and *Latin America by Bike – A Complete Touring Guide* by Walter Sienko. Here are some general pointers on biking in the region:

- Mechanics are competent in Latin America, but they often lack parts; bring plenty of spare parts from home, including inner tubes, patches and the like.

- Take a bike maintenance and repair class before you leave home. You should have a working knowledge of the important parts of your bicycle. Bring a manual just in case you need it.
- Ride defensively. Latin American drivers are not experienced in sharing the road with cyclists and may be startled to come upon you.
- Prepare for all types of weather, including fierce heat. Drink lots of water and carry rehydration salts.
- Equip your bike with mirrors so you can see all traffic clearly.
- Detachable bags (panniers) are a good addition to your gear; you'll want to take them off and into guesthouses or restaurants.
- You can put your bike on the roof of most buses, so if that hill is just too steep for you to climb, wait for a bus and hop on.

HITCHING

There are two types of hitching in Latin America. The first type is when you're in a very remote region where few buses go and you flag down a truck or private car. In this scenario, private vehicles are ersatz public transport and the truck may already be filled with crowds of farmers. You are expected to pay in this instance and the fares are supposedly fixed. Ask the locals what they're paying before handing over your money. This is all perfectly normal and you should encounter few problems. Sometimes there will be a centralised truck park waiting for passengers.

The second type is hitching in the traditional sense, where you stand by the side of the road with your thumb out hoping for a free lift. This is not the safest way to get around and cannot be recommended. If you opt to hitch rides, do it with at least one other person and do not get into a vehicle if you have any suspicious or funny feelings about the driver. Follow your intuition. Women travelling alone are at the greatest risk and should not hitch. The reward of a free ride is not worth the potential dangers. Two women travelling together are advised not to hitch in Mexico. If you are in a car and the situation gets uncomfortable, start asking the driver about his life, and particularly his family. This may take his mind off any malevolent thoughts.

WALKING

When the road dwindles to a dirt track or the last bus of the day has come and gone, or if your taxi runs out of gas, you'll be walking. However, situations don't have to deteriorate this seriously for you to try walking during parts of your trip. There are fantastic walks in this part of the world, for all levels of enthusiasm. Along the beach, through the jungle, up the stairs of the Temple of Inscriptions at the Mayan ruins in Palenque (Mexico), wherever your itinerary takes you, it will certainly involve walking.

If you're a serious walker and want to spend a lot of time exploring on foot, you'll need a good-quality pair of boots and a comfortable pack. Keeping that pack light is a winning strategy (see Equipment in the What to Bring chapter for more on packs and packing). Get in shape or stay that way before your trip; simply strolling leisurely in La Paz (Bolivia) for example, at nearly 4km above

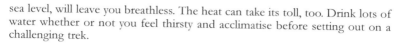

sea level, will leave you breathless. The heat can take its toll, too. Drink lots of water whether or not you feel thirsty and acclimatise before setting out on a challenging trek.

SEA TRAVEL

Travelling by boat can be a blast and there are many popular spots that afford you the opportunity to travel over water. Panama's Archipiélago de San Blas, the Belizean cayes, and the Galápagos Islands are just a few of the wonders you can explore by boat. Inland you can take canoes into the jungle, motorboats across Lake Titicaca and ferries to and from villages along the shores of Lake Atitlán in Guatemala. The Lake District in southern Chile and Argentina should be included on any boater's itinerary. If you're tired of the bus, get off and look for some water; chances are you can hitch a ride to somewhere nearby.

Travelling by boat is usually cheaper than flying, though you won't always have the choice. For example, you must fly to Easter Island (Rapa Nui) off the Chilean coast and the Falkland Islands (Islas Malvinas) off the coast of Argentina. Boat travel also provides opportunities to meet locals and affords you some sightseeing that flying doesn't. Be aware, however, that sea sickness is a very real possibility and can make for a very uncomfortable trip. Travelling by boat also presents dangers that flying doesn't. The condition of the boat is important, and you should give it the once-over before buying your ticket. Locate the life jackets and assess whether there are enough to go around. You may want to don one at the beginning of the voyage. Overcrowding is a serious and all-too-common problem on local vessels. Use your common sense and change your plans if the boat, crew or conditions look dangerous. Here are some other seafaring tips:

- If you're prone to motion sickness, take medication an hour before departure and try to ride on an empty stomach and above deck. Sucking on citrus like lemons or limes is a local remedy for nausea.
- Bring your own food and water. Even if the trip is not long in theory, you never know when a motor will die or some other mitigating circumstance will intervene to stretch an hour's ride to half a day.
- Arrive early to position for a seat, stow your pack and in case there's an early departure.
- Use the toilet before embarking.
- If you're riding on deck, bring something warm to wear, sunblock and sunglasses.
- If you're riding below deck, locate the exits and make sure you'd be able to get out in case of an emergency.
- Watch your luggage or keep it with you.

RIVER TRAVEL

Travelling via the rivers of Latin America can be an excellent way to go: you get to see jungle wildlife, indigenous communities, beaches, Mayan and Incan ruins and mountains, too. The Amazon alone could keep you occupied for a long time. In addition to an Amazonian odyssey, there's the eight hour trip (by slow boat!) to Parque Nacional Tortuguero in Costa Rica, the breeding and nesting place of the green sea turtle; the six day trip up the Río Negro in Brazil to the Venezuelan and Colombian border; or the awesome trip up the Río Manu in Peru into the heart of the Amazonian jungle and one of the most biodiverse places on the planet. The choices are breathtaking and endless, and you will not be disappointed if your adventure finds you on the rivers of the region.

LOCAL TRANSPORT

It can be really intimidating standing on the corner of a Latin American city street, breathing in diesel fumes and wondering how it all works. There are trucks and buses and cars vying with mopeds and motorcycles and bikes. Pedestrians are scurrying in the mix and sometimes you'll have a cart and mule tottering along for good measure. Find a room, dump that pack, wash your face and head out to get your bearings. Once you realise there is a pattern to all the chaos, you'll notice bus stops and taxi stands and maybe light-rail or subway stations. Local transport is cheap, and there's always a crowd that can give you advice if you end up on the wrong bus.

Private transportation is another option. This includes taxis in cities and towns, and the three-wheeled cabs called *triciclos* that are pedalled or motorised and are available in smaller towns. Always agree on a fare before setting off; you may want to write it down so there will be no discrepancy once the trip is completed. Bargain hard for a fair price, especially in a taxi from the airport when you first arrive (see Bargaining in the Money Matters chapter for tips).

Bus

If you plan on spending any amount of time in a Latin American city, your budget will thank you if you take the time to figure out the bus system. In Mexico City, there is also a decent subway system called the Metro, but you are prohibited from riding with anything larger than a day-pack. Figuring out the buses can be frustrating, as route maps are few and far between. Fortunately, buses usually have destination placards in their windshields, giving you a general idea of the route. Otherwise, you can ask someone at a stop, or the bus driver; people are usually anxious to help. In some cities, small buses called *colectivos* or *busetas* are used for inner-city transport. These too should have destination signs in their window or a conductor hanging off the bus shouting the destination and route while trolling for passengers.

Local transportation will be very crowded and people may not appreciate you boarding with a big pack; this is especially bad form during peak hour. Having the exact change is a good idea, though some buses have conductors who take your money and can give change. In some countries, buses will not come to a full stop for male passengers, but will instead simply slow down while the men get on and off. Even the elderly and infirm are subjected to this, and most men have the technique down so that they hit the ground running. Female travellers should expect no special treatment in this regard. Bus drivers and their conductors are generally honest when quoting prices and unless it seems outrageous, you can be confident you're getting a fair deal. Local transport is a favourite milieu for pickpockets, so watch your stuff and remember that thieves can be man, woman or child (see Theft under Hazards & Safeguards in the Issues & Attitudes chapter for some advice on keeping things safe). Here are some other helpful hints:

- Get a route map if you can. Tourist offices or guesthouses might have them.
- Latin American buses often have a driver and a conductor. The conductor collects the fare and is generally helpful. Direct any questions you have to him. If you're not sure how to pay, watch the locals.
- If you're not comfortable with the local language, write your destination on a piece of paper and show it to the conductor or other passengers who will tell you when to get off.
- Avoid peak hours if you can.

Taxi

Taxis in Latin American are fast, plentiful and cheaper than those you're probably used to, so you might find yourself taking them fairly often. Taxi drivers will try to overcharge you, so it's important to try and get a fair or at least acceptable price. Even though lots of Latin American taxis are equipped with meters, the driver may neglect to turn it on or claim it's broken. If this happens, say you'll find another taxi. This may result in a magical meter cure and then you can start your journey. If there is no meter or no intention of using a meter, you'll have to negotiate a fare. Once you've agreed upon the price, say it back to the driver and make sure everyone understands it's for the whole taxi and not per person. You may want to write down the amount so the driver doesn't try to pull a fast one after you arrive at your destination. The longer you're in a country, the more comfortable you'll feel negotiating with taxi drivers. Start with these suggestions:

- Some drivers use meters that tick off the kilometres and money too fast. Try to be aware of what a mile costs in a taxi and if the meter is rigged.
- Taxis congregating around tourist attractions will generally charge more than those just one or two blocks away. Distance yourself from tourist areas and hotels by a block or more to get a better fare.
- Try to have an inkling of the best route to take. Consult a map if necessary and don't be afraid to politely ask about the route if it seems off.
- Taxi fares in some countries are higher at night or may cost more per person.
- Do not pay before arriving at your destination or before retrieving your luggage.
- There are tourist complaint numbers in certain cities. There may even be taxi complaint numbers, which you may want to call if you feel you've truly been ripped off.

Subway, Tram & Local Train

Latin America lags way behind the rest of the world as far as urban rail lines go. There have been pockets of progress though, and cities with trains are easier to negotiate. Among these progressive cities are Quito, Mexico City, Rio de Janeiro, São Paulo, Buenos Aires, Santiago and Caracas. Though trains can get crowded, they are cheap and easy to use. Stations usually have routes and fares posted. If you'll be in a city for a time or anticipate riding trains frequently, see if there are any passes or deals for multiple trips. Thankfully, certain cities have committed to expanding their inner-city train systems, including some in Costa Rica, which is trying to kick-start its urban railway after nearly a century's hiatus.

Great Latin American Train Trips

You have to be very determined to travel by train in Latin America; the rails are in serious disrepair, routes are limited, service is slow and unreliable, and tickets are expensive. Due to neglected rails and some rough geography, train travel is not always safe and certain routes, like the phenomenal Devil's Nose ride in Ecuador, are known for derailments, accidents and even fatalities. Still, governments realise how much travellers enjoy train rides, and programs to restore tracks or privatise entire train systems are afoot in some countries. Usually there is a 1st and 2nd class, with tourists in the strict sense of the word in comfortable 1st class and stalwart backpackers in 2nd. If you're dead set on riding a train in Latin America, here are the possible routes:

Copper Canyon, Mexico – This train runs across the Sierra Madre from Chihuahua to Los Mochis.

Puno/Juliaca to Arequipa, Peru – Train departs from Lake Titicaca and traverses a 4600m pass. Schedules are curtailed in the low season.

La Paz, Bolivia to Arica, Chile – This is a ride going from 4000m to sea level.

Alausí to Durán, Ecuador – This is the infamous Devil's Nose ride, characterised by an exhilarating steep descent via switchbacks. Large portions of track are washed away periodically due to El Niño, thus disrupting services.

Oruro, Bolivia to Calama, Chile – A ride dropping from 4000m to sea level, passing through extinct volcanoes and lunar landscapes.

Salta to San Antonio de Los Cobres, Argentina – Known as the Train to the Clouds, this ride skirts the Andes, passing through many bridges and tunnels.

Curitiba to Paranaguá, Brazil – This is a dramatic ride to the lowlands, with breathtaking views.

Campo Grande to Corumbá, Brazil – This is a popular route going through the Pantanal to the Bolivian frontier.

STAYING IN TOUCH

While you're out gallivanting around Latin America and expanding your horizons, the folks back home are thinking and worrying about you. If you've been on the receiving end of postcards from far-off lands you know how thrilling and reassuring they can be. Friends and family will want postcards and updates periodically and fortunately communications systems in Latin America are such that you can get to a phone or Internet cafe every so often to touch base with them. Hearing familiar voices or logging onto the Net to see if you've got mail will do wonders for your spirits as well.

Keeping in touch will dip in to your budget, so factor this into your trip finances. New technologies such as Net Phone (which allows you to make phone calls over the Internet) facilitate staying in touch at low prices. Keeping a log of when you last called home will help you remember when you should get around to it again; weeks could go by before you realise you haven't let anyone know you're still alive and well.

If any kind of natural disaster, coup, riot or plane crash happens in or near where you're travelling, call home as soon as possible to let your family know you're OK. Here are some more suggestions for staying in touch on the road:

- Give people at home a general itinerary. Don't be too specific as it's bound to change, but saying Chile in March and Brazil in April is a good way to give them some idea of where you'll be.

- If you're heading on a long trek or tour, call home before setting off to let them know your that you may be out of touch for the duration.

- Ask someone at home to hang on to the letters you write them. These are like a second journal with a different perspective, as there's more of a story-telling nuance to letters.

- Some travellers like to make a specific phone schedule whereby they agree to call home every third Tuesday of the month for instance.

- Even if you struggle writing letters, do it! Buy small postcards and write large.

- If you're on a lengthy trip and have a lot of people expecting letters, write one long, detailed missive, make copies and add some personal notes to the end of each one.

- If you have a personal stereo with a record function, you can tape your letters and send recorded messages home.

- Sending along photos you've taken on the road will give others an idea of what you're experiencing.

Telephone

Being deep in the jungle or on top of an Andean peak will put you out of reach of a phone, but you should be able to place international calls in most towns in Latin America. If you're calling within a region or country, remember that the rings and busy signals will sound different from the ones at home. For country-specific details on making phone calls, see the country profiles later in this book.

WHERE TO CALL FROM

Telephone systems are wildly different in individual countries, but the more developed nations generally have pay phones from where you can place international calls. These include Argentina, Chile, Costa Rica, Brazil, French Guiana, Guyana, Mexico and Suriname. The procedure varies for each country and the phones may accept credit cards or phonecards. Prices can be very expensive (eg Argentina) or, where competition flourishes (eg Chile), very cheap. Try to call during off-peak hours for discounts.

In the rest of Latin America, you have to go to a centralised telephone office to place calls; depending on where you are, this may mean jumping through various bureaucratic hoops and queuing. Typically you go to a counter where an operator takes your number and places the call. You'll be pointed to a booth where you take the call. In many countries there is a three minute minimum for international calls, though if you get an answering machine or a busy signal you may be allowed to pay just a nominal fee. Reverse charge (collect) calls are only possible between specific countries. For example, you can make a collect call from Ecuador to Spain, but not from Ecuador to Australia. This is always changing and you'll have to check with the telephone office.

Many Internet cafes now offer Net Phone technology which allows you to place calls over the Internet via a headset. These calls are super-cheap (about one-fifth of what you'll pay at a phone office) and efficient. The connection won't always be the best and there can be lengthy delays between when the person talks

Missed Flight

October 7th was a Sunday – in my mind anyway, but not on the calendar. So convinced was I that Sunday was my departure day, that absolutely nothing seemed wrong when I checked in at the airport in San Salvador.

'Your flight was yesterday,' the attendant muttered. 'But we can put you on today's flight instead.'

For the first time in 48 hours I checked the calendar. Flutters of disbelief thickened into gut-clogging mud. Sure enough, my flight was 24 hours ago: 24 naive hours for me, and a good 18 hours of worry for friends who had gone to the airport to pick me up. I'd spent the last four weeks adventuring from one corner of El Salvador to the other, peeling from my mind tainted reputations of violence and mayhem to find a soulful emerald-green country recovering from its tormented history. Friends back in San Francisco, however, still only knew of its reputation, and without being able to contact me, their imagination fed upon my absence, until 'maybe she missed her flight' turned to 'something is really wrong'. All I could feel was a nauseous stupidity, not just for how foolish it is to completely mistake a departure date, but for the anxiety I'd caused my friends.

Teasing from family and friends eventually dissolved my embarrassment and their frustration, but not before a simple lesson was etched into my mind: It's the ones who are waiting for you who will feel your absence, not you, so check the tickets and check the calendar, and make sure you're on that flight home.

Carolyn Hubbard
Lonely Planet, USA

and you hear them, but the price can't be beaten. Cellular pay phones are also making inroads in Latin America. To place international or local calls from these phones, you need a phonecard specific to the cellular system. These are usually for sale wherever the phones are found, and in hotels and travel agencies.

INTERNATIONAL PHONECARDS

International phonecards are a great way to stay in touch, and because you buy them beforehand, you won't have to worry about squeezing your budget to make scheduled calls home. Lonely Planet's eKno Communication Card is designed specifically for budget travellers. The card gives you free email and affordable international calls from more than 40 countries, plus voice mail that allows you to update your outgoing message periodically. By calling this voice mail, friends and family can listen to the latest news about your adventures and leave messages for you in return. The eKno Card doesn't offer calls from every country covered in this book, but the system is being upgraded all the time. As we go to print, you can use it in Brazil, Chile and Colombia. You can check out and join eKno at www.ekno.lonelyplanet.com or from these three countries. Simply dial the relevant registration number below to join.

TYPES OF CALLS

There are different types of international calls and separate price structures for each kind. You may not have the choice of all these calls in all countries and your options dwindle the further off the beaten track you roam.

Direct (person-to-person) – This is the easiest way to make a call: you pick up the phone and dial. However, you'll be lucky to find this type of call anywhere but in the most technologically sophisticated Latin American cities because it requires the International Direct Dialling (IDD) system. To place an international call you dial the IDD number, the country code, the area code and finally the number of the party you're calling. Phone or credit cards can be used for these calls.

Operator assisted – These are probably the most common calls placed from Latin America. Anytime you go to a centralised telephone office, you're placing an operator-assisted call. These are usually expensive and have a minimum charge.

Reverse charge (collect) – An operator places this type of call for you and the party you're phoning agrees to pay. These are usually very expensive and in certain countries, eg Mexico and Guatemala, prohibitively so. In this case it's better to have the person call you back than pay the reverse charge. Some operators or telephone services will also charge you a small fee for placing this type of call. It's is very difficult to place reverse charge calls from Central America.

Home Country Direct – By calling an access number, Home Country Direct bypasses local operators and connects you directly with an operator in the country you're calling. Once connected, you can place credit card or collect calls. Home Country Direct has been slow to catch on in Latin America, but is currently available in Mexico and a few other countries (see the country profiles for details), and will probably expand. Call your telephone company for more information.

Credit card – The opportunities are rare indeed for credit card calls in Latin America. You'll be much better served by an international phonecard.

Fax

Keeping in touch via fax while you're in Latin America is easy and much cheaper than phone calls. In most countries with centralised telephone centres, you can send a fax for a fraction of the cost of a phone call and receive them for mere pennies in certain cases. Some phone centres will hold faxes for up to a month – a very convenient bonus if you'll be wandering about. Many hotels also offer fax services, but they will charge an arm and a leg to send them, though not too much to receive. Consider giving friends your hotel's fax number if you'll be in one place for a while. Even better are Internet cafes, most of which send and receive faxes, as well as offering email services.

Post

Navigating post offices is part of the travelling regime and you'll visit all kinds, from the hallowed marble halls of the capital city office to the tumbledown shack in a jungle border town. Services are about as varied as facilities. Some countries are so notorious for bad postal services that even the locals don't use them. Air-mail letters to North America and Europe typically take 14 days, but don't be surprised if they take longer. Surface mail can take months to arrive, if it ever does. Any important news should be conveyed by telephone, fax, or email and important documents should be sent through a private courier service or an international shipper such as DHL or Federal Express.

Don't expect postal workers to speak English, even in the biggest cities, though a friendly local will undoubtedly help you negotiate the phalanx of windows. There may be different windows for stamps, certified mail, and local and international post. Have an idea of what it should cost to send a letter or postcard and buy a bunch of stamps at once so you can write and send letters spontaneously. It's pretty deflating to discover a soggy, unstamped postcard with four week old news at the bottom of your day-pack. Mail sent from rural offices usually takes much longer to reach its destination than letters posted from a city. In heavily trafficked tourist destinations, hotels may collect outgoing mail from guests and send it en masse.

Each country has its own postal quirks, so see the Post & Communications sections in the country profiles for details.

RECEIVING MAIL

There are several ways to receive mail while you're on the road, and what a joy it is to have a letter waiting for you in a strange city.

The three basic ways to receive mail are by poste restante (general delivery) at post offices, at American Express offices if you're a card member or carrying its travellers cheques, or at your guesthouse. The first is the most common and presents the greatest opportunity for misdirected or lost mail. The American Express mail service is by all accounts efficient and conscientious, though there may not be offices along your planned route. Having mail sent to your guesthouse or hotel can work, but it's far more practical if it's addressed care of someone specific at the hotel and they've agreed to be responsible for your incoming mail.

POSTE RESTANTE

Poste restante is a good way to receive mail if your itinerary is fairly set and people back home are aware of it. When they want to drop you a line they just send a letter to the main post office of a big city and it is held there. Some rural offices may be unfamiliar with general delivery, so stick to bigger post offices or arrange for mail to be sent to a hotel if you'll be in the sticks. Each country is quite specific about the address lines for poste restante (sometimes known as *lista de correos*), so consult your guidebook for the exact way to address letters.

Poste restante letters are supposed to be filed alphabetically at the post office, though you may think some of the employees are working with a different alphabet! The name line in the address should have your first name, followed by your surname in big, block letters and underlined. It's best not to use titles such as Mr or Ms as you run the risk of having your letter filed under 'M'. Also, drop any middle names. When collecting poste restante mail, have them check under both your first and last initial just in case.

You'll have to show identification to collect poste restante letters and occasionally pay a small fee. There is a maximum time post offices will hold your mail. In most countries it's a month, but you can get authorisation for longer in certain cases. If you're unsure of where you'll be, ask your friends to send copies of the same letter to several different cities. Do not send money through the mail, but instead arrange for a wire money transfer (see International Money Transfers in the Money chapter).

In theory, you can receive packages using this system as well, but don't count on it. If your parcel does arrive, it will have been opened, inspected and perhaps lightened. You'll need to fill out forms and pay import tax if applicable. It would be complete folly to have someone send any questionable or illegal goods via poste restante. If you absolutely must receive a package, have it sent with an expensive, but reliable international shipping company.

SENDING MAIL

Sending mail is easy, the question is whether it will ever arrive. To make things easier on postmasters, clearly address your letters and write the destination country in big letters. Write 'air mail' near the address on all correspondence to speed up delivery. Steaming uncancelled stamps off foreign letters is a common scam in Latin America; have them hand-cancel the stamps right there and then or use a franking machine if the post office has one. Some countries have street mailboxes, but it's always safer to send directly from post offices.

You may want to send more important letters or documents via registered *(certificado)* mail. This will cost a bit more. If you're in a country with expensive postage rates (eg Peru) or with notoriously slow or poor postal services, (eg Venezuela or Guatemala), wait until you cross into a neighbouring country to send your mail. Post offices keep fixed hours, though the lobby may be open at all times and stamps available at vending machines.

SHIPPING ITEMS

Post offices are particular about sending packages and there may be weight and size limits and packaging requirements. Plus, everything has to be inspected by customs. Still, sending things home is a superb way to lighten your pack.

In some countries you will have the choice of sending your package by air or surface mail. Air mail is always more expensive, but it's also more reliable and faster. Sea mail may be your very cheapest option. Packages will arrive four to six months down the line. Skip all these options if you're sending anything valuable, and instead go with a reliable courier or shipping service.

If you have lots of stuff to ship or a few heavy items, you may save some money by using a shipping agent. These companies charge by space rather than weight. One cubic metre is usually the minimum amount and maybe you can team up with friends to maximise your savings. Shipping agents offer door-to-door service, though it's likely you'll have to pick up your goods at the port nearest your destination address. The goods must pass through customs and you may have to pay an import tax before you can collect them.

ADDRESS BOOKS

An address book is essential for keeping track of old friends from home and new friends you'll meet on the road. Make sure you have current addresses for your buddies at home, including email and fax numbers as these are cheap, fast ways to send news. There's a good chance your address book will be lost or damaged on the road, so don't bring the original. Copy down the addresses into a new book or even onto a sheet of paper and take that with you instead.

CASSETTE RECORDINGS

Quick, easy and fun, tape recordings are a spontaneous and ingenious way to capture memories of your trip. Good personal stereos have record functions, and while you may have to summon lots of energy to write a letter, with this method all you have to do is hit record and chat away. It helps if your recorder has a pause button so you can spare your listeners a lot of empty air.

Email

Email can be the most convenient and cheapest way to send news to friends around the globe. A country's Internet (and email) access will only be as good as its phone lines and Internet is still not available everywhere. In Latin America, Chile and Brazil lead the pack in terms of availability, but the rest of South America is not far behind. Guatemala is the front runner in Central America, though elsewhere Internet cafes have yet to become big business. In countries where you can access the Net, you may be limited to the big cities and generally, the fewer Internet resources there are, the more expensive access will be. The main places to access email are Internet cafes and some hotels. For a list of Internet cafes in individual countries in Latin America go to The Internet Café Guide (www.netcafeguide.com). The South American Explorers club in Lima, Cuzco and Quito offers free email services to members (www.samexplo.org).

The easiest email addresses to access in Latin America are through Lonely Planet's eKno communication card free email service (see International Phonecards earlier in this chapter), and Internet providers like Yahoo! and Hotmail. Don't expect to be able to access individual providers like AOL and CompuServe anywhere in Latin America (besides Mexico); the capability is just not there yet, though it probably will be soon. If you travel with a laptop, hooking up to the Internet with your machine will be a challenge and not very likely, unless you're staying in a mid-range or fancy hotel.

FREE EMAIL SERVICES

Even if you're a fierce technophobe or philosophically opposed to the Internet, think about hooking up a free email account before you set off. It is a great tool for staying in touch with your loved ones, which can be especially important on long trips. It's very easy and convenient to set up free email and even if you don't have a computer, you can do it at an Internet cafe. Don't worry if you don't know about computers: the staff at these outfits get paid to help people and they'll give you more advice than you ever wanted! You could wait until you're in Latin America to set up your account, although you may encounter language barriers with this strategy.

With a free email service, you register an email address and you're given a password. The address is your 'mailbox' where you receive email. You can retrieve email from this mailbox on any computer in the world that has Internet access. Internet cafes will often have the most popular providers like Yahoo! and Hotmail in the Bookmarks or Favourite menu of Internet programs. You just have to go to that menu, pull down your provider, enter your password and you're in your mailbox. Here you can read, write, send and save email messages and maintain your electronic address book. Don't fret about the how-to of it all – there will be plenty of people around to help you out.

USING INTERNET CAFES

If you want to use Internet cafes along your route as electronic general delivery mailboxes – where they hold your mail until you show up – you have to research cafes that are willing to provide this service. It will probably be much easier to set up your own email address instead, but to begin your research, go to www.netcafeguide.com to find cafes in the countries you'll be visiting. When friends send you mail, your name should go in the subject line, with your surname in capital letters. You should check for email under your first and last names in case it was filed incorrectly; expect to pay a nominal fee for receiving email this way. There is little privacy with this method, so confidential or sensitive information should not be sent this way.

Media

Keeping abreast of international and local events will help you stay connected to the real world.

RADIO

Unless you have a shortwave radio, you'll have to be satisfied with local stations (meaning it's football, salsa or Madonna in most cases). If you're a news hound or are taking a long trip where your itinerary may depend on international developments, consider investing in a shortwave radio. Affordable models start at about US$40. The two most accessible English-language stations in Latin America are the BBC World Service and the Voice of America; also try Australia's Radio National. For scheduling and frequency information, visit their web sites: www.bbc.co.uk/worldservice; www.voa.gov; www.abc.net.au/ra. A shortwave will also allow you to pick up stations in almost every other language. Radios not only keep you in touch, they keep you entertained.

TELEVISION

Wherever you are in Latin America, if there is a television, it will be on, whatever the quality of the material being broadcast. Satellite dishes are popular because they offer so many channels, and hotel televisions are often tuned to CNN. Sporting events are popular fare in Latin America and you won't soon forget watching your first big football match among an ecstatic local crowd. Sports fanaticism is not limited to football and you can often catch major league basketball and baseball games too. If there is no satellite dish or cable connected to a television, you'll have to be satisfied with local Spanish-language stations showing dubbed reruns of *Miami Vice*.

NEWSPAPERS & MAGAZINES

Most countries have either an English-language daily or weekly. Though these may include more tourist-oriented advertising than hard news, they're worth a glance, especially if you don't speak Spanish. Mexico has two English-language dailies and you should have no problem getting news there. In the largest cities in Latin America, you will find international copies of the *Miami Herald* and the *International Herald Tribune* and you can buy copies of the *New York Times* and the ubiquitous *USA Today*. International copies of *Time* and *Newsweek* may be available and Peace Corps volunteers usually have latter they're all too happy to trade. Airports are the best places to find international newspapers and magazines, though top-end hotels and some bookshops may have them.

Or follow the local lead and simply crowd around newsstands reading the daily edition, displayed in sections for this purpose. It's in Spanish, but it's free.

THE INTERNET

You can get news on the Internet, but this isn't cheap. Expect to pay around US$3 minimum for an hour surfing the Net. Still, you can probably read about what's happening in your home town as almost every newspaper has a web page. See the appendix 'Internet Addresses' for online news service addresses.

COMING HOME

All good things must come to an end, as the cliché goes, and that's all too true for your exhilarating adventures in foreign lands. Returning home will be bitter-sweet and if the thought of falling back in step with the normal world has you feeling down, you're not alone. Still, there are wonderful aspects to coming home, such as reuniting with friends and family, eating home-cooked food, sleeping in a cosy, familiar bed and being liberated from money belts.

Post-Holiday Blues

For a variety of reasons some people in your life may not be interested in hearing your travel tales. Others may not so convincingly feign interest. You may notice their attention wandering as you tell them about the time you were abandoned in the Managua bus station holding a peasant's baby or they may chatter on about a friend's new partner while you try to describe the beauty of an Andean moonrise over Incan ruins. Don't let it get to you and try not to begrudge them their indifference. It may not be indifference after all.

The truth is, if they haven't travelled, they can't possibly relate to what you're talking about because it's too far removed from their experience. Managua? Peasants? Incas? It's nearly impossible for your friends to grasp what you're talking about, just as it was hard for you to understand some of the things you were seeing when you first arrived in Latin America. Envy too can play its part. While you were romping on the beach drinking exotic cocktails, they were working or studying or carrying out their same tired routine. Don't try to cram travel stories down people's throats. You'll know who's truly interested and these are the people to share the really exciting stories with.

Getting yourself mentally prepared for the real world can be a drag. No longer will your days be filled with challenges and triumphs, stimulating highs, natural wonders and cross-cultural excitement. Now it's back to reality. Whether that's study or work, it means old patterns, familiar landscapes and ho-hum horizons. Though you can't be on the road all the time, the best way to fight depression is to plan your next trip! You need money and time to travel, so work with those goals and make another trip a reality. Keeping in touch with friends you made on the road will bolster your spirits and keep you connected with the travelling experience. Get your pictures developed and organise an album. Rent movies about places you visited, snuggle up with a big bowl of popcorn and enjoy.

This advice will go a long way towards alleviating your post-trip blues. Moping around wishing you were still travelling is not going to make another trip happen any faster. Besides, you have to keep fresh all those people-meeting skills you learned while away; get out and about to improve your outlook.

If you're seriously depressed and can't seem to shake it, see a professional and talk about what has you down. Similarly, if you have any physical problems that seem chronic such as loose bowels, skin ailments or chronic fatigue, see a doctor. Some Latin American parasites are very nasty and can procreate in your intestines, so if you think you picked up a bug, seek medical help.

Making the Transition

Culture shock works both ways and to make your re-entry as smooth as possible, give some thought to returning home while you're still on the road. This can be very hard, but will be easier if you have a lover, pet, new job or living situation to return to. All those hours travelling will give you ample time and opportunity to think about your life back home. How do you want it to look ultimately? What can and will you change? Where are there opportunities for you professionally, personally or intellectually? What have you always wanted to do, but never got around to? Travelling can literally give you a new lease of life, so channel all that new energy in a positive way.

Being home may find you depressed or so wildly active your friends won't recognise you. If you're depressed fight through it and take the time to sort it out. Then move on with a vengeance. Put your new skills and confidence to work for you. This will not be a problem if you're excited and full of energy but may be a challenge if you're in a post-holidays blues slump. If you're not feeling up to it all, think back on the single hardest moment of your trip, the time when you really didn't know how or if it was going to turn out and reminisce what you did to get out of it, cope and survive the experience.

Remembering Your Trip

Your trip may all seem like a dream once you've been home for a few days joking and hanging out with your friends. 'Did all that really happen?', you'll ask yourself each morning as you luxuriate in a hot shower with wonderful water pressure. It did happen and here are some ways to keep the memories alive:

- Put together a photo album with the best pictures. Arrange them in chronological order and write captions so you won't forget that the mountain behind you is Illimani in Bolivia. At least write the location on the back of the photo. Put slides in order for future slide shows.
- Host a slide show of your best shots for your travelling friends.
- Keep in touch with foreigners and locals you met. Write letters and include photos of you and friends. If you promised to make copies of photos, do it. Three months down the line you won't get around to it. You could also write thank-you notes to locals who helped you along the way, tour guides, porters or guesthouse owners.
- Gather more knowledge about the culture you explored. Take a class at the local university or college. Learning the language will deepen your understanding of the culture and prepare you for your next trip.
- Try to cook some memorable meals from your trip.
- If you live in a city, see if there's an immigrant community, restaurants, markets or a museum from the countries you visited.
- Reread the journal you kept during your trip. The thoughts you had while living the traveller's life will evoke feelings that pictures can't.

hip-swinging or sombre – there's a fiesta to suit everyone
top: the rio carnival, rio de janeiro, brazil *(guy moberly)*
bottom left: easter celebrations in bogota, colombia *(krzysztof dydynski)*
bottom right: an oaxacan dancer in full flight, mexico *(greg elms)*

rumbling volcanos to climb and dense jungles to trek through ...

top left: laguna verde and volcano licancabur, potsi, bolivia *(woods wheatcroft)*
top right & bottom: some consider parque nacional torres del paine in chile to be
america's finest national park *(woods wheatcroft, aaron mccoy)*

top: farming along the shore of lake titicaca, bolivia *(woods wheatcroft)*
bottom: palma de cera is colombia's national tree *(jason edwards)*

explore an ancient incan empire or just hang out with the locals

top left: ruins at machu piccu, cuzco area, peru *(woods wheatcroft)*
top right: quetzalcoatl, the feathered serpent god, yucatan, mexico *(ross barnet*
bottom: the giant stone moai of easter island *(james lyon)*

top: an apartment block, colombian-style *(krzysztof dydynski)*
bottom left & right: the brightly coloured houses of colombia and brazil
(krzysztof dydynski, guy moberly)

come face-to-face with the abundant wildlife

top: toucans are just one of many colourful birds of the jungle *(john hay)*
bottom left: the ubiquitous llama *(john hay)*
bottom right: a cheeky cotton-top tamarin, peru *(jason edwards)*

top left: a green tree frog *(jason edwards)*
top right: macaws live throughout mexico, central & south america *(krzysztof dydynski)*
bottom: just as pretty as they are tasty — a shiny red crab, argentina *(jason edwards)*

you'll smell the delicious aromas before you even see the food

top: corn grilled with lime juice, mexico *(greg elms)*
bottom left: a handy way to store gourds, chile *(eric wheater)*
bottom right: red hot chillie peppers, mexico *(bruce geddes)*

ARGENTINA

To get a whiff of Europe in the Americas, head to Argentina. The country was incorporated, built and maintained by waves of European immigrants, and continental sensibilities, particularly in Buenos Aires, permeate its architecture, art and attitudes. Modern tourist facilities mean visitors can travel around easily and comfortably. Rarely will foreigners be regarded with curiosity in Argentina.

Though some visitors come to Argentina for the society and culture, the natural attractions are a bigger draw. Argentina was one of the first South American countries to establish national parks and within these protected boundaries are the highest peaks in the western hemisphere, massive glaciers spilling into psychedelic blue lakes, kilometres of Patagonian coastline and vast deserts. In addition are the spectacular Iguazú Falls (Cataratas del Iguazú), on the tripartite border of Argentina, Brazil and Paraguay.

WHEN TO GO

Denizens of the northern hemisphere will delight in the two summers which Argentina enjoys, though the country is so varied geographically that a visit any time will be worth it. Buenos Aires is pleasant year-round, but if Patagonia is on your itinerary, the best time to visit is in summer, from December to February. The Iguazú Falls are most impressive and comfortable in the southern hemisphere's winter or spring when heat and humidity are less oppressive and the water is really flowing.

Winter also offers the opportunity to go skiing.

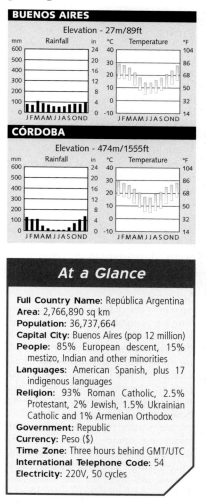

At a Glance

Full Country Name: República Argentina
Area: 2,766,890 sq km
Population: 36,737,664
Capital City: Buenos Aires (pop 12 million)
People: 85% European descent, 15% mestizo, Indian and other minorities
Languages: American Spanish, plus 17 indigenous languages
Religion: 93% Roman Catholic, 2.5% Protestant, 2% Jewish, 1.5% Ukrainian Catholic and 1% Armenian Orthodox
Government: Republic
Currency: Peso ($)
Time Zone: Three hours behind GMT/UTC
International Telephone Code: 54
Electricity: 220V, 50 cycles

HIGHLIGHTS

Argentina has a lot of hidden wonders and while a visit to Buenos Aires and a tour of the Iguazú Falls will be on most itineraries, don't overlook some equally spectacular, though less popular, spots. Here are some of Argentina's top attractions.

Cities

Buenos Aires has always looked to Europe for inspiration and this is apparent in the many museums, plazas, cathedrals, theatres and antique shops that pepper the city. The capital is alive with cultural and intellectual stimulation; take in some tango or Spanish classes during your visit. Known as Argentina's second city, Córdoba gives Buenos Aires a run for its money as regards colonial architecture and ambience. Check out the old market, the Iglesia Catedral and the Jesuit Iglesia de la Compañía. The Museo Histórico Provincial Marqués de Sobremonte here is one of the most important historical museums in the country.

Natural Attractions

Argentina's vast agricultural heartland known as the pampas is the legendary romping ground of the *gauchos* (Latino cowboys). The myth endures in towns like San Antonio de Areco and its environs. This area also has great beaches. If you can get to Patagonia, visits to Moreno Glacier (one of the world's few advancing glaciers) or Península Valdés with its abundant wildlife (whales, penguins, sea lions and more) are unique experiences. The 1km-high Iguazú Falls are dramatic and unforgettable. The marshlands called Esteros del Iberá in the Corrientes province rival the diversity of Brazil's Pantanal and are much less visited. The wine country, especially Cuyo (centred on Mendoza), and the Lake District offer their own natural delights.

Mountaineering

At 6960m, Aconcagua (Roof of the Americas) is the western hemisphere's highest peak and a decent challenge for even seasoned alpinists. The ascent takes from 13 to 15 days. Other popular climbs include those in the Fitzroy Range in Parque Nacional Los Glaciares and Santa Cruz province. The mountains around Bariloche and in Parque Nacional Nahuel Huapi are further possibilities.

Skiing

Great snow, sunny days and killer slopes are the hallmarks of skiing in Argentina (though it's not cheap). The main skiing centres are in the southern Cuyo region; the Lake District, particularly the Cerro Catedral complex near Bariloche and Chapelco near San Martín de los Andes; La Hoya near Esquel; and the most southerly skiing complex in the world, Ushuaia in Tierra del Fuego.

VISA REQUIREMENTS

Visas are required by only a handful of international tourists. Virtually all foreign visitors from western countries don't need visas, but receive a tourist card valid for 90 days upon arrival. Tourist cards are renewable for 90 days at immigration offices in Buenos Aires or in provincial capitals. If you wish to stay in Argentina beyond six months, it's easier to hop into an adjacent country for a spell; upon your return to Argentina you will be eligible for another 180 day stay.

Argentine Embassies

Australia
   (☎ 02-6282 1555) 1st floor, MLC Tower, Woden, ACT 2606

Canada
   (☎ 613-236-2351) Suite 620, 90 Sparks St, Ottawa, Ontario K1P 514
   Consulate: Montreal

UK
   (☎ 020-7584 6494) 53 Hans Place, London SW1 XOLA

USA
   (☎ 202-939-6411) 1600 New Hampshire Ave NW, Washington, DC 20009
   Consulates: Los Angeles and New York

TOURIST OFFICES OVERSEAS

Though Argentina has no formal tourist representation overseas, embassies and consulates usually have a tourist functionary. Travel agents or representatives of Aerolíneas Argentinas, can provide tourist information.

HEALTH

Malaria occurs mainly in rural areas along the borders with Bolivia and Paraguay. Yellow fever is a risk only in the forests in the north-east of the country. Dengue fever can also be a health concern, especially in urban areas in the north of Argentina. Take appropriate precautions against these serious diseases and avoid bites from all insects (especially mosquitoes) to prevent other insect-borne diseases. Be prepared for cold conditions in southern Argentina. Generally, travel in Argentina should present few health concerns, but it's still a good idea to take care with what you eat and drink, because hepatitis, typhoid, dysentery and cholera can all occur. Tap water in Buenos Aires is fine to drink, but outside the capital drink only bottled or purified water.

Itineraries

One Week
Argentina is a huge country and one week will keep you confined to Buenos Aires and nearby attractions; you could fly between the capital and one or two points of interest, but this would be very rushed. Spend two to three days exploring Buenos Aires before setting off for the relaxed, history-laden Isla Martín García. Camp overnight here before heading to the Atlantic coast beaches for a couple of days. Alternatively, you can cross over to the charming colonial Uruguayan capital of Montevideo for a long weekend.

Two Weeks
Two weeks allows you a little more flexibility and you can see a few major attractions. After exploring Buenos Aires for two or three days (perhaps with a visit to Isla Martín García or a ferry ride to Montevideo), check out the Iguazú Falls, followed by a trip to the Moreno Glacier in

Parque Nacional Los Glaciares or to Mendoza in the Cuyo region for a wine tasting trip. This itinerary will require at least two plane rides.

Three Weeks
Follow either the glacier and falls or wine region combinations outlined above, adding a side trip to either the Lake District around Bariloche, with some hiking thrown in, or a visit to the Península Valdés.

One Month
One month will permit a fuller appreciation of Argentina's landscape. Follow all the options for the three week itinerary and add a trekking leg through Chile's phenomenal Parque Nacional Torres del Paine after visiting Los Glaciares. Alternatively, mountain climbers can go for the Aconcagua ascent (allow at least two weeks). If you have any extra time, top off your trip with a visit to Tierra del Fuego.

ARGENTINA HIGHLIGHTS & ITINERARIES

IGUAZÚ FALLS
Dramatic 70m-high falls set in 55,000 hectares of rainforest

BUENOS AIRES
A highly cultural capital, with European-style architecture and stimulating entertainment

THE PAMPAS
The myth of the legendary gauchos lives on in this agricultural heartland

CÓRDOBA
Competes with the capital in terms of colonial architecture and ambience

MENDOZA
The gateway to South America's highest summit, Aconcagua, and ski resorts

ARGENTINE NATIONAL & PROVINCIAL PARKS & RESERVES

1 Monumento Natural Laguna de los Pozuelos
2 PN Baritú
3 PN Calilegua
4 PN Los Cardones
5 PN Finca El Rey
6 RN Formosa
7 PN Río Pilcomayo
8 PN Chaco
9 PN Mburucuyá
10 RP Esteros del Iberá
11 PN Iguazú
12 PN Talampaya
13 PP Ischigualasto
14 PP Aconcagua
15 PP Tupungato
16 PN Sierra de las Quijadas
17 PN El Palmar
18 PN Diamante
19 RN Estricta Otamende
20 PN Lihué Calel
21 PN Laguna Blanca
22 PN Lanín
23 PN Nahuel Huapi
24 PN Los Arrayanes
25 PN Lago Puelo
26 PN Los Alerces
27 RP Península Valdés
28 RP Punta Tombo
29 PN Perito Francisco P Moreno
30 Monumento Natural Bosques Petrificados
31 PN Los Glaciares
32 PN Monte León
33 PN Tierra del Fuego
34 PN Torres del Paine (Chile)

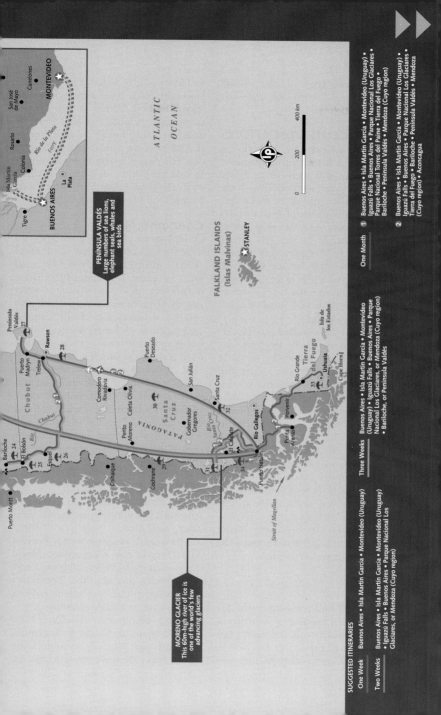

PENINSULA VALDÉS
Large numbers of sea lions, elephant seals, whales and sea birds

MORENO GLACIER
This 60m-high river of ice is one of the world's few advancing glaciers

ATLANTIC

OCEAN

0   200   400 km

MONTEVIDEO

BUENOS AIRES

Rosario

San José de Mayo

Canelones

Colonia

La Plata

Tigre

Isla Martín García

Rio de la Plata

Ferry

Bariloche

El Bolsón

Esquel

Coihaique

Cochrane

Puerto Montt

Chubut

Rio Chubut

Puerto Madryn

Trelew

Rawson

Peninsula Valdés

Comodoro Rivadavia

Caleta Olivia

Santa Cruz

Puerto Deseado

San Julián

Perito Moreno

Gobernador Gregores

Rio Santa Cruz

El Calafate

Puerto Natales

Rio Gallegos

Porvenir

Punta Arenas

Strait of Magellan

Rio Grande

Ushuaia

Cape Horn

Tierra del Fuego

Isla de los Estados

PATAGONIA

SANTA CRUZ

FALKLAND ISLANDS
(Islas Malvinas)

STANLEY

SUGGESTED ITINERARIES

One Week   Buenos Aires • Isla Martín García • Montevideo (Uruguay)

Two Weeks   Buenos Aires • Isla Martín García • Montevideo (Uruguay)
• Iguazú Falls • Buenos Aires • Parque Nacional Los
Glaciares, or Mendoza (Cuyo region)

Three Weeks   Buenos Aires • Isla Martín García • Buenos Aires • Montevideo
(Uruguay) • Iguazú Falls • Buenos Aires • Parque
Nacional Los Glaciares, or Mendoza (Cuyo region)
• Bariloche, or Peninsula Valdés

One Month   ① Buenos Aires • Isla Martín García • Montevideo (Uruguay) •
Iguazú Falls • Buenos Aires • Parque Nacional Los Glaciares •
Parque Nacional Torres del Paine • Tierra del Fuego •
Bariloche • Peninsula Valdés • Mendoza (Cuyo region)

② Buenos Aires • Isla Martín García • Montevideo (Uruguay) •
Iguazú Falls • Buenos Aires • Parque Nacional Los Glaciares •
Tierra del Fuego • Bariloche • Peninsula Valdés • Mendoza
(Cuyo region) • Aconcagua

If you need medical care, health services are good in Buenos Aires and in most cities.

POST & COMMUNICATIONS

Mail and telephone services in Argentina are a frustrating combination of corruption and inefficiency. Postal services especially are frequently hamstrung by strikes and work stoppages, resulting in mountains of mail that sits around forever. Any essential correspondence should be sent via private courier or at least registered. Receiving mail is just as unpredictable and you'll be charged up to US$1.50 for each piece you retrieve. Poste restante mail sent to Buenos Aires should read Capital Federal in the city line.

Despite the substandard service, Argentina has some of the steepest telephone rates in the world. Try to place international calls between 10 pm and 8 am on weekdays or anytime on weekends, when rates are about 20% cheaper. International calls are placed at centralised calling offices owned privately or by the phone company. Not all locations can place reverse charge (collect) calls, so ask first. Credit card and International Direct Dialing calls are available on some phones in some cities. Fax services are available at centralised phone offices.

Email access is becoming easier countrywide as Internet cafes and tech-savvy guesthouses go online.

MONEY
Costs

Travellers will find few bargains in Argentina, as the European style of living is commensurate with the European cost of living; expect to lay out as much here in day-to-day costs as you would in North America or England. Even the most budget-conscious will spend around US$35 a day. Those enjoying a slightly higher level of comfort and dining in restaurants should plan on a whopping US$80 a day. The Argentine economy is subject to wild fluctuations and hyperinflation, so if you're planning a trip here, keep your eye on the exchange rates.

Changing Money

US dollars are currently legal tender in Argentina, so carrying cash or travellers cheques in US currency will make your life a lot easier. If you need to change dollars into pesos, cash nets a better rate than travellers cheques, which also carry a commission. Both can be exchanged at exchange houses, banks, hotels and some travel agencies. MasterCard is the most widely accepted credit card, followed closely by Visa. Most ATMs will honour bank cards and give cash advances on credit cards. Be aware of currency fluctuations when you use your credit card as the exchange rate you're billed at may be dramatically higher (or lower) than the rate at the time of the transaction.

ONLINE SERVICES

Lonely Planet's web site is Destination Argentina (www.lonelyplanet.com/dest/sam/argie.htm).

The English-language weekly Buenos Aires Herald has a homepage (www.buenosairesherald.com) with the latest news, sports and the like. The travel section has interesting pieces written by locals on tourist destinations.

Tango enthusiasts shouldn't miss Art, Literature & Tango in Argentina (www.escapeartist.com/argentina3/art.htm). This page has extensive links on everything from tango and Borges to a Buenos Aires restaurant guide.

Anyone heading to the western hemisphere's tallest mountain must visit the Aconcagua Official Home Page (www .aconcagua.com.ar). Possible routes, weather and equipment suggestions, and a searchable database, make this a great site.

For Patagonia insight, hit the homepage of Mikael and Titti Strandberg, Reports from Expedition Patagonia (www.utsidan.se/mikael/en/patagonien /rapport.htm), which details the duo's year-long adventure through Chile and Argentina to Tierra del Fuego on horseback. Great photos and information (in Spanish) are available at the Patagonia Website (http://newroad .newroad.com.ar/patagonia).

BOOKS

Argentina has produced many literary giants, including Poet Laureate Jorge Luis Borges. Among his more accessible works are the unsurpassable short-story collection *Labyrinths* and the playful *A Universal History of Infamy*.

The very readable *On Heroes and Tombs* by Ernesto Sábato and the world-renowned writings of Manuel Puig, including *Kiss of the Spider Woman* and *Betrayed by Rita Hayworth*, shed light on the Argentine character. Julio Cortázar is another literary beacon. Check out his experimental works *Hopscotch* or *62: A Model Kit*. The landmark film *Blow-Up* was adapted from one of his short stories. The list goes on. Try your library or a searchable Internet database to discover more Argentine authors.

Quality travelogues featuring Argentina, from Charles Darwin's *Voyage of the Beagle* to Bruce Chatwin's *In Patagonia*, are worth a read. Try Gerald

Durrell's entertaining accounts of his travels there including *The Drunken Forest* and *The Whispering Land*.

The Perón years spawned many a publishing effort. The standard biography is *Juan Domingo Perón* by Robert Alexander. More analysis and insight into Perón's legacy can be gleaned from Frederick Turner & José Enrique Miguens' *Juan Perón and the Reshaping of Argentina*. For an account of Perón's ever-popular wife, see JM Taylor's *Eva Perón: The Myths of a Woman*.

The Disappeared: Voices from a Secret War by John Simpson & Jana Bennett is an excellent account of that shadowy period known as the Dirty War. Jacobo Timmerman's *Prisoner Without a Name, Cell Without a Number* is the classic first-person account of that tragic period.

FILMS

Although Hollywood has co-opted Argentina in body and spirit for celluloid atrocities like *Starship Troopers* and *Evita*, the film industry centred in Buenos Aires is a worldwide cinematic powerhouse. María Luisa Bemberg, perhaps Argentina's best known contemporary director, died in 1995. Her historically based films often illuminate the Argentine experience. *Camila* (nominated for a best foreign film Oscar in 1984) and *I Don't Want to Talk About It*, an offbeat love story starring Marcelo Mastroianni, would make a good double feature.

Eliseo Subiela's critically acclaimed *Man Facing Southeast* takes part of its inspiration from Adolfo Bioy Casares' ingenious novella *The Invention of Morel*. Film buffs won't want to miss famed director Héctor Babenco's *Kiss of the Spider Woman*, starring William Hurt and the late great Raúl Julia.

Héctor Olivera's *La Patagonia Rebelde* is a historical account of the anarchist rebellion in Santa Cruz province at the turn of the 20th century. Olivera also adapted Osvaldo Soriano's satirical novels to the big screen in *A Funny Dirty Little War* and *Una Sombra Ya Pronto Serás*.

ENTERING & LEAVING

Argentina is accessible by many international carriers serving Ezeiza airport, outside Buenos Aires. Direct flights are available from many cities in the USA, Canada and Europe. Visitors from Australia or New Zealand might get better fares by purchasing a Round-the-World, Circle Pacific or Circle Americas ticket. The international departure tax is US$13, except on international flights fewer than 300km, when the tax is US$5.

There are more than two dozen official border crossings between Argentina and Chile, Bolivia, Brazil, Paraguay or Uruguay. Some crossings are reached overland (and over mountains!), and some by river or sea. While certain border crossings are quite straightforward, others are difficult and it will take gumption and patience to successfully navigate your way. For example, travel from Chile usually involves a hike through the Andes, while overland travel to Bolivia can go through the border towns of La Quiaca/Villazón (from where you can take a train to La Paz), Aguas Blancas/Bermejo or Pocitos/Yacuiba. Paraguay can be reached by bus and/or river launch, with crossings from Clorinda to Asunción; Posadas to Encarnacíon; and Puerto Iguazú to Ciudad del Este

via Foz de Iguaçu in Brazil. The most common crossing to Brazil is via Foz do Iguaçu or Uruguaiana. Uruguay is linked to Argentina by road bridges, with connections between Montevideo and Buenos Aires via Gualeguaychú, or the quicker land and ferry combination across the Río de la Plata. A ferry and hydrofoil service also runs between Buenos Aires and Colonia to Montevideo.

Routes between Argentina and Chile include Jujuy and Salta to Calama; the popular San Martín de Los Andes to Temuco crossing, where there are regular summer buses across the Paso de Mamuil Malal; La Serena to San Juan (though there is no regular bus service here); and the very popular Buenos Aires-Mendoza-Santiago route. Some of these routes are closed in winter. More interesting are the many Lake District and southern Patagonian routes, with buses and ferries servicing the crossing points between Chile and Argentina. The most popular crossings in the Lake District include Bariloche to Puerto Montt via Parque Nacional Vicente Pérez Rosales and the quick trip from Bariloche to Osorno via Paso Puyehue. For travellers wishing to cross into Patagonia, the Punta Arenas to Tierra del Fuego trip is long and involves a three hour ferry ride and a combination of buses, but is popular nonetheless. Another option for crossing from Chilean Patagonia to Argentina is to go from Puerto Natales to Parque Nacional Torres del Paine via the Río Turbio and El Calafate. This is the gateway to Parque Nacional los Glaciares.

BELIZE

Belize is a gem of a tropical paradise and high on destination lists for diving and snorkelling enthusiasts. Right offshore is the famous Belizean barrier reef, the longest in the western hemisphere. Some of the world's finest diving and snorkelling is in the Belizean cayes, small islands afloat in the Caribbean Sea and flanking the reef.

Belize is something of an anomaly among Central American countries for several reasons. Its government is a democracy that has never had a coup; it's English-speaking; and the population is a diverse mosaic of mestizos, Mayans, Garífunas (Black Caribs) and Creoles – descendants of African slaves and British pirates. Visitors to Belize have to be prepared for a rudimentary, though developing tourist infrastructure. Services can be scarce, accommodation full, transportation slow and it's a bit more expensive than the rest of Central America, but grin and bear all that and you'll enjoy this living Eden.

WHEN TO GO

The dry season is from November to May and many people prefer to travel during this time. July to November is the hurricane season which typically means lots of rain, but it occasionally thumps Belize with a fully fledged natural disaster. Accommodation is more expensive and tends to fill up fast during the dry season, so the best time to visit may be during the shoulder periods, between early May

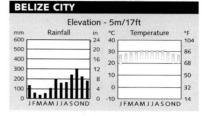

and July or around late November or early December. Whenever you go, expect it to be hot and humid, as most of the country is tropical lowland. The exceptions are the mountains in the west and the cayes, which are blessed by cool ocean breezes.

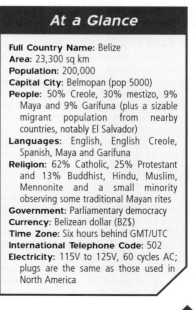

At a Glance

Full Country Name: Belize
Area: 23,300 sq km
Population: 200,000
Capital City: Belmopan (pop 5000)
People: 50% Creole, 30% mestizo, 9% Maya and 9% Garífuna (plus a sizable migrant population from nearby countries, notably El Salvador)
Languages: English, English Creole, Spanish, Maya and Garífuna
Religion: 62% Catholic, 25% Protestant and 13% Buddhist, Hindu, Muslim, Mennonite and a small minority observing some traditional Mayan rites
Government: Parliamentary democracy
Currency: Belizean dollar (BZ$)
Time Zone: Six hours behind GMT/UTC
International Telephone Code: 502
Electricity: 115V to 125V, 60 cycles AC; plugs are the same as those used in North America

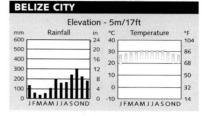
BELIZE CITY — Elevation - 5m/17ft

HIGHLIGHTS

Belize is an ideal destination for exploring stunning submarine worlds with scuba or snorkel gear, but the beaches aren't all that great. Hiking is possible in the highlands and you can also visit the Guatemalan Caribbean coast and the Mayan ruins of Tikal easily from Belize. Here's a list of the best Belize has to offer.

Scuba Diving & Snorkelling

Just off the coast of Belize is the world's second largest barrier reef, and diving and snorkelling enthusiasts will not be disappointed with a visit to the cayes (pronounced 'keys'). The two most popular spots are Caye Caulker and Ambergris Caye, though there are dozens more for those with the time and money to get to them. Underwater visibility reaches up to 60m; you can expect to see all the marine flora and fauna your brain can possibly process. Experienced divers can take advantage of night dives, cave dives and other speciality excursions.

Archaeological Sites

Along with the Yucatán Peninsula and Guatemala, Belize comprises a portion of La Ruta Maya, a tourism concept allowing travellers to experience Mayan culture and ancestry with minimum impact on the environment and local way of life. There are several Mayan sites of note in Belize. In northern Belize, Lamanai is a partially restored site with

Itineraries

One Week

If you have a week, head out of Belize City to Caye Caulker (the super-affordable choice) or Ambergris Caye (the fairly affordable option) for some laid-back fun in the sun. Belize City has few attractions for foreign visitors, so don't waste a moment getting to the cayes. Get your scuba certification, go snorkelling, hang out in a deck chair or go on a manatee tour. Sea kayaks, sailboats, fishing equipment and other items are available for rent. Get a group together, hire a boat and visit some of the pristine, remote beaches further out on the cayes.

Two Weeks

Follow the one week itinerary for the cayes, followed by an inland circuit to visit Mayan ruins. Spend three days in northern Belize visiting Lamanai and Altun Ha. Take a trip up the New River through dense jungle to Orange Walk and stop off at the Crooked Tree Wildlife Sanctuary for some birdwatching.

Alternatively, after one week in the cayes, you can skip all the cultural stuff and head to the beach towns of southern Belize such as Hopkins, Placencia and Punta Gorda, and relax a bit more before returning home.

Three Weeks

Follow the two week itinerary, but between the cayes and the ruins or southern beach portions, fly to Flores in Guatemala for a visit to Tikal. Spend two or three days exploring the ruins with a day trip or two to other ruins deeper in the jungle. Return to Belize City and continue with the two week itinerary, adding a trip to the Mountain Pine Ridge Forest Reserve in the western part of the country if time allows. This beautiful, unspoiled mountain country is dotted with waterfalls and teems with wild orchids, parrots, keel-billed toucans and other exotic flora and fauna. It can be explored by 4WD, on horseback or on foot. Canoeing on the Macal, Mopan and Belize rivers near here is another alternative.

After doing the three week itinerary, you'll find yourself back in Belize City, looking towards Mexico. It's easy to cross to the Yucatán Peninsula from here.

ELIZE HIGHLIGHTS & ITINERARIES

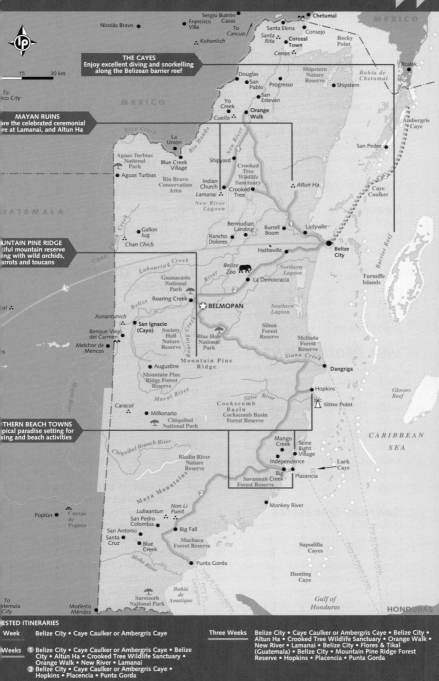

THE CAYES
Enjoy excellent diving and snorkelling along the Belizean barrier reef

MAYAN RUINS
ore the celebrated ceremonial re at Lamanai, and Altun Ha

UNTAIN PINE RIDGE
tiful mountain reserve ng with wild orchids, arrots and toucans

THERN BEACH TOWNS
pical paradise setting for king and beach activities

60 structures, and was a celebrated ceremonial centre until the Spaniards arrived. Altun Ha is the most famous ruin in northern Belize, and though small it served as a powerful trading and agricultural centre. Set on a hilltop overlooking the Belize River, Xunantunich is the pride and joy of Belizean ruins, though it may leave you disappointed if you've already been to Copán in Honduras or to Tikal.

Beaches

Head to southern Belize for beach relaxation. Several small towns along the Southern Highway provide ample settings for a tropical fantasy. The road can be rough, as much of it is unpaved, but that's a small price to pay for paradise. Good beach towns to check out are Hopkins, Sittee River and Placencia.

VISA REQUIREMENTS

Citizens of Commonwealth countries, the USA and the European Union do not need a visa to visit Belize. Technically, everyone is required to have an onward ticket, but only the scruffiest-looking travellers will be asked to produce one. On arrival you'll be given a tourist card valid for 30 days to six months depending on your country of origin.

Belizean Embassies

Belize is a small country with limited resources and many of its overseas diplomatic affairs are handled by British embassies and consulates or honorary consuls. Some of the offices listed below are consular agencies or honorary consuls, but they can usually issue visas and answer whatever questions you may have.

Canada
(☎ 514-871-4741, fax 397-0816) 1080 Beaver Hall Hill, Suite 1720, Montreal, Quebec H2Z 1S8;
(☎ 416-865-7000, fax 865-7048) Suite 3800, South Tower, Royal Bank Plaza, Toronto, Ontario M5J 2J7

UK
(☎ 020-7499 9728, fax 7491 4139) Belize High Commission to London, 22 Harcourt House, 19 Cavendish Square, London W1M 9AD

USA
(☎ 202-332-9636, fax 332-6888) 2535 Massachusetts Ave NW, Washington, DC 20008;
(☎ 213-469-7343, fax 469-7346) 5825 Sunset Blvd, Suite 206, Hollywood, CA 90028

TOURIST OFFICES OVERSEAS

Germany
(☎ 711-233-947) Bopserwaldstrasse 40-G, D-70184 Stuttgart

Mexico
Hotel Parador Lobby, Avenida Tulum 26, Supermanzana 5, Cancún;
Calle 58 No 488-B at Calle 43, Mérida 97000

USA
(☎ 212-563-6011, ☎ 800-624-0686) 421 7th Ave, New York, NY 10001

HEALTH

Malaria exists throughout rural areas, especially in the western and southern parts of the country. Dengue fever also occurs, so take precautions against these mosquito-borne diseases. Avoid bites from all insects, especially in rural areas, to prevent other insect-borne diseases. Drink only treated or bottled water and take care with what you eat to prevent diseases such as cholera, dysentery, typhoid and hepatitis.

Medical care is limited in Belize. If you require serious medical attention, Mexico City has excellent facilities.

POST & COMMUNICATIONS

Belizean mail services are generally reliable and an air-mail letter should arrive in the USA or Canada within two weeks and in Europe within three weeks. You can try to have poste restante mail sent to cities other than Belize City, but you may not receive it. When going to pick up mail, look under both your initials as letters are often filed incorrectly, and bring picture identification.

International calls are most easily and cheaply made from a centralised telephone call centre, and you may be able to place fairly affordable calls from your hotel as well. Fax services are provided by many hotels and private businesses.

Belize is woefully slow on the Internet uptake and you may have trouble getting online. Again, try at your hotel; if it has access, you may be allowed to send and receive email for a small fee.

MONEY
Costs

Prepare yourself for a big dent in your budget if you're travelling from elsewhere in Central America to Belize. It's more expensive than neighbouring countries and even those on the strictest budget can expect to shell out close to US$20 a day. If you're willing to spend a few dollars more a day, you'll notice you're getting much better value for your money as the quality increases exponentially with each extra dollar you spend.

Changing Money

US dollars – cash or travellers cheques – are the easiest items of currency to change and many businesses accept US cash. Banks will change US and Canadian dollars and pounds sterling. Other currencies may be difficult or impossible to exchange. Street money-changers don't offer a significantly better rate than banks, but may be your only choice at borders or if the banks are closed. Belizean bank machines do not accept foreign ATM cards. However, Visa, MasterCard and, to a lesser extent, American Express are accepted in cities and major tourist destinations.

ONLINE SERVICES

For a country so far behind the technological curve, Belize has a lot of web sites, many of them impressive. Lonely Planet's web site is Destination Belize (www.lonelyplanet.com/dest/cam/belize.htm).

Belize Online (www.belize.com) is a good source of information on parks, hotels, and activities in Belize. It also has a calendar of events and guidelines for responsible tourism which are worth a look.

The exhaustive You Better Belize It! (www.belizeit.com) has all the general information you could ever need, plus a chat board, news and weather sections and a searchable database.

The professional and stunning Belize by Naturalight site (www.belizenet.com) is hard to top for ease of navigation and creativity in design. Go here for all your general Belize research, plus added goodies such as the Belizean picture of the day, which is certain to get your travel juices flowing.

If you're going to the cayes, you'll find mountains of specific information on their particular web sites. For Ambergris Caye, go to Ambergris Caye.com (www.ambergriscaye.com), and for Caye Caulker, visit Go CayeCaulker.com (www.gocayecaulker.com).

BOOKS

For a good yarn about travels in the region, try *Time Among the Maya: Travels in Belize, Guatemala and Mexico* by Ronald Wright. Another good read in the same vein is *Tekkin a Waalk* by Peter Ford, which describes travelling up the Caribbean coast from Panama to Belize.

The Maya by Michael D Coe is considered one of the best introductions to the history and culture of the Maya, though some may find it too academic. More accessible is *A Forest of Kings: The Untold Story of the Ancient Maya* by L Shele & D Freidel.

FILMS

Many Hollywood films set in the jungle are filmed in Belize, though they often depict other locales. *The Mosquito Coast* starring Harrison Ford and River Phoenix and based on the novel by Paul Theroux is one such film; it will give you an idea of some of the more unpleasant aspects of the Belizean environment. The classic Joseph Conrad novel *Heart of Darkness* was adapted into a film shot in Belize as well.

ENTERING & LEAVING

Visitors flying into Belize land at Goldson international airport in Belize City. There are direct US flights from Los Angeles, Miami and Houston. Travellers from Europe, Australia or New Zealand will probably have to pass through one of these gateway cities. Departing from Belize by air, there is a US$15 departure tax. In the past there have been regional flights between Cancún and Belize City and there are several airlines that make the trip between Belize City and Flores, Guatemala near Tikal.

Travellers arriving overland from Mexico cross at Chetumal and into Belize at Corozal. To enter Guatemala, you leave Belize at Benque Viejo del Carmen and enter Guatemala at Melchor de Mencos. When crossing Belizean land borders, you have to pay a tax of around US$4. You can also travel by boat from Punta Gorda in southern Belize to Puerto Barrios and Lívingston in Guatemala or from Dangriga and Placencia to Puerto Cortés in Honduras.

BOLIVIA

In colloquial terms, Bolivia is the Tibet of the Americas. Wild, rugged mountains and fertile valleys in the heart of the Andes share the stage with the lowland jungle of the Amazon Basin and the grandeur of Lake Titicaca. In addition to this awesome natural landscape, Bolivia leads all South American countries in colourful and vibrant traditional culture, with more than half of the population boasting pure Amerindian blood.

Outdoor enthusiasts will swoon over Bolivia's snowcapped peaks, volcanoes and lake region. Travellers interested in archaeology, anthropology or history will be occupied visiting the ruins of Tiahuanaco, the Jesuit churches of the Eastern Lowlands and the silver mines at Potosí. Visitors to the jungle and the pampas in the east are treated to superb wildlife viewing and birdwatching. Ironically, Bolivia has yet to register on the gringo radar, with comparatively few independent backpackers making it to this stunning country. Yet you'd be hard-pressed to find a more charming and adventurous destination.

WHEN TO GO

Bolivia has a climate that defies generalisation. Bolivia is in the southern hemisphere, so summer is from November to April and winter from May to October. As opposed to most tropical countries, the Bolivian summer is wet and the winter dry. The best time for a visit to the highlands and altiplano is summer, when it's warmer but then you'll have to contend with torpid, humid lowlands where travel can be difficult. Summer in the jungle means mud, bugs, incessant rain and impassable roads. The ultimate time for a general tour of Bolivia therefore is in winter, particularly from June to September, and this is considered the high tourist season. Bolivia's major festivals also fall in this period and accommodation can be tight and more expensive. You may want to book ahead to avoid disappointment.

At a Glance

Full Country Name: Republic of Bolivia
Area: 1,098,580 sq km
Population: 7,982,850
Capital City: La Paz (pop one million) and Sucre (pop 100,000)
People: 30% Quechua Indian, about 28% mestizo, about 25% Aymara Indian, 16% European (principally Spanish) and 1% African descent
Languages: Spanish but most Indians speak either Quechua or Aymara; composite dialects of Spanish-Aymara and Spanish-Quechua are also widely spoken
Religion: 95% Roman Catholic, plus 5% adhering to syncretic beliefs that blend western and indigenous religious tenets
Government: Democracy
Currency: Boliviano (B$)
Time Zone: Four hours behind GMT/UTC
International Telephone Code: 591
Electricity: 220V, 50 cycles AC, except in La Paz and a few areas in Potosí which run at 110V, 50 cycles; most plugs are the two-pin round type, but two-pronged flat plugs are sometimes used

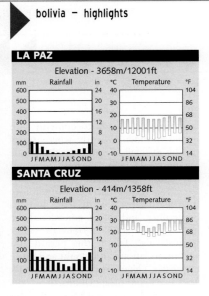

LA PAZ

Elevation - 3658m/12001ft

Rainfall | Temperature

SANTA CRUZ

Elevation - 414m/1358ft

Rainfall | Temperature

HIGHLIGHTS

Bolivia is like many Latin American countries rolled into one and the quantity and type of activities reflects that diversity. Whether your interests are primarily environmental, cultural or historical, Bolivia won't fail to intrigue. In addition to the attractions listed below, Bolivia is one of the better countries in the region for train travel.

Trekking, Camping & Mountain Climbing

From ancient Incan roads in the Cordillera Real to night hikes in the lowland jungle, Bolivia is a trekker's delight. Hard-core alpinists will want to check out the Cordillera Quimsa Cruz, nicknamed the 'South American Karakoram'; the first-ascent opportunities in the Cordillera Apolobamba; and the tricky glacier climbs up Nevado Sajama. Established camp sites are few, but with the right gear, you can backcountry camp almost anywhere in Bolivia.

Wildlife Viewing

The two greatest areas for seeing wildlife are the Chaco, in the southeastern region, and the Amazonian lowlands. The Chaco is an impenetrable, largely inhospitable scrubland that supports rare native flora and fauna. Jaguars, peccaries, tapirs, butterflies and a variety of birds are in abundance here. The jungle lowlands support black caimans, several species of monkeys, hundreds of bird species, anteaters and jaguars, among many other animals. There are several national parks in this region; a popular jumping-off point for jungle tours is Rurrenabaque. Women should only travel with reputable, established guides in the Rurrenabaque area as there have been several reports of rape involving guides here.

Lakes

At 3820m above sea level and 457m deep, Lake Titicaca is an extraordinary natural wonder and a sight visitors will not quickly forget. There are spectacular hikes along the shore, linking different ancient villages, plus offshore islands with camping opportunities. For something completely different, there are lakes Poopó and Uru Uru near Bolivia's largest salt flat, the 12,106 sq km Salar de Uyuni. There is good birding here. The colourful Colorada and Verde lagoons are well worth a look, too.

Cities

Bolivian cities are as varied as their people and a visit to one or two will provide a different flavour to your trip. At nearly 4km above sea level, La Paz is the highest capital in the world and is chock-full of colonial churches and museums. Potosí is the world's highest city at 4090m and the centre of the Bolivian silver mines. Once the richest city in Latin America, and now a UNESCO World Heritage Site, Potosí was built with the sweat and blood of exploited mine workers. Locals consider Sucre, to the north-east, the most beautiful Bolivian city and visitors will be charmed by the colonial mansions, churches and museums which dominate this pleasant place.

VISA REQUIREMENTS

Citizens of most western countries including Canada, New Zealand, Australia, the UK and USA do not need visas to enter Bolivia. Your country of origin dictates how long you are permitted to stay in the country. Citizens of Canada and Australia receive 30 days, with a maximum extension to 90 days. If your paperwork is in order, extensions are easily obtainable at immigration offices in Bolivian cities. Citizens of New Zealand, the USA and UK receive 90 days and are allowed extensions. Minors travelling without both parents need special documentation. Bolivian visa requirements are convoluted and often arbitrary. Check with an embassy before you travel.

Bolivian Embassies

Australia/New Zealand
(☎ 07-3221 1606, fax 3229 7175) Suite 512, Pennys Building, 210 Queen St (GPO Box 53), Brisbane, Qld 4001

Brazil
(☎ 551-1796, fax 551-3047) Bolivia Avenida Rui Barbosa 664, No 101, Flamengo, Rio de Janeiro;
(☎ 881-1688) Bolivia Rua de Eonduras 1147, São Paulo

Canada
(☎ 613-236-5730) 17 Metcalfe St, Suite 608, Ottawa, Ontario K1P 426

Chile
(☎ 232-8180) Avenida Santa María 2796, Santiago

Peru
(☎ 422-8231) Los Castaños 235, San Isidro

UK
(☎ 020-7235 4248) 106 Eaton Square, SW12W London

USA
(☎ 202-483-4410) 3014 Massachusetts Ave NW, Washington, DC 20008
Consulate: New York

TOURIST OFFICES OVERSEAS

Bolivia does not maintain overseas tourist offices, though a well informed travel agent may be able to answer your questions. Contact a Bolivian consulate or embassy for general information and see the web sites listed under Online Services later.

HEALTH

Malaria exists throughout the year in lowland rural areas and yellow fever can occur. Dengue fever occurs in the tropical parts of the country. Avoid mosquito bites both day and night and avoid bites from all insects to prevent other serious diseases. As many Bolivian cities and towns are above 3000m, be aware of the symptoms of altitude sickness (see the Health chapter for more information); trekkers should be prepared for cold conditions. Take care with what you eat and drink to prevent diseases including hepatitis, typhoid, cholera and dysentery. Drink only bottled or purified water and avoid undercooked meat and any suspect seafood.

Medical care in La Paz and other major centres is reasonable, but limited in rural areas.

POST & COMMUNICATIONS

Bolivian postal services are generally reliable, though anything important should be sent by registered post. Receiving poste restante mail is possible in the big cities.

International calls can be placed from centralised call centres or private phones, although reverse charge (collect) calls are possible from private phones only. The cost is outrageous — about US$20 for a 40 second collect call between Bolivia and Europe. Faxes can be sent and received from phone offices in most towns and are charged by the minute.

Email and Internet services (about US$3 an hour online) are available in La Paz and Santa Cruz and should be available soon in other towns.

MONEY
Costs

Budget-conscious travellers who can live with the rough edges will spend around only US$10 a day, while those favouring a little more comfort and style should count on double or even triple that if they splash out. With around US$35 a day or more, you can really live the high life in Bolivia.

Changing Money

Travellers will have trouble changing any foreign currency other than US dollars. In some La Paz exchange houses you can change money from neighbouring countries, but that's about it. Exchange houses will change US cash and travellers cheques and are far more efficient than banks. Unorthodox venues such as jewellery and appliance stores, pharmacies and travel agencies legally serve as exchange houses as well. They'll change cash and travellers cheques, but charge a large commission on the latter. It can be hard to exchange money outside larger towns, especially travellers cheques, so be prepared if you're heading into the

Itineraries

One Week
Spend three days exploring La Paz, including a visit to the ruins at Tiahuanaco and a hike around the extinct volcano of Muela del Diablo in the Valley of the Moon. Head to the shores of Lake Titicaca and the festival town of Copacabana. Spend two days exploring the lakeshore, visiting museums and ancient villages before returning to La Paz.

Two Weeks
Follow the one week itinerary and include a two day hike to the Isla de Sol in Lake Titicaca and a side trip to Coroico in the Yungas. Alternatively, you could hike the Taquesi, La Cumbre to Coroico or Yunga Cruz routes. Or you could do the one week itinerary and a train trip to the impressive salt flats and lakes near Oruro.

Three Weeks
To either of the above two-week itineraries, you could add one of the following: three days hiking in the Sorata area and a couple of days hiking in the Zona Sur; a jungle or pampas trip from Rurrenabaque; or visits to Sucre and Potosí.

One to Two Months
Follow all of the three-week itineraries and include a trip from Sucre through to Santa Cruz, Samaipata and the Jesuit Missions loop and then on to the Chaco towns of Tarija and Tupiza; a trek in the Cordillera Apolobamba with a visit to the Parque Nacional Ulla Ulla; and a trip up to Parque Nacional Noel Kempff Mercado in the country's east.

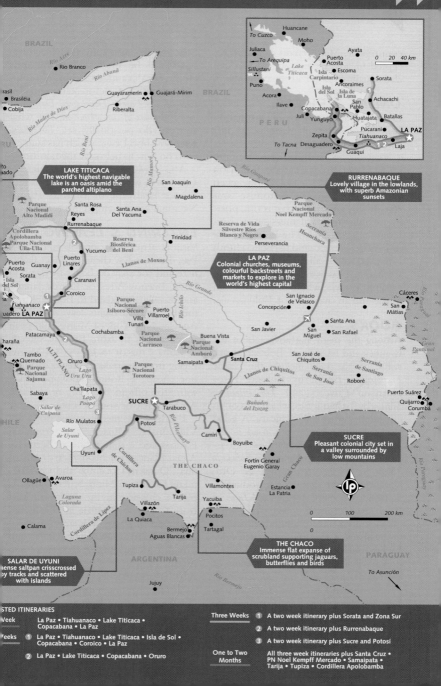

OLIVIA HIGHLIGHTS & ITINERARIES

LAKE TITICACA
The world's highest navigable lake is an oasis amid the parched altiplano

RURRENABAQUE
Lovely village in the lowlands, with superb Amazonian sunsets

LA PAZ
Colonial churches, museums, colourful backstreets and markets to explore in the world's highest capital

SUCRE
Pleasant colonial city set in a valley surrounded by low mountains

THE CHACO
Immense flat expanse of scrubland supporting jaguars, butterflies and birds

SALAR DE UYUNI
mmense saltpan crisscrossed by tracks and scattered with islands

countryside. Major credit cards are accepted in larger cities, where you can also usually get cash advances on them.

ONLINE SERVICES

Lonely Planet's web site is Destination Bolivia (www.lonelyplanet.com/dest /sam/bolivia.htm).

Virtually everything you want to know about Bolivia can be found on the Bolivia Web (www.boliviaweb .com). Here you can customise your research by entering a chat room, posting a bulletin board message or running a classified ad. The Bolivian Café (http//:jaguar.pg.cc.md.us/bolivia.html) is packed full of all the usual tourist information, plus extras like how to set up email in Bolivia, where to buy Bolivian music and an overview of Bolivian art.

BOOKS

Among the many narratives about the beauties and hazards of Bolivian travel, some of the best include the classic *Exploration Fawcett* by Colonel Percy Harrison Fawcett and *The Incredible Voyage* by Tristan Jones, which tells of an adventure across Lake Titicaca. A good read while you're on the road is the humorous *Inca-Kola* by Matthew Parris.

The up-to-date and accurate *Bolivia in Focus* by Paul van Lindert & Otto Verkoren is the definitive introduction to Bolivian society. *The Incredible Incas & Their Timeless Land* by Loren McIntyre is chock-full of photos and information à la *National Geographic* and will give history buffs plenty to chew on.

A fascinating blow-by-blow account of the failed Cuban-style revolution in Bolivia is found in Ernersto Ché Guevara's *Bolivian Diary*. For a trip around the continent with a 22-year-old Ernesto, check out Guevara's *Motorcycle Diaries*.

Conservationists and rainforest enthusiasts will be interested in Susanna Hecht & Alexander Cockburn's complex analysis of deforestation in *The Fate of the Forest: Developers, Destroyers, and Defenders of the Amazon*. For what you can do personally, see *The Rainforest Book* by S Lewis, which has suggestions on how to help save the rainforest.

A C Doyle's science fiction tale, *The Lost World*, was inspired by the mountainous landscape of Bolivia's Parque Nacional Noel Kempff Mercado.

ENTERING & LEAVING

Visitors arriving by air will land in La Paz; there are few cheap or direct flights here and you may do better by flying to Lima, Buenos Aires or Rio de Janeiro and travelling overland to Bolivia. From the USA, most flights leave from Los Angeles, New York or Miami. European travellers can fly from Brussels directly to Santa Cruz or to La Paz via Miami. Flying from Australia or New Zealand is not cheap; a Round-the-World ticket with stop-offs in the USA or in Latin America may be your best bet.

Border crossings at major posts are Villazón-La Quiaca and Yacuiba-Pocitos and a minor one at Bermejo-Aguas Blancas, reached by ferry (Argentina); Quijarro-Corumbà and Guayaramerín to Guajarà-Mirim by ferry (Brazil), plus a crossing in the far north-west from Cobija to Brasiléia in Brazil, and from San Matías to Cáceres; Charaña-Visviri and Avaroa-Ollagüe (Chile); and Yunguyo-Puno and Desaguadero-Puno (Peru). You can cross to Peru via Copacabana and Huatajata across Lake Titicaca. There's a rough three day overland crossing between Boyuibe in Bolivia and Estancia La Patria (heading to Filadelfia) in Paraguay.

BRAZIL

Brazil is one of those countries whose image stays in your mind and heart even if you've never set foot in Rio or Manaus. The mythical magic of the Amazon, the debauchery of Carnaval and the beats and strains of *tropicalismo* have garnered a worldwide reputation and made Brazil the preternatural travel destination of choice. Imagine a country as big as the USA (less Alaska), packed with fun-loving folks of all colour, with stellar beaches, primordial rainforests and towering mountains. Sprinkle in a massive stretch of wetlands, home to the largest concentration of fauna on the planet, and mighty waterfalls, and you'll have some idea of what Brazil has going for it.

WHEN TO GO

There is really no bad time to visit Brazil; the geography is so varied and the country so massive that finding pockets of good weather is no great challenge. The one exception may be in the south, where summer (December to February) can be sticky, hot and humid and winter (June to August) brings interminable downpours. Short, tropical rains can come at all times of the year throughout the country, but rarely affect travel plans. Holidays and festivals – particularly Carnaval – will disrupt travel schedules if you don't plan ahead. December to February and through Carnaval is the holiday period for most Brazilians and accommodation can be difficult, if not impossible, to find in Rio and other popular beach spots.

HIGHLIGHTS

Brazil has so much to offer beyond the Carnaval and Amazon jungle jaunts, that any trip to this vast, fascinating country should include a broader range of activities. The following highlights are just a taste of what Brazil has to offer.

At a Glance

Full Country Name: Federative Republic of Brazil
Area: 8,511,965 sq km
Population: 171,850,000
Capital City: Brasília (pop 1,700,000)
People: 56% European descent, 38% mulatto and 6% African descent; in reality, these figures are skewed by whiteness being equated with social staturel
Languages: Portuguese
Religion: 90% Roman Catholic; 10% have syncretic beliefs such as Macumba and Candomblé
Government: Federal republic
Currency: Real (R$)
Time Zone: There are four time zones: the eastern, north-eastern, southern and south-eastern regions are three hours behind GMT/UTC; Roraima, Rondônia, Mato Grosso, Mato Grosso do Sul, part of Pará and most of Amazonas are four hours behind GMT/UTC; the rest of the country is five hours behind GMT/UTC; and the Fernando de Noronha island is two hours behind GMT/UTC
International Telephone Code: 55
Electricity: Most of Rio de Janeiro and São Paulo run on 110 or 120V, 60 cycles AC; Salvador and Manaus are on 127V and various other cities use 220V – check before you plug in

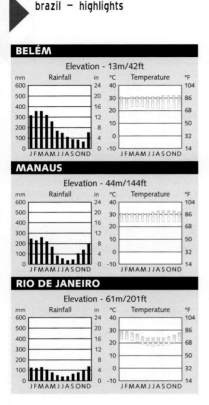

Beaches & Surfing

Brazil lays claim to more than 8000km of coastline and scores of fantastic beaches. Among the most impressive coastal beaches are Prainha near Natal, Praia Ponta do Bicho on Ilha do Mel and Pepino and Barra de Tijuca near Rio de Janeiro. Make sure you don't overlook the excellent river beaches in the north of the country, such as Alter do Chão near Santarém, and Salinópolis at the mouth of the Rio Amazonas. Surfers will be delighted with the fantastic breaks to be had at Praia do Santinho and Praia do Joaquina in Santa Catarina and Saquarema near Rio.

Festivals

Carnaval is the granddaddy of all festivals, and celebrations are held all around Brazil on the two days preceding Ash Wednesday (though the party lasts much longer). The biggest and best Carnaval spectacle takes place in Rio, but locals and travellers also favour the intimate and charming *fête* at Olinda. Other festivals include a return to the Middle Ages in Cavalhadas during a three day celebration featuring dances and medieval tournaments, Semana Santa (Easter Week) in Goiás Velho where locals re-enact Christ's removal from the cross and his interment, and the unforgettable New Year's Eve celebration on Copacabana beach in Rio.

Wildlife Viewing

The Pantanal may be Brazil's (and the world's) best kept secret. While everyone is straining to see elusive wildlife among the foliage of the Amazonian rainforest, visitors to the Pantanal (a vast wetland half the size of France) are checking out all manner of animals in the open. The Pantanal has the most dense concentration of fauna in the world and supports around 270 bird species, jaguars, ocelots, capybaras, monkeys and other animals. Of course, Brazil also boasts the world's largest equatorial rainforest: there are at least 15,000 species living in the Amazon here and parts have yet to be explored. On a tour you may see sloths, peccaries, armadillos (five species), dolphins, manatees, turtles and monkeys.

Music & Dance

No overview of Brazil would be complete without a nod to the incredible music and dance born and bred here.

The north (particularly the state of Bahia) hops with regional music styles including *carimbó*, *boi* and *brega* and every Tuesday and Sunday night in Pelourinho near Salvador there are giant musical dance parties. Afro-Brazilian music called *afoxé* is an important part of the syncretic religion called Candomblé – akin to voodoo in Haiti – and can be appreciated in Bahia. *Samba* is a veritable craze in Brazil and the samba clubs pull out all stops during Carnaval.

Natural Attractions

The Foz do Iguaçu is one of the greatest natural wonders of the world. It dwarfs Africa's Niagara and Victoria falls in grandeur and is a must-see for visitors to the region. There are over 70 national parks, biological reserves and ecological stations in Brazil, so nature enthusiasts will not want for excursions. Within the boundaries of Parque Nacional de Aparados da Serra is the famous Canyon do Itaimbézinho, a narrow canyon dotted with waterfalls and precipitous escarpments dropping 600 to 720m. Camping is possible in Parque Nacional da Chapada dos Guimarães where bizarre rock formations are reminiscent of the American southwest. If you're into remote islands, check out Estação Ecológica de Anavilhanas, an extensive archipelago 100km upriver from Manaus.

Itineraries

One Week
It's a pity to have such a short stint in Brazil, but if this is all you can manage, spend it exploring one interesting city and its environs like Rio or Salvador (known as the Black Rome). If you choose the former, you can visit one of four national parks close to the city or hang out at nearby beaches where surfing and diving are possible. In Salvador, the music, beaches and the island of Itaparica, the largest in the Baía de Todos os Santos, will keep you busy for seven days.

Two Weeks
Choose either Rio or Salvador and add a three day trip to the Pantanal and a trip to the Foz do Iguaçu, spending the balance of your time at the amazing beaches of Santa Catarina around Florianópolis. Alternatively, you can head to the northern state of Amazonas and go on a three or four day jungle trip from a hub such as Manaus, followed by a few days in the colonial towns of Recife and Olinda. Either of these options will require at least one flight to the further reaches of the Pantanal or Amazonas.

Three to Four Weeks
With three weeks you can explore both Rio and Salvador, add a Pantanal or Amazonas trip, and check out the beaches of Santa Catarina in the south or near Fortaleza in the north. Spend the balance of your time visiting Foz do Iguaçu and Parque Nacional Chapada dos Guimarães. A visit to the capital, Brasília, or São Paulo will round out this itinerary.

Two to Three Months
This amount of time allows you to travel by bus, stopping at places that strike your fancy and making new friends. The classic route is overland from Paraguay or Bolivia through Corumbá, spending some time viewing wildlife in the Pantanal. Moving eastward, stop at Foz do Iguaçu and continue to São Paulo and Rio before heading north to Salvador. Hang out there for a while and spend some time at hip beaches like Arraial d'Ajuda, Trancoso or Morro de São Paulo. Make your way along the beaches of the north-east to Belém, followed by a trip to the Amazonas and then on to Peru, Colombia or home.

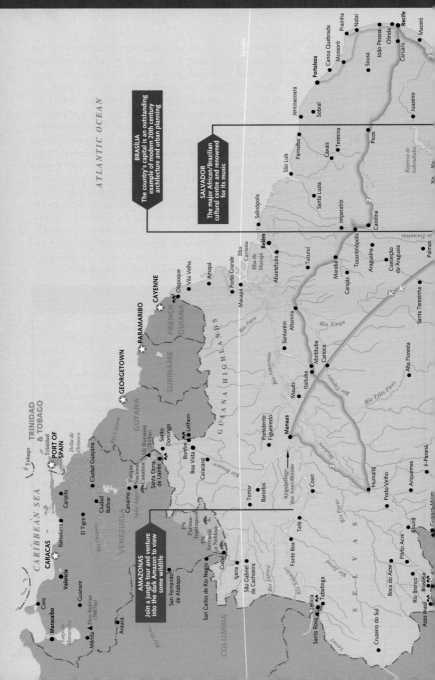

BRAZIL HIGHLIGHTS & ITINERARIES

BRASÍLIA
The country's capital is an outstanding example of modern 20th century architecture and urban planning

SALVADOR
The major African/Brazilian cultural centre and renowned for its music

AMAZONAS
Join a jungle tour and venture into the dark Amazon to view some wildlife

ATLANTIC OCEAN

Equator

CARIBBEAN SEA

CARACAS
Valencia
Maracaibo
Barcelona
Coro
El Tigre
Guanare
Arauca
Mérida ▲ Pico Bolívar (5007m)
Lago de Maracaibo
Río Meta

VENEZUELA
Ciudad Guayana
Ciudad Bolívar
Carúpano
Trinidad
TRINIDAD & TOBAGO
PORT OF SPAIN
Tobago
Delta de Orinoco
Río Orinoco
Río Caroní

GEORGETOWN
GUYANA
PARAMARIBO
SURINAME
CAYENNE
FRENCH GUIANA

Canaima
Salto Ángel
Santa Elena de Uairén
Parque Nacional Canaima
Mt Roraima (2810m)
PN Parima Tapirapecó
PN Serranía La Neblina

Olapoque
Vila Velha
Amapá
Macapá
Porto Grande
Ilha Caviana
Ilha de Marajó
Belém
Abaetetuba
Salinópolis

São Luís
Parnaíba
Caxias
Teresina
Picos
Santa Luzia
Imperatriz
Carolina

Jericoacoara
Sobral
Fortaleza
Canoa Quebrada
Mossoró
Sousa
Juazeiro
Prainha
Natal
João Pessoa
Olinda
Recife
Caruaru
Maceió

Represa de Sobradinho

Bonfim
Lethem
Boa Vista
Caracaraí
Santo Domingo

Tucuruí
Marabá
Carajás
Tocantinópolis
Araguaína
Conceição do Araguaia
Santa Terezinha
Palmas

GUIANA HIGHLANDS
Rio Branco
Tomar
Barcelos
Coari
Rio Negro
Arquipélago das Anavilhanas
Presidente Figueiredo
Manaus
Maués
Itaituba
Carioca
Miritituba
Santarém
Altamira
Rio Xingu
Rio Paru
Rio Amazonas
Rio Tapajós
Rio Teles Pires
Alta Floresta

São Gabriel da Cachoeira
Cucuí
Içana
San Carlos de Río Negro
San Fernando de Atabapo
COLOMBIA
Fonte Boa
Tefé
Rio Japurá
Rio Juruá
Rio Purus
Rio Madeira
Humaitá
Porto Velho
Ariquemes
Ji-Paraná
Abunã
Pôrto Acre
Rio Branco
Boca do Acre
Brasiléia
Assis Brasil
Guajará-Mirim

Leticia
Tabatinga
Santa Rosa
Cruzeiro do Sul
Rio Juruá
SELVAS

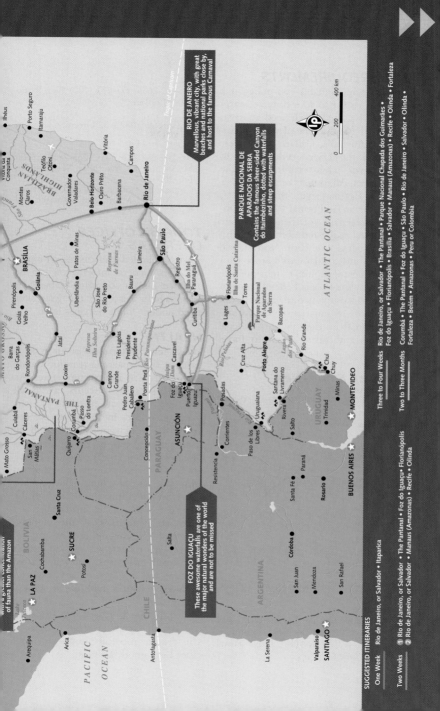

RIO DE JANEIRO
Marvellous, vibrant city, with great beaches and national parks close by, and host to the famous Carnaval

PARQUE NACIONAL DE APARADOS DA SERRA
Contains the famous sheer-sided Canyon do Itaimbézinho, dotted with waterfalls and steep escarpments

FOZ DO IGUAÇU
These awesome waterfalls are one of the major natural wonders of the world and are not to be missed

0   200   400 km

SUGGESTED ITINERARIES

One Week   Rio de Janeiro, or Salvador • Itaparica

Two Weeks   **1** Rio de Janeiro, or Salvador • The Pantanal • Foz do Iguaçu • Florianópolis
                 2 Rio de Janeiro, or Salvador • Manaus (Amazonas) • Recife • Olinda

Three to Four Weeks Rio de Janeiro, or Salvador • The Pantanal • Parque Nacional Chapada dos Guimarães •
                         Foz do Iguaçu • Florianópolis • Brasília • Salvador • Manaus (Amazonas) • Recife • Olinda • Fortaleza

Two to Three Months Corumbá • The Pantanal • Foz do Iguaçu • São Paulo • Rio de Janeiro • Salvador • Olinda •
                         Fortaleza • Belém • Amazonas • Peru or Colombia

VISA REQUIREMENTS

Brazil has an equitable visa policy: if a Brazilian visitor to your home country needs a visa, then you'll need a visa to visit Brazil. At the time of writing, citizens of Australia, Canada, New Zealand and the USA needed visas to enter Brazil, while visitors from the UK did not. All tourists receive a maximum 90 day stay, with the option to renew for an additional 90 days. Onward tickets and sufficient funds are sometimes requested during the renewal process – a chore you should attend to at least 15 days before your visa is due to expire. Extensions are handled by the Polícia Federal in major cities. Unaccompanied travellers under the age of 18 must produce a notarised letter from their parents or legal guardians authorising them to travel alone.

Brazilian Embassies

Argentina
(☎ 394-5227/5260) 5th floor, Carlos Pellegrini 1363, Buenos Aires

Australia
(☎ 02-6273 2372) 19 Forster Crescent, Yarralumla, ACT 2600

Bolivia
(☎ 350 769) 9th to 11th floors, Edificio Foncomin, Avenida 20 de Octubre 2038, La Paz

Canada
(☎ 613-237-1090) 450 Wilbrod St, Ottawa, Ontario K1N 6MB

Colombia
(☎ 571-218 0800) Calle 93 NR 14-20, Piso 8, Apartado Aerea 90540, Bogotá 8

French Guiana
(☎ 30 0467) 23 Chemin Saint Antoine, Cayenne

Paraguay
(☎ 21-44 8069) Calle General Diaz C/14 De Mayo NR 521, Edificio Faro Internacional – Tercero Piso, Caixa Postal 1314, Asunción

Peru
(☎ 446-2635, ext 131, 132) José Pardo 850, Miraflores

UK
(☎ 020-7499 0877) 32 Green St, London W1Y 4AT

USA
(☎ 202-238-2828, fax 238-2818) 3006 Massachusetts Ave NW, Washington, DC 20008
Consulates: Boston, Chicago, Houston, Los Angeles, Miami, San Francisco and New York

TOURIST OFFICES OVERSEAS

Brazil has limited overseas tourist representation. General information can be obtained from a consulate, embassy or travel agent. Also see the web sites listed under Online Services later.

HEALTH

Yellow fever and malaria occur in most parts of the Amazonia regions, mainly in the northern and western states. As dengue fever also occurs, avoid all mosquito bites if possible. Leishmaniasis occurs in the north-eastern areas, so avoid sandfly bites and all other insect bites to prevent serious diseases. Along the coast of Bahia, always wear shoes to prevent infection from the sand-dwelling parasite (bicho de pé). Schistosomiasis is present in the coastal regions of the north-east and there are outbreaks of meningoccal meningitis in the upper Amazon regions. Day to day you should expect few health problems, but watch what you eat and drink to prevent diseases such as hepatitis, typhoid, dysentery and cholera.

Health care is reasonable throughout Brazil, except in remote areas. If you require medical attention, major cities have good facilities.

POST & COMMUNICATIONS

Postal services are pretty reliable in Brazil, though receiving letters can be hit or miss. Air mail letters to North America or Europe typically arrive in a week. Allow about two weeks for air mail to Australia or New Zealand. Poste restante mail is usually held 30 days.

International phone calls are placed from a centralised phone centre called a *posto telefônico*. A clerk places your call, which you take in a booth. You pay after concluding your call. Rates are fairly steep, though discounts are available to many countries at certain times of day. Collect (reverse charge) and Home Country Direct calls are available from all phones. Fax services are offered at post offices.

Email can be accessed at one of the many Internet cafes popping up around the country.

MONEY
Costs

Unfortunately, no longer is cheap travel among Brazil's glorious attractions. Prices increased dramatically in the late 1990s and it now costs about as much to travel here as it would in Australia or south-eastern USA. This means if you really scrimp and eat little but rice and beans, you'll spend around US$30 a day. If you're moving around every few days, staying in hotels and eating in restaurants and/or drinking in bars nightly, you'll spend closer to US$60 a day. Keep in mind that the peak holiday season is from December to February, when prices can increase from 25 to 30%, sometimes more.

Changing Money

With very few exceptions, US dollars are the easiest currency to exchange in Brazil, so carry these to avoid hassles. Money can be exchanged at banks or exchange houses; the latter keep longer hours and offer slightly better rates than banks. Travellers cheques can be hard to change and the rate may be lower than for cash. You'll also probably be charged a 'transaction fee'. For these reasons, cash and credit cards should make up the bulk of your money. Visa is the most widely accepted credit card and cash advances are given without problems; ATMs are found all around the country and accept Visa or MasterCard and bank cards on the Plus system.

ONLINE SERVICES

Lonely Planet's web site is Destination Brazil (www.lonelyplanet.com/dest/sam /bra.htm).

The University of Texas Brazil site (http://lanic.utexas.edu/ilas/brazctr /school.html) is chock-full of useful links, as is the Brazilian Embassy's home page (www.brasil.emb.nw.dc.us /embing6.htm). Go here for consistently updated visa requirements as well.

The massive and informative Virtual Trip to Brazil (www.vivabrazil.com) has a searchable function, chat boards, FAQ section, a Brazilian white pages and just about everything else but the kitchen sink. Bem Vindo Ao Brazil (http://darkwing.uoregon.edu/~sergi ok/brasil.html) is a great introduction to the country and is particularly strong on cultural themes.

Visitors to Rio should check out the trilingual (English, German and Portuguese) site called All About Rio (http: //ipanema.com). As Rio is one of the only Latin American cities that tolerates open homosexuality, it's great to know the Net is cast so wide as to include The

Rio Gay Guide (http://ipanema.com/riôgay/home.htm). Here you'll find gay and lesbian links, good cruising spots and a bit of the local lingo.

BOOKS

Brazilian literature is world-class and inspiring. Read some of the following suggestions and you'll be applying for a visa in no time. Machado de Assis is a literary great and Avon Bard has published several of his books in English translation, including *Philosopher or Dog*, *Epitaph of a Small Winner* and *Dom Casmurro*. Anything you can get by Mário de Andrade is definitely worth a read and his classic *Macunaíma* will have you laughing out loud. Another absolutely hilarious and strange work is *Zero* by Ignácio de Loyola Brandão, which was banned by the military government until the country united in protest.

Jorge Amado is the name that pops up most often in conjunction with Brazilian literature. Among his better works are *Gabriela, Clove and Cinnamon* and *Dona Flor and Her Two Husbands*. The latter work was made into a film starring Sonia Braga. Clarice Lispector, one of a handful of talented women writers, has several collections of short stories, all superb. Gregory Rabassa is generally regarded as the finest translator of Brazilian literature; many of the above selections were crafted into English by him.

For early history, see *Red Gold: The Conquest of the Brazilian Indians* by J Hemming and *The Masters and the Slaves: A Study in the Development of Brazilian Civilization* by Gilberto Freyre, the most famous book on Brazil's colonial past.

Readable travelogues abound. *Brazilian Adventure* by Peter Fleming is a hilarious account of a young journalist's expedition into Mato Grosso in search of the disappeared Colonel Fawcett. *Wizard of the Upper Amazon – The Story of Manuel Córdova-Rios* by F Bruce Lamb is an interesting look at *yagé*, the hallucinogenic drug used by certain tribes of the upper Amazon.

FILMS

With such great musicians, dancers, authors and artists, it's no surprise that Brazil also produces excellent filmmakers. The 1959 *Orfeu Negro* (Black Orpheus) is a stunning re-enactment of the Orpheus and Eurydice myth, set in Rio during Carnaval with music by Luis Bonfa and Antonio Carlos Jobim; it is available on video with English, French or Italian subtitles.

Hector Babenco's 1981 film *Pixote* follows the life of a São Paulo street kid; this work won the best film award at Cannes. Babenco also directed the star-studded *At Play in the Fields of the Lord*, a screen adaptation of Peter Matthiessen's novel. *Carlota Joaquina – Princesa de Brasil* was directed by Brazilian film star Carla Camurut and is a very funny mix of satire, historical drama and fable.

ENTERING & LEAVING

Air passengers usually fly into Rio de Janeiro, though there are international airports at São Paulo, Recife, Fortaleza, Salvador, Belém and Manaus as well. From the USA, the cheapest flights are usually between New York and Rio and Miami and Recife. European travellers will want to get a flight from London to Rio. Visitors from Australia and New Zealand can fly from Sydney or Auckland through Buenos Aires to Rio. Otherwise check out deals like Circle

Pacific, Circle Americas or Round-the-World fares. The international departure tax is around US$36.

Brazil shares borders with every South American country save for Ecuador and Chile, so overland crossings are numerous. From Brazil to Argentina, most travellers pass through Foz do Iguaçu. Between Brazil and Bolivia there are at least four official border crossings, three by land and one by motorised canoe across the Rio Mamoré from Guajará-Mirim to Guayaramerín. Land crossings include Corumbá to Quijarro, Cáceres to San Matías, Brasiléia in the far west of Brazil to Cobija, and the stunning rail journey plied by the 'Death Train'. The Brazilian border town of Tabatinga crosses into Colombia at Leticia. This area is known as the Triple Frontier because you can also cross from Brazil (or Colombia) into Peru here by travelling up the Amazon to Iquitos. Another crossing between Brazil and Peru is at Assis Brasil/Iñapari. To enter French Guiana from Brazil, cross at Oiapoque to St Georges by motorised dugout; the crossing between Brazil and Guyana is at Bonfim, reached via Boa Vista. In addition, there are two major crossings to Paraguay (Foz do Iguaçu to Ciudad del Este and Ponta Porã to Pedro Juan Caballero), five to Uruguay (the most popular is from Chuí to Chuy and Montevideo) and one to Venezuela (Boa Vista to Santa Elena de Uairén). To Paraguay, there are also irregular boat trips from Corumbá to Asunción on the Río Paraguay. It is not possible to cross from Brazil into Suriname; you must cross overland or fly to Cayenne in French Guiana and continue from there.

CHILE

Considered off limits during the bloody dictatorship of General Augusto Pinochet, Chile is now an adventure destination for independent travellers favouring Andean peaks and tropical beaches in an hospitable environment. Chile owes its ecological diversity to its height and length rather than its breadth – at only a handful of points is the country wider than 180km – and nature enthusiasts will find plenty to do around the deserts, canyons, fjords, volcanoes and beaches that exemplify the country's wacky geography. Add to this the friendly and engaging nature of the Chilean people and thriving indigenous communities dotting the landscape and you have the potential for an exotic and memorable trip.

At a Glance

Full Country Name: Republic of Chile
Area: 756,950 sq km
Population: 14,973,843
Capital City: Santiago (pop five million)
People: 90% mestizo, 5% Indians and 5% European descent
Languages: Spanish and a handful of native languages, including Aymara, Mapuche and Rapa Nui
Religion: Over 90% Roman Catholic and 5% Protestant, as well as Lutherans, Jews, Presbyterians, Mormons and Pentecostals
Government: Constitutional republic
Currency: Peso (CH$)
Time Zone: Four hours behind GMT/UTC
International Telephone Code: 56
Electricity: 220V, 50 cycles AC; plugs are the round, two-pronged variety

WHEN TO GO

Varied topography means varied weather and on this score Chile is the champion. As a result of these different weather patterns, there is really no bad time to visit Chile. Santiago and Middle Chile are best visited in spring (September through November) or during the autumn harvest (late February into April), while the Lake District is best in summer (December through March). The ideal time for a skiing vacation is between June and August. Easter Island (Rapa Nui) is cooler, slightly cheaper and much less crowded outside the summer months. The same is true of the Juan Fernández archipelago, which can be inaccessible if winter rains erode the dirt air strip; March is the ideal time to visit.

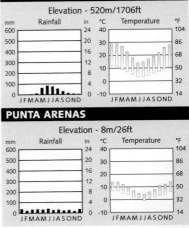

SANTIAGO
Elevation - 520m/1706ft

PUNTA ARENAS
Elevation - 8m/26ft

HIGHLIGHTS

Chile will prove a delight for outdoor fans and sports enthusiasts. Skiing, cycling, rafting and windsurfing are among the popular activities on the mainland. Easter Island (Rapa Nui) and the Juan Fernández islands offer special cultural and wildlife viewing opportunities as well. The following will help you decide what to do while in Chile.

Natural Attractions

From volcanoes and glaciers to deserts and beaches, Chile's natural attractions will not fail to intrigue. Some consider Parque Nacional Torres del Paine to be South America's finest national park and Parque Nacional Laguna San Rafael is not far behind, with its dense floating icebergs skirting massive glaciers. The Norte Grande is a stark desert with geysers and unique wildlife and the southern lake region offers unparalleled beauty. For beaches, head over to La Serena in the Norte Chico department or to Chile's finest beach resort, Viña del Mar, where the national botanical gardens are also located. Volcán Osorno is a picture-perfect volcano with both trekking and skiing opportunities. If you have the money and time, fly out to Archi-piélago Juan Fernández where cast-away Alexander Selkirk lived for over four years, giving Daniel Defoe the inspiration for his classic novel *Robinson Crusoe*.

Archaeological & Cultural Attractions

Chile lays claim to enigmatic Easter Island (Rapa Nui). Its massive stone carvings of disputed origin, and distinct Polynesian flavour are unlike anything else in the world. Norte

Easter Island

Easter Island (Rapa Nui) is the world's most remote inhabited island; you have to travel 1900km in any direction before hitting land again. Basically, Easter Island is a 117 sq km patch of volcanic rock in the middle of nowhere, but it is precisely this isolation that has intrigued and confounded historians, anthropologists and archaeologists for nearly a century.

Social scientists cannot agree how, why or who first colonised Rapa Nui way back in 400 AD. Did the original settlers sail from the eastern coast of South America or, as seems more likely, did they set off from the Polynesian islands of Tonga and Samoa? To further spice the mystery, the original inhabitants carved gargantuan, heavy stone idols called *moai* that they moved the breadth of the island in some cases. How these colossi (the largest soars 21m high) were moved is a matter of great debate. Were they placed on round rocks and rolled or was a complex system of pulleys, sledges and ropes employed? The enigma of Easter Island is like a onion that reveals innumerable layers once you start peeling away and the more you learn, the less you know.

Easter Island is an anomaly and visitors come here mainly to check out the archaeological ruins and surviving culture. There are some decent beaches and camping opportunities as well, but budget travellers will be disappointed with the price tag attached to a visit here. The regular return fare from Santiago, Chile is a steep US$815, but if you take advantage of LanChile's Circle Pacific fare, you get a stop-off in Easter Island and Tahiti before landing in Santiago. This is a particularly good option for travellers from Australia and New Zealand who have to pass over these islands to get to the South American mainland. Visitors from the USA can also take advantage of similar fares.

Grande was once part of the Inca empire and the archaeological sites and surviving indigenous communities here make for interesting travelling. Take a ferry to the Chiloé archipelago

One Week
Start with two days in Santiago and spend the balance visiting nearby wineries and hiking, climbing and rafting in the Cajón del Maipo area south-east of the capital. Visit the hot springs in Parque Nacional El Morado or take a day or two to ski at El Colorado or Portillo if time allows. Alternatively, you can whiz up to the northern desert to visit Parque Nacional Lauca.

Two Weeks
In two weeks you can follow either of the above suggestions and add a quick side trip to superb Patagonia attractions in the south, such as Parque Nacional Torres del Paine. Otherwise, follow the one week itinerary and include a loop of the southern lakes region and several days cruising through the Chilean fjords to Puerto Natales.

Three Weeks
Choose one of the two-week alternatives and add a side trip to Easter Island (Rapa Nui), visiting Valparaíso on the way there or back.

One to Two Months
With this much time you can follow all of the above suggestions, though the long distances involved may require flying between some points. Make sure you explore the beautiful countryside around places in the Lake District like Pucón, Chiloé and Temuco, with its volcanic cones towering above deep blue lakes, ancient forests and verdant farmland.

With two months, you can travel overland on the one month itinerary, and explore the area around the Peruvian border, and the great Atacama Desert in the Norte Grande.

to explore some of the 150 wooden churches serving these picturesque islands.

Trekking
Like all Andean countries, Chile offers fantastic trekking, but here there are established trails and campgrounds. Parque Nacional La Campana is easily accessible from Santiago and day hikes and longer treks abound in Parque Nacional Laguna del Laja. In the Lake District, rivers, lakes and waterfalls punctuate the forested landscape of Parque Nacional Huerquehue and the volcanoes of Parque Nacional Villarrica are easy to get to and a mecca for the hiking set. Parque Nacional Puyehue receives the most visitors annually, which is not surprising given its awesome volcanic setting and spectacular camping and hiking opportunities.

Cities
Big and bustling, the Chilean capital of Santiago is home to a variety of beautiful museums, including the Pre-Columbian Museum and the Palacio de Bellas Artes, which has a fine collection of European and Chilean art. Bellavista, known as the 'Paris quarter', is one of the city's liveliest areas. Valparaíso is Chile's largest port and second largest city. Cobblestoned streets overlooked by precipitous cliffs and hilltop suburbs are accessed by funicular railways and stairway footpaths, forming a maze akin to the medinas of Morocco. Puerto Montt in southern Chile was settled by German colonists and retains a European flavour. The cathedral on the plaza is worth a look and the nearby port of Angelmó and the island of Tenglo are good places to relax.

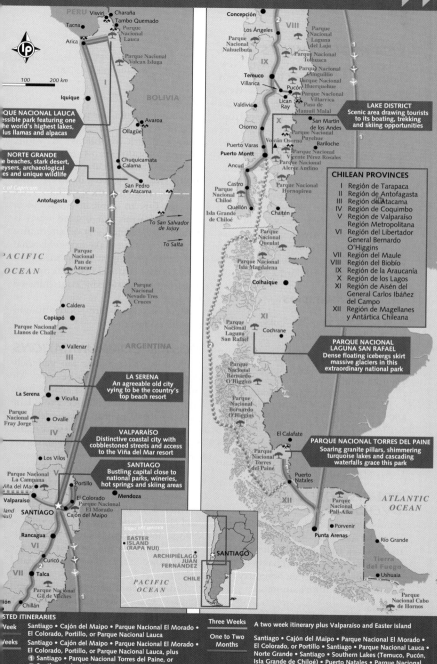

VISA REQUIREMENTS

Citizens of Australia, Canada, New Zealand, the USA and UK do not need visas to visit Chile. Upon arrival, visitors receive a tourist card and stamp valid for 90 days. Tourists from Australia, Canada and the USA are required to pay fees of US$30, US$50 and US$45 respectively upon entry. Tourist cards can be extended in Santiago for an additional 90 days (US$100). Most travellers prefer to cross into Argentina, Peru or Bolivia for a spell and return to Chile to receive a new 90 day tourist card instead. Chile requires visitors to have an onward ticket and airlines may ask to see one before they'll allow you to board a flight.

Chilean Embassies
Australia
(☎ 02-6286 2430) 10 Culgoa Circuit, O'Malley, ACT 2606
Canada
(☎ 613-235-4402) 151 Slater St, Suite 605, Ottawa, Ontario K1P 5H3
New Zealand
(☎ 72 5180) 7th floor, Robert Jones House, 1-3 Welleston St, Wellington
UK
(☎ 020-7580 1023) 12 Devonshire St, London W1N 2DS
USA
(☎ 202-785-3159) 1736 Massachusetts Ave NW, Washington, DC 20036

TOURIST OFFICES OVERSEAS

Tourist information can be obtained from the following offices. Also try representatives of LanChile, the national airline, or the Chilean embassy or consulate in your home country for general tourist information.

Canada
(☎ 613-235-4402) 56 Sparks St, Suite 801, Ottawa, Ontario K1P 5I4

USA
(☎ 202-785-1746) 1732 Massachusetts Ave NW, Washington, DC 20036

HEALTH

As neither malaria nor yellow fever are present, you should experience few serious health problems in Chile. Although, outbreaks of meningoccal meningitis have occurred in Chile in recent years. Be prepared for cold conditions in southern Chile. Tap water is OK to drink in cities and in most rural areas, but bottled water is widely available and a good alternative to the local water. Take care with what you eat, especially avoiding meat and *ceviché* (a raw seafood dish), to prevent diseases transmitted by contaminated food.

Medical services are good throughout the country.

POST & COMMUNICATIONS

Chilean postal services are generally dependable, but tend to be slow. Air mail is the fastest way to send letters. Important correspondence should be sent registered mail to ensure delivery. If you want to receive poste restante mail, keep the address lines simple; do not include titles or middle names. Your letter will probably be filed under the wrong letter, so check under both your first and last initials.

International phone calls are cheap and efficient and you can make reverse charge (collect) and credit card calls easily from phone booths on the street. Fax services are reliable and cheap.

Email access is hard to come by, and Internet cafes few and far between; try to access the web at a tech-savvy guesthouse or computer training centre.

MONEY
Costs

Inflation and revaluation of the Chilean peso make for some expensive travel here. The most frugal traveller should count on spending around US$20 a day, but for most people it will probably be higher. Eating at restaurants, staying in plusher accommodation and taking an occasional taxi could easily shoot your daily expenses into the US$40 range.

Changing Money

Money can be changed at banks, exchange houses, better hotels, travel agencies and on the street. US dollars in cash or travellers cheques are the easiest to change, though you'll lose money because of the commission levied on the latter. It is also difficult to exchange travellers cheques outside the major cities, so carry some cash when you travel further afield. Only in the bigger cities can you use Cirrus and Plus ATM cards for withdrawals. Credit cards are widely accepted for the most part, though local currency revaluations may result in a higher billing rate than you expected.

ONLINE SERVICES

Lonely Planet's web site is Destination Chile (www.lonelyplanet.com/dest/sam /chile.htm).

Check out the Chile Information Project (www.chip.cl) for articles from the Santiago Times, Chile's national English-language daily, which has current ski and surf conditions. Fans of the grape won't want to miss the Wines of Chile site (www.winesofchile .com); winery tours and tastings would make an interesting stop on a Chilean itinerary.

The mysteries of Easter Island (Rapa Nui) are explored and accompanied by fantastic photos at the Easter Island Home Page (www.netaxs.com/~trance /rapanui.html).

To get a blow-by-blow description of an independent traveller's odyssey through Chile, visit Trip Report – Chile (www.travel-library.com/south _america/chile/trip.dowd.html).

Spanish-speakers can head straight to La Brújula (www.brujula.cl/index .html), a comprehensive index of links to everything Chilean on the web.

BOOKS

Literature lovers will not want for Chilean reading material. Pablo Neruda and Gabriela Mistral are both Nobel Prize-winning poets with many works in translation. Try Neruda's *The Heights of Machu Picchu*, *Canto General* or *Passions* to get a feel for his poetry and *Memoirs* for a peek into his life. Langston Hughes translated Mistral's work in *Selected Poems of Gabriela Mistral*. Isabel Allende is a popular fiction writer who dabbles in magic realism in works such as *House of the Spirits* and *Eva Luna*.

For an account of post-Columbian Chilean history, check out either JH Parry's *The Discovery of South America* or Eduardo Galeano's *The Open Veins of Latin America: Five Centuries of the Pillage of a Continent*.

You could fill a small library with books about the Salvador Allende era and the ensuing Pinochet dictatorship. You may want to start with *Crisis in Allende's Chile* by Edy Kaufman and continue with James Petras & Morris Morley's *The United States and Chile: Imperialism and the Overthrow of the Allende Government*. For an insight into the Pinochet years, do not miss José Donoso's novel *Curfew* and Antonio Skármeta's *I Dreamt the Snow was Burning*. Joan Jara, the wife of murdered folk singer Victor Jara, has written the very personal *Victor; An Unfinished Song*.

Chilean writer Luis Sepúlveda's gripping personal odyssey takes him to different parts of the continent and beyond in *Full Circle: a South American journey*, published by Lonely Planet's travel literature series, Journeys.

FILMS

The Chilean film industry has always been prolific and cutting-edge. The 1971 cult classic *The Mole* was directed by Alejandro Jodorowsky and is one of the standout works in the Chilean film canon. Also worth checking out are *Alsino & the Condor*, which was nominated for a Best Foreign Film Academy Award in 1983, and director Gustavo Graef-Marino's *Johnny 100 Pesos*.

Foreign films dealing with Chilean themes include Costa Gavras' 1982 *Missing*, an outstanding adaptation of Thomas Hauser's book *The Execution of Charles Horman: An American Sacrifice*, and *Death and the Maiden* starring Ben Kingsley and Sigourney Weaver. The award-winning *Il Postino* tells an endearing, though fictional, tale of Pablo Neruda's mail carrier. All of these films are available on video.

ENTERING & LEAVING

Travellers arriving by air land at Arturo Merino Benítez international airport in the Santiago suburb of Pudahel. There are direct overseas connections from North America, the UK, Europe and Australia and New Zealand. Travellers from the last two countries may want to purchase a Circle Pacific fare that allows stop-offs in Tahiti and Easter Island (Rapa Nui). There is an international departure tax of about US$12.

The crossing between Arica in Chile and Tacna in Peru provides the only land access to Peru; road and rail connections link Chile with Bolivia, passing through Arica, Visviri, Tambo Quemado (Bolivia) or Calama (Chile). Except from Patagonia, every crossing into Argentina involves crossing the Andes. Routes include Calama to Jujuy and Salta; the popular Temuco to San Martín de Los Andes crossing, where there are regular summer buses across the Paso de Mamuil Malal; La Serena to San Juan (though there is no regular bus service here); and the very popular Santiago to Mendoza and on to Buenos Aires route. Some of these routes are closed in winter. More interesting are the many Lake District and southern Patagonian routes, with buses and ferries servicing the crossing points between Chile and Argentina. The most popular crossings in the Lake District include Puerto Montt to Bariloche via Parque Nacional Vicente Pérez Rosales route and the quick trip from Osorno to Bariloche via Paso Puyehue. For those travellers wishing to cross into Patagonia, the Punta Arenas to Tierra del Fuego trip is long and involves a three hour ferry ride and a combination of buses, but is popular nonetheless. Another option for crossing from Chilean Patagonia to Argentina is to go from Puerto Natales to Parque Nacional Torres del Paine via the Río Turbio and El Calafate. This is the gateway to Argentina's Parque Nacional los Glaciares.

COLOMBIA

As a travel destination, Colombia was blasted off the map thanks to an international media blitzkrieg armed with accounts of drugs, guerrillas, guns and money. These histrionics kept travellers away and so there is little infrastructure, no beaten track and the crowds are, needless to say, thin. In the 1980s and early 90s, all this bad press made for great independent travelling and those who could hack it were treated to a dynamic country with natural wonders, varied indigenous cultures and some of the warmest hospitality in Latin America. But that was in the good old days.

Unfortunately, travel in Colombia became decidedly less fabulous and more treacherous when insurgent groups started targeting tourists in opportunistic fits of violence. In 1998 a tour group on a birdwatching expedition was kidnapped, and in March 1999 three US citizens were kidnapped and murdered. Rural areas are considered off limits to tourists and there are several demilitarised regions over which the government has no control; these are also no-go zones. Though there are still some daredevil travellers visiting Colombia and having a great time, until things cool down, we suggest you stick to the armchair variety of travel when it comes to Colombia.

WHEN TO GO

Colombia's dry season runs from December to March and this is the best time for a visit, especially if you intend to do any trekking. As an added bonus,

many festivals also take place during this time. However, between December and January is when Colombians take their holidays, so transport can be crowded and hotels full. Plan ahead if you'll be here during the holidays.

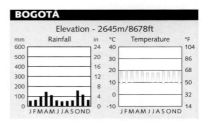

BOGOTÁ
Elevation - 2645m/8678ft

At a Glance

Full Country Name: Republic of Colombia
Area: 1,138,900 sq km
Population: 39,309,422
Capital City: Bogotá (pop five million)
People: 58% mestizo (of European-Indian descent), 20% European descent, 14% mulatto (African-European descent), 4% African descent, 3% African-Indian descent and 1% Indian
Languages: Castilian Spanish, plus over 200 indigenous Indian languages
Religion: 95% Catholic, with the remainder a mixture of traditional, Episcopal and Jewish faiths
Government: Constitutional democracy
Currency: Peso (Col$)
Time Zone: Five hours behind GMT/UTC
International Telephone Code: 57
Electricity: 110V, 60 cycles AC, except for small areas of Bogotá where it's 150V; plugs are the two-pronged North American type.

HIGHLIGHTS

Violent guerrilla activity and the government forces fighting to quell it make travelling in the countryside quite a dangerous proposition. If you do opt to go trekking, contract a guide in Bogotá, check with local authorities about volatile areas and stick to popular trails.

Itineraries

One Week
Spend two days exploring the many museums, cathedrals and plazas of Bogotá. Head north by train to the small town of Nemocón and continue to Guatavita. Visit the sacred Laguna de Guatavita, the birthplace of the infamous El Dorado myth. Push north to the picturesque town of Tenza from where you can travel around the Valle de Tenza before returning to Bogotá.

Two Weeks
Follow the one week itinerary and continue to the Sierra Nevada del Cocuy north-east of Tenza for several days of spectacular hiking and camping. This is a strenuous, technical hike and if you're not a trekker, you may prefer to follow the one week itinerary with a week in and around the laid-back town of Cali.

Three Weeks
Follow either of the two week alternatives and add an excursion to the south-west and the archaeological sites of San Agustín and Tierradentro, plus the colonial city of Popayán. Alternatively, head to the north-west. Here, there is an extensive stretch of tropical rainforest and the lovely Parque Nacional Los Katíos near the Panamanian border.

One Month
Do all the legs of the three week itineraries, plus add a few days in Cartagena and spend the rest of the time snorkelling, scuba diving or relaxing on the Caribbean coast. If the beach isn't your thing, you can add a trip to Leticia in the Amazon lowlands instead.

Mountain & Rock Climbing
Some of Colombia's most challenging mountaineering is in the Sierra Nevada del Cocuy and Sierra Nevada de Santa Marta ranges. The latter includes the Nabusímake to Pico Colón trek near the Caribbean coast. Suesca near Bogotá is good for rock climbing and Parque Nacional Puracé in the south-west has volcanoes, rivers and lakes – spectacular landscapes for some rugged trekking.

Beaches
Colombia has 3000km of coastline, with enough gorgeous sand and surf to impress even the most discerning beach lover. Parque Nacional Tayrona on the Caribbean coast has some of the best beaches, but Cabo de la Vela and Sapzurro, near Capurganá, run a close second. Scuba diving and snorkelling are particularly good off the Archipiélago de San Andrés and Providencia (230km east of the Nicaraguan coast) and near Islas del Rosario, off the Colombian coast near Cartagena.

Jungle Trips
Colombia's Amazon Basin region covers about 400,000 sq km and is characterised by dense, virgin jungle. This area supports more than 200 mammal species, 600 species of birds, 200 species of reptiles and 600 species of fish. In addition, there are many isolated indigenous communities tucked into this part of Colombia; arrangements can be made to visit or stay with them. It's not easy or cheap to get to Leticia (from where most trips start), but if you do, you'll be treated to an authentic experience.

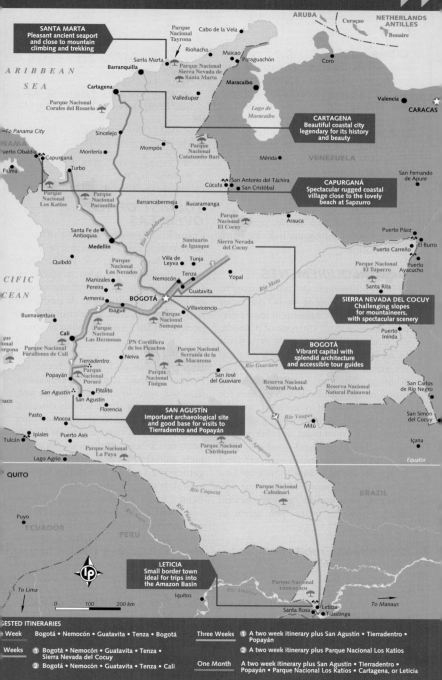

OLOMBIA HIGHLIGHTS & ITINERARIES

SANTA MARTA
Pleasant ancient seaport and close to mountain climbing and trekking

CARTAGENA
Beautiful coastal city legendary for its history and beauty

CAPURGANÁ
Spectacular rugged coastal village close to the lovely beach at Sapzurro

SIERRA NEVADA DEL COCUY
Challenging slopes for mountaineers, with spectacular scenery

BOGOTÁ
Vibrant capital with splendid architecture and accessible tour guides

SAN AGUSTÍN
Important archaeological site and good base for visits to Tierradentro and Popayán

LETICIA
Small border town ideal for trips into the Amazon Basin

CARIBBEAN SEA

NETHERLANDS ANTILLES

ARUBA
Curaçao
Bonaire

Cabo de la Vela
Parque Nacional Tayrona
Riohacha
Maicao
Paraguachón
Coro

Santa Marta
Barranquilla
Parque Nacional Sierra Nevada de Santa Marta
Valledupar
Maracaibo
Valencia
CARACAS

Cartagena
Parque Nacional Corales del Rosario
Lago de Maracaibo

To Panama City

PANAMA
Puerto Obaldia
Palma
Capurganá
Turbo

Sincelejo
Montería
Mompós
Parque Nacional Catatumbo Bari
Mérida
VENEZUELA

Parque Nacional Los Katíos
Parque Nacional Paramillo
Barrancabermeja
Bucaramanga
San Antonio del Táchira
Cúcuta
San Cristóbal

Arauca
Parque Nacional El Cocuy
Puerto Páez
El Burro
Puerto Carreño

Santa Fe de Antioquia
Río Magdalena
Santuario de Iguaque
Sierra Nevada del Cocuy
Parque Nacional El Tuparro
Puerto Ayacucho

Medellín
Quibdó
Parque Nacional Los Nevados
Villa de Leyva
Tunja
Nemocón
Tenza
Yopal
Santa Rita

PACIFIC OCEAN

Manizales
Pereira
Armenia
BOGOTÁ
Guatavita
Villavicencio
Río Meta
Puerto Inírida

Buenaventura
Ibagué
Parque Nacional Sumapaz
Parque Nacional Serranía de la Macarena

Cali
Parque Nacional Las Hermosas
PN Cordillera de los Picachos
Río Guaviare
San Carlos de Río Negro

Parque Nacional Farallones de Cali
Tierradentro
Neiva
Parque Nacional Tinigua
San José del Guaviare
Reserva Nacional Natural Nukak
Reserva Nacional Natural Puinawai

Popayán
Parque Nacional Puracé
Pitalito
San Agustín
Florencia
Río Vaupés
Mitú
San Simón del Cocuy

Pasto
Mocoa
Río Caquetá
Río Apaporis
Içana

Ipiales
Tulcán
Puerto Asis
Parque Nacional Chiribiquete
Equator

Lago Agrio
Parque Nacional La Paya

QUITO

ECUADOR
Puyo
PERU
Río Putumayo
Parque Nacional Cahuinari
BRAZIL

To Lima

Iquitos
Leticia
Tabatinga
Santa Rosa
Parque Nacional Amacayacu
To Manaus

Cities

Bogotá, the country's capital, is the essence of all things Colombian. It's a city of futuristic architecture, vibrant and diverse cultural and intellectual life, splendid colonial churches and brilliant museums. Not to be bested by the capital, Cartagena on the Caribbean coast is considered by many to be the most beautiful Latin American city. The walled old town of this fortified Spanish colonial port is a real gem. It's packed with churches, monasteries, plazas, palaces and noble mansions, replete with overhanging balconies and shady patios.

VISA REQUIREMENTS

Chinese citizens are the only visitors to Colombia who need visas. All other foreigners receive a stamp in their passport upon arrival. Citizens of Canada, the USA and UK receive 90 days, while those from Australia and New Zealand are granted 30 days. You can obtain an additional 30 day visa extension at immigration offices in major cities for around US$18. If you want to stay longer, you'll have to leave Colombia and re-enter to obtain another stamp. If you intend to travel overland, keep in mind that Venezuelan visas are hard to get, so you may want to procure one in your home country before your trip. You may be asked to show an onward ticket before or when you arrive in Colombia.

Colombian Embassies

Australia

(☎ 02-6257 2027, fax 6257 1448) 101 Northbourne Ave, Turner, ACT 2601;
(☎ 02-9955 0311, 9922 5597) 5th floor, 220 Pacific Hwy, Crows Nest, NSW 2065

Canada

(☎ 514-849-4852, 849-2929) 1010 Sherbrooke West, Suite 420, Montreal, Quebec H3A 2R7;
(☎ 416-977-0098) 1 Dundas St West, Suite 2108, Toronto, Ontario M5G 1Z3

UK

(☎ 020-7495 4233) Suite 10, 140 Park Lane, London W1Y 3DF

USA

(☎ 202-387-8338) 2118 Leroy Place, Washington, DC
Consulates: Houston and San Francisco

TOURIST OFFICES OVERSEAS

Colombia maintains a tourist office in New York. You can write to it at: 140E, 57th St, New York, NY 10022. General information is also available at Colombian embassies and consulates, or contact an office of Avianca, the national airline. Also check out the web sites listed later under Online Services.

HEALTH

Both malaria and yellow fever are present in many regions of Colombia. You will need to take appropriate precautions against these serious diseases. Dengue fever also occurs, so avoid bites from mosquitoes and all insects to prevent other serious diseases. Bogotá's high altitude (2600m) may take some getting used to, so take things easy on arrival. It's a good idea to use bottled or treated water and take care with what you eat to avoid diseases such as hepatitis, typhoid, cholera and dysentery.

Medical care is reasonable in Bogotá and most large cities. If you do require serious medical care, Bogotá, or even better Caracas, have the best facilities.

POST & COMMUNICATIONS

Air mail is handled by Avianca, and is generally dependable and efficient. An air-mail letter should take around two weeks to reach its destination. You'll find Avianca offices in every city they serve, usually right next door to the post office. The poste restante mail system is also handled by Avianca and works tolerably well. In theory, you can receive general delivery mail in any city with an Avianca office, but Bogotá is the most reliable. Poste restante mail is generally held for a month.

International calls will be expensive whether you place them from a private phone (eg at a hotel) or at a centralised telephone office. You are charged for a three minute minimum. Reverse charge (collect) calls are permitted to certain countries only. The list is in constant flux, so before you call, check if the country you're phoning can receive reverse charge calls. Faxes can be sent from major telephone offices, and many private companies in bigger cities offer fax services as well.

Email and Internet services are available at a handful of Internet cafes around the country.

MONEY
Costs

Colombia is not the most affordable destination and is becoming more expensive as inflation takes hold; budget travellers used to living on the cheap can get by on US$25 a day. If better accommodation and restaurant meals are more your scene, set aside around US$40 to US$60 a day. If luxury is the only way you can go, budget on around US$70 to US$100 a day.

Changing Money

Changing money in Colombia can be a sticky wicket. Banks are generally the best places to change money, but some banks won't or can't (because they've reached their daily exchange limit by the time you arrive or for a variety of other unfathomable reasons) and still others will just be closed when you show up. Be prepared to wait at least an hour to change money and expect a mountain of paperwork.

Fortunately, exchange houses will change money, but only cash, preferably US dollars. Rather than walk around with wads of US dollars or fight with the bank bureaucracy to change a few travellers cheques, you may want to rely on major credit cards. Getting cash advances in local currency with Visa or MasterCard is the way to go. In addition, there are an increasing number of *cajeros automáticos* (automatic teller machines), which accept Visa and MasterCard, and disperse pesos. The only time you should consider changing money on the street is at land border crossings, and exchange only as much as you'll need until you can get to a bank.

ONLINE SERVICES

Lonely Planet's web site is Destination Colombia (www.lonelyplanet.com/dest/sam/col.htm).

Web pickings are pretty slim for Colombia, but you might try the informative Republic of Colombia site (www.colostate.edu/Orgs/LASO/Colombia/colombia.html). The site is maintained by the Latin American Student's Organization of the Colorado State University.

Visually oriented travellers will appreciate Colombia: Banco de Imagenes (www.uniandes.edu.co/Colombia/Fotos/fotos.html), which has a good selection of photographs. The text is in Spanish.

Macondo (www.rpg.net/quail/libyri nth/gabo) is a web site dedicated to Gabriel García Márquez, the Nobel Prize-winning author and Colombia's prodigal son.

BOOKS

Read up on Colombia before you arrive to maximise your understanding of this complex country. A good place to start is with John Hemming's readable *The Search for El Dorado*. For more history, try the Spanish/English or French/German version of *Colombia* by Françoise de Tailly. Don't confuse this with *Colombia: Portrait of Unity and Diversity* by Harvey F Kline, another good general treatment of Colombian history. For modern history, check out *Colombia: Inside the Labyrinth* by Jenny Pearce.

Kings of Cocaine by journalists Guy Gugliotta & Jeff Leen provides a detailed insight into Colombia's drug cartels and reads like a fast-paced thriller. *The Fruit Palace* by Charles Nicholl is another journalist's account of Colombian culture.

Gabriel García Márquez, prince of magic realism, is Colombia's most famous author. Visitors might carry some of his work in their travels to gain an insider's perspective. Try *The General in His Labyrinth*, *Of Love and Other Demons* or his most famous novel, *One Hundred Years of Solitude*.

FILMS

Colombia has a thriving film industry which has produced some notable movies. Try 1997's *The Debt* (released in 1998 as La Dette in France) or the black-humour favourite *The People at Universal*. For insights into the Colombian mentality and lifestyle, see *Rodrigo D: No Future* or *Oedious Mayor*, co-written by García Márquez.

ENTERING & LEAVING

Colombia serves as a secondary gateway (after Venezuela) to the rest of South America, with cheap flights from the USA and Europe. Most visitors fly into the airport at Bogotá, but there are other international terminals, such as at Cartagena and San Andrés, which may prove convenient. From the USA, you can fly directly, via Central America or through Venezuela. Miami, New Orleans and Houston are common departure cities. Flying from London, Amsterdam, Brussels, Frankfurt or Paris will probably net you the cheapest flight from Europe. From Australia or New Zealand, a Round-the-World or Circle Pacific fare will probably be your best bet. You will need to show an onward ticket before boarding your flight to Colombia. Departure taxes vary with your length of stay; US$17 for up to 60 days and US$30 for longer stays.

If travelling overland, check frequently on the local situation before venturing forth and avoid areas of heavy guerrilla activity. The most popular border crossings are at the Colombian frontiers with Ecuador and Venezuela, because these are the only ones with roads. You can cross into Tulcán, Ecuador at Ipiales in Colombia or try to arrange boat passage from San Lorenzo in Ecuador to Tumaco, Colombia. For travel into Venezuela, try the popular Cúcata to San Antonio del Táchira crossing; the Maicao to Maracaibo route (convenient for travel along the Caribbean coast); or the Puerto Carreño to Puerto Paéz or Ayacucho route. This last option may be dangerous; consult local authorities. Other routes are not recommended at this time due to guerrilla activity. There is also a major land crossing between Colombia (at Leticia), Peru (Santa Rosa) and Brazil (Tabatinga), known as the Triple Frontier.

Truly intrepid travellers can enter Colombia from Panama via the Darién Gap – the dense and dangerous jungle that interrupts the Pan-American Hwy. The trip takes a couple of weeks and will require guides, advance planning, a high degree of self-reliance and good fortune. Guerrillas are active in the area and kidnappings are not uncommon; don't undertake this journey frivolously. If you feel this is something you must do, the place to cross is at Capurganá in Colombia Puerto to Puerto Obaldía in Panama.

Ports on both the Pacific and Caribbean coasts make it possible to arrive and leave by boat. Sea traffic is busier on the Caribbean side: boats frequently come and go between the USA, Mexico, Central America, the Caribbean islands and Venezuela. Colombian ports on the Caribbean include Baranquilla, Cartagena, Santa Marta and Turbo; the major Pacific port is at Buenaventura.

COSTA RICA

Costa Rica is fast becoming one of the world's most popular backpacking destinations. It is safe and peaceful (the government has been democratically elected since the 1800s and the armed forces were abolished in 1948), and it's exotic and 'green'. Conservation is such a powerful item on the political agenda that over 27% of the total land mass boasts some protection status. As a result, ecotourism and Costa Rica are becoming synonymous and there are great opportunities for wildlife viewing, birdwatching and other outdoor activities that emphasise minimum impact travel.

Enthusiasts of all kinds will find beautiful spots for their particular pursuits. Idyllic beaches, snowcapped mountains, virgin rainforest and even an active volcano are among the country's offerings. This is a great destination for campers because of the excellent facilities contained in the extensive national park network. In fact, the tourist infrastructure is well developed throughout Costa Rica, making it a great country to get your feet wet if you're travelling to Latin America for the first time.

WHEN TO GO

Costa Rica's wet season is from the end of April to mid-December, and roads, trails, camp sites and so on can become very wet. The rest of the year is the dry season, with bright sunny days and rain only very occasionally. This is also the high tourist season, and attractions can be very crowded (especially beaches) and hotels more expensive. Try to travel during the shoulder period, just at the end or beginning of either season, to minimise crowds and maximise your budget.

It can be very difficult, if not impossible, to get transport or accommodation during Semana Santa (Easter

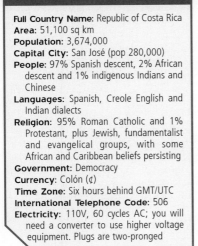

At a Glance

Full Country Name: Republic of Costa Rica
Area: 51,100 sq km
Population: 3,674,000
Capital City: San José (pop 280,000)
People: 97% Spanish descent, 2% African descent and 1% indigenous Indians and Chinese
Languages: Spanish, Creole English and Indian dialects
Religion: 95% Roman Catholic and 1% Protestant, plus Jewish, fundamentalist and evangelical groups, with some African and Caribbean beliefs persisting
Government: Democracy
Currency: Colón (¢)
Time Zone: Six hours behind GMT/UTC
International Telephone Code: 506
Electricity: 110V, 60 cycles AC; you will need a converter to use higher voltage equipment. Plugs are two-pronged

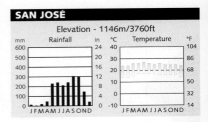

SAN JOSÉ

Elevation - 1146m/3760ft

Week). The major holidays are from December to February and many *ticos* (as locals are called) vacation at this time, making conditions cramped at tourist destinations.

HIGHLIGHTS

Costa Rica is the destination of choice for nature and beach lovers, and outdoor enthusiasts, as well as featuring a cosmopolitan capital city in San José. Here's a list of some of the best the country has to offer.

Natural Attractions

Costa Rica has a wealth of awesome natural attractions. Volcán Arenal regularly spews molten rock, the Península de Osa is crammed with virgin rainforest and wildlife, the beaches are phenomenal and have good surfing, and there are more than 60 protected areas and national parks. You can visit the Monteverde Cloud Forest Reserve, climb 3820m to the top of Cerro Chirripó, or travel several hours by boat up the coast to Tortuguero to watch the nesting of the green sea turtles.

Wildlife Viewing

You would have to work hard in Costa Rica not to see some spectacular tropical wildlife. There are 850 bird species, four species of monkey, all manner of mammals, and marine wildlife as well. Just stroll through any natural setting and you're bound to see Morpho butterflies, hear the eerie call of the oropendola or get splashed by a caiman sliding off a log into the river. The national parks and private reserves are almost tailor-made for checking out wild animals. Among the best are Corcovado, Santa Rosa and Rincón de la Vieja national parks.

Surfing

Costa Rica is a great surfing destination filled with so many wave and point breaks that it feels like one endless summer. The waves aren't as big as in Hawaii, but they're often longer, giving smooth, long rides. Some breaks are very accessible, such as at Puerto Viejo de Talamanca or Jacó, and have a great beach atmosphere and plenty of other surfers. Others, like the left-hand break around Witches Rock at Playa Naranjo, are difficult to reach, but you'll probably have the place to yourself.

Trekking & Camping

From hard-core jungle treks to pleasant strolls in the cloud forest, Costa Rica can satisfy your hiking itch. All the national parks and most of the reserves have good hiking and camping facilities. From a flat patch in the woods to established grounds with showers and toilets, camping is a great way to see the country, meet people and check out the astonishing wildlife. Some popular parks for hiking and camping include Corcovado, Santa Rosa, Monteverde, Manuel Antonio and Chirripó.

VISA REQUIREMENTS

Most visitors do not need a visa to visit Costa Rica, but your nationality will determine how long you can stay. Citizens of the USA, Canada, the UK and most Western European countries are granted 90 days, while citizens of Australia, New Zealand, France, Sweden and most Eastern European and Latin American countries are granted 30 days. Renewals can be arranged in San José. Visas cost US$20 at Costa Rican embassies and can be obtained in neighbouring countries.

237

Costa Rican Embassies

Australia
(☎ 02-9261 1177, fax 9261 2953) 11th floor, 30 Clarence St, Sydney, NSW 2000

Canada
(☎ 613-562-2855, fax 562-2582) 135 York St No 208, Ottawa, Ontario K1N 5T4

Panama
(☎ 264-29/37) Edificio Miraflores, Calle Gilberto Ortega 51-B, Panama City

UK
(☎ 020-7706 8844, fax 7706 8655) Flat 1, 14 Lancaster Gate, London W2 3LH

USA
(☎ 202-234-2945/6, fax 265-4795) 2112 S St NW, Washington, DC 20008

Itineraries

One Week – the Caribbean Coast
Overland transportation is not fantastic in Costa Rica and with only a week, you'll want to fly between some points to maximise your travel time. From San José, fly to Tortuguero and spend two days in Parque Nacional Tortuguero, canoeing the inland waterways, frolicking on the beach and checking out the green sea turtles laying their eggs or breeding (July to early October). Travel down the coast by motorised boat via the Tortuguero Canal to Puerto Limón and continue on to the beach paradise of Puerto Viejo de Talamanca, where you can take a day trip to indigenous communities. Return to the capital by bus.

One Week – the Highlands
From San José, go by bus to the Monteverde Cloud Forest Reserve. Spend two days exploring this wilderness, possibly staying overnight in a refuge. From Monteverde, head to Volcán Arenal and stay for two days, hiking or relaxing at nearby hot springs by day and visiting the volcano at night, which is the best time to see the flaming rocks fly from the crater. Return to San José and take a day trip to Parque Nacional Volcán Irazú for some more smoking crater action. Alternatively, you could visit several small villages and towns around San José, such as Alajuela and Heredia, in the area known as the Central Valley.

One Week – Península de Nicoya
This is the ideal spot if you want to relax on a beach and do little else. From San José, take a bus to Playa del Coco, Playa Hermosa or Playa Panamá. Chill out for a few days, hike in the surrounding tropical forest and, if you can muster the energy, check out Parque Nacional Santa Rosa on a day or overnight trip.

Two Weeks
In two weeks, you can do two of the one week options and travel via river for the round-trip Tortuguero portion. Alternatively, choose one of the one week itineraries and add a trip to Península de Osa and Parque Nacional Corcovado, the wildest rainforest experience available in Costa Rica. You will have to fly at least one way to the peninsula or endure a hot eight hour bus ride.

One Month
A month is a good time frame in which to experience Costa Rica, patiently viewing wildlife and veering off the beaten track. Do the one week Caribbean coast itinerary by public transport and stop off in Parque Nacional Braulio Carrillo on the way back to San José. Or you can do the Osa/Corcovado alternative instead, taking in Isla del Caño which boasts a variety of marine life, fantastic snorkelling and pre-Columbian rock spheres. On the peninsula you can also make a side trip down to Pavones, with some of the best surfing on the Pacific side of Central America. Do the entire highlands itinerary, but hike for two or more days deep into Monteverde, staying at refuges along the way. Next head out to the Península de Nicoya and camp in Parque Nacional Santa Rosa. Make a point to visit the isolated and spectacular Parque Nacional Rincón de la Vieja, with its active volcano and numerous cones, craters and lagoon.

OSTA RICA HIGHLIGHTS & ITINERARIES ▶▶

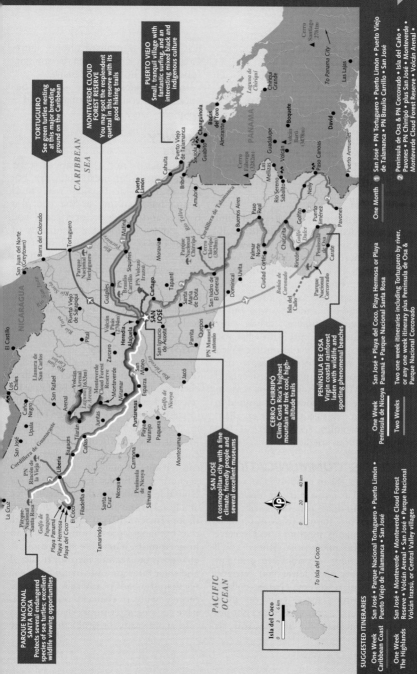

TORTUGUERO
See green turtles nesting at this major breeding ground on the Caribbean

MONTEVERDE CLOUD FOREST RESERVE
You may spot the resplendent quetzal in this reserve with its good hiking trails

PUERTO VIEJO
Small, tranquil village with fantastic surfing and an interesting mix of black and indigenous culture

PARQUE NACIONAL SANTA ROSA
Protects several endangered species of sea turtles; excellent wildlife viewing opportunities

SAN JOSÉ
A cosmopolitan city with a fine climate, friendly people and several excellent museums

CERRO CHIRRIPÓ
Climb Costa Rica's highest mountain and trek cool, high-altitude trails

PENÍNSULA DE OSA
Virgin coastal rainforest laden with wildlife and sporting phenomenal beaches

SUGGESTED ITINERARIES

One Week
Caribbean Coast
San José • Parque Nacional Tortuguero • Puerto Limón • Puerto Viejo de Talamanca • San José

One Week
The Highlands
San José • Monteverde • Monteverde Cloud Forest Reserve • Volcán Arenal • San José • Parque Nacional Volcán Irazú, or Central Valley villages

One Week
Península de Nicoya
San José • Playa del Coco, Playa Hermosa or Playa Panamá • Parque Nacional Santa Rosa

Two Weeks
Two one week itineraries including Tortuguero by river, or one week itinerary plus Península de Osa & Parque Nacional Corcovado

One Month
1. San José • PN Tortuguero • Puerto Limón • Puerto Viejo de Talamanca • PN Braulio Carrillo • San José
2. Península de Osa & PN Corcovado • Isla del Caño • Pavones • PN Chirripó • plus San José • Monteverde • Monteverde Cloud Forest Reserve • Volcán Arenal • Playa del Coco, Playa Hermosa or Playa Panamá • PN Santa Rosa • PN Rincón de la Vieja • San José

Isla del Coco
0   2   4   6 km

0   20   40 km

To Isla del Coco

TOURIST OFFICES OVERSEAS

In the USA, contact the Costa Rican Tourist Board (☎ 305-358-2150, 1-800-343-6332) 1101 Brickel Ave, BIV Tower, Suite 801, Miami, FL 33131. Elsewhere, ask for information at the Costa Rican embassy or consulate in your home country, and check the web sites listed under Online Services later in this chapter.

HEALTH

Malaria occurs mainly in lowland rural areas and dengue fever occurs throughout the country, so take precautions against these serious diseases. Avoid bites from all insects, including sandflies, to prevent other insect-borne diseases. Tap water is OK to drink in San José and other major towns, but in out-of-the-way places, drink only treated water. Take care with what you eat, and especially avoid undercooked meat and raw seafood dishes, to prevent typhoid, hepatitis, dysentery and cholera. Medical facilities are reasonable in the major towns, but limited in rural areas. Mexico City has excellent medical facilities, so fly there if you require serious medical care.

POST & COMMUNICATIONS

The Costa Rican mail system is well developed for this part of the world and in San José you can easily send packages, buy stamps from automated, 24-hour stamp machines and receive mail at the main post office. You'll have to show identification and pay US$0.25 for each letter you retrieve. You can make reverse charge (collect) and operator-assisted calls on most Costa Rican pay phones. Some phones accept international phonecards. If not, go to a centralised phone centre. Faxing from Costa Rica is straightforward and not too expensive.

Internet cafes are few and far between, but you will probably find a couple in San José.

MONEY
Costs

Costa Rica is not as cheap as some other Central American countries, but it's still affordable. If you're really budgeting hard, staying in the cheapest hostels and eating in local cafes, you can expect to spend a minimum of about US$12 a day, although closer to US$20 a day is probably more realistic. If you want to stay in fancier digs with a private bathroom, eat in western-style restaurants and maybe take an internal flight, budget on around US$25 to US$40 a day.

Changing Money

The easiest currency to change is US dollars, whether in cash or travellers cheques, although US$100 bills may be rejected because there are counterfeits in circulation. Make sure your bills are in good condition. Outside of San José, it is very difficult to change any currency other than US dollars. You can change money at hotels, travel agencies and banks. Rates are usually equitable among the three, but service at a hotel or travel agency will be much more efficient than at the bank, where one exchange transaction can take an hour or more. There are street money-changers, but technically they're illegal and their rates are only marginally better than the banks or hotels. Exchange money with freelancers only if you have to – eg after-hours or at borders – to avoid scams or problems with the law. Changing money in small towns can be a challenge, so have plenty of colónes on hand before setting out.

ONLINE SERVICES

Lonely Planet's web site is Destination Costa Rica (www.lonelyplanet.com/dest /cam/costa.htm).

For general information about Costa Rica's attractions, including wonderful photos from the national parks, visit the well presented Costa Rica web site (www.tuanis.com/costarica/costarica .html).

The Complete Costa Rica Web Page (www.cocori.com) has a wealth of information and good maps, an extensive article library and a variety of photos.

An easy to navigate site is Costa Rica.com (www.costarica.com), which is great for researching your itinerary and planning the logistics of your trip.

For a hilarious account of travelling travails in Costa Rica and beyond, hit 2 Guys Travel Central and South America (www.xraydesign.com).

BOOKS

For the travelling literati or literary travellers, a good choice is *Costa Rica: A Traveler's Literary Companion* by Barbara Ras, an anthology of more than two dozen short stories by contemporary Costa Rican writers. Another anthology in the same vein is *When New Flowers Bloomed: Short Stories by Women Writers from Costa Rica and Panama*, edited and compiled by Enrique Jaramillo Levi.

Rainforest enthusiasts should see *In the Rainforest* by Catherine Caufield, which focuses on rainforest devastation; *Life Above the Jungle Floor* by Donald Perry; or *The Enchanted Canopy* by Andrew W Mitchell.

For Costa Rican politics, economics and cultural issues there's *The Costa Rica Reader*, an anthology edited by Marc Edelman & Joanne Kenen, and *The Costa Ricans* by Richard Biesanz et al, which looks at Costa Rican social and political developments in an historical context.

If you'll be roughing it at all in Costa Rica, check out *Backpacking in Central America* by Tim Burford or *Adventuring in Central America* by David Rains Wallace, which have strong Costa Rica sections. *Costa Rica's National Parks and Preserves: A Visitor's Guide* by Joseph Franke has maps and some general information and may also prove handy.

FILMS

Go see *Jurassic Park* in Costa Rica and the groans will be audible as a shot pans from the sign that says 'San José' to Jeff Goldblum sipping a cold beer at a beachside bar; San José is quite inland, though it makes for a quaint shot. Still, this Hollywood blockbuster does have some good nature footage of Costa Rica and is worth renting to get a feel for the landscape. Another Hollywood action flick filmed in Costa Rica is *Congo*, which gives you an idea of how thick the jungle can get.

ENTERING & LEAVING

Most travellers arrive in the Costa Rican capital of San José by air. A secondary international airport is in Liberia, 217km north-west of San José. Flights tend to be cheaper for short stays and a ticket valid for 30 days is the best bargain. From the USA, there are direct flights from Los Angeles, Houston, Miami and New York. Direct flights from London are available or European travellers can connect with gateway cities in the USA, as can Canadians. If flying from Australia or New Zealand, you will have to connect with flights in Hawaii, California or Mexico. The departure tax from Costa Rica is around US$17.

Alternatively, you can travel overland, which may be cheaper and will definitely be a bigger adventure than flying. There are international buses plying the length of Mexico and Central America. The major crossing between Costa Rica and Nicaragua is at the Peñas Blancas border post, but adventurous souls can cross at the Los Chiles post if they have all their paperwork. Between Costa Rica and Panama, most travellers cross at Paso Canoas, though it's also possible to make the crossing at Sixaola-Guabito on the Caribbean coast if you have time and patience. The rarely used Río Sereno crossing near Panama's Parque Nacional Volcán Barú is remote and rugged.

ECUADOR

Straddling the equator with Colombia to the north and Peru to the south, Ecuador is the little known paradise of South America and one of the most biodiverse places on the planet. No matter whether you're interested in beach activities, hiking active volcanoes, visiting rainforest or checking out the wildlife that led to Darwin's theory of evolution, Ecuador can accommodate you. It's the smallest of the Andean nations and you can get from the beach to snowcapped mountains in one day, and hop on a bus to explore the jungle the next. Ecuador is probably best known for its claim to the Galápagos Islands, where you can swim with sharks and loll with elephant seals on a typical day.

Apart from the Galápagos, the country is super-affordable. The Ecuadorian economy has taken a beating in recent years, making it even cheaper for foreign travellers. However, locals are feeling the economic pinch and strikes, protests and transportation stoppages have made travelling here a challenge. Add to these financial woes the unpredictable weather phenomenon called El Niño and you have the ingredients for a rugged adventure. There are plentiful opportunities to get off the beaten track here and if you can dream it, you can do it in Ecuador.

WHEN TO GO

The geography of Ecuador conspires to create fickle weather. Technically, there are two seasons, 'wet' and 'dry', however, they fall at different times

depending on where you are. On the coast and in the Galápagos, the rainy season is from January to April or May, while in the Oriente, the dense jungle region in eastern Ecuador, the rainy season runs from June to August and roads can be impassable. June to August is exactly the time when it's dry and comfortable in the highlands. In Quito, the temperature is pleasant year-round, but remember that the temperature drops around 6°C for every 1000m increase in altitude, so if you're planning on trekking in the Andes, bring warm clothes.

Most foreigners visit from mid-December through January or from June to August and these are the high seasons in Ecuador. Travelling during the off season has some advantages,

At a Glance

Full Country Name: República del Ecuador
Area: 272,045 sq km
Population: 12,562,000
Capital: Quito (pop 1.2 million)
People: 40% mestizo, 40% Indian, 15% Spanish descent and 5% African descent
Languages: Spanish, Quechua, Quichua and other indigenous languages
Religion: Over 90% Roman Catholic, and 10% Christian denominations
Government: Democratic republic
Currency: Sucre (S/)
Time Zone: Five hours behind GMT/UTC
International Telephone Code: 593
Electricity: 110V, 60 cycles AC; sockets take two-pronged, flat plugs of the kind used in North America

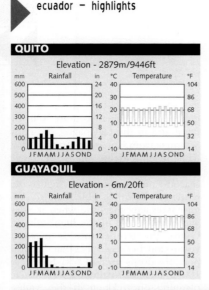

QUITO

Elevation - 2879m/9446ft

GUAYAQUIL

Elevation - 6m/20ft

but the seas can be very rough in the Galápagos in September and October and the weather is uncomfortable, hot and muggy on the coast during the rainy season.

HIGHLIGHTS

Ecuador truly has it all – how your itinerary ends up will depend on your tastes and travel style. Here is a partial list of the opportunities for exploring Ecuador.

Trekking

The long valley corridor between Quito and Cuenca to the south is flanked by parallel mountain ranges containing some of Ecuador's wildest scenery and

The Galápagos Islands

The Galápagos archipelago is a fantasy destination that will ignite your imagination once you realise the possibilities. Here you can snorkel with sharks, swim with sea lions and penguins and picnic with marine iguanas. The animals are so tame you can photograph (no long lens required!) and observe all sorts of unique species in a natural setting. At times you'll be so close to your subjects, you won't believe you're not in a zoo. In short, the wildlife in the Galápagos Islands is like no other on earth and the thrill of being among them is a unique and memorable experience.

Located about 1000km off the coast of Ecuador, the Galápagos are actually dozens of volcanic islands that developed flora and fauna unique from that found on the South American mainland. Only the hardiest plants and animals could adapt and survive in the inhospitable environment of the Galápagos. This interesting fact was noted by Charles Darwin when he visited the archipelago in 1835; he later incorporated his findings into his theory of evolution. While the landscape of the islands is largely unremarkable – lots of scrub and succulents – the wildlife is phenomenal and this is why the Galápagos are worth the time, money and energy a visit requires.

Any way you cut it, a visit to the Galápagos is expensive. Visitors are not permitted to tour the islands without a guide, there's a heavy-duty park tax and most of the best sites are only accessible after several days boat passage. Of course, you also have to fly from the Ecuadorian mainland. This means that even the hardiest and most cunning budget travellers will lay out a minimum of US$800 for a one week tour of the islands, and a budget of US$1000 is probably more realistic. If you want to get certified and scuba dive, visit some of the more far-flung islands or travel on a luxury tour boat, count on spending a whole lot more.

If the economics of Galápagos travel seem prohibitive (and to some independent travellers, unnecessary) the high price of a trip here acts as crowd control and an important conservation measure. Still, once you lay your eyes on a 250kg tortoise, glorious pristine beaches and a sea lion colony hundreds strong, you'll understand why treading lightly and conserving this environment is so crucial.

nine of its 10 highest peaks. Among the most amazing hikes are the climb up Cotopaxi, one of the loftiest active volcanoes in the world at 5897m and to the snowcapped summit of Chimborazo, a 6310m ascent. If you're not prepared to snow-camp or wield ice picks to climb your way to the top, there are many other peaks and hikes suitable for the less gung-ho.

Rainforest Exploration

If you're looking for a *Heart of Darkness* experience, head to the eastern region of Ecuador known as the Oriente. These Amazonian lowlands won't fail to deliver excellent birdwatching and wildlife viewing, flora so strange it defies description and smells and sounds unique to the deep jungle. Tours to the protected Reserva Producción Faunística Cuyabeno, trips up the Napo and Misahuallí rivers and visits to indigenous communities are all popular pursuits in the Oriente. Travellers should be very careful when hiring guides to visit villages in the jungle; try to use agencies that have good relationships with the communities. Tribal tours run by unlicensed and unscrupulous guides can have a zoo-like quality and are unpleasant for everyone.

Studying Spanish

Ecuador is popular for studying Spanish for several reasons, not least among them that Quito is a wonderful place to live and learn, the instruction is good and affordable, and the city is accessible to all the natural and cultural wonders the country has to offer. There's an international student scene in Quito, and Spanish schools are beginning to pop up in other picturesque towns like Otavalo and Cuenca. Programs with dance, cooking and cultural electives are available, as are others with homestay and field-trip options.

Indian Markets

Ecuador has some renowned markets and locals and visitors alike turn out to shop, haggle and enjoy these open-air affairs. The Saturday market in Otavalo dates back to pre-Inca times, while the smaller markets at Saquisilí, Pujilí, Zumbagua, Sigchos and San Miguel de Salcedo are unrivalled for their authenticity. Whether you need a goat, a necklace, a sweater or an aphrodisiac, you'll find it at these markets.

VISA REQUIREMENTS

Most travellers to Ecuador don't need a visa, but receive a free tourist card (T-3) upon arrival. The maximum amount allowable on a T-3 is 90 days, but sometimes you won't get that many; ask for the longest allowance. Extension procedures are fairly easy and straightforward if attended to in Quito. In the recent past, French citizens have needed visas. In addition, any adherents to the Sikh religion will need a visa regardless of their nationality. Visa requirements are always in flux, so check to see if you'll need one. You can get visas in Colombia and Peru or obtain them before you leave home.

Ecuadorian Embassies

Canada
(☎ 613-563-8206, fax 235-5776) 50 O'Connor St, Suite 1311, Ottawa, Ontario K1N 6L2

Colombia
(☎ 91-257 9947) Calle 100 No 14-63, Oficina 601, Bogotá

Peru
(☎ 02-442 4184) Las Palmeras 356, San Isidro

UK
 (☎ 020-7584 1367, fax 7823 9701) Flat 3B, 3 Hans Crescent, Knightsbridge, London SW1X OL5

USA
 (☎ 202-234-7200, fax 667-3482) 2535 15th St NW, Washington, DC 20009

TOURIST OFFICES OVERSEAS

Ecuador has no overseas tourist offices, but a good travel agent will be able to give you most of the information you'll need. Also try the web sites listed under the Online Services section later.

HEALTH

Malaria occurs mainly in the areas along the eastern border area and the Pacific coast. Quito and the central highlands are malaria-free. Yellow fever and dengue fever also occur, so take precautions against these serious diseases. Avoid all insect bites if possible, especially sandfly bites. Food and waterborne diseases such as hepatitis,

---

Itineraries

One Week

From Quito, take a day trip to Otavalo, visiting the 30m-high Mitad del Mundo monument, which marks the 'middle of the world' (ie the equator), on the way back, or take an all day train trip to Parque Nacional Cotopaxi. Then head south to the heart of the Avenue of the Volcanoes, spending two days exploring the highland towns of Saquisilí, Pujilí and Zumbagua and hiking around Laguna Quilotoa, west of Latacunga. Try to time this leg so you're in one of these towns on market day. Continue south through Riobamba and take the train from Alausí to Huigra along the infamously scary and breathtaking Devil's Nose route.

Two Weeks

Before heading south, as in the one week itinerary, hop over to Baños with its gorgeous box canyon setting and hot springs. Hike, bike or river-raft in the area for a day or two before moving on to the Avenue of the Volcanoes. After riding the Devil's Nose, stop at the Inca ruins of Ingapirca before hitting Cuenca. Hike and explore the ethereal Area Nacional de Recreación Cajas west of Cuenca before continuing south to 'The Valley of Longevity', as Vilcabamba is known.

One Month

Barring any serious transportation nightmares, you'll be able to see a good part of Ecuador in a month. Follow the two week itinerary, but from Baños head into the Oriente for a jungle tour. Spend a day or two organising the tour in Tena, Puyo or Misahuallí and at least four days exploring the deep Ecuadorian rainforest. Alternatively, you can leave Quito for Lago Agrio and tour the isolated Cuyabeno reserve. Complete the rest of the two week itinerary, return to Quito and head to the coast south of Manta to hang out on the beach. Do a day tour of the Isla de la Plata (known as the paupers' Galápagos), which is part of Parque Nacional Machalilla.

Two Months

This will allow you to explore all of the above in the detail they deserve. If you can't afford to go to the Galápagos, spend the balance of your time heading north to Ibarra and taking the train to San Lorenzo. Camp and hike in the wilds of the páramo (humid, high-altitude grassland) of Reserva Ecológica El Angel. Visit the African enclave of Borbón on the Río Cayapas, canoe up the Río San Miguel and spend time in the Reserva Ecológica Cotacachi-Cayapas. Following the above itineraries, veer off from Baños either before or after your jungle tour to visit Parque Nacional Sangay. Continue with the above itineraries, but return from the coast via the scenic route through the mountains.

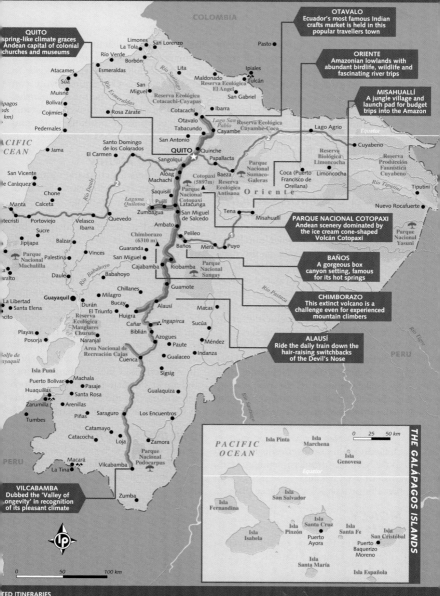

ECUADOR HIGHLIGHTS & ITINERARIES

QUITO
spring-like climate graces Andean capital of colonial churches and museums

OTAVALO
Ecuador's most famous Indian crafts market is held in this popular travellers town

ORIENTE
Amazonian lowlands with abundant birdlife, wildlife and fascinating river trips

MISAHUALLÍ
A jungle village and launch pad for budget trips into the Amazon

PARQUE NACIONAL COTOPAXI
Andean scenery dominated by the ice cream cone-shaped Volcán Cotopaxi

BAÑOS
A gorgeous box canyon setting, famous for its hot springs

CHIMBORAZO
This extinct volcano is a challenge even for experienced mountain climbers

ALAUSÍ
Ride the daily train down the hair-raising switchbacks of the Devil's Nose

VILCABAMBA
Dubbed the 'Valley of longevity' in recognition of its pleasant climate

THE GALAPAGOS ISLANDS

typhoid, cholera and dysentery all occur. Stick to treated water in all areas and take care with what you eat; generally day to day health problems are few. Take things easy on arrival in Quito, which at 2850m could leave you breathless for the first couple of days.

Medical care is reasonable throughout Ecuador, but for serious medical care, Caracas or Lima provide more extensive medical facilities.

POST & COMMUNICATIONS

Important documents shouldn't be sent through the mail as the Ecuadorian postal service is somewhat unreliable. Personal mail can be sent to the main post office. It's filed alphabetically, so make sure that your last name is clear. If you're a member of the South American Explorers Club, you can receive mail securely and conveniently at its Quito clubhouse (see Online Services).

Ecuador is struggling to join the 21st century as far as telephone service goes. New cellular pay phones that only take phonecards are popping up in the cities and larger towns; you can make international calls at these or at centralised phone centres.

Internet cafes are wildly popular in Quito and other tourist destinations and you'll have no problem sending faxes, email or even talking on the phone with Net Phone technology at these places.

MONEY
Costs

Travelling in Ecuador on the cheap is completely realistic. Expect to spend around US$7 to US$15 a day if you stay in backpackers hostels and eat at small, local places. Add about US$1 for every hour you spend on public transportation. If you move up to a mid-range hotel, eat at western-style or upmarket restaurants and take a taxi once in a while, you'll spend closer to US$50 a day. Of course, you can splash out, stay in the most expensive hotels, eat only at exclusive restaurants and deny yourself nothing, and spend about US$90 to US$150 a day.

Changing Money

Your best bets for changing money are banks and exchange houses. They have about the same exchange rates and only differ slightly in the rate for cash as opposed to travellers cheques, but exchange houses are usually much more efficient and keep longer hours. You may have to change money on the street occasionally, eg if everything is closed or you're at the border. The rates won't be terrific and you should be aware of scams involving counterfeit bills or fixed calculators. It's harder to change money off the beaten track, so stock up before heading off into the wilderness. Only the biggest cities and most popular tourist destinations will accept Visa and MasterCard. ATMs in the cities accept foreign bank cards.

ONLINE SERVICES

Lonely Planet's web site is Destination Ecuador & The Galápagos Islands (www.lonelyplanet.com/dest/sam/ecu.htm.

Ecuador Explorer (www.ecuadorexplorer.com) has good descriptions of Ecuador and its attractions.

The Ministry of Tourism homepage (www.ecua.net.ec/mintur/ingles) is a readable site with current events, visa requirements, historical data and the like. Similar is the site of the Ecuadorian Embassy in the US (www.ecuador.org).

The South American Explorers Club (www.samexplo.org) maintains an up-to-date site, with an efficient search feature and good links.

BOOKS

One of the best regional history books is *The Conquest of the Incas* by John Hemming; there are several chapters on Ecuador.

For an academic look at recent history and political science, there's David Corkill & David Cubitt's *Ecuador: A Fragile Democracy*.

Even if the Galápagos Islands aren't on your itinerary, no visitor to Ecuador should pass up reading Charles Darwin's *On the Origin of Species by Means of Natural Selection*. After all, the animals of those islands gave him the theory! A more contemporary take on the same topic is *Darwin for Beginners* by J Miller & BV Loon. If wildlife is your game, see the definitive *Galápagos: A Natural History Guide* by Michael H Jackson, which discusses the fauna, plants and geology of the islands. On a lighter note is Kurt Vonnegut's funny evolutionary tale *Galápagos*.

Travels Amongst the Great Andes of the Equator is the great alpinist Edward Whymper's account of his 1880 expedition that made eight seminal ascents of Ecuador's tallest peaks. *The Panama Hat Trail* by Tom Miller is an interesting account of Ecuadorian life in the guise of a novel about a guy searching for Panama hats.

If you want to hike or camp on your trip, get *Climbing & Hiking in Ecuador* by Rob Rachowiecki et al.

ENTERING & LEAVING

Most people fly to Ecuador, though it's possible to come overland or by sea. There are international airports in Quito and Guayaquil with direct services from Houston, Los Angeles, Miami and New York. Most flights from Europe have stopovers in the USA or the Caribbean. Flights from Australasia also stop in the USA. There are some direct flights from other major South or Central American cities. There is a US$25 departure tax from Ecuador.

It can be cheaper to fly to Lima, Peru from where you'll have a 24 hour bus ride to Quito. The overland bus from Peru is long but safe; the same cannot be said for the Colombia-Ecuador bus route, and this is not recommended as violence against tourists is on the rise. The main crossing into Colombia is at Tulcán, going to Ipiales.

The most popular border crossings between Peru and Ecuador are at Huaquillas and Macará, with the former being much better trodden. In 1998 Peru and Ecuador settled a long-standing border dispute and agreed to jointly manage a system of national parks in the Oriente region. Travellers wishing to cross between the two countries along Ecuador's eastern border should consult local authorities or the staff at the South American Explorers Club.

EL SALVADOR

El Salvador is fast on the mend since the end of the brutal civil war that raged in the mountains and flatlands from 1980 to 1992. This small Central American country (about the size of Wales) is peppered with volcanoes, rivers and mountains in a rugged landscape still healing from war wounds; unexploded land mines are strewn about and many private citizens and former guerrillas still tote guns.

El Salvador is not a top backpacking destination and there is little tourist infrastructure. However, several non-governmental organisations from the USA, Australia and Europe sponsor development projects here and it's a gratifying place to work as a volunteer. Talking to locals about their experiences and discussing the triumphs of the peace process can provide a fulfilling and memorable trip. The popular Gringo Trail bypasses El Salvador altogether, providing an opportunity for adventurous travellers to explore new frontiers.

WHEN TO GO

From May to October is the wet season in El Salvador and heavy rains can make roads impassable and travelling very uncomfortable. The Parque Nacional Montecristo-El Trifinio is also closed at this time of year. You won't have to worry about foreign crowds during the dry season (from November to April), but conditions can be hot and dusty, with average temperatures reaching 34°C. Probably the best time to go is during the shoulder periods abutting the wet and dry seasons.

At a Glance

Full Country Name: Republic of El Salvador
Area: 20,752 sq km
Population: 5.9 million
Capital City: San Salvador (pop 493,000)
People: 94% mestizo (Spanish-Indian), 5% Indian and 1% European descent
Languages: Spanish, and some Nahua
Religion: 75% Roman Catholic and 25% Protestant and other Christian denominations, including the Baptist Church and Jehovah's Witnesses
Government: Republic
Currency: Colón (¢)
Time Zone: Six hours behind GMT/UTC
International Telephone Code: 503
Electricity: 110V, mostly 60 cycles AC; two-pronged, flat plugs like those used in North America are the norm

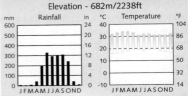

SAN SALVADOR
Elevation - 682m/2238ft

HIGHLIGHTS

Without a doubt, the best part of El Salvador is the people. Mingle with the locals during your travels and you're bound to have a good time. Here are some sights to check out in between fraternising.

Volcanoes

There are more than 25 extinct volcanoes in El Salvador and a handful of active ones. Among the most impressive are Volcán Izalco (1910m) in Parque Nacional Cerro Verde and Volcán de Santa Ana (2365m), the highest volcano in the country. Cerro Verde affords spectacular views of the lake and valley below, punctuated by the still steaming cone of Volcán Izalco. There is good hiking around and into the crater of Boquerón, part of Volcán San Salvador.

Natural Attractions

Although El Salvador lags behind neighbouring countries in conservation efforts, there are several areas worth visiting for wildlife viewing and unspoiled nature. Parque Nacional Montecristo-El Trifinio, straddling the borders of El Salvador, Guatemala and Honduras, is a cloud forest supporting at least 87 bird species, and animals including two-fingered anteaters, spider monkeys, pumas and agoutis. Isla Montecristo on the coast is an undeveloped and pristine area with all kinds of wildlife. It takes some effort to get this far afield, but friendly local families will put you up once you do. This is a great chance to combine cultural and natural experiences.

Volunteering & the Peace Process

Visiting the northern reaches of El Salvador, previously the stronghold of the FMLN (the principal guerrilla group during the war), affords a chance to witness peacetime reconstruction. The districts of Chalatenango and Morazán were important battle sites and the village of La Palma is also

worth a visit. For volunteer opportunities, check out Committee for Solidarity with the People of El Salvador (CISPES; ☎ 212-229-1290 in the USA), a long-standing activist organisation affiliated with the FMLN that places volunteers in programs dealing mostly with workers' rights.

VISA REQUIREMENTS

Citizens of most western countries don't need visas, but get a tourist card valid for 90 days whether you're arriving by land or air. Cards cost US$10 and you must buy a new one every time you re-enter El Salvador. Citizens of other countries need visas. The single-entry visa stamp is good for 90 days from the date of issue, not the date of entry. You can renew visas twice for a total stay of three months. Renewals are processed at the immigration office in San Salvador. If you want to stay longer than three months you must apply for a temporary resident's permit.

El Salvadoran Embassies

Canada
(☎ 613-238-2939) 209 Kent St, Ottawa, Ontario K2P 1Z8

Guatemala
(☎ 334-3942, fax 360-1312) 18a Calle 14-30, Zona 13, Guatemala City

Honduras
(☎ 36-8045, fax 36-9403) Colonia San Carlos, 2a Av, No 205, Tegucigalpa; (☎ 53-4604, fax 52-8215) Agencias Panamericana de Sula, San Pedro Sula

New Zealand
Ross, France, Barristers, Union Law Centre, PO Box 22-544, Otahuhu

UK
(☎ 020-7436 8282) Tennyson House, 159 Great Portland St, London W1N 5FP

USA
(☎ 202-265-9671) 2308 California St NW, Washington, DC 20008

TOURIST OFFICES OVERSEAS

El Salvador doesn't maintain tourist offices overseas but a good travel agent should be able to answer most of your

Itineraries

One Week

Venture out of San Salvador to explore the sleepy, charming village of Suchitoto, perhaps catching a jazz concert, before heading south-west to hike the Boquerón (Big Mouth) crater of Volcán San Salvador. On day two, head west to laid-back Santa Ana, El Salvador's second largest city. In the next few days, you can visit Parque Nacional Cerro Verde, hike Volcán Izalco, pass a day at beautiful Lago de Güija or visit the Mayan ruins of Tazumal before returning to the capital.

Two Weeks

Follow the one week itinerary, continuing on to Parque Nacional Montecristo-El Trifinio, via Metapán. This is a hard place to get to and most of it is closed from May to November, but is well worth the effort. Camp overnight before heading south via La Palma, visiting the cooperative of El Salvadoran painter Fernando Llort. He has popularised the bright, cartoonish depictions of farmers and mountain villages now considered so typical of El Salvador.

Three Weeks to One Month

Follow the two week itinerary, spending some time in the northern region of El Salvador, particularly in the war-torn districts of Chalatenango and Morazán, visiting isolated towns such as Dulce Nombre de Maria and Chalatengo. There is no tourist infrastructure up here and you will have to rely on your wits and the kindness of strangers. Continue south to the coast, visiting Isla Montecristo, staying with local families and exploring the area's beaches. Follow La Costa de Bálsamo to La Libertad and use that town as a base for wandering the beaches of the coast, before returning to the capital.

questions. Also see the web sites listed under Online Services below or check with an El Salvadoran consulate or embassy in your home country.

HEALTH

Malaria is a risk in El Salvador's rural areas and dengue fever can also be a health concern, so take precautions against mosquito-borne diseases. Avoid all insect bites, especially sand flies, to prevent other insect-borne diseases. Food and waterborne diseases, such as hepatitis, typhoid, cholera and dysentery occur. Take care with what you eat, especially seafood and undercooked meat, and drink only treated water.

In San Salvador and in rural areas medical care is limited. Travel to Mexico City if you require serious medical care.

POST & COMMUNICATIONS

You have three choices for sending mail from El Salvador: surface, air or express service. Surface is the cheapest and takes the longest – some letters never arrive. Express mail is the most expensive and, in theory, the fastest. A letter to the USA or Canada using this service should take five days, while a letter to Australia or Europe should take 10 days. You can, again in theory, receive poste restante mail at the main post office in San Salvador.

Some public telephones will place international calls, though mostly you'll have to go to a centralised call centre. These are in every city and town and you can send faxes and telegraphs from these offices as well. Hotels may be able to place international reverse charge (collect) calls for you, but this is very expensive.

Internet access is not currently available in El Salvador.

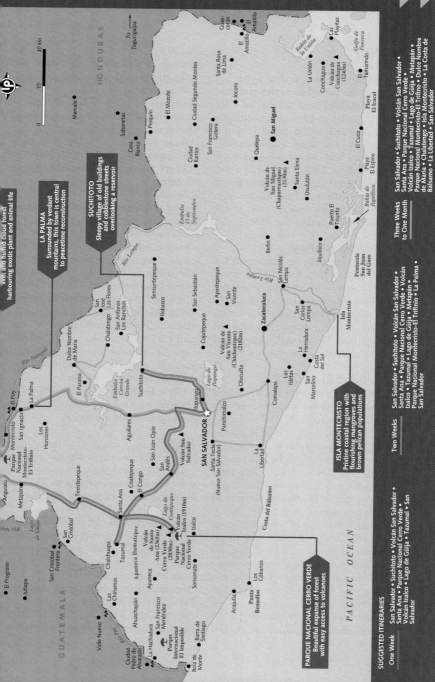

SALVADOR HIGHLIGHTS & ITINERARIES

LA PALMA
Surrounded by verdant mountains, this town is central to peacetime reconstruction

SUCHITOTO
Sleepy village of old buildings and cobblestone streets overlooking a reservoir

Wet and humid cloud forest harbouring exotic plant and animal life

ISLA MONTECRISTO
Pristine coastal region with flourishing mangroves and brown pelican populations

PARQUE NACIONAL CERRO VERDE
Beautiful expanse of forest with easy access to volcanoes

SUGGESTED ITINERARIES

One Week
San Salvador • Suchitoto • Volcán San Salvador • Santa Ana • Parque Nacional Cerro Verde • Volcán Izalco • Lago de Güija • Tazumal • San Salvador

Two Weeks
San Salvador • Suchitoto • Volcán San Salvador • Santa Ana • Parque Nacional Cerro Verde • Volcán Izalco • Tazumal • Lago de Güija • Metapán • Parque Nacional Montecristo-El Trifinio • La Palma • San Salvador

Three Weeks to One Month
San Salvador • Suchitoto • Volcán San Salvador • Santa Ana • Parque Nacional Cerro Verde • Volcán Izalco • Tazumal • Lago de Güija • Metapán • Parque Nacional Montecristo-El Trifinio • Dulce Nombre de María • Chalatengo • Isla Montecristo • La Costa de Bálsamo • La Libertad • San Salvador

MONEY
Costs

Tourist services are few and far between in El Salvador. Hotel and restaurant owners are aware of the limited choices and charge accordingly. You can squeak by on about US$15 a day, but if you want a comfortable hotel room and decent food, plan on spending about US$20 to US$25 a day. You can spend even more than this if you want to live the El Salvadoran high life, and should budget on about US$35 a day if that's your style.

Changing Money

The easiest currency to exchange is US dollars (cash only). Travellers cheques are still novel in El Salvador and some bank branches won't change them. To make matters worse, the policy seems to differ not only between banks but between branches as well. Change any leftover colónes before you leave.

ONLINE SERVICES

Lonely Planet's web site is Destination El Salvador (www.lonelyplanet.com /dest/cam/els.htm).

A good place to start researching volunteer opportunities is the CISPES homepage (www.blank.org/sweatgear /cispes.html£labor). This site lists campaigns and fundraising drives and what you can do both at home or in El Salvador to help.

Country Tips on El Salvador (www .maya-travel.com/salvador/sctips.htm) should keep you occupied with its great links and information on everything from studying Spanish to what to eat.

BOOKS

If you're hell-bent on travelling independently through El Salvador, *On Your Own in El Salvador* by Jeff Brauer, Julian Smith & Veronica Wiles is a guide you should not leave home without.

More literary is Joan Didion's *Salvador*, which is a quick read. Be sure also to read some of the moving poetry by El Salvador's most famous poet, Roque Dalton. His work is available in English translations.

There are many books dealing with El Salvador's civil war, including *El Salvador: The Face of Revolution* by Robert Armstrong & Janet Shenk and *Witness to War: An American Doctor in El Salvador* by Charles Clements MD, who worked in the war-zone district of Chalatenango in 1982 and 1983. *The Massacre in El Mozote* by Mark Danner is an emotional account of the brutal killing of 900 men, women and children in this small town in northern El Salvador. For a woman's point of view, read *I Was Never Alone: A Prison Diary from El Salvador* by Nidia Diaz, a guerrilla commander captured and shot by the military in 1985.

On a lighter note is PJ O'Rourke's *Holidays in Hell*, a devilishly funny travelogue about the region.

FILMS

El Salvador doesn't really have a film industry. For insights into the civil war, there are *Romero*, produced by Ellwood Kieser, and Oliver Stone's *Salvador*.

ENTERING & LEAVING

El Salvador is a Central American hub, so there are flights from all major regional cities, plus international flights from Atlanta, Dallas, Houston, Los Angeles, Miami, New York and San Francisco. Flights from Europe and Australia will fly through one of these cities. All international flights arrive at

Comalapa international airport, near the Pacific coast 44km south of San Salvador. There's a departure tax of US$23 on international flights.

Overland, San Salvador, Santa Ana and San Miguel are linked to Tegucigalpa (Honduras) and Guatemala City by bus. You can cross from El Salvador to Guatemala at the Anguiatú, Las Chinamas, La Hachadura and San Cristóbal border posts. The main crossings to Honduras are at El Amatillo and El Poy, both posts on the border. A departure tax is payable to border guards. There are also buses to Costa Rica, Nicaragua and Panama.

FALKLAND ISLANDS (ISLAS MALVINAS)

If you really feel like you need to get away from it all, make a beeline for the Falkland Islands (Islas Malvinas), some 500km east off Argentina's Patagonian mainland in the southern Atlantic Ocean. Both the location of the Falklands and the lifestyle of the inhabitants are far removed from the modern world. It's a fine destination for an off-the-beaten-track sojourn.

The Falkland Islands are British in government and habit (you can set your watch by teatime) and have become decidedly more so since Argentina invaded in 1982. Britain quickly dispatched naval units to defend the unarmed islanders and Argentine forces eventually surrendered. With astounding braggadocio, Argentine politicians have been heard to say that the islands will once again belong to Argentina. Though Falklands politics (or at least rhetoric) can still be tense on occasion, the natural splendour and hospitality of the islands are unforgettable.

WHEN TO GO

The Falkland Islands, so far out to sea, are notorious for awful and changeable weather. Still, you don't come here for fun in the sun. You come to the Falklands to see the wildlife, and that is most abundant between October and March. This is when migratory birds – including penguins – call in and marine mammals return to the headlands. Of course, these months see the most tourists, though so few people make it out here, that's not saying much. December and January are good months to visit because the extended daylight hours let you check out wildlife late into the evening. These are also, however, the wettest months. Between Christmas and New Year's Eve there are fantastic horse-racing, bull-riding and sheepdog competitions in Stanley.

At a Glance

Full Country Name: Colony of the Falkland Islands
Area: 12,170 sq km
Population: 2050 permanent residents
Capital City: Stanley (pop 1750)
People: British
Languages: English
Religion: Predominantly Anglican
Government: Colony of the UK
Currency: Falkland Islands pound (£)
Time Zone: Four hours behind GMT/UTC
International Telephone Code: 500
Electricity: 220/240V, 50 cycles AC; plugs have three square pins, of the kind used in the UK

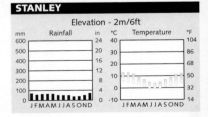

STANLEY
Elevation - 2m/6ft

HIGHLIGHTS

Like the Galápagos Islands off the coast of Ecuador, the Falkland Islands support a varied and unique array of wildlife. Most visitors come here for the

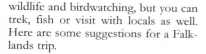

wildlife and birdwatching, but you can trek, fish or visit with locals as well. Here are some suggestions for a Falklands trip.

Wildlife Viewing

The Falkland Islands are the stomping ground for five penguin species, black-browed albatrosses, crested caracaras, cormorants, falcons, hawks and swans, to name but a few. Birders will be well occupied. Elephant seals, sea lions, dolphins and killer whales also ply the waters and are so unaccustomed to humans, their boldness may shock you. To check out the colony of king penguins, head to Volunteer Beach; Sea Lion Island is the place to mingle with elephant seals by the hundreds and take in some phenomenal birdwatching.

Fishing

A land of so much water and so few people is bound to have good fishing and the Falklands don't disappoint. Sea trout, smelt and mullet abound and there are rich fishing spots within walking distance of the capital. September to April is fishing season, and March to late April is the prime time to hook sea trout; there are many places jumping with fish right off the main highway on East Falkland Island.

Trekking

Trekking is a good option, although many landowners and the tourist board now discourage camping because of fire danger and disturbances to stock and wildlife. The stretch from Seal Bay to Volunteer Point on the northern coast of East Falkland Island offers a magnificent mixture of broad sandy beaches and rugged headlands with penguins in view. Hiking through the

1982 battlefields on East and West Falkland islands makes for an interesting trek. Saunders Island off West Falkland has ruins and good wildlife viewing.

VISA REQUIREMENTS

Visa requirements for the Falkland Islands are generally the same as those for the UK. Citizens of Australia, Canada, New Zealand and the USA are usually given a maximum stay of four months. An onward ticket may have to be produced upon entry. British subjects must have a passport. Argentines may have a very difficult time obtaining a visa for the Falkland Islands.

Falklands Embassies

For information on visas, contact the islands' UK representative at Falkland House (☎ 020-7222 2542) 14 Broadway, Westminster, London SW1H 0BH. In Chile, you can direct your inquiries to the British Consul John Rees (☎ 61-22 8312), Roca 924, Punta Arenas.

TOURIST OFFICES OVERSEAS

The following contacts represent the Falklands overseas tourist offices. British embassies may also be able to provide information.

Chile
(☎ 61-22 8312) Broom Travel, Roca 924, Punta Arenas
UK
(☎ 020-7222 2542, fax 7222 2375) 14 Broadway, Westminster, London SW1H 0BH
USA
(☎/fax 510-525-8846) Leo Le Bon & Associates, 190 Montrose Ave, Berkeley, CA 94707

HEALTH

There are few health problem on the Falkland Islands. Come prepared for some harsh weather − the wind and sun can combine to burn unsuspecting visitors and it can get very cold. As always, take care with food and water. Should you require serious medical care, Stanley has excellent facilities.

POST & COMMUNICATIONS

Postal services from the Falklands are very reliable as mail goes through London; there are two weekly air-mail services. Parcels over 450g, however, are shipped by sea only four or five times a year. To receive mail in the islands, use the following address lines: Name, Post Office, Stanley, Falkland Islands, via London, England.

Cable and Wireless PLC are the local and long-distance telephone carriers. International calls are charged in six-second increments. Reverse charge calls are only possible to the UK.

There is currently no Internet access in the Falklands.

MONEY
Costs

Visiting the Falklands is a financial commitment. The air fare is expensive, transportation is costly (unless you walk) and accommodation isn't cheap (except for camping). Travellers staying in moderate lodging and eating at restaurants should budget about US$50 a day; this high figure can be seriously mitigated by camping and preparing your own meals. For slightly better accommodation and food, allot closer to US$100 a day. Going all out in the Falklands could cost you up to US$200 daily.

Changing Money

The Falkland Islands pound is pegged to the UK pound sterling, which circulates alongside the local currency. Credit cards are not widely used, but travellers cheques are readily accepted. Brits with guarantee cards can cash personal checks up to £50 at the Standard Chartered Bank in Stanley.

ONLINE SERVICES

Lonely Planet's web site is Destination Falkland Islands (www.lonelyplanet.com /dest/sam/fal.htm).

Itineraries

There are no buses in the Falklands, so you have to fly point to point or rent a vehicle; both of these options are expensive, but you have little choice. If you make it out this far, make the most of it. The following itineraries assume you'll splurge on transport.

One Week

Spend two days in and around Stanley, visiting the 1982 battlefields and the penguin colony along Penguin Walk and Gypsy Cove. Spend the remaining days trekking from Seal Bay to Volunteer Point on the north coast of East Falkland. This will take you through Port Louis (the oldest settlement) to Seal Bay where you can camp with permission. Then it's on to Dutchman's Brook. You can camp overnight here before finishing at Volunteer Bay, with the largest king penguin colony on the islands.

Two Weeks

Follow the one week itinerary, adding a day trip to Sea Lion Island, before heading to West Falkland. Spend the remainder of your time here, taking in Pebble Island and Saunders Island before continuing to Port Stephens. From this pretty port you can see an amazing diversity of wildlife, but there are no facilities. Visit Carcass Island or New Island before returning to Stanley.

LKLAND ISLANDS HIGHLIGHTS & ITINERARIES

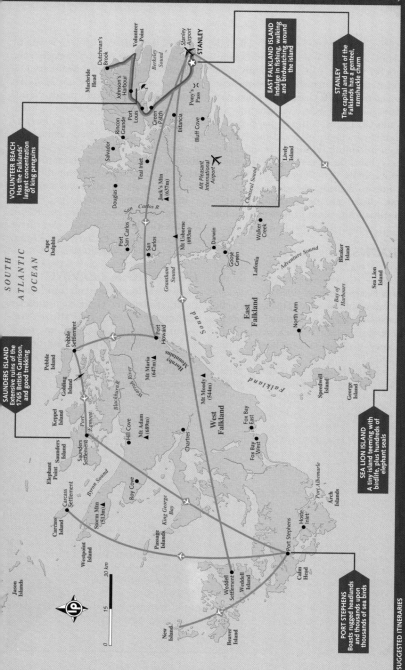

VOLUNTEER BEACH
Has the Falklands' largest concentration of king penguins

SAUNDERS ISLAND
Extensive ruins of the 1765 British Garrison, and good trekking

EAST FALKLAND ISLAND
Indulge in fishing, walking and birdwatching around the island

STANLEY
The capital and port of the Falklands has a genteel, ramshackle charm

SEA LION ISLAND
A tiny island teeming with birdlife, plus hundreds of elephant seals

PORT STEPHENS
Boasts rugged headlands and thousands upon thousands of sea birds

SUGGESTED ITINERARIES

One Week Stanley • Port Louis • Volunteer Point • Dutchman's Brook

Two Weeks Stanley • Port Louis • Volunteer Point • Dutchman's Brook • Stanley •
Port Howard • Pebble Island • Saunders Island • Port Stephens •
New Island or Carcass Island • Stanley • Sea Lion Island

The official site of the Falkland Islands Tourist Board (www.tourism.org.fk) will get you started with tour and weather information, tips on how to get there and what to do once you arrive. The UK's Association of National Tourist Offices page (www.tourist-offices.org.uk/Falkland_Islands/gen-info.html) is more substantial and less gloss. Go here for RAF flight information.

For a detailed analysis of the 1982 war, check out the Falkland Islands/Malvinas War homepage (www.yendor.com/vanished/falklands-war.htm).

BOOKS

For a readable introduction to the general history and geography of the islands, see the aptly titled *The Falkland Islands* by Ian Strange. This is not to be confused with *The Falkland Islands* by Paul Morrison or *The Falklands* by Tony Chater, two more recent books on the subject.

Among the dozens of books about the 1982 war, Max Hastings & Simon Jenkins' *Battle for the Falklands* is one of the best. If that doesn't quench your thirst for the nitty-gritty details, try *One Hundred Days: Memoirs of the Falklands Battle Group Commander* by Sandy Woodward & Patrick Robinson. Pierre Boulle (author of *Planet of the Apes* and *Bridge Over the River Kwai*) penned *The Whale of the Victoria Cross*, a novel about a British warship that mistakes a whale for a submarine during the Falklands War and then takes it as a mascot.

Bird enthusiasts should get a copy of *Falkland Islands Birds* by Robin Woods and hikers will do well to have on hand Julian Fisher's *Walks and Climbs in the Falkland Islands*.

ENTERING & LEAVING

Transportation to the Falkland Islands is strictly by air. There are biweekly civilian flights from RAF Brize Norton in Oxfordshire, England, and regular weekly flights from the airports of Santiago and Punta Arenas in Chile. Mt Pleasant international airport is about 60km west of Stanley.

FRENCH GUIANA

Imagine France in a tropical setting with a spicy twist and you've basically got French Guiana. Historically, French Guiana is best known as the penal colony where Captain Alfred Dreyfus (a French army officer wrongfully convicted of treason in 1894) and Papillon were imprisoned, but it is now home to the French aerospace program. French Guiana is a lot of swamp and jungle and outside of the French government compounds, there's substantial poverty.

This may be the perfect destination for adventure travellers: getting around is hard and getting comfortable even harder. It's hot and isolated. Still, there are fantastic stands of virgin rainforest and a biodiversity to rival any on earth. What doesn't make French Guiana an absolutely perfect destination is the price tag; you really will think you're in Paris for the amount of money you'll shell out travelling here.

WHEN TO GO

It will probably be hot and humid no matter when you show up in French Guiana. Over 90% of the country is classified as equatorial rainforest and this is not surprising considering more than 250cm of rain drenches the country each year. January to June are the rainiest months, when the humidity is palpable. It may be drier from July to December, but not much more comfortable. Carnaval is in February and though no match for its bigger sibling down south in Brazil, it's still a fun time to be in French Guiana.

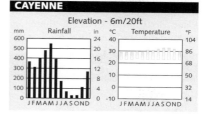

HIGHLIGHTS

Many travellers steer clear of French Guiana because of the cost and the climate. However, those that do go find that there is a certain *je ne sais quoi* to the place. Most likely it's the combination of tropical ambience, French style and the dearth of tourists. If you make it out this way, here are some suggested highlights.

At a Glance

Full Country Name: Guyane Française
Area: 91,250 sq km
Population: 134,000
Capital City: Cayenne (pop 40,000)
People: 70% Creole (of mixed African/Afro-European descent), 10% European, 8% Asian, 8% Brazilian and 4% Amerindian
Languages: French, French Guianese creole and Amerindian languages
Religion: Predominantly Catholic
Government: Overseas department of France
Currency: French franc (FF)/Euro
Time Zone: Three hours behind GMT/UTC
International Telephone Code: 594
Electricity: 220V, 50 cycles

Cities

Cayenne is like a European city in a tropical environment, with the architecture and food of the old world engulfed by the heat and seduction of the new. The liveliest areas are the Place de Palmistes, where there are many cafes and outdoor food stalls, and the neighbourhood known as 'Chicago', where you can catch some quality music in any number of small clubs. A handful of historic forts in and around the capital are also worth a visit, mainly for the views. Kourou has grown from a backwater town to a legitimate city with the help of the European space programs that have their headquarters here.

Penal Colonies

This isn't for everyone, but the islands that comprise the former penal colonies can be fascinating in terms of history and natural settings. Île Royale, the largest of the three islands collectively known as the Îles du Salut (Salvation Islands), was the administrative headquarters for the prison settlement. Nearby Île St Joseph was reserved for solitary confinement. Île du Diable (Devil's Island), a tiny islet now covered with coconut palms, was home to the bulk of prisoners. The atmospheric ruins are the islands' main attraction, but their abundant wildlife – including macaws, agoutis and sea turtles – provides another reason to visit.

Wildlife Viewing

Although French Guiana is prime territory for an ecotourism industry, the infrastructure just isn't there yet. Trips through the interior rainforest are popular and exciting, but expensive. Head to the Kaw River, 65km from Cayenne, by bus and then boat for good birdwatching and wildlife viewing. You can see leatherback turtles near Mana between April and September.

VISA REQUIREMENTS

Visitors from the EU countries, Australia, Canada, New Zealand and the

---

Itineraries

One Week

There are few roads in French Guiana besides the one hugging the coast, so your choices are limited if you're only here for a week. Hang out in Cayenne for two days, soaking up the culture and a little sun at the very good beach of Rémire-Montjoly, 10km south-east of town. Then head to Cacao, a village of Hmong refugees, some 75km west of the Cayenne-Régina paved highway. There is a fascinating Sunday market here. Finally, head up the coast to Kourou and spend the next two days visiting the space programs there and the penal colony islands, before returning to Cayenne.

Two Weeks

With a two week itinerary, you can do an in-depth version of the one week itinerary, spending more time among different Laotian communities south of Cayenne. Also make your way to the accessible, but isolated wildlife area of Kaw before heading north to Kourou.

Three Weeks

Follow the two week itinerary, extending the northern leg after Kourou to include Mana (for turtle watching) and St Laurent du Maroni. This town has historical significance as the reception camp for newly arrived convicts, but its real appeal lies in its geography. On the northern bank of the Maroni (Marowijne) River, you can take river trips into the rainforest from St Laurent du Maroni and spend time in Maron and Amerindian communities. You can also take a ferry into Suriname from here.

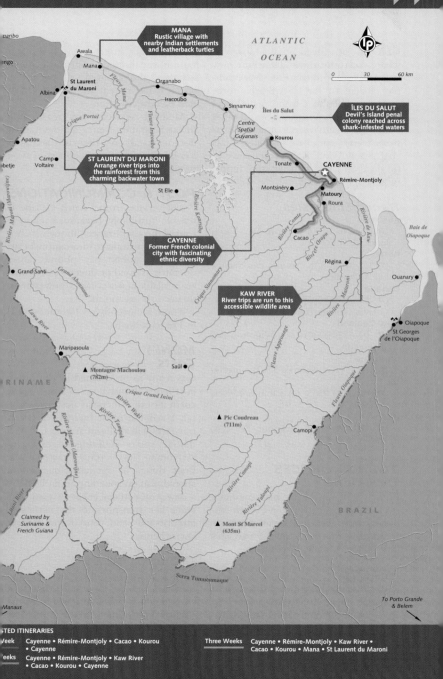

FRENCH GUIANA HIGHLIGHTS & ITINERARIES

MANA
Rustic village with nearby Indian settlements and leatherback turtles

ÎLES DU SALUT
Devil's Island penal colony reached across shark-infested waters

ST LAURENT DU MARONI
Arrange river trips into the rainforest from this charming backwater town

CAYENNE
Former French colonial city with fascinating ethnic diversity

KAW RIVER
River trips are run to this accessible wildlife area

ATLANTIC OCEAN

0   30   60 km

Paramaribo
Awala
Mana
St Laurent du Maroni
Albina
Apatou
Camp Voltaire
bebetje
Grand Santi
Maripasoula
SURINAME
Claimed by Suriname & French Guiana
Manaus

Organabo
Iracoubo
Sinnamary
Centre Spatial Guyanais
Kourou
Tonate
CAYENNE
Rémire-Montjoly
Montsinéry
Matoury
Roura
Cacao
Régina
Ouanary
Oiapoque
St Georges de l'Oiapoque
St Elie
Saül
Montagne Machoulou (782m)
Pic Coudreau (711m)
Camopi
Mont St Marcel (635m)
BRAZIL
Serra Tumucumaque
To Porto Grande & Belem

Fleuve Mana
Crique Portal
Fleuve Iracoubo
Rivière Maroni (Marowijne)
Rivière Kourou
Rivière Sinnamary
Grand Abounami
Lawa River
Crique Grand Inini
Rivière Waki
Rivière Tampok
Rivière Maroni (Marowijne)
Litani River
Rivière Camopi
Rivière Yaloupi
Rivière Comté
Rivière Orapu
Rivière Mataroni
Fleuve Approuague
Fleuve Oiapoque
Rivière de Kaw
Baie de Oiapoque
Îles du Salut

USA do not need visas. However, where you're from will determine how long you're permitted to stay. For example, citizens of the USA receive three months, while those from Australia get just one month. Visitors from all other countries need visas, obtainable at French embassies or consulates. Visas cost around US$25 and you'll have to produce an onward ticket and supply two passport photos.

French Embassies

Australia
(☎ 02-6216 0100) 6 Perth Ave, Yarralumla, ACT 2600
Brazil
(☎ 312-9100) SAS, Avenida das Nacoes, lote 4, Brasília
Canada
(☎ 613-789-1795) 42 Sussex Drive, Ottawa, Ontario K1M 2C9
New Zealand
(☎ 04-472 0200) 1-3 Willeston St, Wellington
Suriname
(☎ 476-455) Gravenstraat 5-7, Paramaribo
UK
(☎ 020-7823 9555) 6A Cromwell Place, London SW7
USA
(☎ 202-328-2600) Belmont Rd NW, Washington, DC

TOURIST OFFICES OVERSEAS

French Guiana does not maintain overseas tourist offices, but French embassies and consulates can answer basic travel questions. Also see the web sites listed under Online Services later.

HEALTH

Malaria is a health concern throughout French Guiana and yellow fever can also occur. Dengue fever and leishmaniasis can occur, so avoid mosquito and all other insect bites. Food and waterborne diseases, such as dysentery, hepatitis and typhoid, all occur, so watch what you eat and stick to purified or bottled water.

Medical services are reasonable throughout the country, although most doctors speak only French. Caracas in Venezuela is a better option if you require serious medical care.

POST & COMMUNICATIONS

Postal service from French Guiana is reliable (probably because it all gets routed through France!) though it's not cheap. You can place international calls from any public pay phone, either operator-assisted or direct. Phonecards are available at post offices, newsstands, tobacco shops and the like.

There is currently no Internet access in French Guiana.

MONEY
Costs

Get ready to be stunned by the prices in French Guiana, as it's the most costly South American destination by far. Even the most budget-conscious travellers will shell out at least US$45 a day. If you're counting on eating in restaurants and getting a taste of the finer things in French Guiana, you should plan on spending about US$100 a day. Any extravagances in your itinerary like transport to the rainforest interior will send your overall budget skyrocketing.

Changing Money

French Guiana, as an overseas department of France, is in the process of switching its official currency from the French franc to the Euro. Although the franc is still circulating, it is considered a denomination of the Euro which begins circulating after 1 January 2002. US dollars and travellers cheques are easy to change in Cayenne, but the rates you get are about 5% below the published exchange rates. You can hedge this by bringing some francs with you. Credit cards are widely accepted and ATMs give cash advances on Visa and MasterCard. Eurocard and Carte Bleue are also widely accepted and you can use Cirrus or Plus cards at ATMs in the post offices.

ONLINE SERVICES

Lonely Planet's web site is Destination French Guiana (www.lonelyplanet.com .au/dest/sam/fgu.htm).

The web site of the Guiana Shield Media Project (www.gsmp.org) features good information on environmental issues. Similar information is provided by the Rainforest Information Center (www.mdi-guyane.fr/pouagouti/index .asp) based in St Laurent du Maroni.

BOOKS

Probably the best known book about French Guiana is Henri Charrière's novel *Papillon*, about the Devil's Island penal colony. The novel was adapted into a Hollywood movie starring Steve McQueen as Charrière and a young Dustin Hoffman. A nonfiction work about the same island is the readable *Devil's Island: Colony of the Damned* by Alexander Miles.

For a laugh-out-loud read, check out *Equator* by Thurston Clarke, which describes the author's travels in French Guiana, among other places. A good overview of the country is featured in *France's Overseas Frontier* by R Aldrich & J Connell.

ENTERING & LEAVING

There are daily direct flights from Paris, some with stop-offs in Martinique or Guadeloupe. From the USA, there are regular flights from Miami and other gateway cities. Within South America, there are flights to Brazil, Ecuador, Suriname and Venezuela. There is a US$20 departure tax on all international flights, except those going to France.

It's possible to cross over to Suriname from St Laurent du Maroni by taking the passenger ferry to Albina. From there, there are road connections to Suriname's capital, Paramaribo. There are also launches from St Georges to Oiapoque in Brazil, but first you'll have to fly from Cayenne to St Georges, as the road doesn't yet extend that far.

GUATEMALA

Despite decades of civil war, Guatemala has remained a hot spot on the backpacker trail, and not simply because it's cheap. Guatemala remains the centre of the Mayan universe with fantastic ruins, markets and a thriving culture; it has the highest and most active volcanoes in Central America; and it offers many opportunities to get off the beaten track and into the heart of the indigenous world. Still, there's an established infrastructure along the Gringo Trail and a plenitude of Spanish schools if hanging out with your compatriots or language study are among your priorities.

The peace accord signed in 1996 put an end to the civil war, during which an estimated 200,000 Guatemalans were killed and countless 'disappeared'.

Many provisions of the accord attempt to address the rights and needs of the indigenous population, including political representation, health care and education. Integrating former guerrillas into normal Guatemalan life is another challenge. Developing a lasting peace is rife with paradoxes, eg men with big guns keeping that peace, and these will be evident all through the country.

WHEN TO GO

Guatemala's dry season is from October to May, when travelling is most pleasant. The typically humid, torpid Pacific coast – temperatures average around 38°C – chills out slightly during this time and the highlands are warm. During the rest of the year, however, the coast roasts and the highlands are wet and cold with freezing night-time temperatures. The northern Petén region, home to the soaring ruins at Tikal and Guatemala's jungle lowlands, varies from hot and humid to hot and slightly less humid. March and April are the hottest months here, while December and January are the coolest.

At a Glance

Full Country Name: Republic of Guatemala
Area: 109,000 sq km
Population: 12 million
Capital City: Guatemala City (pop two million)
People: 56% Spanish descent and 44% Mayan descent
Languages: Spanish, Garífuna and 21 Mayan languages
Religion: Roman Catholic, Pentecostal and Mayan-Catholic fusion
Government: Democracy
Currency: Quetzal (Q)
Time Zone: Six hours behind GMT/UTC
International Telephone Code: 502
Electricity: 115V to 125V, 60 cycles AC; plugs are the flat-pronged type used in North America

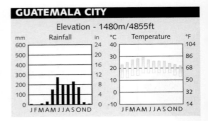

GUATEMALA CITY
Elevation - 1480m/4855ft

HIGHLIGHTS

All things authentic, indigenous and colourful are intrinsic to the Guatemalan experience. Natural wonders – some of the best in Central America – are also tucked away here and travellers who check out the surrounding environment will be well rewarded. Here are some starting points.

Markets

The vibrant culture of the Mayan people is evident everywhere. Rainbow-coloured *huipiles* (traditional women's blouses) are intricately embroidered. Weavings, textiles and tablecloths all explode with colour from the many Indian markets throughout the country. Some of the best and brightest markets are in Chichicastenango, Antigua Guatemala and in smaller villages such as Sololá and Momostenango. In Chichi (as it's called), market day is punctuated with processions by *cofradías* (brotherhoods) that combine Mayan rituals and Catholic rites. Incense, food and drink are offered to ancestors to ensure the continued fertility of the earth.

Archaeological Sites

The Mayan ruins of Tikal represent one of the monumental wonders of the world, and if you're anywhere near Guatemala try to get to the Petén region to explore these relics of a lost dynasty. Tucked into the jungle, the plazas, pyramids and temples of Tikal share an environment with monkeys, parrots, tree frogs and snakes. The major ruins have been excavated from the wild growth, but many more remain hidden and the surrounding rainforest is still intact. Many ancient Mayan sites lurk in the jungle and visitors are encouraged to venture further afield to visit Uaxactún and Ceibal. The easily accessible sites of Quiriguá, with the tallest stelae in the Mayan world, and Iximché, the capital of the Cakchiquel Maya when the Spaniards arrived, are also worth visiting.

Natural Attractions

Three volcanoes ring the beautiful Lago de Atitlán, a collapsed volcanic cone fed by several rivers and dotted with charming small towns. Hiking, soaking in thermal springs and paddling around the lake are all popular pursuits. Scuba diving certification is also available on the lake. The caves at Lanquín, north of Guatemala City near Cobán, are so deep they remain unexplored for the most part, though visitors can venture in for a few hundred metres and frolic in the underground river. Nearby, Semuc-Champey is a stunning feat of nature. Here, a limestone bridge 300m long looms over several natural pools filled by a rushing underground river.

Wildlife Viewing

The jungle lowlands in the Petén region are phenomenal for wildlife viewing. Birdwatchers should head to Biotopo del Quetzal to check out quetzals or to the Biotopo Monterrico-Hawaii where birdwatching in the coastal mangrove swamp is rewarding. At this same reserve you can see endangered leatherback and Ridley turtles laying their eggs on the beach between June and November. A total of nine biological reserves and wildlife refuges, some remote and some easily accessible, are open to visitors in Guatemala.

Studying Spanish

Antigua Guatemala is one of the most popular places in Latin America to learn Spanish. Programs are plentiful and varied and you can combine one-on-one Spanish instruction with a homestay or dancing, cooking or weaving classes. Quetzaltenango is a growing centre for Spanish schools and is favoured by visitors who want a more authentic and indigenous atmosphere than exists in the backpackers haven of

Antigua. There are other small towns with Spanish schools, and private tutors are another option.

VISA REQUIREMENTS

Most visitors to Guatemala do not need a visa but the length of your stay will depend on your country of origin. Citizens of many European countries and the USA usually receive 90 days upon arrival while citizens of Australia, Canada, New Zealand and the

Itineraries

One Week

Arrive in Guatemala City and shuttle directly to Antigua Guatemala, the country's original capital. Explore the colonial churches and museums for a day and arrange for a flight to Flores in the Petén region. Here, spend two or three days exploring the ruins of Tikal, with an optional day trip to the Ceibal ruins deeper in the jungle. Return to Antigua and visit the nearby town of San Antonio Aguas Calientes, famous for its weaving, or hike to one of the three volcanoes around Antigua. With an extra day you can visit Lago de Atitlán and stay overnight before returning to Guatemala City.

Two Weeks

Follow the one week itinerary, spending one or two days on the shores of Lago de Atitlán, preferably at one of the small towns accessible by ferry. Continue to the highland towns of Chichicastenango and Momostenango for two or three days to explore the Indian markets. Visit the nearby ruins of K'umarcaaj, the ancient capital of the Quiché Maya, perhaps going further to the remote town of Nebaj high in the mountains for an overnight stay. Alternatively, you can travel east from Chichi to the Honduran border and visit the Mayan ruins at Copán, a two day trip at least.

One Month

A month allows you to add a little cultural and natural variety to your travelling diet. Follow the two week itinerary, but continue east

from Nebaj over very rugged roads to Cobán. From this city you can visit the caves at Lanquín and the beautiful natural limestone pools at Semuc-Champey. Head south-east to the Honduran border, visit the Mayan ruins at Copán in Honduras for two or three days and then make for the Caribbean coastal town of Lívingston, perhaps stopping off on the way on the shores of Lago de Izabal at Río Dulce for some wildlife viewing or water activities. From Lívingston you can easily cross into Belize by ferry or make your way back to Guatemala City.

Two Months

Two months will let you get off the beaten path and into areas rarely visited by foreigners, where a knack for Mayan dialects will serve you better than the best Spanish skills. Follow the one week itinerary, but travel overland to Tikal, perhaps taking the back door route over unpaved, rough roads and stopping in Poptún to gather your strength. Continue to Tikal and spend several days exploring the surrounding jungle areas. Complete the one month itinerary, with some time spent in one of the biological reserves, such as the Biotopo del Quetzal (on the way from Cobán to Copán), or one of the national parks such as the remote Parque Nacional los Cuchumatanes (north of Heuheutenango). Hike to a volcano or two, take Spanish classes or get certified for scuba diving to broaden your horizons and round out your itinerary.

UATEMALA HIGHLIGHTS & ITINERARIES

TIKAL
Lofty Mayan temples rise above a jungle canopy filled with monkeys and exotic birds

LÍVINGSTON
Laid-back fishing town of black Guatemalans, coconut palms and gaily painted buildings

NEBAJ
Remote village where locals aintain a traditional life-style, nown for its excellent textiles

LAGO DE ATITLÁN
ollapsed volcanic cone fed y several rivers and dotted with charming towns

CHICHICASTENANGO
Chichi boasts extraordinary mountain scenery and a traditional Mayan market

ANTIGUA GUATEMALA
A charming colonial city and a popular place for studying Spanish

Map labels

MEXICO · BELIZE · Belize City · BELMOPAN · CARIBBEAN SEA · HONDURAS · EL SALVADOR · SAN SALVADOR · PACIFIC OCEAN

Parque Nacional-Mirador Dos Lagunas-Río Azul
Biotopo Laguna del Tigre-Río Escondido
Reserva de la Biosfera Maya
Uaxactún
Tikal
Parque Nacional Tikal
El Naranjo
Melchor de Mencos
Benque Viejo del Carmen
Dangriga (Stann Creek)
Parque Nacional Sierra del Lacandón
Flores
El Cruce
Lago de Petén Itzá
Big Creek
To Mexico City
Yaxchilán
Bonampak
Bethel
El Subín
Sayaxché
Ceibal
Parque Nacional Ceibal
Reserva Aguateca-Dos Pilas
Poptún
Cuevas de Poptún
Punta Gorda
Bahía de Amatique
Golfo de Honduras
Comitán
Benemérito
Reserva Machaquilá
Modesto Méndez
Livingston
Biotopo Punta de Manabique
Puerto Barrios
Lagunas de Montebello
Playa Grande
Parque Nacional Lachuá
Sebol
Fray Bartolomé de las Casas
El Golfete
Parque Nacional Río Dulce
El Cinchado
Corinto
a de la ostura
Ciudad htémoc
La Mesilla
Sierra de Chamá
Reserva Natural Cerro Bisis Nebaj
Lanquín
Semuc-Champey
El Estor
Río Dulce
Lago de Izabal
La Ruidosa
zintla
Parque Nacional los Cuchumatanes
Zaculeu
Huehuetenango
Sierra de los Cuchumatane
Cobán
Purulhá
Bocas del Polochic
Río Polochic
Mariscos
Río Motagua
Santa Bárbara
Volcán Tajumulco (4220m)
Sacapulas
Biotopo del Quetzal
Reserva de la Biosfera de Sierra de Las Minas
Salamá
Sierra de las Minas
Quiriguá
Río Ulúa
El Carmen
Momostenango
Santa Cruz del Quiché
Purulhá
Río Hondo
Zacapa
Quetzaltenango
Totonicapán
Chichicastenango
Sololá
Sierra de Cuacús
El Florido
Copán Ruinas
Copán
Santa Rosa de Copán
ad Hidalgo
Ciudad Tecún Umán
Panajachel
Iximché
Chimaltenango
Chiquimula
Ocós
Retalhuleu
Volcán Atitlán (3537m)
Santiago Atitlán
Lago de Atitlán
Antigua Guatemala
GUATEMALA CITY
San Antonio Aguas Calientes
Esquipulas
Agua Caliente
Nueva Ocotepeque
Maza-tenango
San José Pinula
Laguna de Ayarza
El Progreso (Guastatoya)
Anguiatú
Anguiatú
Metapán
Champerico
Santa Lucía Cotzumalguapa
Esquintla
Cuilapa
San Cristóbal Frontera
Valle Nuevo
San Cristóbal
Lago de Güija
To Tegucigalpa
Nueva Venecia
La Democracia
Chiquimulilla
Ciudad Pedro de Alvarado
Las Chinamas
Santa Ana
Embalse Cerrón Grande
Sipacate
Puerto San José
Iztapa
Monterrico
Biotopo Monterrico-Hawaii
La Hachadura
Sonsonate
Lago de Coatepeque
Lago de Ilopango
Embalse 15 de Septiembre

30 · 60 km

SUGGESTED ITINERARIES

UK will typically get 30 days. Stay extensions can be obtained at immigration offices in Guatemala.

Guatemalan Embassies

Canada
(☎ 613-233-7188/237, fax 233-0135) 130 Albert St, Suite 1010, Ottawa, Ontario K1P 5G4

UK
(☎ 020-7351 3042, fax 7376 5708) 13 Fawcett St, London SW 10

USA
(☎ 202-745-4952, fax 745-1908) 2220 R St NW, Washington, DC 20008

TOURIST OFFICES OVERSEAS

There is a Guatemalan tourist office (☎ 305-443-0343, fax 443-0699) in the USA at 300 Sevilla Ave, Suite 210-A, Coral Gables, FL 33134. See the web sites listed under Online Services.

HEALTH

Malaria exists in the lowland rural areas, but there is no risk in the central highlands. Dengue fever is present, mainly in urban areas, so take precautions against both these mosquito-borne diseases. Avoid insect bites, especially in rural areas, to prevent other serious insect-borne diseases. Hepatitis, typhoid, cholera and dysentery all occur, so take care with all food and water. Tap water is not safe to drink; bottled water is widely available.

Full medical services are available in Guatemala City, but services are otherwise limited. If you do require serious medical care, Guatemala City has many private hospitals and clinics.

POST & COMMUNICATIONS

Incoming and outgoing mail service is notoriously unreliable in Guatemala, with reports of lost or stolen poste restante mail commonplace. Locals use private courier services and you may want to follow suit, especially for anything important. When you pick up poste restante mail, be prepared to show your passport and check under both of your initials.

International telephone calls are very expensive from Guatemala and you're better off having someone call you back at an appointed time and number. Reverse charge (collect) calls are only allowed between Guatemala and countries with reciprocal telecommunications agreements. Your best and cheapest bet is to use the telephone, fax and email services offered by private companies or Internet cafes, which are plentiful in bigger cities and popular tourist destinations.

MONEY
Costs

Costs and value can vary greatly in Guatemala, but if you're budget-wise and can take a bit of rough travelling, you can survive on about US$12 a day. Even if you splurge a little on better accommodation with a private bathroom and eat well two or three times a day, you'll only be spending around US$25 a day. Solo travellers will find few bargains on accommodation as a single and double room usually cost about the same.

Changing Money

As you'll find throughout Central America, the US dollar is king and you'll have problems changing anything else. Carry US dollars or travellers cheques and change sufficient amounts of money before you head off the beaten track. If you're travelling with money other than US dollars, you can change them at the airport exchange houses in Flores or Guatemala City. Banks are the best places to change money and rates are similar for cash or travellers cheques. The street moneychangers don't offer a better rate than the banks, but they may be your only option at borders or after-hours; change only what you'll need for the immediate future.

ONLINE SERVICES

Lonely Planet's web site is Destination Guatemala (www.lonelyplanet.com/dest/cam/gua.htm).

The Guatemala Web (www.guatemalaweb.com) is an exhaustive, easy-to-navigate site with good logistical information on markets, natural attractions and bus schedules. There are good links to other sites as well.

The Quetzaltenango Pages (www.xelapages.com) has everything you want to know about Xela (the Mayan word for this town, pronounced 'shayla'). There are lists of Spanish schools, volunteer opportunities, Internet cafes and the like. A similar site is The Antigua Journal (www.theantiguajournal.com), detailing everything about that city.

BOOKS

One of the most influential books to ever come out of Guatemala is *I, Rigoberta Menchú: An Indian Woman in Guatemala* by Rigoberta Menchú. This Nobel Peace Prize winner's testimonial introduced the world to the plight of Mayans in Guatemala and their murderous repression by the government. Anyone interested in Mayan culture should definitely check out the eminently readable *Popol Vuh*, the

Mayan creation story. *Time and the Highland Maya* is an anthropological account of the Quiché Maya of Momostenango by Barbara Tedlock.

Mayans in modern society and their role in recent history can be found in Victor Perera's *Unfinished Conquest: The Guatemalan Tragedy*. David Stoll's *Between Two Armies* is an investigation of the Mayan people and their position between a rock and a hard place in the recent civil war, with the army on one side and guerrillas on the other.

Stephen Benz travels the Ruta Maya and along the Mosquito Coast in his *Green Dreams: Travels in Central America*. This exploration of ancient cultures and modern travel is published by Journeys, Lonely Planet's travel literature series.

Clamor of Innocence: Central American Short Stories, edited by Barbara Paschke & David Volpendesta, contains 31 short stories by writers from the region.

FILMS

One movie not to be missed by anyone travelling to Guatemala is Gregory Nava's *El Norte*, which tells the story of two refugees fleeing the violence and repression of Guatemala. The movie follows the pair as they leave their homeland to make a new life in the USA.

Guatemala doesn't have what you could call a domestic film industry, but several Hollywood extravaganzas have been filmed there. To give you an idea about the environment, check out the James Bond film *Moonraker* or *New Adventures of Tarzan*. Trivia buffs may be interested to know that parts of the first *Star Wars* film were shot at Tikal.

ENTERING & LEAVING

Visitors arriving by air touch down at La Aurora international airport in Guatemala City. There are several gateway cities in the USA, one of the most important being Los Angeles; visitors from Australia and New Zealand will probably fly through here, while European travellers will go through Cancún, Mexico on the cheapest flights. Some international flights go directly to Flores in the Petén region, but unless you're on a package tour you'll most likely land in Guatemala City.

Sharing borders with Mexico, Belize, Honduras and El Salvador means many travellers enter Guatemala overland. Along the lengthy border between Guatemala and Mexico, there are five border crossings: La Mesilla to Cuauhtémoc; Ciudad Tecún Umán to Ciudad Hidalgo; El Naranjo to La Palma; Bethel to Frontera Corozal; and Sayaxché to Benemérito. The last three involve boat passage, and travellers should check the security situation in Chiapas, Mexico before attempting the Sayaxché to Benemérito crossing. From Guatemala to Belize, there is an overland crossing from Melchor de Mencos to Benque Viejo del Carmen, and a ferry crossing from Puerto Barrios and Lívingston to Punta Gorda, across the Bahía de Amatique.

There is a crossing from El Florido in Guatemala to Copán Ruinas in Honduras, and another at the Agua Caliente border post. If you're aching for adventure, you can try the remote border crossing at El Cinchado in eastern Guatemala to the town of Corinto in Honduras. An unofficial border crossing known as the 'Jungle Trail' exists between Puerto Barrios in eastern Guatemala and Puerto Cortés or Omoa in Honduras. Once arduous, there are now well synchronised transport connections on the trail; it crosses the borders via Finca La Inca in Guatemala, El Límite on the Río Montagua and Cuyamelito in Honduras.

You can cross between El Salvador and Guatemala at the Anguiatú, Las Chinamas, La Hachadura and San Cristóbal border posts.

GUYANA

Adventurous travellers rejoice! There is still a pocket of unspoiled, rarely trodden, tropical land and it's known as Guyana. It's hot and muggy and the coast is all mangroves with no beach (just a few of the reasons why Spanish and Portuguese settlers passed it by), but if you can stand it, you'll be well rewarded. Some of the world's most spectacular virgin rainforest survives in the Guyanese interior and the remote Kaieteur Falls are an awesome force, plunging 250m from a jungle plateau to the Potaro River below. Wildlife is thriving in Guyana's remote forests; the more spectacular creatures include jaguars, sloths, monkeys and blue arrow frogs. There are endemic orchids, butterflies and hundreds of bird species.

Guyana is not the destination for everyone, however. Travel here is either prohibitively expensive or absurdly rough. The tourist infrastructure is largely nonexistent in the interior and conditions can be uncomfortable, to put it mildly. Of course, if you decide to travel to Guyana you'll also have to hear ad nauseum about the Jonestown massacre, the 1979 murder/suicide orchestrated by Jim Jones of nearly 1000 of his cult followers.

WHEN TO GO
Guyana has the quintessential equatorial climate: it's hot and humid almost all the time and the only way to differentiate between the seasons is by how much rain is falling. There are actually two rainy seasons. The first runs from May to mid-August, while the second is from mid-November to late January. Kaieteur Falls is most impressive directly following either of the rainy seasons (late January or late August is best), when they are gushing with run-off. If you want to explore the interior overland, visit during the dry season because most roads are impassable after a heavy wet-season.

GEORGETOWN

Elevation - 2m/6ft

At a Glance

Full Country Name: Co-operative Republic of Guyana
Area: 215,000 sq km
Population: 705,200
Capital City: Georgetown (pop 200,000)
People: 51% East Indian, 43% Afro-Guyanese, 4% Amerindian and 2% European and Chinese
Languages: English (although most Guyanese speak Creole), Hindi and Urdu
Religion: 57% Christian, 33% Hindu and 10% Muslim
Government: Democracy
Currency: Guyanese dollar (G$)
Time Zone: Four hours behind GMT/UTC
International Telephone Code: 592
Electricity: 110V in Georgetown, 220V elsewhere; power outages are frequent

HIGHLIGHTS

If you're not into hot, sweaty and dirty travelling, Guyana may not be for you. The greatest attraction is the interior region which has large tracts of jungle and inspiring wildlife viewing. The Rupununi Savanna is a vast grassland teeming with spectacular wildlife, including cowboys! There are some attractive small towns such as Bartica, but the capital of Georgetown is dangerous and can be seen in a day.

Jungle Trips

Getting into the thick of the Guyanese jungle can be a labour of love and is only recommended for well prepared and thick-skinned travellers. Luckily, there are many tour operators offering different adventures including plane trips over the Kaieteur and Orinduik falls, customised interior treks and camping excursions. Other natural attractions include the vast Rupununi Savanna and white-water rafting on the Essequibo, Kamuni and Mazaruni rivers. For the experienced jungle-trekker, the overland route from Georgetown to Lethem near the Brazilian border will be an unforgettable experience. This is only possible during the dry season.

VISA REQUIREMENTS

Citizens from Australia, Canada, New Zealand, the USA and the UK don't need a visa, but make sure your passport is valid for at least six months from when you plan to enter Guyana. Upon entry, you'll be granted a three month maximum stay, which should be plenty. If you do need a visa, submit your application at least six months in advance.

Guyanese Embassies Abroad

Canada
(☎ 613-235-7249) 151 Slater St, Suite 309, Ottawa, Ontario K1P 5H3. Consulate: Toronto

UK
(☎ 020-7229 7684, fax 7727 9809) 3 Palace Court, Bayswater Rd, London

USA
(☎ 202-265-6900) 2490 Tracy Place, Washington, DC;
(☎ 212-527-3215) 866 United Nations Plaza, New York, NY

TOURIST OFFICES OVERSEAS

Guyana maintains no overseas tourist offices, but a good travel agent should

---

Itineraries

One Week
You will probably feel rushed in a week, as there isn't much to do in this amount of time aside from organised tours. You could arrange to fly over the Kaieteur or Orinduik falls or hook up with a multiday interior trip.

Two Weeks
Arrange a multiday trip to the interior and fly over the falls, but do as much as you can overland and incorporate some camping into your itinerary. The hike from Bartica, the closest town to Kaieteur Falls, is a difficult four day round trip. If you have some time remaining, hang out in Bartica at the confluence of the Essequibo, Kamuni and Mazaruni rivers and do some white-water rafting, visit the colourful market and go swimming.

Three Weeks
This will be too long in Guyana for most people. However, if your dream trip is to hike through the jungle in a test of endurance and sanity, this is the place for it. You may want closer to four or even five weeks in Guyana if you plan to explore the jungle on foot. Go in the dry season and try the Georgetown to Lethem overland route.

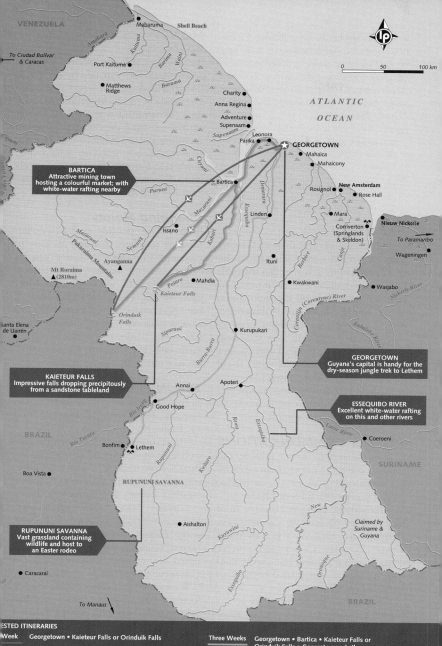

GUYANA HIGHLIGHTS & ITINERARIES

VENEZUELA

To Ciudad Bolívar & Caracas

Mabaruma
Shell Beach
Port Kaituma
Matthews Ridge
Charity
Anna Regina
Adventure
Supenaam
Leonora
Parika

GEORGETOWN
Mahaica
Mahaicony

ATLANTIC
OCEAN

BARTICA
Attractive mining town hosting a colourful market; with white-water rafting nearby

Bartica

Rosignol
New Amsterdam
Rose Hall

Linden
Mara
Corriverton
(Springlands
& Skeldon)
Nieuw Nickerie

Issano

To Paramaribo

Wageningen

Ituni

Mt Roraima
(2810m)
Ayanganna

Kwakwani

Wasjabo

Mahdia
Kaieteur Falls

Orinduik Falls

Kurupukari

Santa Elena de Uairén

GEORGETOWN
Guyana's capital is handy for the dry-season jungle trek to Lethem

KAIETEUR FALLS
Impressive falls dropping precipitously from a sandstone tableland

Annai
Apoteri

ESSEQUIBO RIVER
Excellent white-water rafting on this and other rivers

Good Hope

Coeroeni

BRAZIL

Bonfim
Lethem

SURINAME

Boa Vista

RUPUNUNI SAVANNA

Claimed by Suriname & Guyana

RUPUNUNI SAVANNA
Vast grassland containing wildlife and host to an Easter rodeo

Aishalton

Caracarai

BRAZIL

To Manaus

ESTED ITINERARIES

Week   Georgetown • Kaieteur Falls or Orinduik Falls

Weeks   Georgetown • Bartica • Kaieteur Falls or Orinduik Falls

Three Weeks   Georgetown • Bartica • Kaieteur Falls or Orinduik Falls • Georgetown • Lethem

be able to answer basic questions. Guyanese consulates and embassies may also be of help. For more detailed information, try contacting the private Tourism Association of Guyana (representatives listed below). It publishes the useful *Guyana Tourist Guide*.

UK
Guyanese High Commission
(☎ 020-7229 7684, fax 7727 9809) 3 Palace Court, Bayswater Rd, London
USA
Ms Mary Lou Callahan
(☎ 203-431-1571) Unique Destinations, 307 Peaceable St, Ridgefield, CT

HEALTH

Malaria occurs in rural areas of Guyana and yellow fever occurs throughout the country. Dengue fever is also a health concern, particularly in the interior, so take care and avoid all mosquito bites. Avoid sandfly bites, as leishmaniasis occurs, and try to avoid bites from all other insects. Take care with food and water as hepatitis, typhoid and cholera all occur. Stick to treated water in all areas, including Georgetown.

Medical facilities are reasonable, but for serious medical care Caracas in Venezuela is a better option.

POST & COMMUNICATIONS

The postal service is not reliable and sending and receiving mail can be dicey. Try registered mail or use a private freight service like UPS or DHL.

International calls can be made from blue public phones in Georgetown, Berbice and Linden. You can make Home Country Direct and reverse charge (collect) calls, but credit card calls have been suspended because of frequent fraud.

There is no public Internet access available in Guyana.

MONEY
Costs

Put the squeeze on your Guyanese dollars and you can get by on about US$10 a day here. Travellers preferring a modicum of comfort and style in their accommodation and a bit of variety in their diet should plan on spending about US$20 to US$30 a day. If you're accustomed to finer living, don't visit Guyana, though a relatively upmarket travel experience can be had here for US$40 a day or more.

Changing Money

Both British pounds and US dollars (cash or travellers cheques) are easy to exchange in Guyana. Money can be exchanged at banks or exchange houses; the latter are more convenient and efficient. There is no black market, but hotels may exchange money for you as a convenience at around the same rate as the banks are proffering. Credit cards are accepted at Georgetown's swanky hotels and restaurants.

ONLINE SERVICES

Lonely Planet's web site is Destination Guyana (www.lonelyplanet.com/dest /sam/guy.htm).

The Guyana: Land of Six Peoples web site (www.lasalle.edu/~daniels/guy exp/bgintro.htm) is a great resource, full of useful information including weather, history and current events.

Guyana News and Information (www.guyana.org) is a factual site with some useful information; it's heavily biased towards foreign policy as it's based on releases flowing from the Guyanese embassy in Washington, DC.

Wayne's Guyana Page (www.vaxxine .com/wmoses/guyana.html) is a fun, informative site with added touches like Guyanese proverbs (eg 'Yuh can't suck cane and blow whistle') and recipes.

The multilingual Guiana Shield Media Project (www.gsmp.org) focuses primarily on environmental issues and ongoing conservation projects.

BOOKS

There is little Guyanese literature, so take advantage of what's out there, particularly ER Braithwaite's *To Sir, With Love*, an entertaining read, even though it doesn't take place in Guyana.

Many foreigners have written about this tropical land. Check out VS Naipaul's candid travelogue *The Middle Passage* or his brother Shiva's satire of Guyanese intellectuals in *The Hot Country*. Shiva Naipaul also wrote about the depressing waste of life at the Jonestown massacre in *Journey to Nowhere: a New World Tragedy* (also published as *Black and White*). Evelyn Waugh described a rugged trip from Georgetown through the Rupununi Savanna in *Ninety-two Days*.

David Lowenthal's *West Indian Societies* looks at all of the Guianas with an emphasis on history and geography.

ENTERING & LEAVING

International flights land at Georgetown. The most direct European route is from the UK, with a stop-off in Barbados or from Germany via Trinidad. There are daily direct flights from New York and Miami in the USA. Other flights leave from Toronto, Canada and stop in Trinidad or Curaçao before continuing to Georgetown. Some travellers arrive by air from Venezuela via Trinidad. There is a US$8 departure tax on international flights.

There is a land border crossing between Guyana and Brazil and a ferry crossing between Guyana and Suriname. There are no road connections to Venezuela and no legal border crossing points. From Bonfim, Brazil you can cross the river to Lethem, in Guyana's south-western Rupununi Savanna. Bonfim has a good road connection to the larger Brazilian city of Boa Vista, but the road from Lethem to Georgetown is rough, and may be impassable in wet weather. To get to Suriname, take the ferry from Corriverton (Springlands) to Nieuw Nickerie.

HONDURAS ▶▶

Honduras is a paradise waiting to be discovered. Though long popular in scuba diving circles for the magnificent Bay Islands (Islas de la Bahía), Honduras is still rarely explored by the backpacking set. Mayan ruins, long, white-sand beaches watched over by coconut palms and dense tropical rainforest are all part of its appeal. Travelling here is relatively easy and inexpensive, making Honduras an even more attractive destination.

Unfortunately, the long Caribbean coastline that harbours so many fabulous beaches also gets pummelled during the hurricane season. Honduras was slammed by Hurricane Mitch in November 1998. Hotels, bridges, roads and electrical lines were wiped out, and the country is still recovering.

WHEN TO GO

The rainy season in Honduras is from May to October, though it can rain on the Caribbean coast at any time of year. September, October, January and February are the rainiest months there. February to April are the best times to visit the Caribbean coast and the Bay Islands, when it's relatively dry and not as humid. This is the peak travel period and you can expect crowds and higher prices at popular tourist destinations. The interior highland region is cool year-round, with temperatures averaging between 25 and 30°C. The hurricane season runs from July to November.

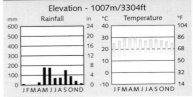

HIGHLIGHTS

It's fairly easy to get around Honduras and you can design a varied itinerary, visiting ancient Mayan sites and pristine beaches with few problems. Here are some suggestions for a Honduran trip.

Archaeological Sites

The Mayan ruins at Copán are awesome and rivalled only by Tikal in

At a Glance

Full Country Name: Republic of Honduras
Area: 112,492 sq km
Population: Six million
Capital City: Tegucigalpa (pop 785,000)
People: 90% mestizo, 7% Indian and 3% Garífuna and immigrants of various nationalities
Languages: Spanish, Creole English and Indian dialects
Religion: Predominantly Roman Catholic, plus other Christian denominations and indigenous forms of worship
Government: Constitutional democracy
Currency: Lempira (L)
Time Zone: Six hours behind GMT/UTC
International Telephone Code: 504
Electricity: 110V, mostly 60 cycles AC (some places use 220V); two-pronged, flat plugs like the kind used in North America are the norm

Guatemala. Archaeologists are making new discoveries all the time at Copán and you can watch excavation of this city that was occupied for more than 2000 years. The pleasant town of Copán Ruinas, with its cobbled stone streets and white adobe homes, is an excellent place to spend a few days. Nearby, the ruins at El Puente in La Entrada are also worth a visit.

Diving & Snorkelling

Roatán, Utila and Guanaja comprise the Bay Islands, located 50km off Honduras' northern coast, where there is some of the best scuba diving and snorkelling on the planet. The reef surrounding the Bay Islands is a continuation of the Belizean barrier reef and the diversity of flora and fauna is stunning. The Bay Islands are one of the cheapest places to get PADI scuba diving certification, particularly on Utila where a four day course costs around US$125. Challenging dives, including night dives, cave dives and wreck diving, are available for the experienced. The Hog Islands (Cayos Cochinos) are a privately owned biological marine reserve with abundant marine life and black coral reefs.

Beaches

Honduras has some beautiful tropical beaches that will make you feel like you've strolled into a postcard. Trujillo is not to be missed; it boasts all the typical tropical beach loveliness, plus the grave of would-be Central American despot William Walker. Nearby Barrio Cristales is home to the Garífuna people. This is the place for music, dancing and revelry. If relaxing is the extent of your beach itinerary, head to gorgeous Tela, considered by some to

be the best Caribbean beach town on the Central American isthmus (though this may change when the proposed multimillion dollar Tela Bay Development Project is built).

Wildlife Viewing

The Mosquitia region in the north-east offers some of the best chances to see endangered wildlife in Central America. This is the famed Mosquito Coast; it is very hard to reach and there is no tourist infrastructure, so travellers making the effort to get here are rewarded with privacy and excellent wildlife viewing. Animals and birds to look for are manatees, monkeys, crocodiles, toucans, egrets, macaws and other birds. You will see all this and more on a trip up the Río Plátano Biosphere Reserve (a World Heritage Site). Expect very rugged travel in this region. Visitors should have lots of time, a working knowledge of Spanish and copious amounts of good insect repellent for a trip here.

VISA REQUIREMENTS

Visitors from Australia, Canada, New Zealand, the USA and UK, plus citizens of most Western European countries don't need visas, but receive a 30 day tourist card upon entry. Every 30 days you can get another extension, for up to six months in total. You can usually apply for extensions at any immigration office, and they cost from US$1 to US$2 depending on your citizenship. Visa requirements change frequently, so double-check before you go.

Honduran Embassies
Australia
(☎ 02-9252 3779) 19/31 Pitt St, Sydney, NSW 2000

Canada
(☎ 613-233-8900, ☎/fax 232-0193) 151 Slater St, Suite 908A, Ottawa, Ontario K1P 5H3

UK
(☎ 020-7486 4550, fax 7486 4596) 115 Gloucester Place, London W1H 3PJ

USA
(☎ 202-966-7702/4596, fax 966-9571) 3007 Tilden St NW, Washington, DC 20008

TOURIST OFFICES OVERSEAS

In the USA, the Honduran Tourist Institute (☎ 1-800-410-9608) is at 2100 Ponce de Leon Blvd, Suite 1175, Coral Gables, FL 33134. Otherwise, Honduras maintains few tourist offices overseas. Travel agents will be able to answer most questions and Honduran consulates or embassies in your home country may be able to help. See the web sites listed under Online Services.

HEALTH

Malaria is a health risk in rural areas and especially on the north coast, including the Bay Islands and the Mosquitia region. Dengue fever also occurs, so avoid bites from all insects, especially in rural areas. Food and waterborne diseases occur, including hepatitis, typhoid, dysentery and cholera, so take care with food and water. Tap water is not safe to drink anywhere in Honduras; bottled water is widely available.

Medical services vary throughout the country. If you need medical attention, Tegucigalpa has many hospitals

Itineraries

One Week
Tegucigalpa is not particularly pleasant, but spend one day going to museums and exploring nearby villages such as Suyapa and Santa Lucía. Head north to the original Honduran capital of Comayagua and explore a bit before pushing north-west to San Pedro Sula. The following day, make your way to Copán Ruinas and spend at least two days exploring the Copán ruins before flying back to Tegucigalpa.

Two Weeks
Do the one week itinerary but rather than flying from Copán to Tegucigalpa, make your way by bus to the Caribbean coastal town of La Ceiba and take a boat to the Bay Islands. Spend the balance of your time diving, snorkelling, swimming and hiking. You can fly back to Tegucigalpa or return overland from La Ceiba.

Three Weeks
Do the two week itinerary, but sprinkle some visits to national parks throughout your trip. Near Tegucigalpa, you can visit the lush cloud forest of La Tigra and near San Pedro Sula, visit Parque Nacional Cusuco. Hike the 2242m-high peak of Cerro Jilinco here. This cloud forest is also a great birdwatching destination, and from April to June quetzals can be seen. Augment your time on the Caribbean coast with visits to the excellent beach towns of Tela and Trujillo, perhaps visiting a couple of nearby Garífuna villages for some partying in between.

One Month
With a month in Honduras, you can do the two week itinerary followed by a full two weeks on the Mosquito Coast. La Ceiba is the hub for flights to Mosquitia, with services to Palacios, Puerto Lempira and Ahuas, and other towns in the region. Alternatively, you can do the three week itinerary with more exploration of national parks and the coast. This alternative could include visits to Celaque and Cerro Azul near Copán, Capiro-Calentura near Trujillo or Punta Sal near Tela. A visit to the Hog Islands would be a good treat on this itinerary.

HONDURAS HIGHLIGHTS & ITINERARIES

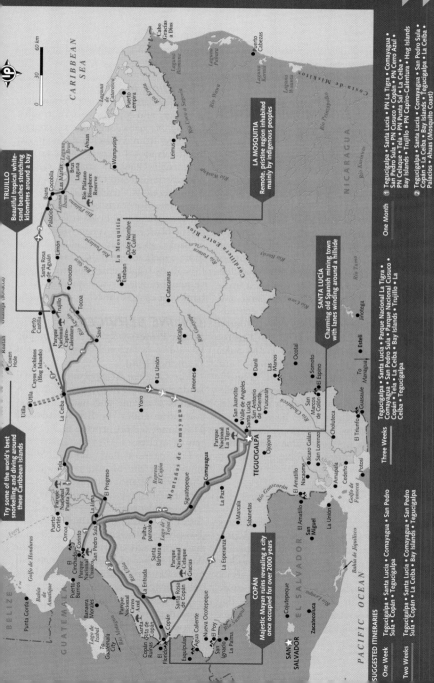

TRUJILLO
Beautiful tropical white-sand beaches stretching kilometres around a bay

LA MOSQUITIA
Remote, pristine region inhabited mainly by indigenous peoples

SANTA LUCÍA
Charming old Spanish mining town with lanes winding around a hillside

COPÁN
Majestic Mayan ruins revealing a city once occupied for over 2000 years

Try some of the world's best snorkelling and diving around these Caribbean islands

SUGGESTED ITINERARIES

One Week
Tegucigalpa • Santa Lucía • Comayagua • San Pedro Sula • Copán • Tegucigalpa

Two Weeks
Tegucigalpa • Santa Lucía • Comayagua • San Pedro Sula • Copán • La Ceiba • Bay Islands • Tegucigalpa

Three Weeks
Tegucigalpa • Santa Lucía • Comayagua • Parque Nacional La Tigra • Comayagua • San Pedro Sula • Parque Nacional Cusuco • Copán • Tela • La Ceiba • Bay Islands • Trujillo • La Ceiba • Tegucigalpa

One Month
1 Tegucigalpa • Santa Lucía • PN La Tigra • Comayagua • San Pedro Sula • PN Cusuco • Copán • PN Cerro Azul • PN Celaque • Tela • PN Punta Sal • La Ceiba • Bay Islands • Trujillo • PN Capiro-Calentura • Hog Islands

2 Tegucigalpa • Santa Lucía • Comayagua • San Pedro Sula • Copán • La Ceiba • Bay Islands • Tegucigalpa • La Ceiba • Palacios • Ahuas (Mosquito Coast)

and clinics, but for serious health matters, it may be better to leave for Mexico City which has excellent medical facilities.

POST & COMMUNICATIONS

In theory, letters posted via air mail from Honduras to the USA or Canada should arrive in about a week. Mail to Europe will take two weeks and to Australia about three weeks. Receiving mail from the USA can be dicey as many Hondurans living there send money to their families back in Honduras, so letters bearing a US postmark are often pilfered. Poste restante mail sent to Tegucigalpa will be held for 60 days and you'll have to pay a small fee and show identification to pick it up.

International phone calls and fax transmissions can be made at centralised call centres operated by Hondutel. There are 24-hour offices in Tegucigalpa, La Ceiba and San Pedro Sula. Operating hours are usually from 7 am to 9 pm in the rest of the country. International calls are expensive, while sending faxes is surprisingly affordable.

Internet cafes have been slow to catch on in Honduras, but private businesses in Tegucigalpa and the Bay Islands will often connect travellers to the Internet for a fee.

MONEY
Costs

Honduras can be cheap or expensive depending on how you travel. Super-thrifty folks who stay in backpacker hostels or camp, and eat local food or cook their own, can get by on about US$12 a day. Prices will be more expensive in Tegucigalpa and the Bay Islands, especially during the February to April peak tourist season. With a bit more splurging, you'll spend closer to US$20 a day.

Changing Money

US dollars are the easiest currency to exchange and you may have trouble finding a bank willing to change currency from Guatemala, Nicaragua or El Salvador. In Tegucigalpa, Lloyd's Bank will change Canadian dollars, pounds sterling and Deutschmarks, but that's about it. You'll get nearly the same rate for cash as for travellers cheques. The same holds true for rates on the black market versus official rates in banks, so stick to the latter. Visa is more widely accepted than MasterCard, though in bigger cities and towns you should be able to use either card at banks for cash advances.

ONLINE SERVICES

Lonely Planet's web site is Destination Honduras (www.lonelyplanet.com/dest/cam/hon.htm).

The Coconut Telegraph (www.bayislands.com) is the homepage of the Bay Islands Magazine and has general information about the Bay Islands and Honduras, feature articles and a calendar of events.

For current and detailed information on the Mosquitia region and the Río Plátano Biosphere Reserve, visit La Mosquitia (www.txinfinet.com/mader/planeta/0597/0597mosquitia.html). A Walkabout in the Río Plátano Biosphere (www.generation.net/~derekp) has mountains of information on the Mosquitia region, including a map, lists of volunteer opportunities, ongoing relief programs and travelogues.

Honduras This Week Online (www.marrder.com/htw) will keep you abreast of the latest local developments.

BOOKS

Several books deal with Honduras' tortured legacy as the original 'banana republic'. *Honduras: The Making of a Banana Republic* by Alison Acker and the famous *Prisión Verde* (in Spanish) by Ramón Amaya Amador are two good places to start. Two other informed choices for understanding Honduran social, political and economic paradigms are Richard Lapper's *Honduras: State for Sale* and *Honduras: Portrait of a Captive Nation* edited by Nancy Peckenham & Annie Street. *So Far from God* is a no-holds-barred appraisal of Central America, its Spanish legacy, its current problems and its troubled relationship with the USA.

Anyone intent on heading to the Mosquitia region should tote a copy of *La Mosquitia: A Guide to the Savannas, Rain Forest and Turtle Hunters* by Derek Parent. This is probably the most comprehensive information you can get on this isolated, little explored area; there are maps. To order a copy, write to the The Adventurous Traveler Bookstore (☎ 1-800-282-3963), PO Box 1468, Williston, VT 05495, USA. You can also visit the author's web site at www.generation.net/~derekp for more information.

If you're craving travel stories about Honduras, check out *Through the Volcanoes* by Jeremy Paxman, which is an account of his travels through all seven Central American countries with a political emphasis, or *Tekkin a Waalk* by Peter Ford, an entertaining narrative describing a trek along the Caribbean coast from Belize to Panama.

ENTERING & LEAVING

Most flights land at the international airport in Tegucigalpa, though it's possible to get flights into San Pedro Sula. Direct flights from Houston, Miami and New Orleans are available to Roatán in the Bay Islands. Travellers from Europe, Australia or New Zealand have to connect with flights in the USA or Mexico. If you fly out of Honduras, the departure tax is about US$9.

There are many border crossings from Honduras to Guatemala, El Salvador and Nicaragua; some more frequently travelled than others. The fee to cross is US$2. From Honduras to Guatemala, the main crossings are from Copán Ruinas to El Florido and the Agua Caliente border post. There is a rough, difficult crossing by foot between Corinto (Honduras) to El Cinchado (Guatemala) and another challenging crossing, the 'Jungle Trail', from Puerto Cortés in Honduras to Puerto Barrios in Guatemala.

Going from Honduras to El Salvador, you can cross at the busy post of El Amatillo on the Interamericana Hwy with no difficulty. Alternatively, you can try the more remote crossing at the El Poy border post, near Nueva Ocotepeque in Honduras and near La Palma in El Salvador.

The most used crossing between Honduras and Nicaragua is near San Marcos de Colón on the Interamericana Hwy in Honduras and El Espino in Nicaragua. Other crossings include those at Las Manos (Honduras) and El Triunfo/Guasaule.

You can also travel by boat from Dangriga or Placencia in Belize to Puerto Cortés in Honduras.

MEXICO

Mexico is a country of paradox, where rugged mountains cradle isolated communities and the jet-setting elite pop in and out of glamorous beach resorts. Meanwhile, frontier *madquiladoras* (sweatshops) crank out consumer goods for the masses while Aztec and Maya descendants strive to maintain their traditional culture. Just when you think you know the place, a watershed experience will reveal a different Mexico you had no idea existed.

Despite recurring flare-ups in the Chiapas region in the east and the rise of crime due to Mexico's simmering financial woes, this is a great place for independent travellers. There are rivers, volcanoes, beaches and ruins, plus fiestas and great food, lots of art, history and a vibrant culture that etches itself on the psyche. Public transportation is for the most part efficient, costs are reasonable and there is a lot of space to roam around and get lost if you wish.

WHEN TO GO

Whenever you can afford to go to Mexico, do it! The country is so large, you'll always be able to find good weather and accommodation somewhere. The coastal and lowland regions can get pretty hot and humid from May to September, especially in the southern states. Otherwise, altitude moderates the heat and the inland mountainous regions are pleasant and can even get downright cool between December and February.

July and August are the most popular months to travel for both locals and foreigners, and you may find hotel rooms are expensive and hard to come by, particularly in the coastal resorts. Other peak periods include the stretch between December and January before Christmas and after New Year and on

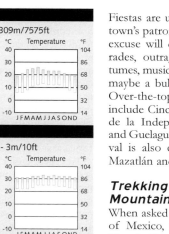

MEXICO CITY
Elevation - 2309m/7575ft

ACAPULCO
Elevation - 3m/10ft

MONTERREY
Elevation - 528m/1732ft

either side of Semana Santa (Easter Week).

HIGHLIGHTS

Whether you enjoy the mountains for a challenging hike, perusing local markets for handcrafts or sitting on a beach with a nice cold beer, you can do it in Mexico. Here is a necessarily abbreviated list of some of the interesting things to do in Mexico.

Fiestas

In addition to festivals, fairs and national holidays, every Mexican city, town and village has its own fiesta days and these folks know how to party.

Fiestas are usually held to honour the town's patron saint, though almost any excuse will do. Festivities include parades, outrageous or traditional costumes, music, dancing and drinking and maybe a bull run through the streets. Over-the-top fiestas and observances include Cinco de Mayo in Puebla, Día de la Independencia in Mexico City and Guelaguetza in Oaxaca City. Carnaval is also celebrated in Cuernavaca, Mazatlán and Veracruz.

Trekking & Mountain Climbing

When asked to describe the geography of Mexico, the Spanish conquistador Hernán Cortés answered by crumpling up a piece of paper; this gives you an idea of the trekking and mountain climbing opportunities here. Indeed, hiking through Mexico could be your whole itinerary. Some of the most extraordinary hikes are in and around the Barranca del Cobre (Copper Canyon) and in Baja California. Climbing volcanoes is an exciting option as many are still active, such as Popocatépetl east of Mexico City, which is off limits to hikers when it starts belching volcanic debris. Other volcano hikes include Volcán Paricutín, Volcán Nevado and Volcán de Fuego de Colima. There are also more than 40 national parks and biosphere reserves that can be explored on foot.

Water Sports

Both the Caribbean and Pacific coasts have good snorkelling and diving opportunities, though the visibility is generally better on the Caribbean side. There, divers favour Isla Mujeres, Playa del Carmen, Cozumel and Xcalak. On the Pacific coast, Puerto Vallarta,

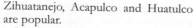
Zihuatanejo, Acapulco and Huatulco are popular.

Head to the Pacific coast if you want to surf. The breaks here are stellar, especially during summer. Check out the stretch in Baja between San José del Cabo and Cabo San Lucas, and Puerto Escondido's 'Mexican Pipeline' in Oaxaca State. There are many other breaks around Mazatlán, Ensenada, Manzanillo and Zihuatanejo.

Archaeological Sites

The Mayans ruled and flourished from several seats of power in Mexico and these magnificent ruins are alone worth the trip. In the Chiapas region, there is the ancient city of Palenque, with 20 sq km of ruins; the even larger site at Yaxchilán above the banks of Río Usumacinta; and the important ruins of Izapa. Part of La Ruta Maya, a tourism route devised to allow travellers to visit Mayan sites with minimum impact and maximum exposure, the Yucatán Peninsula is peppered with ruins. Among the most impressive are Chichén Itzá, Tulum, tucked along a tropical beach and Uxmal, an important site with many more ruins still to be uncovered. Near Mexico City is the awesome Mayan city of Teotihuacán, the capital of Mexico's first civilisation.

VISA REQUIREMENTS

Citizens of almost all Western European countries and the USA, Canada, Australia and New Zealand do not need visas to enter Mexico. Rather, these visitors receive a tourist card on arrival. The cards are free and the time you are allowed in Mexico will vary depending on your country of citizenship. Most visitors receive 180 days, though citizens of France, Austria, Greece and Argentina only get 90 days. Sometimes immigration officers will try to give you 30 days; ask for more if you intend a longer stay. Extensions are available at immigration offices in many Mexican cities, though it may be tricky to get more time than the allowable maximum stay. Visitors who stay longer than permitted on their tourist cards are subject to fees of around US$50 for each month they've overstayed.

Travellers under 18 years of age not accompanied by one or both of their parents are required to show a notarised consent form signed by both parents or the absent parent. If you're a minor planning a trip to Mexico, contact an embassy or consulate to find out exactly what paperwork you'll need to enter the country.

Mexican Embassies

Australia
  (☎ 02-6273 3905) 14 Perth Ave, Canberra, ACT 2600
  Consulate: Sydney

Belize
  (☎ 02-30 193, ☎ 30 194) 20 North Park St, Fort George Area, Belize City

Canada
  (☎ 613-233-8988/6665) 45 O'Connor St, Suite 1500, Ottawa, Ontario K1P 1A4
  Consulate: Montreal

Guatemala
  (☎ 333-72 54) Edificio Central Ejecutivo, 7th floor, 15a Calle No 3-20, Zona 10, Guatemala City

New Zealand
  (☎ 04-472 5555/6) 8th floor, 111-115 Customhouse Quay, Wellington

UK
  (☎ 020-7235 6393) 8 Halkin St, London SW1X 7DW

USA
  (☎ 202-728-1633/36) 1911 Pennsylvania Ave NW, Washington, DC 20006

There are many other Mexican consulates in US cities, especially in the

Itineraries

One Week – The Beach

Explore Mexico City for a day or two before heading to the Pacific coastal resort of Acapulco. Skirt the crowds as swiftly as possible and head north-west about 10km to Pie de la Cuesta. Here you can swim, water-ski and birdwatch. You can take day trips to Puerto Marqués and go for a sail or ride a horse along the beach at Playa Revolcadero, where there is also a good surf break. Alternatively, you can head to Zihuatanejo up the Pacific coast for a couple of days of beach relaxation in this old fishing village.

One Week – The Cities

Exploring Mexico City can eat up a week of your itinerary with no problem. Spend two days exploring the museums, the Zócalo, the Alameda, and the Bosque de Chapultepec, Mexico City's largest park. Don't miss the Palacio Nacional, with its Diego Rivera murals or the Basilica de Guadalupe. Take a third day to visit the tremendous pyramids at Teotihuacán before heading south-east to the charming colonial city of Puebla for three days. The 70 churches, dozens of museums and the Africam Safari Park should keep you entranced until you have to head home. If you still have time, visit the Pirámide Tepanapa – the Great Pyramid of Cholula 10km west of Puebla. This is the biggest pyramid ever built.

Two Weeks

You can follow both of the one week itineraries outlined above or select one and include a trip to the Yucatán Peninsula for some serious beach and archaeology action. You'll have to fly because the 20 hour bus ride will not fit well with this schedule. Fly into Mérida and hop on a bus to Chichén Itzá, spending the night there so you can enjoy the ruins either late that day or early the next morning. When you've had your fill of the ruins, head east to the beautiful Caribbean coast, staying in Playa del Carmen or Isla Mujeres. Spend the rest of your trip lying on some of the world's most beautiful beaches south of Cancún, explore the ruins of Tulum or go snorkelling or diving.

Three Weeks

With three weeks in Mexico you'll find yourself becoming immersed in the country. Do the one week cities itinerary, followed by the Yucatán alternative, except take the bus one way and head into the indigenous highlands of the Tabasco and Chiapas states. You can visit ruins at Bonampak and Yaxchilán, hang out in cool and mysterious San Cristóbal de Las Casas and take a phenomenal boat ride in the 1000m-deep Cañón del Sumidero.

One Month

You can't do it all in a month, but this will give you time to see why people fall in love with Mexico so easily. Take public transportation throughout this itinerary to maximise your cultural immersion. Follow the one week cities itinerary and the one week beach portion, but before heading to the Yucatán, make your way to Guadalajara. This is the country's second largest city and the birthplace of mariachi music, tequila and the Mexican Hat Dance. If the city's plazas, churches and museums start to wear thin, venture to the suburbs and check out the many galleries, markets and museums there. Continue on to the Yucatán and complete the remainder of the three week itinerary.

Two Months

Your Mexican odyssey begins when you have this kind of time. Do all the legs mentioned above, but from Guadalajara make your way by train or bus to Mazatlán and hang out at the beaches and offshore islands there before heading north along the coast to Los Mochis. This is the beginning (or end) of the famous Copper Canyon railway. You can stay at hotels or guesthouses along the rail route or hop off at Creel and camp and explore. Make your way south through the highlands stopping in Zacatecas, San Luis Potosí and the super-cool town of Guanajuato before continuing on to the Yucatán and Chiapas, checking out Oaxaca en route. If you have any time left you can cross into the Petén region of northern Guatemala to see the phenomenal Mayan ruins at Tikal.

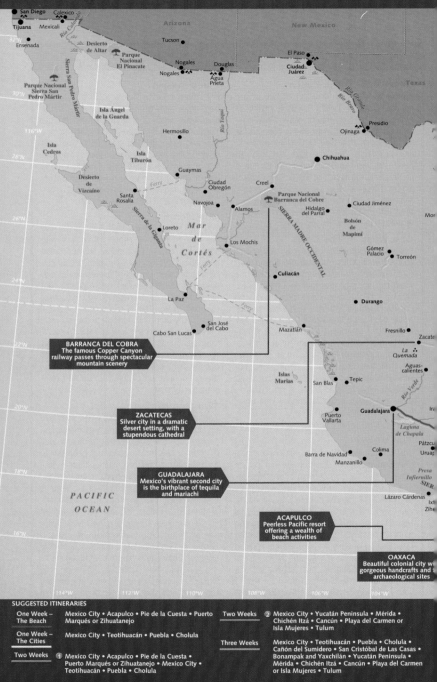

MEXICO HIGHLIGHTS & ITINERARIES

BARRANCA DEL COBRA
The famous Copper Canyon railway passes through spectacular mountain scenery

ZACATECAS
Silver city in a dramatic desert setting, with a stupendous cathedral

GUADALAJARA
Mexico's vibrant second city is the birthplace of tequila and mariachi

ACAPULCO
Peerless Pacific resort offering a wealth of beach activities

OAXACA
Beautiful colonial city wi
gorgeous handcrafts and
archaeological sites

SUGGESTED ITINERARIES

One Week – The Beach
Mexico City • Acapulco • Pie de la Cuesta • Puerto Marqués or Zihuatanejo

One Week – The Cities
Mexico City • Teotihuacán • Puebla • Cholula

Two Weeks ①
Mexico City • Acapulco • Pie de la Cuesta • Puerto Marqués or Zihuatanejo • Mexico City • Teotihuacán • Puebla • Cholula

Two Weeks ②
Mexico City • Yucatán Peninsula • Mérida • Chichén Itzá • Cancún • Playa del Carmen or Isla Mujeres • Tulum

Three Weeks
Mexico City • Teotihuacán • Puebla • Cholula • Cañón del Sumidero • San Cristóbal de Las Casas • Bonampak and Yaxchilán • Yucatán Peninsula • Mérida • Chichén Itzá • Cancún • Playa del Carmen or Isla Mujeres • Tulum

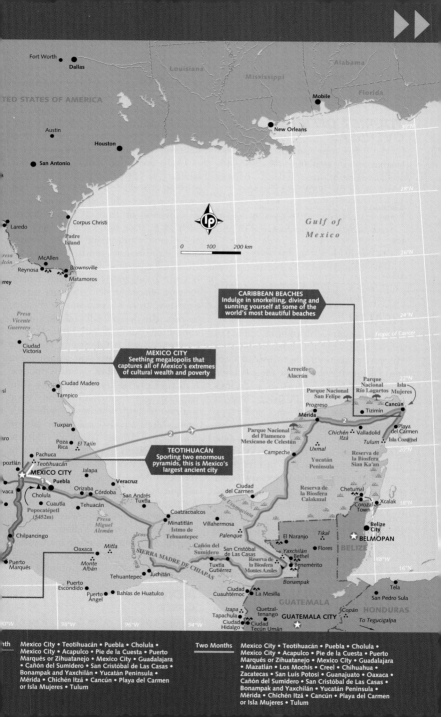

CARIBBEAN BEACHES
Indulge in snorkelling, diving and sunning yourself at some of the world's most beautiful beaches

MEXICO CITY
Seething megalopolis that captures all of Mexico's extremes of cultural wealth and poverty

TEOTIHUACÁN
Sporting two enormous pyramids, this is Mexico's largest ancient city

Gulf of Mexico

UNITED STATES OF AMERICA

Louisiana
Mississippi
Alabama
Florida

Fort Worth
Dallas
Austin
Houston
San Antonio
Laredo
Corpus Christi
Padre Island
McAllen
Reynosa
Brownsville
Matamoros
Ciudad Victoria
Ciudad Madero
Tampico
Tuxpan
Poza Rica
El Tajín
Pachuca
Teotihuacán
MÉXICO CITY
Jalapa
Puebla
Cholula
Orizaba
Córdoba
Cuautla
Popocatépetl (5452m)
Tehuacán
Veracruz
San Andrés Tuxtla
Chilpancingo
Oaxaca
Mitla
Monte Albán
Tehuantepec
Juchitán
Puerto Escondido
Puerto Ángel
Bahías de Huatulco
Puerto Marqués
SIERRA MADRE DE CHIAPAS
Coatzacoalcos
Minatitlán
Istmo de Tehuantepec
Villahermosa
Cañón del Sumidero
San Cristóbal de Las Casas
Tuxtla Gutiérrez
Ciudad Cuauhtémoc
La Mesilla
Ciudad Cuauhtémoc
Izapa
Tapachula
Ciudad Hidalgo
Quetzaltenango
Ciudad Tecún Umán
GUATEMALA CITY
Palenque
Bonampak
El Naranjo
Yaxchilán
Bethel
Benemérito
Reserva de la Biosfera Montes Azules
Tikal
Flores
Copán
To Tegucigalpa
San Pedro Sula
Tela
HONDURAS
GUATEMALA
BELIZE
Belize City
BELMOPAN
Chetumal
Corozal Town
Xcalac
Reserva de la Biosfera Calakmul
Ciudad del Carmen
Río Usumacinta
Campeche
Parque Nacional del Flamenco Mexicano de Celestún
Uxmal
Yucatán Peninsula
Reserva de la Biosfera Sian Ka'an
Mérida
Progreso
Tizimín
Chichén Itzá
Valladolid
Tulum
Isla Cozumel
Playa del Carmen
Cancún
Isla Mujeres
Parque Nacional Río Lagartos
Parque Nacional San Felipe
Arrecife Alacrán

Presa Falcón
Presa Vicente Guerrero
Presa Miguel Alemán

0   100   200 km

Tropic of Cancer

30°N
28°N
26°N
24°N
22°N
20°N
18°N
16°N

98°W   96°W   94°W   92°W   90°W   88°W

border states. Look in the front of a phonebook for more information.

TOURIST OFFICES OVERSEAS

In the USA and Canada, tourist information is available (☎ 800-446-3942). There are several offices throughout the USA and Europe.

Canada
(☎ 514-871-1052) 1 Place Ville Marie, Suite 1526, Montreal, Quebec H3B 2B5
UK
(☎ 020-7734 1058) 3rd floor, 60-61 Trafalgar Square, London WC2N 5DS
USA
(☎ 212-755-7261) 405 Park Ave, Suite 1041, New York, NY 10022

HEALTH

Malaria occurs throughout most of rural Mexico but it is not a concern in the resort areas on the Mexican Gulf and Pacific coasts. Dengue fever occurs; take precautions against these serious diseases and avoid all insect bites if possible. Take things easy when you first arrive in Mexico City as the air pollution and high altitude can take some getting used to. Generally travel in Mexico presents few health problems, but contaminated food and water can transmit diseases such as typhoid, hepatitis, cholera and dysentery. Drink only treated water and take care with food, especially avoiding undercooked meat, and seafood. If you need serious medical attention, Mexico City has excellent facilities.

POST & COMMUNICATIONS

The postal service in Mexico is inconsistent and all letters should be marked air mail *(correo aéreo)* to help ensure delivery. Letters sent to the USA or Canada via air mail should take four

to 14 days to arrive. A letter to Europe takes between one and three weeks and to Australasia a month or more. In theory you can receive poste restante mail at any post office in Mexico, and mail will be held for a month.

There are three main places from where you can place phone calls: pay phones, *casetas telefónicas* (where an operator places the call and you take it in a booth), or from a private phone such as in your hotel. Pay phones are cheap and work mainly with phonecards. Connections can be bad. Casetas are more expensive than public phones, but the connections are usually better. Reverse charge (collect) calls are super-expensive from Mexico and it's cheaper to have the person call you back at an appointed number and time. If you have an AT&T, MCI, Sprint, Hello! or Canadian calling card, you can use these to call other parts of North America. Call your phone company before your trip to get information on your phonecard and whether it will work from Mexico. Also ask your phone company about Mexico's Home Country Direct system, where you're connected directly with an operator in the country you're calling. Fax service is ubiquitous and cheap in Mexico; look for the signs that read 'Fax Público'.

Internet cafes are popular in Mexico City, Oaxaca, Puerto Vallarta and San Miguel de Allende, among many other tourist destinations. You can expect to pay around US$3 for 30 minutes.

MONEY
Costs

Budget travellers who camp or stay in bottom-end hotels, eat in local places and take the bus, can expect to spend about US$15 a day. If you throw in a taxi here and there, eat at better restaurants and have a private bath in your hotel room, you'll be looking at around US$25 to US$35 a day. Mexico has all the modern amenities and if you want to travel in deluxe style, spending hundreds of dollars a day, that's also an option. Keep in mind that prices at popular resorts and in bigger cities are higher than elsewhere in the country.

Changing Money

Credit cards and ATMs are widely accepted in Mexico and you should have no problems using Visa, MasterCard and even American Express in big cities. You can get cash advances on credit cards from most ATMs or you can use your own bank card if it's on the Cirrus or Plus system. Bank cards are good because you get a reasonable exchange rate and are spared the commission fees usually tacked onto transactions with travellers cheques or cash. Keep your US cash to a minimum in Mexico as robberies are all too common. Prices in pesos are preceded by a dollar ($) sign. Don't confuse this with prices in US dollars, which are preceded by US$ or USD.

ONLINE SERVICES

Lonely Planet's web site is Destination Mexico (www.lonelyplanet.com/dest /nam/mexico.htm).

Mexico: An Endless Journey (www .mexico-travel.com) is the official site of Mexico's Ministry of Tourism and is chock-full of detailed information on natural attractions and notable buildings and museums. Along the same lines is the Excite City.Net Mexico web site (http://city.net/countries/mexico).

Art enthusiasts should go directly to The Original Frida Kahlo Home Page (www.cascade.net/kahlo.html), which has links and information galore relating to everything Frida. Fans of Diego Rivera's work should check out the WWW's Riverinos site (www.chapingo .mx/cultura/Capilla/www-riv.html).

If you dig archaeology (groan), hit A Mesoamerican Archaeology WWW Page (http://copan.bioz.unibas.ch/meso .html). Another good resource for Mexican archaeology and anthropology information is the Maya/Aztec/ Inca Center web site (www.realtime .com/maya/index.html).

Two good sites related to ecotourism are Escolar Mazunte (www.laneta.apc .org/mazunte) and Eco Travels in Mexico (www.txinfinet.com/mader/ec otravel/mexico/mexinterior.html).

If you're still hankering for more, use one of the specific search engines dealing with all things Mexican. The Mexico Web Guide (http://mexico .web.com.mx) and Mexico's Index (www.trace-sc.com/index1.com) are a good place to start.

BOOKS

One of the best general books on Mexico from pre-Columbian times to the present is the anthology *Many Mexicos* by Lesley Byrd Simpson. For a strictly historical account, see *The Course of Mexican History* by Michael C Meyer & William L Sherman.

For good reads on ancient Mexican civilisations, try Richard F Townsend's *The Aztecs* or *Daily Life of the Aztecs* by Jacques Soustelle. Those interested in Mayan culture should check out the appropriately titled *The Maya* by Michael D Coe. *Ancient Kingdoms of Mexico* by Nigel Davies is a compact, scholarly study of the Olmec, Teotihuacán, Toltec and Aztec civilisations.

History of the Conquest of New Spain by Bernal Díaz del Castillo is an eyewitness account of the Spanish arrival by one of Cortés' lieutenants and not to be missed by enthusiasts of Latin American history and culture. The extremely well researched *Conquest: Montezuma, Cortes & The Fall of Old Mexico* by Hugh Thomas is a tome about the same period.

For contemporary Mexican society and how it works, especially in relation to the USA, see Alan Riding's *Distant Neighbors*. Patrick Oster deals with many similar themes in his work *The Mexicans*.

Carlos Fuentes is one of Mexico's most famous novelists. Probably his best known work is *The Old Gringo*, which was made into a Hollywood film starring the improbable pairing of Jimmy Smits and Jane Fonda. If you want a real challenge, check out *Terra Nostra* by Fuentes. Octavio Paz is another intellectual luminary and his fame was duly earned with the fabulous essay collection *Labyrinth of Solitude*. Paz is also a wonderful poet.

Many foreigners have written about Mexico as well. Try Graham Greene's *The Power and the Glory*, Malcolm Lowry's *Under the Volcano* or Carlos Castaneda's *Don Juan* series.

FILMS

Mexico has a thriving film industry and a visit to a decent video store should reap scores of Mexican movies. Try the classic tale of conquest dramatised in Nicolás Echevarría's *Cabeza de Vaca* or the most awarded film in Mexican history *El Callejón de los Milagros* (English title: Midaq Alley), starring Salma Hayek. Another popular Mexican film is *Como Agua Para Chocolate* (Like Water for Chocolate), a romantic drama.

Then there's the disturbing *Santa Sangre* by Alejandro Jodorowsky.

ENTERING & LEAVING

There are over a dozen US cities servicing more than 30 destinations in Mexico on direct flights. The cheapest departure cities from Europe are London, Amsterdam, Paris and Frankfurt. Travellers from Australasia may consider purchasing a Round-the-World ticket with a Mexico stop-off, as these can be cheaper than a regular return fare. The Mexican cities with the most international air traffic are Mexico City, Guadalajara, Cancún, Monterrey and Acapulco, in that order. There is a departure tax of US$12 from Mexico.

Travellers can cross into Mexico by road from the USA at one of 20 official crossing points. US buses connect with Mexican buses at the border. There are two major land crossings between Mexico and Guatemala (road and rail): La Mesilla to Cuauhtémoc; and Ciudad Tecún Umán to Ciudad Hidalgo. There are also three little known and relatively hair-raising jungle routes by backcountry bus and riverboat. One leaves from the Bethel in the Petén region in Guatemala to Frontera Corozal in Mexico; another crossing is between El Naranjo and La Palma via the Río San Pedro; lastly is the route (growing in popularity) between Sayaxché in Guatemala and Benemérito in Mexico via the Río Usumacinta. This last takes you to Sayaxché by bus and then down the Río de la Pasión to Benemérito, where you can catch a bus to Palenque. Travellers should check the security situation in Chiapas before attempting this crossing. There is one road crossing point between Mexico and Belize near Chetumal and Corozal.

NICARAGUA

Mention Nicaragua and most people conjure up images of the 1979 Sandinista revolution and the ensuing Contra War, a bloodbath incited by the US-sponsored army of anti-insurgents known as the Contras. No matter what you may imagine about Nicaragua, a visit will prove revelatory and exciting. You'll witness a society rebuilding and redefining itself in the aftermath of war and meet people who lived through it.

Geographically, Nicaragua is a wonder for independent travellers, with volcanoes and rivers, beaches and mountains. This largest Central American country has little tourist infrastructure and an adventure in Nicaragua is by definition off the beaten track. Visitors prepared for rugged, basic conditions will be amply rewarded with fond memories of this country.

WHEN TO GO

Nicaragua has an alpine climate, where seasons and temperatures vary with altitude and the time of year. The Pacific lowlands and Managua are hot year-round, though things cool off a bit during the dry season from December to the end of April. The highland region is much cooler than the coasts, but suffers from heavy rainfall during the May to November wet season. On the Caribbean coast, there is a shorter dry season, from about March to May, though it can rain then too and is still quite hot. The best time to visit is from December to April, when there's little rain and lower humidity, but before everything gets

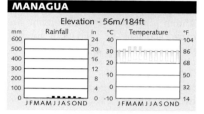

parched and dusty in the heat of the dry season.

Semana Santa (Easter Week) is a very big deal in Nicaragua and rooms by the beach are booked weeks or months in advance; this is a good time to head to the hills. Nicaragua was devastated by Hurricane Mitch in November 1998 and may still be suffering the after-effects by the time you read this.

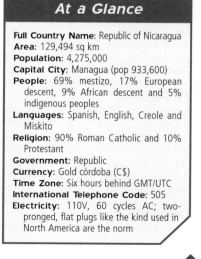

At a Glance

Full Country Name: Republic of Nicaragua
Area: 129,494 sq km
Population: 4,275,000
Capital City: Managua (pop 933,600)
People: 69% mestizo, 17% European descent, 9% African descent and 5% indigenous peoples
Languages: Spanish, English, Creole and Miskito
Religion: 90% Roman Catholic and 10% Protestant
Government: Republic
Currency: Gold córdoba (C$)
Time Zone: Six hours behind GMT/UTC
International Telephone Code: 505
Electricity: 110V, 60 cycles AC; two-pronged, flat plugs like the kind used in North America are the norm

HIGHLIGHTS

Probably the greatest highlight of a Nicaragua trip is the sociopolitical and historical air that permeates daily life and allows even the casual visitor a peek into the postrevolutionary process. Within this electric environment are many activities to keep your interest peaked.

Trekking

In northern Nicaragua there is good hiking in the Selva Negra near Matagalpa. Just a hop and skip from Managua are volcanoes worth a climb. Parque Nacional Volcán Masaya, with its steaming, belching crater, is a good trekking option, as are the spectacular volcanoes on Isla de Ometepe in Lago de Nicaragua. The Archipiélago de Solentiname, a little further afield in Lago de Nicaragua, also has good hiking.

Water Sports

The Corn Islands (Islas del Maíz), about 70km off the Caribbean coast, have great diving in idyllic surrounds. The water is clear, the coral reefs teeming and there's a sunken Spanish galleon that can be seen by snorkellers. Gear is unavailable, so bring your own.

Surfing is also possible and there are good breaks at Playa Poneloya, near León and at Playa Popoyo near Rivas. Nicaragua's beaches offer some fantastic swimming – check out Pochomil and San Juan del Sur. Swimming is also popular at various volcanic crater lakes such as Laguna de Xiloá, 20km northwest of Managua.

Colonial Cities

León and Granada were Nicaragua's principal colonial cities and still retain their Spanish character. The university town of León boasts the biggest cathedral in Central America. This is the intellectual centre of the country and was a hotbed of Sandinista revolutionary rhetoric and action during the war. History buffs and socialists will appreciate León's many murals and monuments to the movement. In Granada, on the shores of Lago de Nicaragua, colonial plazas are overlooked by dramatic churches, and horse-drawn carriages still ply the streets. Another interesting old city is Masaya, home to the most famous handcrafts market in the country.

Off the Beaten Track

Getting off the beaten path in Nicaragua means getting down to serious wildlife viewing and crosscultural exchanges. A group of 356 islands in the northern portion of Lago de Nicaragua known as Las Isletas are superb for birdwatching and hanging out with local farmers. Parque Nacional Isla Zapatera, the largest island of Las Isletas, has birds and huge pre-Columbian statues. Isla del Muerto has tombs and rock carvings.

Some parts of the virgin rainforest stretching along Nicaragua's Caribbean coast are so dense they're impenetrable. This is the famed Mosquito Coast (Costa de Miskitos) that stretches north into Honduras. Most travellers visit Bluefields, where a fascinating population of Miskitos, Ramas and Sumos Indians mixes with Blacks and mestizos. Dancing and parties are the hallmarks of Bluefields and those venturing on the 10 hour combination bus and boat ride from Managua won't be disappointed. Intrepid travellers with a lot of time and patience can attempt to penetrate the thick jungle covering the coast.

VISA REQUIREMENTS

Citizens of the USA and UK do not need visas to visit Nicaragua and are issued a tourist card (US$5) good for 90 days upon arrival. Citizens of Australia, Canada, New Zealand and most Western European countries do need visas; these are good for 30 days after the date of issue. Visas can be extended twice for a total of three months at immigration offices in Managua.

Nicaraguan Embassies

You can obtain a visa either at home or in a neighbouring country, but if you need one you must get it prior to your arrival at the Nicaraguan border or airport.

Canada
(☎ 613-234-9361/2, fax 238-7666) 130 Albert St, Suite 407, Ottawa, Ontario K1P 5G4

Costa Rica
(☎ 222-2373/3479, fax 221-5481) Av Central No 2540, Calles 25 and 27, Barrio La California, San José

Honduras
(☎ 32-7218/24, fax 31-1412) Colonia Lomas del Tepeyac, Bloque M-1, Calle 11, Tegucigalpa

UK
(☎ 020-7584 4365/3231) 84 Gloucester Rd, London SW 4PP

USA
(☎ 202-939-6570, fax 939-6542) 1627 New Hampshire Ave NW, Washington, DC 20009

TOURIST OFFICES OVERSEAS

Nicaragua maintains few tourist offices overseas, though a good travel agent should be able to answer most of your questions. A Nicaraguan consulate or embassy in your home country will also have some tourist information. For other research help, see the web sites listed under Online Services below.

HEALTH

Malaria occurs in most rural areas of Nicaragua, as does dengue fever, so take precautions against these serious mosquito-borne diseases. Pay attention to basic food and water hygiene, as hepatitis, dysentery, typhoid and cholera can occur. Especially avoid undercooked meat and suspect seafood. Some of Nicaragua's lakes, including Lago de Managua and Laguna de Masaya, are seriously polluted, so stick to the beaches for swimming. Outside Managua, where tap water is safe, drink only purified or bottled water.

Medical facilities are reasonable in Managua, but services are limited outside the capital. For serious medical care, it may be a good idea to leave for Mexico City, where there are excellent medical services.

POST & COMMUNICATIONS

Mail sent from Nicaragua will take a long time to reach its destination. Postcards sent to the USA can take up to three weeks to arrive and the delivery times to Europe and Australia are more like a month or two. Important mail should be sent *certificado* (registered). You are more likely to successfully receive poste restante mail in a big city. Technically the post office is supposed to hold it for a month, but it might be tossed out after a week or two.

Telephone calls and faxes are also handled at centralised phone offices; every city and town has one. It may not be possible to place reverse charge (collect) calls to every country.

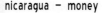
Itineraries

One Week

With only a week, you'll be zooming around with little time to meet and converse with locals, which is the most exciting part of a trip here. Still, if that's all the time you have, take a day to explore the areas around Managua, including Parque Nacional Volcán Masaya, Laguna de Xiloá (off the road to León) and El Trapiche (near Tipitapa), where water from natural springs has been channelled into large outdoor pools. Spend two days in Granada, with side trips offshore to Las Isletas, visiting Isla Zapatera and San Pablo Island in Lago de Nicaragua. Spend the balance of your trip in the colonial city of León.

Two Weeks

Follow the one week itinerary with three more days in Lago de Nicaragua, visiting Isla de Ometepe and hiking a volcano or two there and venturing further south to the Archipiélago de Solentiname. This is a sort of artists' colony that also has great hiking and fishing. From San Carlos, wend your way along the coast to León, stopping at the undeveloped and beautiful beaches just north and south of San Juan del Sur.

Three Weeks

Follow the two week itinerary, but head north from León to the Matagalpa area for some fantastic hiking in the Selva Negra. Many people like this part of the country the best, with its refreshing climate and distinct culture; you may find yourself lingering. Check out the pleasant towns of Estelí and Jinotega before making your way back to Managua.

Alternatively, you can follow the two week itinerary and spend the balance of your time exploring Bluefields and the Mosquito Coast, taking in the Corn Islands. If things are really going your way, you may be able to squeeze in a quick visit to Matagalpa.

There are only around half a dozen companies providing email and Internet services in Nicaragua.

MONEY
Costs

The very frugal budget traveller will spend between US$5 and US$10 a day for a spartan room, local dining and a bus or two. If you hire a taxi once in a while, stay in slightly better accommodation and eat in restaurants, you can expect to spend more like US$15 to US$30 a day. Costs are higher on the Caribbean coast than elsewhere in the country.

Changing Money

Except in Managua and at border crossings, travellers cheques are difficult to cash in Nicaragua. You may get lucky and find an exchange house that will do it for you, but don't count on it. It's better to rely on cash and credit cards. Visa and MasterCard are accepted at most mid-range hotels and restaurants and even some cheapies, especially in Ometepe. Outside of Nicaragua it is nearly impossible to convert córdobas, so use them before you leave the country.

ONLINE SERVICES

Lonely Planet's web site is Destination Nicaragua (www.lonelyplanet.com/dest /cam/nic.htm).

The University of Texas Latin American web site (www.lanic.utexas .edu/la/ca/nicaragua) is comprehensive, with academic and general resources on everything Nicaraguan.

The Spanish/English bilingual Sandino's Main Page (www.pagusmundi .com/sandino/sandino.htm) covers all possible topics related to Nicaragua's

CARAGUA HIGHLIGHTS & ITINERARIES

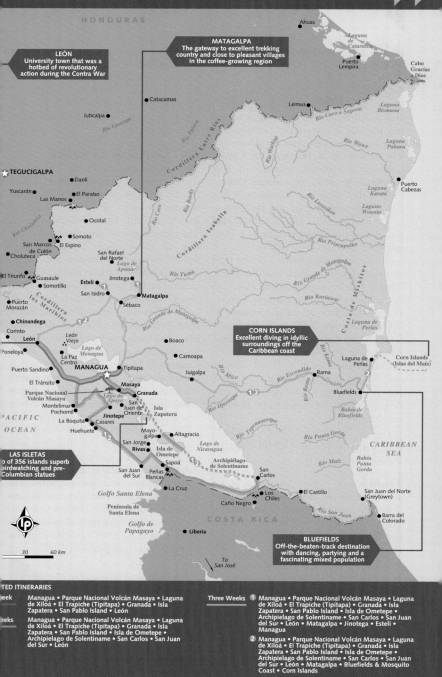

LEÓN
University town that was a hotbed of revolutionary action during the Contra War

MATAGALPA
The gateway to excellent trekking country and close to pleasant villages in the coffee-growing region

CORN ISLANDS
Excellent diving in idyllic surroundings off the Caribbean coast

LAS ISLETAS
...o of 356 islands superb ...irdwatching and pre-Columbian statues

BLUEFIELDS
Off-the-beaten-track destination with dancing, partying and a fascinating mixed population

HONDURAS

Ahuas
Laguna de Caratasca
Puerto Lempira
Cabo Gracias a Dios

Catacamas
Leimus
Laguna Bismuna

Juticalpa
Río Guayape
Río Coco o Segovia
Laguna Pahara

TEGUCIGALPA
Danlí
Puerto Cabezas

Yuscarán
El Paraíso
Cordillera Isabella
Laguna Karatá
Laguna Wounta

Las Manos
Ocotal
Río Bocay
Río Prinzapolka

Somoto
San Marcos de Colón
El Espino
San Rafael del Norte

Choluteca
San Isidro
Jinotega
Lago de Apanás
Río Tuma
Río Grande de Matagalpa

El Triunfo
Guasaule
Somotillo
Estelí
Matagalpa
Sébaco
Río Kurinwas

Puerto Morazán
Cordillera los Marlblos
Boaco
Costa de Mosquitos
Laguna de Perlas

Chinandega
Corinto
León
León Viejo
Camoapa
Juigalpa
Río Mico
Río Escondido
Laguna de Perlas
Corn Islands (Islas del Maíz)

Poneloya
La Paz Centro
Lago de Managua
MANAGUA
Tipitapa
Río Rama
Rama
Bluefields

Puerto Sandino
Masaya
Granada
Bahía de Bluefields

El Tránsito
Parque Nacional Volcán Masaya
Lago de Apoyo
San Juan de Oriente
Isla Zapatera

Montelimar
Pochomil
Jinotepe
Casares
Mayo-galpa
Altagracia
Lago de Nicaragua
Río Tepenaguasapa

La Boquita
Huehuete
San Jorge
Rivas
Isla de Ometepe
Sapoá
Archipiélago de Solentiname
San Carlos
Río Punta Gorda
CARIBBEAN SEA

San Juan del Sur
Peñas Blancas
La Cruz
Caño Negro
Los Chiles
El Castillo
San Juan del Norte (Greytown)
Bahía Punta Gorda

PACIFIC OCEAN
Golfo Santa Elena
Península de Santa Elena
COSTA RICA
Río San Juan
Barra del Colorado

Golfo de Papagayo
Liberia

To San José

30   60 km

...TED ITINERARIES

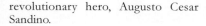

revolutionary hero, Augusto Cesar Sandino.

BOOKS

Many books exploring the political and social history of Nicaragua focus on the 1979 Sandinista revolution. Among these, *Fire from the Mountain: The Making of a Sandinista* by Omar Cabezas is a classic account of the Sandinista guerrilla experience. Shirley Christian's *Nicaragua: Revolution in the Family* is a narrative of the revolution by a leading US journalist on the ground at the time. *Sandino* is a biographical account of Sandino.

For an interesting analysis of the US-sponsored Contra War, see *Comandos: The CIA & Nicaragua's Contra Rebels* by newspaper correspondent Sam Dillon. For another account of shameless US imperialism, see William Walker's account of his failed takeover of Central America in *The War in Nicaragua*.

On a lighter note is *Death, Dreams and Dancing in Nicaragua* by Australian journalist Penny O'Donnell, an entertaining account of public radio stations Sandinista-style.

Poets of Nicaragua, 1918-1979, edited by Stephen White, is a useful bilingual anthology.

FILMS

The remarkable documentary *Pictures from a Revolution* by noted photographer Susan Meiselas offers a realistic perspective of Nicaraguan life during the revolution. Director Alex Cox's *Walker* takes a surreal, satirical look at the narcissistic doings of William Walker in Nicaragua and Central America. It stars Ed Harris as Walker and Peter Boyle as Cornelius Vanderbilt and features a soundtrack by Joe Strummer, formerly of The Clash.

ENTERING & LEAVING

Most visitors arrive by air, landing at the Augusto C Sandino airport 12km east of Managua. There are flights from Miami, Houston and Los Angeles in the USA and from Madrid, Spain. Most travellers have to connect through one of these cities. There are also flights between Managua and most other Central American and Caribbean cities. There is an airport departure tax from Nicaragua of US$20.

Travellers can cross into Nicaragua from two points in Costa Rica and three in Honduras. In addition, there is an international bus service from Guatemala City to Panama City, which passes through Managua. From Costa Rica, the main crossing is at Peñas Blancas on the Interamericana Hwy. There is also a river crossing at Los Chiles, accessible by boat from San Carlos. Into Honduras, the overland border crossings are at Las Manos, El Espino/San Marcos de Colón and Guasaule/El Triunfo. Fishing and cargo boats from Bluefields and Puerto Cabezas, both on the Caribbean coast, are constantly coming and going; you may be able to hitch a ride to another Central American port or island.

PANAMA

Few foreigners know much about Panama beyond the canal and the nefarious shenanigans of General Manuel Noriega (now under the control of US penal authorities), which does this beautiful and dynamic country a disservice. While tourists make a mad rush at neighbouring Costa Rica, Panama continues to be a well kept travellers secret, where stands of virgin rainforest and abundant wildlife are just waiting to be discovered. In addition, Panama has vital indigenous communities and the attractive pride and hospitality of the Panamanian people.

Panama also boasts deserted tropical beaches and river rapids to challenge even the greatest white-water aficionados. There are 1518 islands off the coasts of Panama and some, like the Archipiélago de San Blás, are quite notable for their distinctive culture and handcrafts. Panama is a thin country and while the morning may find you snorkelling in the Caribbean, by the afternoon you could be dipping your toes in the Pacific.

WHEN TO GO

Panama is a tropical country so it's hot and steamy a lot of the time. This is especially true on the coasts, where the humidity can become quite overbearing. The dry (summer) season runs from mid-December to about April and this is the most popular time to travel. Those who like to party should try to be in Panama City during Carnaval, which is one of the world's largest celebrations of its kind, held during the four days preceding Ash Wednesday. At this time hotel rooms can be very hard to find; reservations are essential and should be made well in advance. The dry season is the best time for trekking, or you'll be trudging through mud. For divers, the dry season

PANAMA CITY

Elevation - 33m/118ft

At a Glance

Full Country Name: Republic of Panama
Area: 78,000 km
Population: 2,779,000
Capital City: Panama City (pop 610,000)
People: 64% mestizo, 14% African descent, 10% Spanish descent, 5% mulatto and 5% Indian
Languages: Spanish, English and Indian languages
Religion: 84% Roman Catholic, 5% Protestant and 5% Islamic, plus small numbers of Jews, Hindus and various Indian tribes with their own belief systems
Government: Democracy
Currency: Balboa (B)
Time Zone: Five hours behind GMT/UTC
International Telephone Code: 507
Electricity: 110V, mostly 60 cycles AC; currents vary wildly and power surges and outages are not uncommon. Sockets are two-pronged

is the best time for the Caribbean coast; otherwise you'll be fighting high winds and powerful currents. Strong winds are common in February and March on the Pacific side.

HIGHLIGHTS

Panama has unspoiled beaches and reefs, decent mountain climbing and a host of other natural attractions not overrun with crowds. The following is a taste of what Panama has to offer.

Scuba Diving & Snorkelling

The best diving in Panama is off the Archipiélago de San Blás on the Caribbean coast and near Isla de Coiba and the Archipiélago de las Perlas on the Pacific coast. Visibility is better on the Caribbean side. There are very few dive operators (and only a handful of decompression chambers) in Panama and some dive sites require special permission, so consult a guidebook before planning a diving trip here. For a unique dive experience, visit the sunken train in the Panama Canal, or dive in both the Caribbean and Pacific in one day. Other good sites include Bahía Piña and Punta Mariato (on the Península de Azuero) on the Pacific side and Cayos Zapatillas (south-east of Isla Bastimentos in the Bocas del Toro) and Portobelo on the Caribbean.

Surfing

The best surfing in Panama is on the Pacific side and when the southern swells are rolling at Santa Catalina, you'll be treated to the best right-hand break in all of Central America. The best time for a visit here is between February and mid-August. Other good breaks (both left and right) are at Playa Teta and Playa Río Mar, both close to

San Carlos. On the Caribbean coast, surfers can try the party capital of Isla Grande or the mellower Playa Palenque west of El Porvenir. Equipment is not available for rent so bring your own.

Trekking

Hike to the top of Panama's highest peak, Volcán Barú (3478m), for a memorable view encompassing both the Caribbean and Pacific coasts, or try the six hour, deep jungle hike in the same area in the country's extreme west. There are many great walks in Panama's national parks including the old Sendero Las Cruces trail used by the conquistadors in Parque Nacional Soberanía and the nature trail in Parque Natural Metropolitano outside of Panama City. Then there's the infamous Darién Gap trek through the unmarked jungle vastness between Panama and Colombia. This can only be done during the dry season and even then it's dangerous, due to bandits and smugglers. Still, there are some fantastic hikes in this region, especially within the Parque Nacional Darién, where beaches, mountains and superb birdwatching collide.

Birdwatching

There are 940 bird species (and counting) in Panama and even the casual observer will be treated to sightings, perhaps some rare. Panama's location between two continents and its narrow girth mean native, migratory and endemic species all flock around the shores and valleys here. The oft-mentioned, but rarely seen, resplendent quetzal is more abundant in western Panama than anywhere else in Central America. Other notable birds include the harpy eagle, the king vulture and four species of macaws.

Fishing

There is topnotch fishing throughout Panama and whether you prefer the deep-sea, angling or river variety, you won't be disappointed. World-class deep-sea fishing is available at Bahía Piña, Isla de Coiba and the Pearl archipelago. There is good bass fishing in Lago Gatún and trout fishing in rivers around Volcán Barú.

VISA REQUIREMENTS

Citizens of the USA, Canada, Australia, New Zealand and the UK do not need visas to enter Panama. Visitors from these countries do need to purchase a tourist card (US$5) at their point of entry or a Panamanian embassy. Tourist cards receive a 30 day stamp. Border posts sometimes run out of tourist cards, and in this case you will be refused entry. Visas are also good for 30 days and cost around US$20. Visitors are typically asked to show an onward ticket and may be asked to produce sufficient funds (usually US$500 per month). After 30 days, a 60 day extension can be obtained at immigration offices in Panama. If you stay more than 30 days, you must obtain an exit stamp from immigration. These requirements change often; check with an embassy as to the paperwork you'll need to enter and exit Panama.

Panamanian Embassies

You can obtain visas in neighbouring countries as well as at home. Some countries have several Panamanian consulates in addition to the embassy.

Canada
(☎ 613-236-7177, fax 236-5775) 130 Albert St, Suite 300, Ottawa, Ontario ON K1P

Colombia
(☎ 1-257-5067, fax 257-5068) Calle 92, No 7-70, Bogotá

Costa Rica
(☎ 257-3241, fax 257-4864) Calle 38, Avenidas 5 and 7, 275m from the centre of Colon, north of San José

UK
(☎ 020-7493 4646, fax 7493 4499) 48 Park St, London W1Y 3PD

USA
(☎ 202-483-1407, fax 483-8413) 2862 McGill Terrace NW, Washington, DC 20008
Consulates: Miami, New York and San Francisco

TOURIST OFFICES OVERSEAS

Panama does not have any overseas tourist offices, but Panamanian embassies and consulates can supply general information. Also visit the web sites listed under Online Services.

HEALTH

Yellow fever exists in Darién Province and malaria occurs throughout the year in the San Blás islands and the Darién region in the east, in the Bocas del Toro area in the west and around Lago Bayano and Lago Gatún. You will need to take precautions against both these serious diseases if you plan on travelling to these areas. Dengue fever occurs, so avoid bites from all insects, especially mosquitoes. Take care with food and water as diseases including hepatitis, typhoid, dysentery and cholera can all occur. Generally tap water is OK to drink in most parts of Panama, but it's not a bad idea to stick with bottled or purified water. Being so close to the equator, the sun can be very strong in Panama. Be sure to keep drinking, preferably water, to avoid dehydration and cover up to avoid sunburn.

Panama City has good medical services, but medical care is limited in rural areas. If you do require serious medical attention, Panama City or Mexico City, where medical services are excellent, are the best options.

POST & COMMUNICATIONS

The postal service is reliable and air mail is the most efficient way to send letters or postcards from Panama. Airmail letters should take about five to 10 days to reach Canada and the USA and 10 days to reach Europe or Australia. Travellers can receive poste restante mail at main post offices in large cities and large towns. It's important to write República de Panamá in the address: letters with Panama only may be returned. In 1998, a five year plan was launched to modernise Panama's badly outdated and inefficient phone service. Until 10,000 pay phones are installed as promised, you'll have to go to centralised call centres or track down one of the few working pay phones. You can place international calls from hotels, but the charge is usurious. Fax services are also available at centralised phone offices.

Email is available at Internet cafes in Panama City.

Itineraries

One Week

Spend two days exploring Panama City, with time set aside to check out Panamá La Vieja, catch some live music and dine on delicious and varied food. Arrange a visit to Isla Taboga, 20km south for some fun in the sun and wildlife viewing. Head out to the Panama Canal and spend a day checking out the locks, the Summit Botanical Gardens & Zoo and hiking the section of the Sendero Las Cruces in Parque Nacional Soberanía. Returning to Panama City, continue to the pleasantly cool, elevated town of El Valle and enjoy two days of hiking. Be sure to visit the exquisite Sunday handcrafts market. Finally, hit the beach at Santa Clara for a day or two.

Two Weeks

Follow the one week itinerary and continue on to Boquete near the Costa Rican border to hike and take in some wildlife at Volcán Barú, soak in the therapeutic hot springs at Caldera and walk the Sendero Los Quetzales trail. Camp at Parque Internacional La Amistad, with its gorgeous rainforest, if you're up for it. Alternatively, you can follow the one week itinerary and spend the second week on the Península de Azuero birdwatching at Playa El Aguillito, an extraordinary centre for migratory seabirds including the roseate spoonbill, black-necked stilt and yellow-crowned Amazon. Visit also the well preserved colonial city of Parita and hit the many beaches in and around Pedasí.

Three Weeks

Choose either of the two week options, followed by a trip to the Caribbean coast for a bit of sand, sun and surf. In the west of the country, head up to Chiriquí Grande for the Bocas del Toro and in the east try the San Blás islands (near Colón); both have great diving. The latter, reached from the nearest major town El Porvenir, offer a unique cultural experience as they are ruled by the fiercely traditional Kuna Indians. Kuna textiles known as molas are world-renowned for their intricate, colourful and well executed designs. Enjoy the deserted beaches near Isla Grande, reached by boat from La Guayra, before heading home. If the sea is not your cup of tea, follow a two week itinerary and spend another week trekking around the remote and pristine Parque Nacional Darién.

PANAMA HIGHLIGHTS & ITINERARIES

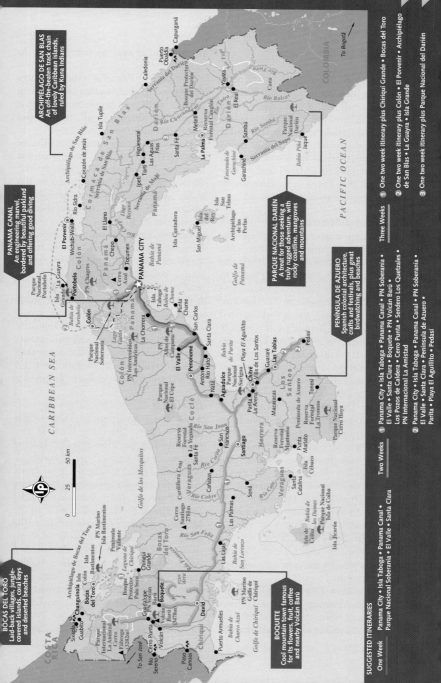

ARCHIPIÉLAGO DE SAN BLAS
An off-the-beaten track chain of lovely Caribbean islands, ruled by Kuna Indians

PANAMA CANAL
An engineering marvel, bordered by beautiful parkland and offering good diving

BOCAS DEL TORO
Laid-back villages, jungle-covered islands, coral keys and deserted beaches

BOQUETE
Cool mountain town famous for its flowers, fruit, coffee and nearby Volcán Barú

PENÍNSULA DE AZUERO
Spanish colonial architecture, crafts and festivals, plus great birdwatching and beaches

PARQUE NACIONAL DARIÉN
A treat for those seeking a truly rugged adventure, with rocky coastline, mangroves and mountains

SUGGESTED ITINERARIES

One Week
• Panama City • Isla Taboga • Panama Canal •
Parque Nacional Soberanía • El Valle • Santa Clara

Two Weeks
1 Panama City • Isla Taboga • Panama Canal • PN Soberanía •
El Valle • Santa Clara • Boquete • PN Volcán Barú •
Los Pozos de Caldera • Cerro Punta • Sendero Los Quetzales •
PN Internacional La Amistad

2 Panama City • Isla Taboga • Panama Canal • PN Soberanía •
El Valle • Santa Clara • Península de Azuero •
Parita • Playa El Aguillito • Pedasí

Three Weeks
1 One two week itinerary plus Chiriquí Grande • Bocas del Toro

2 One two week itinerary plus Colón • El Porvenir • Archipiélago
de San Blas • La Guayra • Isla Grande

3 One two week itinerary plus Parque Nacional del Darién

MONEY
Costs

Panama is not the cheapest of Central American countries, but the budget-conscious will still be able to get by on about US$15 a day. Accommodation will typically take the largest bite and if you prefer a more comfortable room with a bath, plan on spending closer to US$20 or US$30 a day. Food, transportation and entry fees throughout the country are reasonable.

Changing Money

Panamanian currency is called the balboa, but everyone else in the world calls it the US dollar. Since 1904, the dollar has been the legal tender in Panama. Though Panama issues coins (in the same denominations, size and metal as US coins), the only bills used are US dollars. Outside of the airport and a couple of exchange houses in Panama City, it is nearly impossible to change foreign currencies. Travellers cheques in currencies other than US dollars cannot be exchanged at all. American Express is the most widely honoured, as other brands have been expertly counterfeited in Panama, but even these are sometimes rejected. Basically, cash is the best way to deal with finances here, because credit cards can only be used in Panama City. You may have better luck with ATM cards, as ATMs are catching on fast.

ONLINE SERVICES

Lonely Planet's Destination Panama page is at www.lonelyplanet.com/dest/cam/pan.htm.

The Panama: Places, Folklore, Festivals and Museums web site (http://gringo.ent.ohiou.edu/~medina/panama.html) is a useful site on Panamanian culture and is easy to navigate via its map.

Focus on Panama (www.iaehv.nl/users/grimaldo/panama.html) is a bit grating with its first-person, purple prose, but among it all, it provides some decent information.

If you're toying with the idea of visiting the Bocas del Toro, visit the homepage at www.bocas.com. It may all look like one big advertisement, but there are some good facts for the visitor and history of the islands buried within it.

Birders will not want to miss the Panama Audubon Society's site (www.pananet.com/audubon). Here you'll find a catalogue of birds in Panama and a field-trip calendar, both of which can help you define your itinerary. The homepage of the Smithsonian Tropical Research Institute (www.stri.org), which maintains its headquarters in Panama and a research station on Isla Barro Colorado (in Lago Gatún) will interest conservationists.

BOOKS

A good introduction to Panamanian history from 1513 to 1964 is the readable *Panama: Four Hundred Years of Dreams and Cruelty* by David A Howarth. For history and society from the 1960s to the present, check out Tom Barry & John Lindsay-Poland's *Inside Panama*. The title of Luis E Murillo's tome, *The Noriega Mess: The Drugs, the Canal, and Why America Invaded*, pretty much says it all. Another decent read on this debacle is Kevin Buckley's *Panama: The Whole Story*.

For good reading on the construction of the Panama Canal, see David McCullough's riveting *The Path Between the Seas: The Creation of the Panama*

Canal. A tad less thrilling is *And the Mountains Will Move* by Miles P Du Val.

Literary fans will appreciate *When New Flowers Bloomed,* a collection of stories by women writers from Panama and Costa Rica, edited by Enrique Jaramillo Levi.

FILMS

The Academy Award-winning documentary *The Panama Deception* by filmmaker Barbara Trent pulls no punches in its investigation into the US invasion of Panama. The film caused an uproar and anyone interested in foreign policy or Panama should check it out.

ENTERING & LEAVING

Most international flights arrive at Tocumen international airport 35km from Panama City. There are direct flights form Miami, Houston, New York, Washington, DC and Los Angeles. European travellers will probably have to stopover in one of these US cities or in the Caribbean. Some flights, particularly those serving other Central American cities, may land at the international airport in David. Before you are allowed to board your plane in your origin city, you will be required to show an onward ticket. There is a departure tax of US$20.

Crossing by land between Costa Rica and Panama is easy. The most popular crossing is at Paso Canoas, on the Interamericana Highway, followed by Sixaola-Guabito near the Caribbean coast. A third is the rarely used crossing at Río Sereno. Despite the huge amount of shipping passing through the Panama Canal, it's hard to catch a ride on a boat.

No roads connect Colombia and Panama and crossing the Darién Gap between the two countries is not easy. The stretch is fraught with natural dangers and the drug-runners and bandits plying it make it even more potentially dangerous. If you feel this is something you must do, the place to cross is at Puerto Obaldía in Panama to Capurganá in Colombia. You can take this route without too much difficulty if you travel by boat. Going overland is another story, as there is no trail through the first part of dense jungle. Do your research and hire a guide before attempting this crossing.

PARAGUAY

Little known to its immediate neighbours let alone the outside world, Paraguay has distanced itself from the rest of Latin America and remained outside the mainstream until very recently. Much of its isolation is due to geography and the violent regime of General Alfredo Stroessner, who kept the country in a tight grip for 35 years until his government was overthrown in 1989. Since then, Paraguay has made a conscious effort to become more open and accessible and travellers will delight in the vast wilderness of the Gran Chaco, the placid and scenic capital of Asunción and the handful of little explored national parks.

WHEN TO GO

Paraguay is blessed with a springlike climate during winter (May to about

ASUNCIÓN
Elevation - 139m/456ft

September), but becomes brutally hot during summer. About 1500mm of rain falls evenly throughout the year and shouldn't disrupt travel plans. Carnaval in Asunción is a wild celebration held over the two days prior to Ash Wednesday.

HIGHLIGHTS

Independent travellers who want to get off the beaten track need only to visit Paraguay. So rare are the foreign tourists here, there's hardly a track to speak of. Here is a list of some of the country's most intriguing attractions.

Cities & Towns

Asunción is perched on the banks of the Río Paraguay and is one of Latin America's oldest cities (founded in 1537). Though few colonial buildings remain, Asunción boasts superior parks and decent museums. For colonial ruins, head to the area around the southeastern city of Encarnación, where important missions erected by the Jesuits rival any found in the Americas. Caacupé, Paraguay's most important religious centre and the site of an annual pilgrimage, is also worth a trip.

National Parks

Parque Nacional Ybycuí, just 150km from the capital, is an accessible, well preserved tract of tropical rainforest where visitors can hike and camp. A good adventure destination is the subtropical Parque Nacional Serranía San Luis near the Brazilian border. For superb exposure to native flora and fauna, try the little visited Parque Nacional Defensores del Chaco in the semi-arid north-west region. Camping and lodging are available at the picturesque Parque Nacional Cerro Corá, one of Paraguay's most scenic parks.

Itaipú Dam

At 1350 sq km, this is the world's largest hydroelectric project and well worth a peek if you're in south-eastern Paraguay. Before the construction of a gigantic reservoir for the project, the waterfalls here (Sete Quedas) were larger than even nearby Iguazú Falls. You can visit these famous falls in Brazil from the boomtown of Ciudad del Este.

VISA REQUIREMENTS

Most visitors to Paraguay require visas. The notable exceptions are citizens from neighbouring countries and those from the USA and the UK, who are given tourist cards upon arrival. Visas and tourist cards are good for a stay of 90 days. To obtain a visa you will have to show a clean police record and a bank statement and pay a fee of US$10. Paraguay has strict paperwork requirements for travellers under the age of 20 not accompanied by their parents. If you fall into this category, check at a Paraguayan embassy before you travel to ascertain what certification you'll need to be admitted to the country.

Paraguayan Embassies

Paraguay has limited representation abroad; your best bet may be to visit an embassy or consulate in a neighbouring country.

Argentina

(☎ 011-4812 0075) Viamonte 1851, Buenos Aires;
(☎ 03783-426576) Gobernador Ruiz 2746, Corrientes;
(☎ 03752-423850) San Lorenzo between Santa Fe and Sarmiento, Posadas

Bolivia

(☎ 322018) Av Arce, Edificio Venus, La Paz

Brazil

(☎ 045-523 2898) Bartolomeu de Gusmão 738, Foz do Iguaçu;
(☎ 242-9671) No 1208, Rua do Carmo 20, Centro, Rio de Janeiro;
(☎ 255-7818) 10th floor, Av São Luis 112, São Paulo

UK

(☎ 020-7937 1253) Braemar Lodge, Cornwall Gardens, London SW7 4AQ

Uruguay

(☎ 400-3801) Bulevar Artigas 1256, Montevideo

USA

(☎ 202-483-6960, fax 234-4508) 2400 Massachusetts Ave NW, Washington, DC 20008
Consulates: Los Angeles, Miami and New York

TOURIST OFFICES OVERSEAS

Paraguay does not maintain overseas tourist offices, though the larger consulates or embassies will be able to provide general information. The national airline, Líneas Aéreas Paraguayas (Lapsa; ☎ 800-795-2772), can supply information. See also the web sites listed under Online Services below.

HEALTH

Malaria occurs in rural areas, particularly in the regions bordering Brazil and around the Itaipú Dam. Dengue fever can occur, so take precautions against these insect-borne diseases. Also avoid bites from insects to prevent leishmaniasis. Hepatitis, typhoid and dysentery can occur, so watch what you eat and drink – when in doubt drink only bottled or purified water.

Itineraries

One Week
With one week in Paraguay you can spend a few days in Asunción, taking a day trip to the east on the antique, wood-burning train that runs for 28km between the capital and Areguá on the shores of Lago Ypacaraí. The balance of your trip can be spent exploring the fascinating towns of the region including Caacupé, Piribebuy, Yaguarón and Itá. Alternatively, you can zoom north for a quick circuit of the Gran Chaco wilderness.

Two Weeks
Follow the one week itinerary and add a camping and hiking trip to Parque Nacional Ybycuí. Follow up with a trip to the Jesuit missions of Encarnación, Trinidad and Jesús in the south before returning to Asunción.

Three Weeks
Follow the two week itinerary, continuing north-east from the missions to Ciudad del Este for a visit to the Itaipú Dam and the Iguazú Falls in Brazil. A quick visit to the Gran Chaco will round out your trip.

One Month
This will give you enough time to see almost everything Paraguay has to offer. Take in all of the suggestions outlined above, travelling overland so you can experience the local culture and witness the landscape up close. Be sure to check out the historical Mennonite town of Filadelfia, from where you can also explore some of Paraguay's remaining indigenous communities. Also hike and camp through the isolated Parque Nacional Defensores del Chaco near the Bolivian border.

Medical care is reasonable in cities, but limited in rural areas. If you do require medical attention, head for one of the hospitals or clinics in Asunción.

POST & COMMUNICATIONS

For the most part, Paraguayan mail services are reliable, though important correspondence should be sent via registered mail. It's possible to receive poste restante mail in Paraguay by addressing letters to the central post office. It costs around US$0.25 for each piece retrieved.

To place international calls, you have to trudge to a centralised calling centre. Every town has at least one and the centres in Asunción are equipped with fibre optic lines that can connect callers with international operators in several countries including the USA, the UK, Australia, Germany and Japan. Reverse charge (collect) and credit card calls are the cheapest way to go.

You may be able to find one or two Internet cafes in the capital from where you can send faxes or email.

MONEY
Costs

Budget travellers arriving from Argentina or Uruguay will rejoice in Paraguay's cost of living, where US$10 is about the daily minimum outlay. For a bit more comfort in accommodation and variety in your diet, expect to spend more like US$15 to US$30 a day.

Changing Money

As in most Latin American countries, the US dollar is the foreign currency of choice, though German deutschmarks are accepted in Asunción. Exchange houses are the most convenient places

PARAGUAY HIGHLIGHTS & ITINERARIES

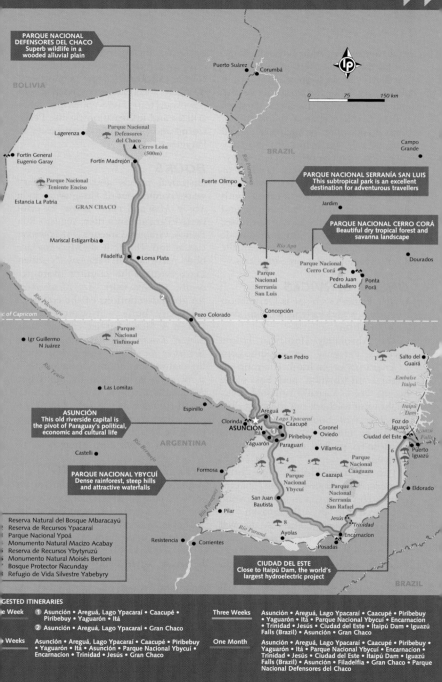

PARQUE NACIONAL DEFENSORES DEL CHACO
Superb wildlife in a wooded alluvial plain

PARQUE NACIONAL SERRANÍA SAN LUIS
This subtropical park is an excellent destination for adventurous travellers

PARQUE NACIONAL CERRO CORÁ
Beautiful dry tropical forest and savanna landscape

ASUNCIÓN
This old riverside capital is the pivot of Paraguay's political, economic and cultural life

PARQUE NACIONAL YBYCUÍ
Dense rainforest, steep hills and attractive waterfalls

CIUDAD DEL ESTE
Close to Itaipú Dam, the world's largest hydroelectric project

Reserva Natural del Bosque Mbaracayú
Reserva de Recursos Ypacaraí
Parque Nacional Ypoá
Monumento Natural Macizo Acabay
Reserva de Recursos Ybytyruzú
Monumento Natural Moisés Bertoni
Bosque Protector Ñacunday
Refugio de Vida Silvestre Yabebyry

BOLIVIA
BRAZIL
GRAN CHACO
ARGENTINA

Puerto Suárez • Corumbá
Lagerenza
Parque Nacional Defensores del Chaco
▲ Cerro León (500m)
Fortín General Eugenio Garay
Fortín Madrejón
Fuerte Olimpo
Parque Nacional Teniente Enciso
Estancia La Patria
Jardim
Campo Grande
Mariscal Estigarribia
Filadelfia • Loma Plata
Parque Nacional Serranía San Luis
Rio Apa
Parque Nacional Cerro Corá
Dourados
Pedro Juan Caballero • Ponta Porã
Pozo Colorado
Concepción
Igr Guillermo N Juárez
Parque Nacional Tinfunqué
San Pedro
Salto del Guairá
Embalse Itaipá
Las Lomitas
Espinillo
Areguá
Lago Ypacaraí
Caacupé
Itaipú Dam
Foz do Iguaçú
Iguazú Falls
Clorinda
ASUNCIÓN
Itá
Piribebuy
Coronel Oviedo
Ciudad del Este
Puerto Iguazú
Yaguarón
Paraguarí
Villarrica
Castelli
Formosa
Parque Nacional Ybycuí
Parque Nacional Caaguazu
Caazapá
Eldorado
Parque Nacional Serranía San Rafael
San Juan Bautista
Pilar
Jesús • Trinidad
Encarnación
Resistencia • Corrientes
Ayolas
Posadas
BRAZIL

SUGGESTED ITINERARIES

One Week
① Asunción • Areguá, Lago Ypacaraí • Caacupé • Piribebuy • Yaguarón • Itá
② Asunción • Areguá, Lago Ypacaraí • Gran Chaco

Two Weeks
Asunción • Areguá, Lago Ypacaraí • Caacupé • Piribebuy • Yaguarón • Itá • Asunción • Parque Nacional Ybycuí • Encarnación • Trinidad • Jesús • Gran Chaco

Three Weeks
Asunción • Areguá, Lago Ypacaraí • Caacupé • Piribebuy • Yaguarón • Itá • Parque Nacional Ybycuí • Encarnación • Trinidad • Jesús • Ciudad del Este • Itaipú Dam • Iguazú Falls (Brazil) • Asunción • Gran Chaco

One Month
Asunción • Areguá, Lago Ypacaraí • Caacupé • Piribebuy • Yaguarón • Itá • Parque Nacional Ybycuí • Encarnación • Trinidad • Jesús • Ciudad del Este • Itaipú Dam • Iguazú Falls (Brazil) • Asunción • Filadelfia • Gran Chaco • Parque Nacional Defensores del Chaco

to change money, though they'll charge a commission and offer lower rates for travellers cheques than cash. Some places may ask you to produce the receipt for your travellers cheques before they'll exchange them. In the interior and more remote places, you'll have to rely on banks for currency exchange. Freelance street money-changers can be useful at borders or after-hours, though be aware of possible scams when dealing with them. Better hotels, restaurants and shops in Asunción accept credit cards, but their use is less common outside the capital. Paraguayan ATMs generally do not recognise foreign bank cards.

ONLINE SERVICES

Lonely Planet's web site is Destination Paraguay (www.lonelyplanet.com/dest /sam/par.htm).

The Absolutely Unofficial Home Page of Paraguay (www.eskimo.com /~krautm/tourism.html) is strong on cultural information and has some decent links. Visually oriented folks might want to check out the site called The Heart of South America (www .pla.net.py/intertours), which has lots of detailed photos of attractions in Paraguay.

The Guaraní Home Page (http: //merece.uthscsa.edu/gram/guarani /index-eng.html) is a must for anyone interested in the Paraguayan indigenous language. The site is well organised with an interactive Guaraní to German or Spanish dictionary, a Guaraní tutorial and information on indigenous cultures in Paraguay.

Spanish-speakers will be interested in Paraguay Para Todo El Mundo (www .canit.se/~carbar/cover.html), which has all kinds of fun facts about Paraguay. The Friends of Paraguay, a nonprofit organisation founded by former Peace Corps volunteers, maintains a web site (www.pipeline.com /~ybycui/fop). Here you'll find news articles and information on the Peace Corps and other ongoing projects in Paraguay.

BOOKS

Historical novels and other literary works coming out of Paraguay include *Son of Man* and *I the Supreme* by celebrated Paraguayan writer Augusto Roa Bastos. Graham Greene's *The Honorary Consul* and *Travels With My Aunt* are both partly set in Paraguay. Norman Lewis visited the country more recently. See his work, *The Missionaries*, for good descriptions of the country.

History buffs will want to read Elman & Helen Service's *Tobatí: Paraguayan Town* and Gaylord Warren's *Rebirth of the Paraguayan Republic*, which highlights the country's incomplete recovery from the War of the Triple Alliance. For general works on authoritarian nastiness, see *Rule by Fear: Paraguay After Thirty Years Under Stroessner* published by Americas Watch and *The Stroessner Era* by Carlos Miranda.

ENTERING & LEAVING

Asunción is a convenient hub for air traffic to the Southern Cone countries and if you can snag a cheap fare to the Paraguayan capital, you can travel overland to neighbouring nations. There are several direct flights a week between Miami and Asunción; all other flights connect through nearby South American cities such as Rio de Janeiro, Buenos Aires, or Santa Cruz in Bolivia. The international departure tax is around US$15.

The geographic isolation of Paraguay is apparent in the paucity of land border crossings. Between Paraguay and Argentina there are three: Asunción and Clorinda; Encarnacíon and Posadas; and Ciudad del Este to Puerto Iguazú via Foz de Iguaçu in Brazil. Travelling from Paraguay to Brazil you can cross at the Ciudad del Este to Foz do Iguaçu post or at Pedro Juan Caballero to Ponta Porã. If you prefer travelling by boat, there are irregular trips from Asunción on the Río Paraguay to the Brazilian city of Corumbá. The overland crossing between Estancia La Patria (reached via Filadelfia) in Paraguay and Boyuibe in Bolivia is one of the most challenging on the South American continent and has a lot of fans as a result. There is no public transport and you may get stuck on a deserted road waiting for a ride.

PERU

Peru is a mystical and mysterious destination, where formations like the Nazca Lines and the desertion of the great Incan city of Machu Picchu still defy explanation. From the steamy jungles of the Amazonian lowlands to Lake Titicaca soaring above sea level, Peru has natural wonders to rival its cultural phenomena and travellers will be hard-pressed to decide which of the many things to do and see here.

Violent guerrilla activity, particularly by the Sendero Luminoso (Shining Path), has decreased substantially in the past decade, allowing for exploration of areas previously considered too dangerous for foreigners. Peru has a burgeoning tourist industry as a result and all manner of transport, accommodation, food and guides are available.

At a Glance

Full Country Name: República del Perú
Area: 1,285,216 sq km
Population: 26,624,000
Capital City: Lima (pop over seven million)
People: 54% Indian, 32% mestizo, 12% Spanish descent, 2% Black and an Asian minority
Languages: Spanish, Quechua and Aymara
Religion: Over 90% Roman Catholic, plus a small Protestant population
Government: Democracy
Currency: Nuevo sol (S/)
Time Zone: Five hours behind GMT/UTC
International Telephone Code: 51
Electricity: 220V, mostly 60 cycles AC, except for Arequipa which runs on 50 cycles; two-pronged, flat plugs like those used in North America are the norm

WHEN TO GO

Much like all the Andean nations, Peru has wet and dry seasons which vary depending on where you are. The rainy season in the highlands and the Amazonian lowlands runs from December to April, when it can get very wet. In the rainforest, this means a downpour or two each day, but with sunny breakthroughs often enough to make it worth the trip. In the highlands, however, rain means cold weather and mud – not ideal conditions if you want to hike to Machu Picchu. The dry season

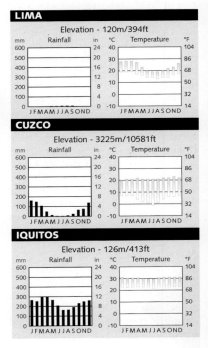

in the highlands is from June to August, exactly when most westerners take their holidays, and so tourist destinations are mobbed at this time.

The sunny, dry season on Peru's coast is from December to March. For the remainder of the year, however, the coast is cloaked in fog.

HIGHLIGHTS

There are so many enticing things to see and do in Peru, you'll have to decide beforehand what most piques your interest. The following suggestions should help pare down the options.

Archaeological Sites

Machu Picchu, known as the Lost City of the Incas, is the most visited attraction in South America, and with good reason. These ruins tower above the Río Urubamba, nestled in a crook of the Andes. The ruins were not discovered by the Spanish conquistadors and remained hidden until 1911. The mystery of why the Incans abandoned this city endures. You can hike into the ruins along the Inca Trail. There are other important archaeological sites sprinkled throughout Peru, the most striking of which are at Chan Chan, Sillustani, Kuélap, and the 2500-year-old ruins of the Chavín, near Huaraz. The Nazca Lines are tremendous designs etched in the desert by the Nazca civilisation and must be seen from an airplane to be fully appreciated.

Natural Attractions

Some of the world's most pristine and diverse rainforest lies within the boundaries of Peru's Parque Nacional Manu in the Amazon Basin region. The 1.8 million hectare park is well protected and only about 20% is open to visitors.

Here you'll see many species of monkeys and birds including macaws, green ibis and herons, river turtles, caimans, snakes and, if you keep your eyes peeled, perhaps a jaguar, tapir, peccary or a giant anteater or two. This is serious jungle and not for those squeamish about bugs!

In the south-eastern corner of Peru is Lake Titicaca which is jointly administered by Bolivia and Peru. Travellers frequently pass between the two countries in this area. Lake Titicaca is 3820m above sea level and at 170km long, it's the largest lake in South America. A visit to Lake Titicaca will leave you breathless because of the altitude and the scenery. The island communities in the middle of the lake are friendly and make an intriguing trip.

Trekking & Mountain Climbing

Some alpinists argue that Peru has the finest trekking in South America. If you're coming here for the mountains, head straight to Huaraz, where many of the ascents are higher than 6000m and permanently covered in snow. The Cordillera Blanca near Huaraz includes Huascarán (6768m), Alpamayo (5947m) and Champará (5850m). You can hire guides and rent gear in Huaraz.

VISA REQUIREMENTS

Citizens of most western countries do not need visas, but receive a free tourist card upon arrival. The maximum stay is 90 days, but immigration officials will sometimes give you fewer; request the maximum 90 days and you should get it. Visitors requiring visas can usually get them from Peruvian embassies in adjacent countries, or should obtain one before leaving home.

Renewing tourist cards is straight-forward if you've the required paper-work, including an onward ticket. It costs US$20 for each additional 30 days, and you're only allowed to renew for 180 days. Lima is the best place to renew.

Peruvian Embassies

Australia
(☎ 02-6257 2953, fax 6257 5198) Suite 1, 9th floor, Qantas House, 97 London Circuit, Canberra, ACT 2601. Mailing address: PO Box 971, Civic Square, ACT 2608

Bolivia
(☎ 2-35 3550, fax 36 7640) Avenida 6 de Agosto y Guachalla, Edificio Alianza, La Paz

Brazil
(☎ 61-242 9435, fax 243 5677) SES, Av das Nações, Lote 43, 70428-900, Brasília DF

Canada
(☎ 613-238-1777, fax 232-3062) 170 Laurier Ave West, Suite 1007, Ottawa, Ontario K1P 5V5

Chile
(☎ 2-235 2356, fax 235 8139) Avenida Andrés Bello 1751, Providencia 9, Casilla 16277, Santiago
Consulate: Arica

Itineraries

One Week
Peru is so large and the geography so rugged, you'll be challenged with only a week to explore it. This is especially true in cities like Cuzco or Puno where adjusting to the altitude can take a day or longer. After landing in Lima, head directly to Cuzco by air and visit the ruins of Machu Picchu for two days. From Cuzco take the train to Puno and spend two days on the shores of Lake Titicaca, perhaps taking a day trip to the island village of Taquile or to the pre-Inca ruins at Sillustani.

Two Weeks
Follow the one week itinerary, continuing on to the colonial city of Arequipa by train from Puno. Spend the balance of your time enjoy-ing the myriad activities in and around Arequipa: visit the colonial churches and monasteries; travel to the popular Cañon del Colca; climb El Misti volcano; or check out the petroglyphs at El Toro Muerto.

Return to Lima, stay in the suburbs of Miraflores or Barranco and enjoy the cafes and bars. If you want to hike into Machu Picchu on the Inca Trail (four to five days), shave off the Arequipa portion of this itinerary and spend that time in Cuzco arranging and doing the hike.

One Month
This is the sort of time you'll need to really experience Peru. Follow the two week itiner-ary, but before heading south to Lake Titicaca, arrange a tour to Parque Nacional Manu from Cuzco. Spend a week in this stunning jungle paradise, then schedule some recovery time, perhaps two days in Cuzco, before taking the train to Lake Titicaca. Arrange to spend a night with a local family on the island of Taquile in the middle of the lake.

Resume the two week itinerary with either the Arequipa or Machu Picchu options. Alter-natively, you can spend just two days in Arequipa and then head to Nazca for a flight over the Nazca Lines before returning to Lima.

Two Months
Two months will allow you to explore the major sites and see the best attractions with enough days to chill out in between.

Follow the one month itinerary with both the Machu Picchu and Arequipa options, con-tinuing on to Nazca. From there, return to Lima and either explore the coast with a few days in Trujillo or head to Huaraz, Peru's mountain climbing and hiking mecca. From Trujillo you could head even further north to Chachapoyas to see the magnificent Kuélap archaeological site.

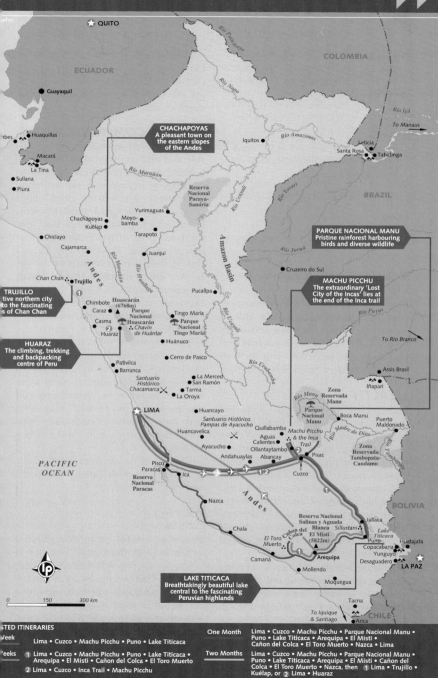

PERU HIGHLIGHTS & ITINERARIES

★ QUITO

COLOMBIA

ECUADOR

● Guayaquil

To Manaus

● Huaquillas

Macará

La Tina

● Sullana

● Piura

CHACHAPOYAS
A pleasant town on the eastern slopes of the Andes

Iquitos

Leticia
Santa Rosa ✈ Tabatinga

BRAZIL

Reserva Nacional Pacaya-Samiria

● Chachapoyas
Kuélap

Moyo-bamba

Yurimaguas

Tarapoto

Juanjui

PARQUE NACIONAL MANU
Pristine rainforest harbouring birds and diverse wildlife

● Chiclayo

Cajamarca

● Cruzeiro do Sul

MACHU PICCHU
The extraordinary 'Lost City of the Incas' lies at the end of the Inca trail

Chan Chan ∴ ● Trujillo ①

TRUJILLO
tive northern city to the fascinating s of Chan Chan

Pucallpa

To Río Branco

Chimbote
Caraz ● Huascarán (6768m)
Casma ● Parque Nacional Huascarán
Huaraz ② ∴ Chavín de Huántar

Tingo María ●
Parque Nacional Tingo María

Assis Brasil

HUARAZ
The climbing, trekking and backpacking centre of Peru

● Huánuco

Iñapari

Pativilca ●
Barranca ●

Santuario Histórico Chacamarca ✕

● Cerro de Pasco

Zona Reservada Manu

Parque Nacional Manu

Boca Manu

★ LIMA

La Merced ●
San Ramón ●
Tarma ●
La Oroya

Huancayo ●

Santuario Histórico Pampas de Ayacucho

Quillabamba
Aguas Calientes
Machu Picchu & the Inca Trail

Puerto Maldonado

PACIFIC OCEAN

Huancavelica ●

Ayacucho ●
Andahuaylas

Ollantaytambo
Abancay ● ① ②
Pisac
Cuzco

Zona Reservada Tambopata-Candamo

Pisco ●
Paracas ● ✈ ✈ ✈ 🚲 ① ②
Ica ●

Reserva Nacional Paracas

Andes

① ①

● Nazca

BOLIVIA

Chala ●

Reserva Nacional Salinas y Aguada Blanca
El Misti (5822m) ▲
Sillustani

Juliaca

El Toro Muerto ✕ Cañón del Colca
Camaná ●

Lake Titicaca
Puno
Huatajata
Copacabana
Yunguyo
Desaguadero

① Arequipa

★ LA PAZ

● Mollendo

LAKE TITICACA
Breathtakingly beautiful lake central to the fascinating Peruvian highlands

● Moquegua

Tacna ●

To Iquique & Santiago

CHILE

Arica

0   150   300 km

Colombia
  (☎ 1-257 6292, fax 257 3753) Carrera 10 bis, No 94-48, Santa Fe de Bogotá, DC
Ecuador
  (☎ 2-554 161, fax 562 349) Edifico España, Penthouse, Amazonas 1429 y Colón, Quito
New Zealand
  (☎ 4-499 8087, fax 499 8057) Level 8, Cigna House, 40 Mercer St, POB 2566, Wellington
UK
  (☎ 020-7235 1917, fax 7235 4463) 52 Sloane St, London SW1X 9SP
USA
  (☎ 202-833-9860, fax 659-8124) 1700 Massachusetts Ave NW, Washington, DC 20036

TOURIST OFFICES OVERSEAS

Peru maintains few overseas tourist offices, but a travel agent will be able to answer questions. Peruvian consulates or embassies in your home country may also be able to help. Also visit the web sites listed under Online Services below.

HEALTH

Malaria exists in areas below 1500m, but there is no malaria in Lima, Cuzco, Machu Picchu or Lake Titicaca. Yellow fever occurs in the central and northern areas, so take precautions against both these serious diseases. Dengue fever also occurs, so avoid mosquito bites and avoid bites from all insects to prevent other insect-borne diseases. Take care travelling in the highlands, as altitude sickness can occur and trekkers should be prepared for cold conditions. Food and waterborne diseases, including typhoid, cholera, hepatitis and dysentery all occur, so watch what you eat and drink. Tap water is not safe to drink in Lima; you should stick to bottled or purified water throughout Peru.

Medical care is generally good in Lima and in most other cities. Health care in rural areas is limited, so head for the capital if you require serious medical care.

POST & COMMUNICATIONS

Peruvian postal services are more reliable and efficient than those in neighbouring Andean countries. Air mail to the USA or Europe will take from one to two weeks if sent from Lima; longer from other cities and smaller towns. For receiving poste restante mail, use the Lima post office. Remember that letters are filed alphabetically so you should check under both your initials. If you are a member of the South American Explorers Club (see Online Services), you can receive mail at its Cuzco and Lima clubhouses, both of which are secure and convenient.

The telephone service is suffering growing pains as the national system modernises. You used to have to go to a centralised telephone centre to place international calls, but increasingly you can use regular pay phones in big cities and tourist towns. Some only take coins, but in major cities you can buy phonecards.

Email and fax services are available at decent prices in Lima, its suburbs and Cuzco.

MONEY
Costs

Peru is reasonably cheap, though more expensive than Bolivia and Ecuador. If you're on a super-tight budget, you can get by on US$15 a day by staying in the cheapest backpacker hostels and eating set meals in local restaurants. If you want to stay in better hotels, take a taxi every so often and vary your diet, you can expect to spend about US$40 a day. Keep in mind that for each extra dollar you spend on accommodation, the quality typically jumps threefold.

Changing Money

The main places to change money in Peru are at banks, finer hotels and exchange houses. These last are the most efficient, keep the longest hours and offer similar rates to banks. The areas around banks are usually mobbed with moneychangers, but they don't offer better rates than banks or exchange houses and so are really only useful when everything else is closed or you're at a border. The finer hotels will also exchange money, but you'll pay extra for this service. Cash will get you a slightly better rate than travellers cheques and Visa is widely accepted in the major cities and tourist towns. Beware of foreign credit card commissions, which can be as much as 8%, though cash advances are usually exempt.

ONLINE SERVICES

Lonely Planet's web site is Destination Peru (www.lonelyplanet.com/dest/sam/peru.htm).

The South American Explorers Club (www.samexplo.com) has a wealth of Peruvian information, links, trip reports and travellers tips. Other Latin American countries are also discussed.

The Lost Cities Adventure site (www.destination360.com/lostcities.htm) will show you what the latest computer technology can do as it takes you on a panoramic, full 360° tour of Peruvian sites like Lake Titicaca, Cuzco and Machu Picchu.

The bilingual English-Spanish site Peru Online (www.peruonline.com) is nothing spectacular but has great links.

BOOKS

Conquest of the Incas by John Hemming is recognised as one of the finest books written on that civilisation and its subjugation by Spanish conquistadors. *Monuments of the Incas* by the same author and illustrated with black and white photographs by Edward Ranney is also worth a look.

Mario Vargas Llosa is Peru's most celebrated novelist. Try *Real Life of Alejandro Mayta* or *Aunt Julia and the Scriptwriter* for a taste of his work.

There are many travelogues about Peru. Among the best are the realistic *Cut Stones & Crossroads: A Journey in the Two Worlds of Peru* by Ronald Wright and *Journey Along the Spine of the Andes* by Christopher Portway, who travelled through the Andes from Colombia to Bolivia. Both of these books will give you a good idea of what you can expect while travelling in Peru. Also check out Matthew Parris' *Inca-kola: A Traveller's Tale of Peru.*

If you want to hike, get a copy of *Backpacking & Trekking in Peru & Bolivia* by Hilary Bradt which describes popular treks like the Inca Trail, but also has descriptions of hikes further off the beaten path. *The Peruvian Andes* by Philippe Beaud is a paperback guide to mountain climbing and trails in French, English and Spanish.

FILMS

Peru doesn't have much of a film industry to brag about, but the scenery is so stunning that the country is the location for many tropical movies.

One of the most famous filmed in Peru is Werner Herzog's *Fitzcarraldo*. Although the story takes place in Brazil, it was shot in the Peruvian Amazon and will give you a good feeling for the jungle lowlands. Another stunning film shot in Peru is *The Big Blue*, starring the fabulous French actor Jean Reno.

Peru is also a favourite setting for nature documentaries and one worth tracking down is *Manu: Peru's Hidden Rainforest*, produced by Reader's Digest and PBS for the Living Edens series. At the end of this documentary, the filmmakers even demonstrate the equipment and techniques they used to get certain shots because the footage is so extraordinary it seems fake. You can order this video online (www.pbs.org/edens/manu).

ENTERING & LEAVING

Lima is an international hub and many flights to the South American mainland pass through or terminate here. Visitors from Australia and New Zealand will probably find a Circle Pacific fare is the way to go, with stopoffs in Tahiti, Hawaii or Los Angeles before the connecting flight to Lima. Flying from other South and Central American cities is not a problem if you can afford it. There is a US$20 departure tax if you fly out of Peru.

Many travellers pass through Peru to neighbouring countries. There are crossings into Ecuador at Macará and Huaquillas. In 1998 Peru and Ecuador settled a long-standing border dispute and agreed to jointly manage a system of national parks in the Oriente region. Travellers wishing to cross between the two countries along Ecuador's eastern border should consult local authorities or the staff at the South American Explorers Club. The only crossing from Peru into Chile is from Tacna to Arica. You can cross overland into Bolivia at Desaguadero and Yunguyo to Puno and via Copacabana and Huatajata across Lake Titicaca. The determined, patient and unflappable can shoot for the three way Peruvian, Colombian and Brazilian border by travelling the Amazon upriver from Iquitos to Santa Rosa in Peru, crossing into Brazil at Tabatinga. Another border crossing between Peru and Brazil is at Iñapari/Assis Brasil.

SURINAME

The Spanish and Portuguese never colonised Suriname because the weather and heat are so awful. Eventually, however, the British and Dutch laid roots in Suriname. To make their miserable lives easier, the colonists spread the misery around by importing African slaves and later indentured workers from India and Indonesia. These are the origins of the wild, anomalous culture that survives in Suriname today, making it a unique destination in Latin America. Aside from culture, Suriname has some of the least explored and best preserved stands of rainforest in the world.

WHEN TO GO

The dry seasons are from early February to late April and from mid-August to early December. These are the best periods to visit. It rains most between late April and July. It is hot and humid almost all of the time.

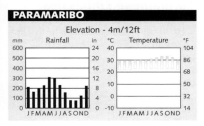

PARAMARIBO

Elevation - 4m/12ft

Rainfall / Temperature

HIGHLIGHTS

Most people come to Suriname to see the unspoiled, rarely explored virgin rainforest in the well managed system of parks and reserves. There are other interesting things to do, and here's a sampling.

Cities

Suriname's capital city, Paramaribo (frequently called just 'Parbo') is an intriguing blend of Europe and Asia set in tropical South America. You can tour the Roman Catholic Kathedraal, main Mosque and Dutch Israeli Synagogue before dining on Javanese satay under a swaying palm tree. Suriname's second city is Nieuw Nickerie near the mouth of the Nickerie River. You can chill

---

At a Glance

Full Country Name: Republic of Suriname
Area: 163,270 sq km
Population: 440,000
Capital City: Paramaribo (pop 240,000)
People: 35% East Indian, 32% Afro-Surinamese, 15% Indonesian and 10% Bush Negroes (descendants of ex-slaves who inhabit the upland forests), plus smaller numbers of Amerindians, Chinese and Europeans
Languages: Dutch, English, Sranan (an English-based Creole), Hindi, Javanese and Chinese
Religion: 27% Hindu, 25% Protestant, 23% Roman Catholic and 20% Muslim, plus small numbers of Buddhists, Jews and followers of Amerindian beliefs
Government: Republic
Currency: Suriname guilder (Sf)
Time Zone: Three hours behind GMT/UTC
International Telephone Code: 597
Electricity: 127V and very reliable; European-style plugs with two round pins are used

out here for a while or take a ferry over to Guyana.

Wildlife Viewing & Natural Attractions

Brownsberg Nature Park, less than two hours south of the capital, is a stand of montane tropical rainforest. There are good views, hikes and waterfalls and overnight stays can be arranged. Albina is a remote village on the Marowijne (Maroni) River which forms the border with French Guiana. From Albina you can hire a canoe and a guide to visit the nearby Galibi Nature Reserve, where

---

Itineraries

One Week
It takes about a week to see the major, accessible sights in Suriname. Start by hanging out in Parbo for a couple of days, soaking up the western-cum-tropical ambience and partaking of some delicious food – it is said that the best Indonesian food outside of Indonesia is in Suriname. A good side trip is to Brownsberg Nature Park where you might stay overnight before heading north to Nieuw Nickerie for a couple of days. Return to Parbo, leaving one day to hop off the bus at whichever coastal town may strike your fancy.

Two to Three Weeks
Follow the one week itinerary, then hook up on a guided tour to Raleighvallen/Voltzberg Nature Reserve in the middle of the country; an expedition to Mt Kasikasima in the south; or a river tour of Kumalu and the Awarra Dam in the heart of Maroon country.

Tours are also available to Tafelberg Nature Park, the easternmost of the 'Lost World Mountains' in the central region and Tonka Island in Brokopondo Lake. Multiday trips to the interior or along the reserves of the coast can also be arranged. Either before or after a tour, take a side trip to Albina and the adjacent Galibi Nature Reserve.

Ridley, green and leatherback turtles nest in June and July.

There are nature reserves and national parks throughout Suriname, both along the coast and inland. Travellers should splurge on an organised tour or guide to explore the nether reaches of this jungle wonderland.

VISA REQUIREMENTS

Unless you are a citizen of Denmark, Finland, Guyana, Israel, Norway, Sweden, Switzerland or the UK, you will need a visa to enter Suriname. You can get visas at home or in neighbouring countries. Visa applications have to be filled out in duplicate and accompanied by two passport photos and the appropriate fee – between US$30 and US$42 depending on your nationality. You may be asked to produce an onward ticket and sufficient funds before your visa is granted. Officially, visas are good for two months, but you will probably receive only a one week stamp upon arrival. Extensions are available at the immigration office in Paramaribo.

Surinamese Embassies
French Guiana
　(☎ 30-0461) 38 Rue Christophe Colomb, Cayenne
Guyana
　(☎ 67844) 304 Church St, Georgetown
USA
　(☎ 202-244-7488) 4301 Connecticut Ave NW, Suite 108, Washington, DC;
　(☎ 305-593-2163) 7235 NW 19th St, Miami, FL

TOURIST OFFICES OVERSEAS

Suriname has a few overseas tourist offices. The embassy in Washington, DC has excellent tourist information,

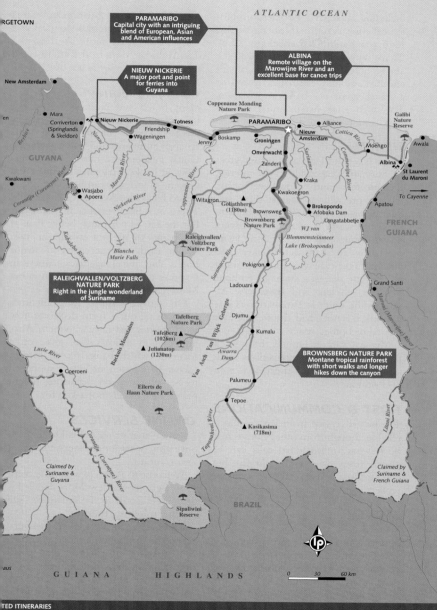

PARAMARIBO
Capital city with an intriguing blend of European, Asian and American influences

NIEUW NICKERIE
A major port and point for ferries into Guyana

ALBINA
Remote village on the Marowijne River and an excellent base for canoe trips

RALEIGHVALLEN/VOLTZBERG NATURE PARK
Right in the jungle wonderland of Suriname

BROWNSBERG NATURE PARK
Montane tropical rainforest with short walks and longer hikes down the canyon

ATLANTIC OCEAN

GEORGETOWN
New Amsterdam
Mara
Corriverton (Springlands & Skeldon)
Nieuw Nickerie
Friendship
Wageningen
GUYANA
Kwakwani
Wasjabo
Apoera
Blanche Marie Falls
Coppename Monding Nature Park
Totness
Jenny
Boskamp
PARAMARIBO
Alliance
Nieuw Amsterdam
Groningen
Onverwacht
Zanderij
Kraka
Kwakoegron
Witagron
Goliathberg (1180m)
Brownsweg
Brownsberg Nature Park
Raleighvallen/Voltzberg Nature Park
Pokigron
Ladouani
Djumu
Tafelberg Nature Park
Tafelberg (1026m)
Julianatop (1230m)
Coeroeni
Eilerts de Haan Nature Park
Palumeu
Tepoe
Kasikasima (718m)
Lucie River
Backalis Mountains
Van Asch Van Wijck Gebergte
Awarra Dam
Tapanahoni River
Claimed by Suriname & Guyana
Sipaliwini Reserve
BRAZIL
GUIANA HIGHLANDS
Corantijn (Corentyne) River
Moengo
Albina
St Laurent du Maroni
To Cayenne
Apatou
Langatabbetje
WJ van Blommensteinmeer Lake (Brokopondo)
Brokopondo
Afobaka Dam
Kumalu
Grand Santi
Galibi Nature Reserve
Awala
FRENCH GUIANA
Maroni (Marowijne) River
Claimed by Suriname & French Guiana
Litani River
Cottica River
Commewijne River
Suriname River
Coppename River
Saramacca River
Nickerie River
Marowijne River
Nanni River
Kabalebo River

30   60 km

SUGGESTED ITINERARIES

One Week Paramaribo • Brownsberg Nature Park • Nieuw Nickerie • Paramaribo

Two to Three Weeks Paramaribo • Brownsberg Nature Park • Nieuw Nickerie • Paramaribo • Raleighvallen/Voltzberg Nature Park • Lake Brokopondo • Kumalu • Awarra Dam • Mt Kasikasima • Tafelberg Nature Park • Albina • Galibi Nature Reserve

including a superb booklet on biological conservation. To obtain a copy, send a self-addressed envelope (22 by 28cm) with US$2.50 in postage to the above address. Otherwise, consult another embassy, Surinam Airways or a travel agent for basic information. The web sites listed under Online Services later are also good resources.

HEALTH

There is a risk of malaria in rural areas of Suriname, especially in the interior. Dengue fever and yellow fever occur, so take precautions against these serious diseases. Avoid all insect bites to prevent diseases transmitted by insects. Schistosomiasis occurs, so don't swim or bathe in freshwater lakes and streams. Take care with food and water to prevent diseases such as typhoid, hepatitis, cholera and dysentery. Although the water in Paramaribo is safe to drink, it is not a bad idea to stick with treated or bottled water.

Medical care is limited throughout Suriname. If you require serious medical care, Caracas in Venezuela is your best option.

POST & COMMUNICATIONS

The postal service from Paramaribo is reliable, though from other cities it may be less so. International calls can be placed from blue public phones, but you must use tokens, call reverse charge (collect) or use a Home Direct service.

MONEY
Costs

Suriname is relatively expensive, though you'll be dancing a financial jig of joy if you've just arrived from very expensive French Guiana. The frugal can get by in Suriname for around US$20 to US$25 a day, but throw in any extras like a taxi or a western-style meal and you'll be spending more like US$50 a day. Multiday tours to the interior and natural reserves start at about US$400.

Changing Money

Many hotels and business will accept US dollars at the official bank rate as this is the most common foreign currency in Suriname. Still, you can change Dutch guilders and other foreign currency at banks. Changing Brazilian and Guyanese currency can be tricky, so try not to have a pocket full of these bills. There is a black market in Suriname, but the rate is not much better than at the bank, so it's not worth the risk. Credit cards are accepted at major hotels and travel agencies. American Express is more common than either MasterCard or Visa.

On arrival, visitors are sometimes asked to fill out a form declaring how much money they have with them. Also, immigration officers may give you a form on which banks record foreign exchange transactions; this is supposed to be submitted on departure, but in practice it's usually not asked for.

ONLINE SERVICES

Lonely Planet's web site is Destination Suriname (www.lonelyplanet.com/dest /sam/sur.htm).

Welcome to Parbo (www.parbo.com) gives a good overview. More detailed is Suriname Tourism Foundation's site (http://mhw.org/tourism).

The overwhelming Gateway to Suriname site (www.surinam.net) is chock-full of more information than you'll ever need on this tropical locale.

For those out for a visual experience, there's Tropical Rainforest in

Suriname (www.euronet.nl/users/mb leeker/suriname/suri-eng.html), which is a virtual rainforest tour that can be viewed in 10 languages.

For scientific and academic articles on conservation projects in Suriname and beyond, visit the Amazon Conservation Team site (www.ethnobotany .org).

BOOKS

For a general introduction to Suriname, see *Suriname: Politics, Economics & Society* by Henk E Chin & Hans Buddingh. A good follow-up read to this is *The Dutch Caribbean: Prospects for Democracy* edited by Betty Sedoc-Dahlberg.

Tales of a Shaman's Apprentice by Mark Plotkin touches on history, anthropology and environmental issues as it recounts the search for medicinal plants in the forests of Suriname and Brazil.

ENTERING & LEAVING

Most visitors will arrive by air in Paramaribo. There are direct European flights from Amsterdam, though it may be cheaper to fly from Paris to Cayenne, French Guiana and travel overland to Suriname. From the USA, there are flights from New York, Atlanta and Miami; some flights are via the Netherlands Antilles.

You can travel overland between Suriname and Guyana or French Guiana. From Suriname to French Guiana, you take a ferry-bus combination from Albina across the Marowijne (Maroni) River to St Laurent du Maroni. From Nieuw Nickerie, Suriname to Corriverton (Springlands), Guyana there is a passenger ferry across the Corantijn (Corentyne) River. To come from Brazil, you must fly or travel overland to Cayenne in French Guiana and then to Suriname.

URUGUAY

For a lot of travellers, Uruguay is more a place to pass through than to visit. Sandwiched between Argentina and Brazil, Uruguay acts as a buffer country between these two powerhouses and lingers in relative obscurity as a result. Still, hopping into Uruguay from Buenos Aires is very convenient and visitors will be pleasantly surprised by the charming capital, colonial towns and renowned beach resorts here.

WHEN TO GO

Uruguay is blessed with a year-round temperate climate, so any time is good for a visit weather-wise. During summer, however, crowds flock to the beaches and popular destinations are crowded. Make sure you book ahead at this time. The littoral region tends to be cloyingly hot during summer, though the interior is cooler.

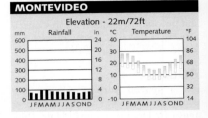

MONTEVIDEO

Elevation - 22m/72ft

Rainfall — Temperature

HIGHLIGHTS

Most visitors come to Uruguay to visit the beach. From Buenos Aires, the Uruguayan capital of Montevideo makes a good weekend trip. Here are some of the best things to do while in Uruguay.

Water Sports

Uruguay offers terrific fishing, boating, swimming and yachting. Riverside Carmelo are both good fishing spots and Punte del Este on the so-called Uruguayan Riviera is one of South America's most glamorous and exclusive beach destinations. Just offshore are Isla Gorriti, which has superb beaches and the ruins of an 18th century fortress, and Isla de Lobos, a nature reserve that is home to a large sea lion colony.

Cities & Towns

Backed by picturesque hills, Montevideo has a photogenic quality. It is packed with colonial charm, especially along the narrow streets and port area of the Ciudad Vieja (Old City). Don't miss the Mercado del Puerto, a colourful, lively centre filled with markets, restaurants, artists and street

At a Glance

Full Country Name: República Oriental del Uruguay
Area: 176,220 sq km
Population: 3,308,523
Capital City: Montevideo (pop 1,400,000)
People: 88% European descent, 8% mestizo and 4% Black
Languages: Spanish
Religion: 96% Roman Catholic, 2% Protestant and 2% Jewish
Government: Republic
Currency: Peso (Ur$)
Time Zone: Three hours behind GMT/UTC
International Telephone Code: 598
Electricity: 220V, 50 cycles

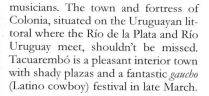

musicians. The town and fortress of Colonia, situated on the Uruguayan littoral where the Río de la Plata and Río Uruguay meet, shouldn't be missed. Tacuarembó is a pleasant interior town with shady plazas and a fantastic *gaucho* (Latino cowboy) festival in late March.

VISA REQUIREMENTS

Citizens of most Western European countries, Israel, Japan and the USA do not need visas to enter Uruguay. Visitors from these countries receive tourist cards upon entry which are good for a 90 day stay. All other foreign tourists need visas. Visas cost around US$30; an onward ticket and passport photo must be provided with the application. Both tourist cards and visas can be extended at the immigration office in Montevideo for an additional 90 days.

Uruguayan Embassies

Argentina
(☎ 01-4803 6030) Las Heras 1907, Recoleta, Buenos Aires;
(☎ 03446-426168) Rivadavia 510, Gualeguaychú;
(☎ 0345-421 0380) Pellegrini 709, 1C, Concordia

Australia
(☎ 02-6282 4800) MLC Tower, 1st floor, Suite 107, Woden, ACT 2606

Brazil
(☎ 224-2415) SES Av Das Naçoes, Lote 14, Brasília DF;
(☎ 553-6033) Praja de Botafogo 242, 6 Andar, CEP 22250, Rio de Janeiro

Canada
(☎ 613-234-2937) 130 Albert St, Suite 1905, Ottawa, Ontario K1P 5G4

UK
(☎ 020-7584 8192) 2nd floor, 140 Brompton Rd, London SW3 1HY

USA
(☎ 202-331-4219) 1918 F St NW, Washington, DC 20006
Consulates: Santa Monica & San Francisco

TOURIST OFFICES OVERSEAS

There are a number of overseas tourist offices that can provide you with information about Uruguay. Some addresses are:

Australia
Direct tourist inquiries to the Uruguayan Consulate General (☎ 02-9232 8029) GPO Box 717, Sydney, NSW 2001

Canada
(☎ 613-234-2937) 130 Albert St, Suite 1905, Ottawa, Ontario K1P 5G4

UK
Tourist information can be obtained from the Uruguayan embassy (see previously)

USA
(☎ 212-755-1200 ext 346) 541 Lexington Ave, New York, NY 10012

HEALTH

There are few serious health concerns for travellers in Uruguay. Neither malaria nor yellow fever occur here, but it's still a good idea to avoid all insect bites. Take care with what you eat and drink to prevent diseases transmitted by contaminated food and water. Avoid undercooked meat and raw seafood, and stick to bottled or purified water.

Medical care is reasonable in Montevideo but limited in other areas. If you require serious medical care, good facilities are available in Buenos Aires.

POST & COMMUNICATIONS

Uruguayan postal services vary in reliability and any mail suspected of containing something valuable is likely to be rifled. Important correspondence should be sent by registered mail or private courier service. Poste restante mail to Montevideo should, in theory, be held for up to a month.

International calls are placed from centralised calling offices run by Antel, the state telephone monopoly. Discount rates (40% off) are in effect between 9 pm and 9 am weekdays, and all day Saturday, Sunday and holidays. Reverse charge (collect) and credit card calls can be made to most countries.

You may be able to find Internet cafes providing email services in the capital.

MONEY
Costs
Annual inflation in Uruguay is about 45%, but steady devaluations keep prices from rising rapidly in dollar terms. Budget travellers can get by on about US$15 a day; if you're looking for a bit more comfort and nutrition, expect to spend closer to US$30 a day.

Changing Money
In Montevideo, popular beach towns and Colonia, exchange houses provide efficient moneychanging services, but you'll be forced to resort to banks in the interior. There is no black market for moneychanging. Cash, especially US dollars, is the easiest to exchange; travellers cheques can be changed, but sometimes carry a commission. Major credit cards are accepted by finer restaurants, hotels and shops, but Uruguayan ATMs will not accept North American or European credit or bank cards.

ONLINE SERVICES
Lonely Planet's web site is Destination Uruguay (www.lonelyplanet.com/dest /sam/uru.htm).

The web isn't otherwise swimming with Uruguay sites. Try the homepage of the Embassy of Uruguay (www .embassy.org/uruguay) for general tourist information and current events and Moving to Uruguay (www.escape artist.com/uruguay/uruguay.htm) for consular information, background on arts and culture and links to related sites.

BOOKS
A good overview of modern Uruguayan society and politics is *Contemporary Uruguay: Problems and Prospects* by Henry Finch. Follow this up with Martin Weinstein's *Uruguay, Democracy at the Crossroads* and you'll have plenty of political analysis to gnaw on.

The grotesque tale of Uruguay's military dictatorship is told in Lawrence Weschler's *A Miracle, A Universe: Settling Accounts with Torturers.*

Travel with translated editions of *No Man's Land*, *The Shipyard* or *A Brief Life* by Juan Carlos Onetti, or anything from the pen of Mario Benedetti, two of Uruguay's best known contemporary

Itineraries

One Week
Spend two days checking out the churches, markets and museums of the capital before heading off for some coastal splendour along the Uruguayan Riviera. Visit the offshore islands, using Punta del Este as a base, before escaping the crowds and cruising further along the coast to La Paloma or Aguas Dulces.

Two Weeks
Follow the one week itinerary, but add a week in the littoral region. Visit Colonia and Mercedes and Tacuarembó in the interior before returning to Montevideo.

Three Weeks
This is quite a bit of time to spend in tiny Uruguay, but you could follow the two week itinerary with a ferry trip to Buenos Aires and spend four or five days exploring that capital city and its environs.

RUGUAY HIGHLIGHTS & ITINERARIES

ARGENTINA

BRAZIL

TACUAREMBÓ
Pleasant interior town that draws visitors to its annual gaucho festival

MERCEDES
Popular for boating, swimming and fishing, and its resort on the Río Negro

CARMELO
Excellent centre for exploring the Paraná delta by boat, with good swimming and fishing

COLONIA
Colonial town set in the wheatfields of the Uruguayan littoral

MONTEVIDEO
Picturesque capital boasting colourful markets and a lively tradition of street musicians

PUNTA DEL ESTE
Glamorous beach resort in the scenic Uruguayan Riviera

0   40   80 km

Monte Caseros
Barra do Quaraí
Bellá Unión
Artigas
Quaraí
Santana do Livramento
Rivera
Tranqueras
Bagé
oncordia
Salto
Termas de Guaviyú
Tacuarembó
Aceguá
To Pelotas, Porto Alegre & Río de Janeiro
Valle Edén
Río Arapey Grande
Río Queguay
Melo
Cuchilla de Haedo
ón
Paysandú
Jaguarão
San Gregorio del Polanco
Paso de Los Toros
Río Branco
Lago Artificial de Rincón del Bonete
Vergara
Laguna Merín
uaychú
Río Yí
Treinta y Tres
ay
tos
Mercedes
Durazno
José Batlle y Ordóñez
Río Olimar Grande
no
Dolores
Trinidad
Cuchilla Grande Inferior
Lascano
Chuí
Chuy
Nueva
almira
Río San Salvador
Cardona
Parque Nacional Santa Teresa
Carmelo
Florida
Laguna Negra
Rosario
San José de Mayo
Aiguá
Villa Serrana
Castillos
Aguas Dulces
ENOS AIRES
Colonia
Juan L Lacaze
Canelones
Minas
Rocha
Parque Forestal Cabo Polonio
Río de la Plata
La Paloma
Atlántida
Piriápolis
José Ignacio
MONTEVIDEO
Maldonado
Punta del Este
ATLANTIC OCEAN
Ferry
Ferry

TED ITINERARIES

| eek | Montevideo • Punta del Este • La Paloma, or Aguas Dulces |
| eeks | Montevideo • Punta del Este • La Paloma, or Aguas Dulces • Montevideo • Colonia • Mercedes • Tacuarembó • Montevideo |

Three Weeks   Montevideo • Punta del Este • La Paloma, or Aguas Dulces • Montevideo • Colonia • Mercedes • Tacuarembó • Montevideo • Buenos Aires (Argentina)

writers. The classic *Ariel* by José Enrique Rodó is an early 20th century essay contrasting North American and Latin American civilisation, with heavy Shakespearean symbolism.

FILMS

The intriguing and famous *State of Siege* by Costa-Gavras tells the story of the Tupamaro guerrillas' kidnapping and execution of supposed CIA officer Dan Mitrione during the height of the Uruguayan dictatorship. *A Place in the World* is a fine Uruguayan movie and *Alive: A Miracle in the Andes* tells the incredible story of a Uruguayan rugby team whose airplane crashed in the mountains.

ENTERING & LEAVING

Uruguay's international airport is in Montevideo, though cheaper flights may be available to Buenos Aires, from where you can easily cross into Uruguay. The main US gateway city is Miami; European visitors can fly directly from Madrid to Montevideo or go from Amsterdam via Rio de Janeiro and São Paulo in Brazil. The international departure tax is US$2.50 to Argentina, US$6 to other South American countries and US$7 to other destinations.

To get to Buenos Aires you can take a bus from Montevideo via Gualeguaychú or the quicker land and ferry combination across the Río de la Plata. A ferry and hydrofoil service runs between Colonia and Buenos Aires. There are also launches from Carmelo to Tigre, a suburb of Buenos Aires.

There are several land and river crossings between Uruguay and Brazil. The most popular is on the excellent paved highway connecting Montevideo and Chuy in Uruguay with Chuí in Brazil. Those heading from Colón, Argentina to Brazil via Tacuarembó in Uruguay typically use the crossing at Rivera and Santo do Livramento.

VENEZUELA

Venezuela is one of those mosaic destinations with a range of attractions likely to satisfy even the most discerning travellers. The country has a modern road network and well developed tourist infrastructure built with oil money in the 1970s and 80s. Still, the interior rural and indigenous communities hearken back to a simpler, traditional way of life that for the most part has remained unchanged for generations. The landscape is as varied as the people, with snowcapped Andean peaks, gorgeous Caribbean beaches and lush tropical rainforests.

With its developed infrastructure and attendant amenities, first-time travellers to Latin America will appreciate the ease and comfort with which they can enjoy the natural attractions of Venezuela. At the same time, old hands who want to get off the beaten track will probably find themselves exploring the Venezuelan interior on their own.

WHEN TO GO

The most pleasant time to travel in Venezuela is during the summer dry months between about November and May. Christmas, Carnaval and Semana Santa (Holy Week) also fall within this period and transportation and accommodation can be hard to find (you may want to book ahead). The rest of the year is the wet season, and though heavy rains can make hiking and mountain climbing arduous or even dangerous, this is the time to visit Salto Angel (Angel Falls), the world's highest waterfall.

HIGHLIGHTS

Venezuela has a lot to offer nature and beach lovers and can accommodate many tastes and travel styles. Here's a short list of some of the country's best attractions.

Natural Attractions

Salto Angel is on most Venezuelan itineraries with good reason. This spectacular 1km waterfall is the highest in the world and boasts one of the longest uninterrupted drops at 807m. There are over 40 national parks with trails ranging from easy to strenuous in

At a Glance

Full Country Name: Republic of Venezuela
Area: 912,050 sq km
Population: 23,203,466
Capital City: Caracas (pop 3,435,795)
People: 67% mestizo, 21% European descent, 10% African descent, 2% Indian and approximately 200,000 Amerindians (remnants of diverse semi-nomadic hunter-gatherer societies)
Languages: Spanish is the official language, but more than 30 Amerindian languages still survive, predominantly belonging to the Arawak, Cariban and Chibcha ethnolinguistic categories
Religion: 96% Roman Catholic and 2% Protestant, plus small populations of Jews and Muslims
Government: Democracy
Currency: Bolívar (Bs)
Time Zone: Four hours behind GMT/UTC
International Telephone Code: 58
Electricity: 110V 60, cycles AC; outlets take two-pronged flat plugs like those used in North America

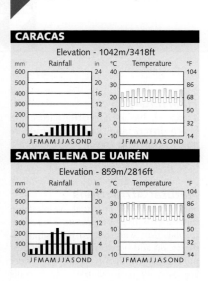

CARACAS

Elevation - 1042m/3418ft

SANTA ELENA DE UAIRÉN

Elevation - 859m/2816ft

alpine, coastal and jungle settings. Spelunkers will delight in the several hundred caves sprinkled throughout the country and the *tepuis* (flat-topped mountains looming more than 1000m above rolling savanna), will inspire even the most jaded geography buffs. Venezuela has 3000km of coastline and beach; diving and snorkelling enthusiasts will revel in the area around Parque Nacional Mochima and the Archipiélago Los Roques on the central north coast.

River Activities

Covering 25,000 sq km, the Delta del Orinoco is the second largest delta in South America after the Amazon, and the mighty Río Orinoco and its many tributaries offer plenty of fun for river enthusiasts. Rafting is becoming highly popular here and on other Venezuelan rapids, and the fishing in the Orinoco is world-class. Along this river you can also visit indigenous communities and there is decent wildlife viewing.

Trekking & Mountain Climbing

Venezuela marks the start of the Andean Cordillera, which stretches the length of the continent and provides great hiking. Adventurous travellers should try the ascent of Roraima tepui (2810m) on the Brazilian-Venezuelan-Guyanese border. The Sierra Nevada de Mérida is the best trekking region, and there are opportunities for technical and rock climbing here too. Interesting hikes with varying degrees of difficulty can be found in Parque Nacional Henri Pittier, Venezuela's oldest national park.

VISA REQUIREMENTS

Visitors from most western countries, including Australia, Canada, New Zealand, the USA and UK do not need visas if they fly into Venezuela. Upon arriving at the airport, visitors are issued a tourist card valid for 90 days. These are not renewable. Until recently, all tourists entering Venezuela overland required a visa and few consulates in neighbouring countries issued them. In short, overland travel to Venezuela could be a real drag. Thankfully, this requirement is being loosened somewhat, but if you plan to travel overland and want to play it safe, apply for a Venezuelan visa in your home country. Onward tickets are sometimes asked for at Venezuelan border crossings.

Venezuelan Embassies

Australia
(☎ 02-6282 4828) MLC Tower, Phillip, ACT 2606
Brazil
(☎ 552-6699, fax 551-5248) Praia de Botafogo 242, 5th floor, Rio de Janeiro
Canada
(☎ 613-235-5151) 32 Range Rd, Ottawa, Ontario K1N 8J4

Colombia
(☎ 256-3015) Avenida 13 No 103-16, Bogotá
Guyana
(☎ 60841) Thomas St, between Quamina and Church Sts, Georgetown
UK
(☎ 020-7581 2776/7) 1 Cromwell Rd, London SW7 2HW
USA
(☎ 202-342-2214) 1099 30th St NW, Washington, DC 20007

TOURIST OFFICES OVERSEAS

There are few tourist offices outside of Venezuela. One office which can provide general information and maps is the Venezuelan Tourist Association (VTA; ☎ 415-331-0100), PO Box 3010, Sausalito, CA 94966, USA. Consulates, embassies and travel agencies may also provide basic information. Also see the web sites listed under Online Services.

HEALTH

Malaria exists in rural areas in southern Venezuela, particularly in the Amazon and Los Llanos regions. Yellow fever can occur; take precautions and avoid all mosquito bites as dengue fever can also occur in Venezuela. In the north-central region, schistosomiasis occurs, so avoid bathing or drinking freshwater in this area. Avoid all insect bites, including bites from sandflies, to prevent diseases transmitted by insects. Tap water is generally safe to drink in Caracas and most large towns, but in rural areas stick to bottled or purified water and take care with what you eat.

If you require serious medical attention, Caracas has a number of hospitals and clinics, but medical care outside Caracas can be limited, especially in rural areas.

POST & COMMUNICATIONS

Usually two out of three ain't bad. Unfortunately, Venezuela's postal service is slow, inefficient and unreliable. Air-mail letters sent to Europe or North America can take a month to arrive, if they get there at all. Any important mail should be sent registered or, better yet, with a private courier service. The news on receiving mail is as discouraging. In theory, it's possible to receive poste restante (general delivery) mail, though letters take a long time to arrive and some never do. If you must give it a try, stick

Itineraries

One Week
Spend one to three days in and around Caracas, with a side trip to Archipiélago Los Roques for some snorkelling. The remainder of the trip can be spent at Choroní and/or Rancho Grande in Parque Nacional Henri Pittier and on a tour to Canaima/Salto Angel.

Two Weeks
Follow the one week itinerary and add one of these three options: Mérida and the surrounding mountains of the Sierra Nevada de Mérida; Ciudad Bolívar and La Gran Sabana; or a trek to the top of Roraima tepui.

One Month
Take all of the above suggestions for the two week itinerary and if you have time remaining, from Mérida include a tour to Los Llanos, centred around San Fernando de Apare.

Two Months
To the one month itinerary, add a circuit of Coro and its environs, including a jaunt to Parque Nacional Morrocoy. Follow this with a visit to Parque Nacional Mochima, Cueva del Guácharo (home to the unusual oilbird) and the Península de Paria in the east. If time and money allow, conclude your trip with a tour to the Delta del Orinoco and/or Río Caura.

VENEZUELA HIGHLIGHTS & ITINERARIES

ARCHIPIÉLAGO LOS R...
Beautiful archipela...
small coral islands, b...
and extensive coral...

SIERRA NEVADA DE MÉRIDA
Popular trekking area
ranging from lush forest
to permanent snow

PARQUE NACIONAL MOCHIMA
Scenic park including a wealth of islands, deep bays and white-sand beaches

DELTA DEL ORINOCO
Marshy green carpet crisscrossed by water channels; provides great rafting and fishing

MT RORAIMA
One of the country's largest and highest table-topped sandstone mountains

SALTO ANGEL
The county's number one attraction is this remote and spectacular waterfall

CARIBBEAN SEA

GRENADA
Grenada

Isla La Blanquilla

La Orchila

Isla La Tortuga

Nueva Esparta
Isla de Margarita
La Asunción
Porlamar

TRINIDAD & TOBAGO

Tobago

Parque Nacional Mochima

Carúpano

Península de Paria

Cumaná
Sucre
Güiria

Trinidad

PORT OF SPAIN

Puerto La Cruz
Barcelona
Piritu
Cueva del Guácharo
Caripe

Caripito

Anzoátegui

Maturín

Delta Amacuro

Zaraza

Anaco

Monagas

Tucupita
Delta del Orinoco

San José de Amacuro

El Tigre

Barrancas

Río Orinoco

Ciudad Bolívar
Ciudad Guayana

Mabaruma

Upata

Maripa

Ciudad Piar

Embalse de Guri

Matthews Ridge

Charity

Supenaam

El Callao
Tumeremo

GEORGETOWN

La Paragua

El Dorado

GUYANA

Bartica

Bolívar

Río Paragua

Canaima

Salto Angel (Angel Falls)

LA GRAN SABANA

Kavac
Kavanayén
Parque Nacional Canaima

Linden

Kwakwani

Mt Roraima (2810m)

Santa Elena de Uairén

Icabarú

Santo Domingo

Annai

amazonas

Río Caura

Río Caroni

Río Uraricoera

BRAZIL

Bonfim
Lethem

Boa Vista

Río Maruaca

Río Matacuni

Río Ocamo

Río Orinoco

Parque Nacional Parima-Tapirapecó

Caracarai

To Manaus

acional Neblina

to the post office in Caracas and have correspondence clearly addressed. Mail sent to a post office box in Venezuela is much more likely to arrive.

International calls are best placed from public phone booths using a phonecard or by making a reverse charge (collect) call. Reverse charges calls are not possible to all countries. Rates drop dramatically at night; off-peak rates depend on where you are calling to. Fax services are available throughout Venezuela at centralised phone offices, private businesses and some hotels. The last is an expensive option.

Internet cafes are just starting to catch on in Venezuela and your best bet for email and Internet service is in Caracas and university towns.

MONEY
Costs

Budget travellers used to a bit of discomfort, who stay in cheaper hotels and travel by bus can visit Venezuela on around US$20 a day and still have some money for a beer, movie or occasional taxi ride. Travellers wanting finer accommodation and better eats should plan on spending US$40 a day or more.

Changing Money

It's the same old story here: US dollars are the foreign currency of choice and the easiest to exchange. Cash is efficiently converted to bolívars at exchange houses in all cities, most tourist towns and at border crossings.

American Express travellers cheques are the most widely accepted, but keep in mind that changing cheques in Venezuela is a big hassle. For this reason, most travellers prefer to rely on credit and ATM cards. In fact, it is easier to find an ATM that accepts foreign bank or credit cards, than it is to find a bank that will exchange dollars! Visa is the most widely accepted, but MasterCard is a close second. You can get cash advances or pay for better rooms or meals with either of these cards.

ONLINE SERVICES

Lonely Planet's web site is Destination Venezuela (www.lonelyplanet.com/dest /sam/ven.htm).

All the links you'll ever need have been collected by Venezuela's Web Server (venezuela.mit.edu). The official web site of the Embassy of Venezuela (www.embavenez-us.org) provides all the typical cultural, historical and tourism information governments like to spoon-feed tourists.

Infinitely more interesting is the Catholic Apparitions of Jesus and Mary homepage (www.biddeford.com/~del orged/betania) which details the recurring appearance of these icons in Betania.

BOOKS

The Search for El Dorado by John Hemming is a good general overview of the colonisation period. Edward J Goodman's account of the personas involved in the conquest, *The Explorers of South America*, is also a good read. For more current history, read Judith Ewell's *Venezuela, a Century of Change*.

Travellers interested in Venezuela's indigenous cultures should take a look at Robin Hanbury-Tenison's *Aborigines of the Amazon Rain Forest: The Yanomami*.

FILM

Venezuela's film industry is alive and well and you may want to check out titles on video to see what's available.

Perennial favourites include *Oriana*, *Jericho* and *Amanecio de Golpe*.

A handful of Hollywood movies have been filmed on location in Venezuela and these are good for putting the landscape and environment in context, if nothing else. With this in mind, you may want to see *Arachnophobia*, *Jungle 2 Jungle* or *What Dreams May Come*.

ENTERING & LEAVING

Venezuela serves as a gateway to South America and air-fare deals abound to Caracas. There are direct flights from Miami, New York and Los Angeles in the USA, though the last is no bargain. Travellers from Canada have to connect through Miami.

Several European carriers serve Caracas and there is usually some deal afoot. Traditionally, it has been cheapest to fly from London, Amsterdam, Brussels, Frankfurt and Paris. There are no deals (in time or money) for visitors from Australia or New Zealand, however. Try flying to Argentina or Chile on a Circle Pacific or Circle Americas fare and travel overland to Venezuela to save money. Alternatively, fly to London and take advantage of cheap fares there. There is an international departure tax of US$21 from Venezuela.

There are road connections with Colombia and Brazil only. To travel to Guyana overland from Venezuela, you must go via Brazil (from Bonfim in Brazil and across the river to Lethem via Boa Vista). There are four crossings between Venezuela and Colombia, but some of these are particularly dangerous and travel to Colombia is not encouraged at this time. The most popular crossing is from San Antonio del Táchira to Cúcata; if you enter Colombia here, you'll have to pay a departure tax of between US$3 and US$10. The road to Brazil leaves Venezuela at Santa Elena de Uairén and enters Brazil at Boa Vista. There is also a seldom used river and road crossing through the Amazon rainforest at San Simón de Cocuy to São Gabriel in Brazil; a definite chance for adventure. There is also a very rough road to Georgetown in Guyana.

Entry by sea is possible from the USA – travellers can take a cargo ship from one of several ports on the Gulf of Mexico. Alternatively, ferries run from the Lesser Antilles to Venezuela.

INTERNET ADDRESSES

ACTIVITIES
CameraSurf Homepage: www.uol.com.br/camerasurf
PADI: www.padi.com
Surfline: www.surfline.com
Surf Reports: www.centralamerica.com/cr/surf

AIR FARES
eXito: www.exitotravel.com
Expedia: www.expedia.msn.com/daily/home/default.hts
Flight Info.Com: www.flifo.com
Preview Travel: www.previewtravel.com
Travelocity: www.travelocity.com

AIRLINES
AeroContinente: http://200.4.197.130/Acerca-in.htm
Aerolineas Argentinas: www.aerolineas.com.ar
AeroMexico: www.aeromexico.com
Air Courier Association: www.aircourier.org
Air France: www.airfrance.fr
Air New Zealand: www.airnz.com
Alitalia: www.alitalia.com/english/index.html
American Airlines: www.americanair.com
Ansett Australia: www.ansett.com.au
Avensa: www.avensa.com
Avianca: www.avianca.com.co
British Airways: www.british-airways.com
Canadian Airlines: www.cdnair.ca
Continental Airlines: www.flycontinental.com
Grupo Taca: www.grupotaca.com
Guyana Airways: www.turq.com/guyana/guyanair
Iberia: www.iberia.com
International Association of Air Travel Couriers (IAATC): www.courier.org/index.html
LanChile: www.lanchile.cl
Lauda Air: www.laudaair.com
Lloyd Aéreo Boliviano: www.labairlines.com
Lufthansa: www.lufthansa.com

336

Mexicana Airlines: www.mexcicana.com
Qantas Airways: www.qantas.com
United Airlines: www.ual.com
Varig: www.varig.com.bra

CAR & MOTORCYCLE
American Automobile Association: www.aaa.com/vacation/idp.html
Australian Automobile Association: www.aaa.asn.au
British Automobile Association: www.theaa.co.uk/membership/offers/idp.html
Canadian Automobile Association:
   www.caa.ca/CAAInternet/travelservices/frames14.htm

FILM & RADIO
BBC World Service: www.bbc.co.uk/worldservice
Internet Movie Database: www.imdb.com
Radio America: www.voa.gov
Radio Australia: www.abc.net.au/ra

HEALTH
Altitude Sickness: www.princeton.edu/~oa/altitude.html;
   www.gorge.net/hamg/AMS.html
American Society of Tropical Medicine & Hygiene: www.astmh.org
British Airways Travel Clinics:
   www.britishairways.com/travelqa/fyi/health/health.html
CDC (US Centers for Disease Control & Prevention): www.cdc.gov
Health Canada: www.hc-sc.gc.ca/hpb/lcdc/osh
International Association for Medical Assistance to Travellers: www.sentex.net
International Planned Parenthood Federation: www.ippf.org
International Society of Travel Medicine: www.istm.org
Lariam Action USA: www.suggskelly.com/lariam
MASTA (Medical Advisory Services for Travellers): www.masta.org
Medical College of Wisconsin Travelers Clinic: www.intmed.mcw/travel.html
Mefloquine: www.travelhealth.com/mefloqui.htm;
   www.geocities.com/TheTropics/6913/lariam.htm
Shorelands: www.tripprep.com
Travel Health Information Service: www.travelhealth.com
Travellers Medical and Vaccination Centre: www.tmvc.com.au
WHO (World Health Organization): www.who.ch

INTERNET & TELEPHONE ACCOUNTS
eKno: www.ekno.lonelyplanet.com
Internet Cafe Guide: www.netcafeguide.com

MAPS

Hagstrom Map and Travel Center: www.hagstromstore.com
International Travel Maps: www.nas.com/~travelmaps
Rand McNally – The Map & Travel Store: www.randmcnallystore.com
World of Maps & Travel Books: www.worldofmaps.com

MONEY MATTERS

Credit Cards: www.mastercard.com/atm;
www.visa.com/cgi-bin/vee/pd/atm/main.html
Oanda Online Currency Converter: www.oanda.com/converter/classic

NEWSPAPERS & MAGAZINES

The Australian: www.news.com.au
Bicycling: www.bicyclingmagazine.com
Big World Magazine: www.bigworld.com
Chicago Tribune: www.chicagotribune.com
The Globe & Mail (Toronto): www.theglobeandmail.com
The Independent (UK): www.independent.co.uk
LA Times: www.latimes.com
Mountain Bike: www.mountainbike.com
National Geographic: www.nationalgeographic.com
New York Times: www.nytimes.com
Outside: http://outside.starwave.com
San Francisco Examiner: www.examiner.com
South American Explorer: www.samexplo.org
Southern Cross (UK): www.southerncross.co.uk
Surfer Magazine: www.surfermag.com
Sydney Morning Herald: www.smh.com.au
The Times: www.the-times.co.uk
Time Out: www.timeout.com/london
TNT: www.tntmag.co.uk
Traveller Magazine: www.travelmag.co.uk
Vancouver Sun: www.vancouversun.com

NICHE TRAVELLERS

Access-Able Travel Source: www.access-able.com
Accessible Journeys: www.disabilitytravel.com
American Association of Retired Persons (AARP): www.aarp.org
Gay Scape: www.gayscape.com
International Gay & Lesbian Travel Association (IGTLA): www.IGLTA.org
Mobility International USA: www.miusa.org
NICAN: www.nican.com.au

Royal Association for Disability & Rehabilitation (RADAR): www.radar.org.uk

Society for the Advancement of Travel for the Handicapped (SATH): http://sath.org/index.html

PASSPORTS & VISAS

Passports Australia, Department of Foreign Affairs & Trade: www.dfat.gov.au/passports/passports_faq_contents.html

Passport Office, Department of Foreign Affairs & International Trade (Canada): www.dfait-maeci.gc.ca/passport/paspr-2.htm

Passport Office, Department of Internal Affairs (New Zealand): http://inform.dia.govt.nz/internal_affairs/business es/doni_pro/fees.html

Passport Services, the State Department (USA): http://travel.state.gov/passport_services.html

UK Passport Agency, The Home Office: www.open.gov.uk/ukpass/ukpass.htm

TEACHING RESOURCES

Association of American Schools in South America: www.aassa.com

Dave's ESL Café: www.pacificnet.net/~sperling/eslcafe.html

English Expert Page: www.englishexpert.com

International House: www.international-house.org

Job Registry Online Directory: www.edulink.com/JOBS_FILES_LIST/jobopenings.html

Learn Spanish: www.studyspanish.com

New World Teachers: www.goteach.com

Teach English in Mexico: www.teach-english-mexico.com

TEFL Job Centre: www.jobs.edunet.com

WorldTeach: www.igc.org/worldteach

TRAVEL ADVISORIES

British Foreign & Commonwealth Office: www.fco.gov.uk

Conservation International's Ecotravel Center: www.ecotour.org/ecotour.htm

Council Travel: www.counciltravel.com

Ecotour: www.ecotour.org/ecotour.htm

Encounter Overland: www.encounter.co.uk

Exodus: www.exodustravels.co.uk

Flight Centre: www.flightcentre.com

Global Exchange: www.globalexchange.org

Green Travel Network: www.greentravel.com

Intrepid Travel: www.intrepidtravel.com.au

Journeys International: www.journeys-intl.com

Latin American Travel Consultants: www.amerispan.com/lata

Serious Sports: www.serioussports.com/core.html

South America Explorers Club: www.samexplo.org

Specialty Travel: specialtytravel.com
STA Travel: www.sta-travel.com
Tourism Concern: www.gn.apc.org/tourismconcern
Tourism Offices Worldwide Directory: www.towd.com
Trailfinders: www.trailfinder.com
Travel CUTS: www.travelcuts.com

TRAVEL EQUIPMENT
Karrimor: www.karrimor.com.uk
Lowe Alpine Packs & Apparel: www.lowealpine.com
Macpac: www.macpac.com.nz
Photo.net: www.photo.net/photo
REI: www.rei.com

VOLUNTEER ORGANISATIONS
Australian Volunteers International: www.ozvol.org.au
AmeriSpan: www.amerispan.com/volunteer
Council on International Educational Exchange: www.ciee.org/vol
Earthwatch Institute: www.earthwatch.org/australia/html;
    www.earthwatch.org/t/Toeuropehome.htm
Global Volunteers: www.globalvolunteers.org
International Voluntary Service: www.ivsgbn.demon.co.uk
Peace Corps of the USA: www.peacecorps.gov
Tx Serve: www.txserve.org/general/volopp2.html
Voluntary Service Overseas (VSO): www.oneworld.org/vso
Volunteer Service Abroad: www.tcol.co.uk/comorg/vsa.htm

OTHER USEFUL SITES
AmeriSpan/Latin American Travel Consultants Travel Resources:
    www.amerispan.com/resources/default.htm
Federation of International Youth Travel Organisations: www.fiyto.org/index-old.html
FEMA Tropical Storm Watch: www.fema.gov/fema/trop.htm
Habitat for Humanity: www.habitat.org
Hostelling International: www.iyhf.org
International Student Travel Confederation: www.isic.org/index.htm
Internet Guide to Hostelling: www.hostelling.com
Oxfam International: www.oxfaminternational.org
Planeta.com: www2.planeta.com/mader
Rain or Shine: www.rainorshine.com
Transitions Abroad: www.transabroad.com
US State Department Travel Warnings & Consular Information Sheets:
    http://travel.state.gov/travel_warnings.html
World Events Calendar: www.travel.epicurious.com

GLOSSARY

COMMON WORDS

albergue juventile – youth hostel

altiplano – Andean high plain of Peru, Bolivia, Chile and Argentina

apunamiento – altitude sickness

arroz con pollo – rice with chicken

bahía – bay

baño – place for bathing

buseta – minivan

buenos días – 'good morning'

cabaña – bungalow, usually on the beach

cajeros automáticos – automatic teller machines

carnet de passage – official paper for vehicles going to Central America

casa de cambio – exchange house (for changing money)

casa de familia – family house available for homestays

casa de huéspede – guesthouse

casetas telefónica – phone booth for taking operator assisted calls (Mexico)

caye – small island of sand/coral fragments

cerro – hill

certificado – registered mail

ceviche – a raw seafood dish

chifa – Chinese restaurant

ciudad – city

colectivo – minivan

comedore – basic local eatery

comida corrida – set meal (Mexico and Central America)

cómo está? – 'how are you?'

cofradía – brotherhood (Guatemala)

cordillera – mountain range

correo aéreo – air mail

criollo – Creole, born in Latin America of Spanish descent; on the Caribbean coast it refers to someone of mixed Black and European descent

cueva – cave

el menú – set meal (Ecuador)

finca – plantation, ranch

Garifúna, plural Garinagu – refers to a mixed race of descendants of Africans and Carib Indians from the Caribbean island of St Vincent, who first came to Central America in the late 18th century

gaucho – Latino cowboy

gringo/gringa – non-Latin American, especially from the USA; sometimes, not always, derogatory

hospedaje – guesthouse

huipil – woven white dress from Mayan regions with intricate, colourful embroidery (Guatemala)

Inca – the dominant indigenous civilisation of the Central Andes at the time of the Spanish conquest

indígena – native American (Indian)

lago – lake

laguna – lagoon; shallow lake

lista de correos – post restante mail

mariachi – small ensemble of street musicians playing traditional ballads (Mexico)

mate bombillo – hot chocolate stirrer

mercado – market

mestizo/a – a person of mixed Indian and Spanish ancestry

mulato/a – a person of mixed African and European ancestry

palapa – open-air structure with a palm-thatched roof and no walls (Panama)

páramo – humid, high-altitude grassland of the northern Andean countries

parque nacional – national park

plato del día – set meal (Mexico and Central America), *see also* comida corrida

playa – beach

posada – inn

prato do dia – set meal (Brazil)

Quechua – indigenous language of the Andean highlands, spread by Inca rule and widely spoken today

refugio – national park cabin

río – river (in Brazil, *rio*)

salar – salt lake or salt pan, usually in the high Andes or Argentine Patagonia

Semana Santa – Holy Week; the week before Easter

servicio – toilet

sierra – mountain range

stela – carved stone monument of the ancient Maya

tapir – large hoofed animal; a distant relative of the horse

ticos – Costa Rican locals

tricolo – three-wheeled motorised cab

vicuña – wild relative of the domestic llama and alpaca, found only at high altitudes in the south-central Andes

volcán – volcano

AIR TRAVEL TERMS

baggage allowance – Written on your ticket and usually includes one 20kg item to go in the hold, plus one item of hand luggage.

bucket shops –These are unbonded travel agencies specialising in discounted plane tickets.

cancellation penalties – If you have to cancel or change a discounted ticket, there are often heavy penalties involved; insurance can sometimes be taken out against these penalties. Some airlines impose penalties on regular tickets as well, particularly against 'no-show' passengers.

check-in – If you fail to check in on time (usually one to two hours before departure time on international flights) and the flight is overbooked, the airline can cancel your booking.

confirmation – Having a ticket written out with the flight and date you want doesn't mean you have a seat until the agent has checked with the airline that your status is 'OK' or confirmed.

full fares – Airlines traditionally offer 1st class (coded F), business class (coded J) and economy class (coded Y) tickets. With so many promotional and discounted fares available, few passengers pay full economy fare.

ITX – An ITX, or 'independent inclusive tour excursion', is often available on tickets to popular holiday destinations. Officially it's a package deal combined with hotel accommodation, but many agents will sell you one of these for the flight only and give you phoney hotel vouchers in the unlikely event that you're challenged at the airport.

lost tickets – If you lose your plane ticket an airline will usually treat it like a

travellers cheque and, after inquiries, issue you with another one. Legally, however, an airline is entitled to treat it like cash and if you lose it then it's gone forever.

MCO – An MCO, or 'miscellaneous charge order', is a voucher that looks like a plane ticket but carries no destination or date. It can be exchanged through any International Association of Travel Agents (IATA) airline for a ticket on a specific flight. It's a useful alternative to an onward ticket in those countries that demand one, and is more flexible than an ordinary ticket if you're unsure of your route.

no-shows – These are passengers who fail to show up for their flight. Full-fare passengers who fail to turn up are sometimes entitled to travel on a later flight. The rest are penalised.

on request – An unconfirmed booking for a flight.

onward tickets – An entry requirement for many countries is that you have a ticket out of the country. If you're unsure of your next move, the easiest solution is to buy the cheapest onward ticket to a neighbouring country or a ticket from a reliable airline which can later be refunded if you don't use it.

open-jaw tickets – Return tickets where you fly into one place but out of another.

overbooking – Since every flight has some passengers who fail to show up, airlines often book more passengers than they have seats. Occasionally somebody gets 'bumped' onto the next available flight and this is most likely to be passengers who check in late.

point-to-point tickets – Discount tickets that can be bought on some routes in

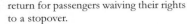

return for passengers waiving their rights to a stopover.

promotional fares – Officially discounted fares available from travel agencies or direct from the airline.

reconfirmation – If you don't reconfirm your flight at least 72 hours prior to departure, the airline may delete your name from the passenger list.

restrictions – Discounted tickets often have various restrictions on them – such as needing to be paid for in advance, incurring a penalty to be altered, or restrictions on the minimum and maximum period you must be away.

round-the-world tickets – RTW tickets give you a limited period (usually a year) in which to circumnavigate the globe. You can go anywhere the carrying airlines go, as long as you don't backtrack. The number of stopovers or total number of separate flights is decided before

you set off and they usually cost a bit more than a basic return flight.

stand-by – A discounted ticket where you only fly if there is a seat free at the last moment, and usually available only on domestic routes.

transferred tickets – Plane tickets cannot be transferred from one person to another. Travellers sometimes try to sell the return half of their ticket, but officials can ask you to prove that you are the person named on the ticket. This is less likely to happen on domestic flights, but on an international flight tickets are compared with passports.

travel periods – Ticket prices vary depending on the time of year – low (off-peak) season, high (peak) season or shoulder season. Usually the fare depends on your outward flight. If you depart in the high season you pay the high fare.

INDEX

Italics indicates maps

LONELY PLANET

ON THE ROAD

Lonely Planet **travel guides** explore cities, regions and countries in depth, with restaurants, accommodations and more for every budget. With reliable, easy-to-use maps, practical advice, great cultural background and sights both on and off the beaten track. There are over 200 titles in this classic series covering nearly every country in the world.

 Lonely Planet Upgrades extend the usefulness of existing travel guides by detailing any changes that may affect travel in each region since the book has been published. Upgrades can be downloaded for free on www.lonelyplanet.com/upgrades

For travellers with more time than money, **Shoestring guides** offer dependable, first-hand information with 100s of detailed maps, plus insider tips for stretching money as far as possible. Covering entire continents in most cases, the six-volume shoestring guides have been known as 'backpackers' bibles' for over 25 years.

For the discerning short-term visitor, **Condensed** guides highlight the best a destination has to offer in a full-colour pocket-sized format designed for quick access. From top sights and walking tours to opinionated reviews of where to eat, stay, shop and have fun.

Lonely Planet **CitySync** lets travellers use their Palm™ or Visor™ handheld computers to quickly search and sort hundreds of reviews of hotels, restaurants, major sights, and shopping and entertainment options, all pinpointed on scrollable street maps. CitySync can be downloaded from www.citysync.com

ESSENTIALS

Read This First books help travellers new to a destination hit the road with confidence. These invaluable pre-departure guides give step-by-step advice on preparing for a trip, from budgeting and arranging a visa to planning an itinerary, staying safe and still getting off the beaten track.

Healthy Travel pocket guides offer practical advice for staying well on the road, with user-friendly design and helpful diagrams and tables.

Pocket-sized, with colour tabs for quick reference, extensive vocabulary lists easy-to-follow pronunciation keys and two-way dictionaries, Lonely Planet **Phrasebooks** cover the essential words and phrases travellers may need.

Lonely Planet's eKno is a communication card developed especially for travellers, with low phone rates, free email and a toll-free voicemail service so that you can keep in touch while on the road. Check it out on www.ekno.lonelyplanet.com

LONELY PLANET

ACTIVITY GUIDES

For those who believe the best way to see the world is on foot, Lonely Planet's **walking guides** detail everything from family strolls to difficult treks, with expert advice on when to go and how to do it, reliable maps and essential travel information.

Cycling guides map out a destination's best bike tours, long and short, in day-by-day detail. With all the information a cyclist needs, including advice on bike maintenance, places to eat and stay, and innovative maps with detailed cues to the rides and elevation charts.

The **Watching Wildlife** series is perfect for travellers who want authoritative information but don't want to tote a field guide. Packed with advice on where, when and how to view a region's wildlife, each title features photos of over 300 species and engaging insights on their lives and environments.

With underwater colour photos throughout, **Pisces Books** explore the world's best diving and snorkelling areas. Each book contains listings of diving services and dive resorts and detailed information on depth, visibility, levels of difficulty and marine life you're likely to see.

MAPS & ATLASES

Lonely Planet's **City Maps** feature downtown and metropolitan maps as well as transit routes, walking tours and a complete index of streets and sights. Plastic-coated for extra durability.

Road Atlases are an essential navigation tool for serious travellers. Cross-referenced with Lonely Planet guidebooks, they also feature distance and climate charts and a complete site index.

LONELY PLANET

FOOD & RESTAURANT GUIDES

Lonely Planet's **Out to Eat** guides recommend the brightest and best places to eat and drink in top international cities. Arranged by neighbourhood and packed with dependable maps, scene-setting photos and quirky features, Out to Eat serves up the lot.

For people who live to eat, drink and travel, **World Food** guides are full of gorgeous, evocative photos and packed with details on regional cuisine, guides to local markets and produce, recipes, useful phrases for shopping and dining, and a comprehensive culinary dictionary.

OFF THE ROAD

Journeys is a travel literature series that captures the spirit of a place, illuminates a culture, recounts an adventure or introduces a fascinating way of life. These books are tales to read while on the road or at home in your favourite armchair.

Lonely Planet's new range of lavishly illustrated **Pictorial** books is just the ticket for both travellers and dreamers. Quirky tales and vivid photographs bring the adventure of travel to life, before the journey begins or long after it is over.

Entertaining and adventurous, Lonely Planet **Videos** encourage the same independent approach to travel as the guidebooks. Currently airing throughout the world, this award-winning series features all original footage and music.

TRAVELLERS NETWORK

Lonely Planet online. Lonely Planet's award-winning web site has insider information on hundreds of destinations from Amsterdam to Zimbabwe, complete with interactive maps and colour photographs. The site also offers the latest travel news, recent reports from travellers on the road, guidebook upgrades and a lively traveller's bulletin board www.lonelyplanet.com or AOL keyword: lp

Lonely Planet produces two free newsletters. **Planet Talk** is the quarterly print version, **Comet** comes via email once a month. Each is loaded with travel news, advice, dispatches from authors and letters from readers. Contact your nearest Lonely Planet office to subscribe.

LONELY PLANET

Guides by Region

L onely Planet is known worldwide for publishing practical, reliable and no-nonsense travel information in our guides and on our web site. The Lonely Planet list covers just about every accessible part of the world. Currently there are fifteen series: travel guides, Shoestrings, Condensed, Phrasebooks, Read This First, Healthy Travel, Walking guides, Cycling guides, Pisces Diving & Snorkeling guides, City Maps, Travel Atlases, Out to Eat, World Food, Journeys travel literature and Pictorials.

AFRICA Africa on a shoestring • Africa – the South • Arabic (Egyptian) phrasebook • Arabic (Moroccan) phrasebook • Cairo • Cape Town • Cape Town city map • Central Africa • East Africa • Egypt • Egypt travel atlas • Ethiopian (Amharic) phrasebook • The Gambia & Senegal • Healthy Travel Africa • Kenya • Kenya travel atlas • Malawi, Mozambique & Zambia • Morocco • North Africa • Read This First Africa • South Africa, Lesotho & Swaziland • South Africa, Lesotho & Swaziland travel atlas • Swahili phrasebook • Tanzania, Zanzibar & Pemba • Trekking in East Africa • Tunisia • West Africa • Zimbabwe, Botswana & Namibia • Zimbabwe, Botswana & Nambia Travel Atlas • World Food Morocco
Travel Literature: The Rainbird: A Central African Journey • Songs to an African Sunset: A Zimbabwean Story • Mali Blues: Traveling to an African Beat

AUSTRALIA & THE PACIFIC Auckland • Australia • Australian phrasebook • Bushwalking in Australia • Bushwalking in Papua New Guinea • Fiji • Fijian phrasebook • Healthy Travel Australia, NZ and the Pacific • Islands of Australia's Great Barrier Reef • Melbourne • Melbourne city map • Micronesia • New Caledonia • New South Wales & the ACT • New Zealand • Northern Territory • Outback Australia • Out To Eat – Melbourne • Out to Eat – Sydney • Papua New Guinea • Pidgin phrasebook • Queensland • Rarotonga & the Cook Islands • Samoa • Solomon Islands • South Australia • South Pacific • South Pacific Languages phrasebook • Sydney • Sydney city map • Sydney Condensed • Tahiti & French Polynesia • Tasmania • Tonga • Tramping in New Zealand • Vanuatu • Victoria • Western Australia
Travel Literature: Islands in the Clouds • Kiwi Tracks: A New Zealand Journey • Sean & David's Long Drive

CENTRAL AMERICA & THE CARIBBEAN Bahamas, Turks & Caicos • Bermuda • Central America on a shoestring • Costa Rica • Cuba • Dominican Republic & Haiti • Eastern Caribbean • Guatemala, Belize & Yucatán: La Ruta Maya • Jamaica • Mexico • Mexico City • Panama • Puerto Rico • Read This First Central & South America • World Food Mexico
Travel Literature: Green Dreams: Travels in Central America

EUROPE Amsterdam • Amsterdam city map • Andalucía • Austria • Baltic States phrasebook • Barcelona • Berlin • Berlin city map • Britain • British phrasebook • Brussels, Bruges & Antwerp • Budapest city map • Canary Islands • Central Europe • Central Europe phrasebook • Corfu & Ionians • Corsica • Crete • Crete Condensed • Croatia • Cyprus • Czech & Slovak Republics • Denmark • Dublin • Eastern Europe • Eastern Europe phrasebook • Edinburgh • Estonia, Latvia & Lithuania • Europe on a shoestring • Finland • Florence • France • French phrasebook • Germany • German phrasebook • Greece • Greek Islands • Greek phrasebook • Hungary • Iceland, Greenland & the Faroe Islands • Istanbul City Map • Ireland • Italian phrasebook • Italy • Krakow •Lisbon • London • London city map • London Condensed • Mediterranean Europe • Mediterranean Europe phrasebook • Munich • Norway • Paris • Paris city map • Paris Condensed • Poland • Portugal • Portuguese phrasebook • Portugal travel atlas • Prague • Prague city map • Provence & the Côte d'Azur • Read This First: Europe • Romania & Moldova • Rome • Russia, Ukraine & Belarus • Russian phrasebook • Scandinavian & Baltic Europe • Scandinavian Europe phrasebook • Scotland • Slovenia • Spain • Spanish phrasebook • St Petersburg • Switzerland • Trekking in Spain • Ukrainian phrasebook • Venice • Vienna • Walking in Britain • Walking in Ireland • Walking in Italy • Walking in Spain • Walking in Switzerland • Western Europe • Western Europe phrasebook • World Food Italy • World Food Spain
Travel Literature: The Olive Grove: Travels in Greece

INDIAN SUBCONTINENT Bangladesh • Bengali phrasebook • Bhutan • Delhi • Goa • Hindi & Urdu phrasebook • India • India & Bangladesh travel atlas • Indian Himalaya • Karakoram Highway • Kerala • Mumbai (Bombay) • Nepal • Nepali phrasebook • Pakistan • Rajasthan • Read This First: Asia & India • South India • Sri Lanka • Sri Lanka phrasebook • Trekking in the Indian Himalaya • Trekking in the Karakoram & Hindukush • Trekking in the Nepal Himalaya
Travel Literature: In Rajasthan • Shopping for Buddhas • The Age Of Kali

LONELY PLANET

Mail Order

Lonely Planet products are distributed worldwide. They are also available by mail order from Lonely Planet, so if you have difficulty finding a title please write to us. North and South American residents should write to 150 Linden St, Oakland CA 94607, USA; European and African residents should write to 10a Spring Place, London, NW5 3BH; and residents of other countries to PO Box 617, Hawthorn, Victoria 3122, Australia.

ISLANDS OF THE INDIAN OCEAN Madagascar & Comoros • Maldives • Mauritius, Réunion & Seychelles

MIDDLE EAST & CENTRAL ASIA Arab Gulf States • Central Asia • Central Asia phrasebook • Dubai • Hebrew phrasebook • Iran • Israel & the Palestinian Territories • Israel & the Palestinian Territories travel atlas • Istanbul • Istanbul to Cairo • Jerusalem • Jerusalem City Map • Jordan & Syria • Jordan, Syria & Lebanon travel atlas • Lebanon • Middle East on a shoestring • Syria • Turkey • Turkey travel atlas • Turkish phrasebook • Yemen
Travel Literature: The Gates of Damascus • Kingdom of the Film Stars: Journey into Jordan • Black on Black: Iran Revisited

NORTH AMERICA Alaska • Backpacking in Alaska • Baja California • California & Nevada • California Condensed • Canada • Chicago • Chicago city map • Deep South • Florida • Hawaii • Honolulu • Las Vegas • Los Angeles • Miami • New England • New Orleans • New York City • New York city map • New York Condensed • New York, New Jersey & Pennsylvania • Oahu • Pacific Northwest USA • Puerto Rico • Rocky Mountain • San Francisco • San Francisco city map • Seattle • Southwest USA • Texas • USA • USA phrasebook • Vancouver • Washington, DC & the Capital Region • Washington DC city map
Travel Literature: Drive Thru America

NORTH-EAST ASIA Beijing • Cantonese phrasebook • China • Hong Kong • Hong Kong city map • Hong Kong, Macau & Guangzhou • Japan • Japanese phrasebook • Japanese audio pack • Korea • Korean phrasebook • Kyoto • Mandarin phrasebook • Mongolia • Mongolian phrasebook • North-East Asia on a shoestring • Seoul • South-West China • Taiwan • Tibet • Tibetan phrasebook • Tokyo
Travel Literature: Lost Japan • In Xanadu

SOUTH AMERICA Argentina, Uruguay & Paraguay • Bolivia • Brazil • Brazilian phrasebook • Buenos Aires • Chile & Easter Island • Chile & Easter Island travel atlas • Colombia • Ecuador & the Galapagos Islands • Healthy Travel Central & South America • Latin American Spanish phrasebook • Peru •Quechua phrasebook • Rio de Janeiro • Rio de Janeiro city map • South America on a shoestring • Trekking in the Patagonian Andes • Venezuela
Travel Literature: Full Circle: A South American Journey

SOUTH-EAST ASIA Bali & Lombok • Bangkok • Bangkok city map • Burmese phrasebook • Cambodia • Hanoi • Healthy Travel Asia & India • Hill Tribes phrasebook • Ho Chi Minh City • Indonesia • Indonesia's Eastern Islands • Indonesian phrasebook • Indonesian audio pack • Jakarta • Java • Laos • Lao phrasebook • Laos travel atlas • Malay phrasebook • Malaysia, Singapore & Brunei • Myanmar (Burma) • Philippines • Pilipino (Tagalog) phrasebook • Read This First Asia & India • Singapore • South-East Asia on a shoestring • South-East Asia phrasebook • Thailand • Thailand's Islands & Beaches • Thailand travel atlas • Thai phrasebook • Thai audio pack • Vietnam • Vietnamese phrasebook • Vietnam travel atlas • World Food Thailand • World Food Vietnam

ALSO AVAILABLE: Antarctica • The Arctic • Brief Encounters: Stories of Love, Sex & Travel • Chasing Rickshaws • Lonely Planet Unpacked • Not the Only Planet: Travel Stories from Science Fiction • Sacred India • Travel with Children • Traveller's Tales

Are you sure you've packed everythin

Lonely Planet's eKno is all you need to stay in touch
while you're away.

Join eKno today and get 10% bonus free usage by
quoting RTGIV2699 when you register.

To join just contact us with a toll free call to custom
service on USA +1 213 927 0101 or online at
www.ekno.lonelyplanet.com. All you need to do is
charge up your account with your credit card, and
it's rechargeable anytime from anywhere.

Cheaper International Phone Calls

You can currently make calls at budget rates from over 50 cou
and the list is growing all the time. This is similar to using a ca
card. It's simple – just dial the access number of the country y
in and then follow the voice prompts.

Free email

Get a free email address that works anywhere in the world. All
have to do is log onto a computer and pick up your email via y
eKno address.

Voicemail

You can send, leave and receive voice messages, so friends can
leave you messages from home or on the road and you can rep
even forward the message to others. Give your eKno number to
friends and family or swap eKno numbers with friends you ma
the road – this way you can always keep in touch.
  You can also listen to your voice messages via the eKno web s
(www.ekno.lonelyplanet.com) for free.